Workplace Justice

Employment Obligations in
International Perspective

Studies in Industrial Relations

Hoyt N. Wheeler and Roy J. Adams, Editors

Workplace Justice
Employment Obligations in International Perspective

Edited by
Hoyt N. Wheeler
University of South Carolina
and
Jaques Rojot
University of Paris I, Sorbonne

University of South Carolina Press

Copyright © 1992 University of South Carolina

Published in Columbia, South Carolina, by the
University of South Carolina Press

Manufactured in the United States of America

Library of Congress Cataloging-in-Publication Data

Workplace justice : employment obligations in international
  perspective / edited by Hoyt N. Wheeler and Jacques Rojot.
    p. cm. — (Studies in industrial relations)
    Includes bibliographical references and index.
    ISBN 0-87249-781-X (hardback : acid-free paper)
    1. Employee rules. 2. Labor discipline—Law and legislation.
  3. Employees—Dismissal of—Law and legislation. I. Wheeler, Hoyt
  N. II. Rojot, Jacques. III. Series.
  K1765.W67 1992
  344′.012598—dc20
  [342.412598]   92–16829

Contents

CONTENTS

vi

Workplace Justice

Employment Obligations in
International Perspective

INTRODUCTION

A custodian leans on his mop, resting from two hours of hard labor cleaning a hallway. His supervisor approaches, surveys the work, and says, "Do it again. That's just not good enough." The custodian, angered, throws down his mop and walks away, saying, "Do it yourself." Has the custodian violated an obligation of his employment? If so, can he lawfully be fired? Only reprimanded? Does it matter what country he is in?

A scenario such as this one is typical in all industrialized countries, as are the questions that it raises. Human beings are employed by other human beings in work organizations. The organizations survive and have their raison d'etre by virtue of their ability to efficiently produce goods or services. This requires certain behaviors, such as work performance, and the avoidance of others, such as insubordination or stealing the employer's property. In the hierarchical social structures found in these organizations, employees who fail to engage in required behaviors or do engage in prohibited behaviors are disciplined or dismissed. In all industrial societies there have grown up sets of rules spelling out the substantive obligations of employment that indicate which behaviors are required and which are to be avoided.

Looking at a widely dispersed set of industrialized countries, this book speaks to the questions raised above across a range of obligations of employment. Our concern is with those obligations that can lead to discipline or termination of employment if they are

1

violated. An explicit assumption of this analysis is that, as indicated above, there is fundamental commonality across national systems in the human relationship that we call employment. We believe that the crux of this relationship is the undertaking of certain obligations, primarily subordination, on the part of one person (the employee) in exchange for obligations, primarily the payment of money, by another person or organization (the employer). Our study is of the identity, nature, and boundaries of the substantive obligations of employees, and the penalties for failing to meet those obligations, across countries.

In each of our countries there is a system of industrial, or workplace, justice that exists for dealing with violations of employee obligations. Its purpose is justice as to these workplace obligations. In most countries this is initially a matter of private justice, with employers imposing penalties upon their employees for alleged violations of their obligations—misconduct. In some countries the initiation of punishment is dependent upon joint private management–labor mechanisms. In some these determinations are reviewed by joint private management–labor semijudicial tribunals—arbitration. At some point these employer actions become matters of public justice, subject to review by government-established courts—either ordinary law courts, arbitration tribunals, or specialized labor courts. It is the entire set of a country's private and public institutions pertaining to discipline and dismissal, and its procedures and substantive rules, to which we refer when speaking of a national industrial justice system.

There are both practical and theoretical reasons for our inquiry. Practically, managers need to know what the law is in order to follow it. Trade unionists and other worker representatives need this knowledge in order to insist effectively on lawful behavior by managers. These needs increase, and the difficulty in meeting them grows exponentially, as both business and labor look across national boundaries, as they must in the modern world. Subjects such as the obligations of employment need to be understood in a general cross-national context in order to be worked with, as a practical matter. It is especially useful to identify commonalities across national systems. This simplifies both training and practice. Even where management action is not subject to joint or government regulation, as in the nonunionized sector in the United States, the body of norms developed in other systems can furnish guidance for management policy.

2

Policy makers engaged in the practical task of making laws also have reason to be interested in this. In many countries statutory law regulates this area in great detail. In others it is a matter of court- or arbitrator-made law. Whatever the source of law in a particular system, it is clear that there is a need for government concern as to its substance. Even the most emphatically private industrial justice system, such as that in the United States, is ultimately and, it appears, increasingly accountable for its actions through the judicial system. The pressures for this arise, in our view, from the centrality of the employment relationship in a modern society. It is out of this relationship that goods and services are produced. The productive capacity of the economy depends upon it. Quite as importantly, basic issues of human rights and dignity are involved. There is always a public interest in justice and in the citizens of a free society being free from arbitrary and oppressive treatment, whether at the hands of government or private persons. In Europe at present there is also a strongly felt need to deal with questions of harmonization of social policy, including those dealing with employment. This requires knowing what the rules are in various countries and having a strong grasp of cross-national commonalities.

As to theory, there are several possible benefits to be derived from our inquiry. First, it goes to the very heart of the employment relationship, thereby holding out some promise of elucidating its essential nature. Second, it explores the boundaries of the obligations attached to employment, furnishing information on its extensiveness. Third, its method reduces the subject to concrete terms which are understandable and capable of generating hypotheses. Fourth, it has implications for basic questions of comparative law involving the universality of principles of justice. Last, it should be kept in mind that broad fields of academic investigation have the employment relationship as their focus. This is true of industrial relations, industrial psychology, industrial sociology, labor law, human resources management, and labor history. Improving our understanding of the fundamentals of this relationship could be useful for any and all of these fields.

PUBLIC POLICY

Termination of the employment relationship by the employer has drawn increasing attention from lawmakers in recent years. This has been especially true on the two sides of the

3

Atlantic. There have been significant changes in the law in both Europe and the United States. Curiously, the changes have been in opposite directions.

EUROPE

In Europe the 1980s saw a strong move toward greater flexibility for management in general. This included flexibility in getting rid of unwanted employees. The argument of European managers was that the many constraints imposed upon them by government and unions, compared to those of competing nations, had rendered their industries uncompetitive. These fetters on their actions were blamed for the development of an unfavorable comparison with the United States in unemployment rates, which had developed after years of European superiority in this regard. Because of a conjunction of the apparent functionality of acceding to this argument, the force available to employers at a time of high unemployment and decreasing union strength, and the facile use of the normative language of "flexibility," these arguments essentially prevailed.[1] This included facilitating the employer's power to fire employees for alleged misconduct.[2] However, it did not move Europe toward greater harmonization of laws in this regard. More importantly, there is little or no evidence that it operated to reduce unemployment.

UNITED STATES

Perhaps the most important development in the American law of employment in the 1980s was the weakening of the employment-at-will doctrine, under which an employer can dismiss an employee at its discretion. This rule, invented by the courts under the common law, is in the process of being substantially modified by them through the creation and expansion of exceptions to the rule on a case-by-case basis. As a result, employers who have fired employees in violation of public policy, contrary to implied in fact or implied in law contractual obligations, or in an abusive manner, have been successfully sued for quite large amounts of money. One state, Montana, has adopted legislation requiring just cause for termination of employment. Similar legislation is being considered in a number of other states, and a significant effort is being made to develop and lobby for a national model state law.

At the same time that the courts have been changing the

4

common law in ways that make it more difficult to terminate employees, the U.S. Congress has also acted. In the late 1980s plant-closing legislation was passed, requiring employer notice of a closing or a mass layoff. The use of polygraph (lie detector) tests was limited. Protections for handicapped employees have been enacted. All of this has occurred during a period when, for the first time in many years, the legal minimum wage has been increased.

THE LITERATURE

There exists a substantial literature on discipline and termination of employment for employees failing to meet the obligations of employment. In the United States this subject is dealt with in standard arbitration treatises,[3] journal articles on arbitration,[4] and some fairly recent work on discipline in nonunion settings.[5] Similar literature, cited in our national chapters, exists in other countries. There is also something of a body of work on an international comparative basis. However, none of it engages in the type of comparative systematic analysis of concrete employment obligations that we do in our study.

Beginning in 1985 and ending in 1988 *European Industrial Relations Review* ran a series of articles on termination of employment in particular European countries. This series covered Italy, Austria, Switzerland, Greece, Finland, Iceland, Norway, Sweden, Portugal, Spain, Belgium, the United Kingdom, France, West Germany, Denmark, and Malta.[6] These highly useful pieces all spoke briefly to the substantive rules of the employment obligation but attempted no international comparisons.

One interesting paper that makes international comparisons is by M. E. Banderet, published in *International Labour Review* in 1986.[7] This author analyzes disciplinary offenses in a number of countries, using a rather interesting conceptualization. In addition, two issues of the journal entitled, at different times, *Comparative Labor Law* and *Comparative Labor Law Journal* contain international comparisons of the rules of discipline and dismissal. In the first of these, published in 1982, there is a general paper on termination of employment, followed by country reports on Britain, Israel, Romania, Singapore, and the United States, as well as a paper on ILO rules.[8] The later, 1987, issue is entitled "The Role of Neutrals in the Resolution of Shop Floor Disputes."[9] It includes an introductory note and country reports on Australia, Austria, Belgium, Finland, France, Germany, Israel, Italy, Japan, the Netherlands, Sweden, and the United Kingdom. All of these papers deal with many of the same substantive questions as those examined in our study. However, being of quite different design, they are chiefly descriptive and speak at a more general level.

Our review of both the national and international literature leaves us with the impression that, while useful, it could be added to by analysis that is structured somewhat differently. What would be especially helpful, we believe, is a study that is rigorously planned and designed, specific as to obligations of employment and factual settings, and utilizes the same structure of analysis for a number of different countries. This is essentially the task that we have set before us.

PLAN OF THIS STUDY

The object of this study is to improve our understanding of the obligations of employment, both within the several country systems and across them. To that end we have adopted a strategy that identifies important and interesting obligations, constructs specific factual scenarios on each of them, develops a set of factors that have the potential for affecting their legal outcome, devises a set of specific factual variations that exemplify these factors, sets out the general substantive rules in each country, analyzes the particular obligations in each country, and then makes cross-national comparisons.

Perhaps the best way to explain how this strategy operates is to tell the story of how we went about it. It began with the codirectors of the project, who are from the United States and France, putting together a list of potential obligations of employment to which the study might relate. We had a list of perhaps twenty-five of these. By combining and culling them, we reduced the list. We then wrote factual scenarios, similar to the one that opened this chapter, for a dozen of these. Having then assembled a group of scholars, mainly in Europe, who were interested in being involved in such a project, we obtained funding from the Center for International Business and Research at the University of South Carolina for Professor Wheeler to travel to Europe and meet with Professor Rojot and the other participants for the purpose of completing the design of the study.

What might be called the Wheeler European Grand Tour

6

portion of the design phase began with Wheeler and Rojot meeting in Paris to further discuss the particular obligations to be used and the design of the scenarios. Quite importantly, we also created a tentative list of factors that might affect the outcomes on these obligations. Wheeler then visited study participants in Belgium, the Netherlands, Spain, Switzerland, Italy, and the United Kingdom, and returned to Paris to meet with Rojot. The result of these meetings was agreement on a set of ten obligations of employment, a set of factors, and an extensive set of factual variations that were drawn from the scenarios and factors. After returning to the United States, Wheeler sent these to the European participants, made changes based upon their suggestions, and then wrote up final versions of the scenarios, factors, and variations.

The obligations agreed upon as subjects of our study are subordination, sobriety, security of employer's property, peaceful workplace, off-duty conduct, attendance, performance, loyalty, restrict collective action, and avoid conflict of interest. The factors are set out in the outline at the end of this chapter. It is worth noting that we formed the view that the specific factors could be usefully classified as having to do with either: (1) seriousness, (2) mitigation, or (3) enforceability. The factual scenarios and variations are given following the outline.

Using the obligations, factors, scenarios, and variations agreed upon, each participant undertook to write a country paper, utilizing a common outline. Also, additional countries— Australia, Canada, and Israel—were added, and the participants from those countries agreed to write papers according to the common design. With the support of the Council for European Studies, the Center for International Business Education and Research at the University of South Carolina, the University of South Carolina School of Law, and the Riegel and Emory Human Resources Research Center of the College of Business Administration of the University of South Carolina, a meeting of the research group was held in Columbia, South Carolina, in November 1990. Country papers were prepared for this meeting for Australia, Belgium, Canada, France, Israel, Italy, Spain, the United Kingdom, the United States, and West Germany. We discussed the issues on an obligation-by-obligation basis, reaching some collective conclusions. In addition, we planned another stage of the overall project of which this book is a part. This last stage involves a study of the actual practices as to discipline and dismissal, drawing its hypotheses mainly from the legal analysis. It is hoped that the results of this research will be published at a later date.

This volume is the result of these labors. It contains a set of country papers and a concluding chapter that reflects our principal conclusions. Each national chapter sets out, for the particular country, the framework of the industrial justice system, the history of the substantive law of employment obligations, and the general principles of that law. It then applies the law to the case scenarios and variations in order to reveal the workings of the law in concrete situations. Our purpose is to provide a reference guide of some depth and detail for each country, both as to the system of industrial justice and the substantive law of the obligations of employment of that country. In our concluding general comments we draw some comparative conclusions.

It should be kept in mind that this is a study of the *law* of the obligations of employment as they can lead to discipline or dismissal. Questions of practice, which are of equal importance, await our later efforts.

Factors Affecting Discipline or Dismissal

Seriousness

Degree of severity of offense

Probability of reoccurrence

Nature of offense
  Threat to managerial
    authority
  Threat to important policy
    or rule
  Cost
  Precedent establishment
  Moral turpitude

Mitigation

Needs of employee
  Old age
  Financial need
  Poor health
  Low market demand
    for employee

Personal characteristics
  High seniority
  Good discipline record
  Good performance record
  Status as employee
    representative

Accompanying circumstances
  Urgent need to act
  Provocation
  Other offenses absent
    (aggravation if present)

Value to organization
  High performance
  Critical skills
  Skills difficult to replace

Enforceability

Due process
  Lack of procedural standards

Procedural standards not followed	Implicit by failure to enforce against others
Failure to enforce against other employees	Implicit by failure to enforce against employee
Reasonableness	Clarity of rule
	Lack of written rule
Waiver	Ambiguous rule
Explicit	Lack of notice of rule

Industrial Justice Scenarios, Factors, Variations

The following materials represent imaginary situations that might give rise to discipline or termination of employment. PI indicates a positive inference for the employee. NI indicates a negative inference.

I. SUBORDINATION

Scenario

JD, a janitor at the A Manufacturing Company, is assigned the task of waxing office hallways. He completes one hallway. His supervisor, FF, inspects the hallway and says to JD, "Do this floor again." JD replies "No," and walks away.

Factors and Variations

Seriousness
1. Degree of antagonism in refusal
PI. "I do think it is waxed well enough. If you don't mind, I'll leave it." NI. "Go to hell. I'm not doing it again."
2. Threat to supervisor
PI. Walks away. NI. JD pushes FF away, saying, "If you know what's good for you, you won't give me another stupid order like that."
3. Repeated refusal
PI. JD had never previously refused to obey an order. NI. JD had previously refused to obey orders and had been warned against this conduct.
4. Presence of other employees
PI. No other employees present. NI. Five other employees present.

9

5. Belief safety or health threatened
   PI. JD reasonably believed that the fumes from the stripping compound would cause damage to his eyes if he immediately rewaxed the floor. NI. No reason to believe any health hazard present.
6. Belief order contrary to rules
   PI. A company rule existed prohibiting immediate rewaxing of floors. NI. No company rule involved.
7. Belief order foolish or incompetent
   PI. JD reasonably believed that immediately rewaxing the floor would not improve its appearance and that it was necessary to wait before doing this. NI. No reason to believe that redoing the floor would be ineffective.
8. Order beneath dignity of employee
   PI. FF says, "Get down on your knees and scrub that floor clean with this toothbrush and then wax it again." NI. FF says, "Do this floor again."
9. Degree of interference with production
   PI. The hallway is seldom used and its condition is fully usable. NI. As JD has waxed the floor, which is a heavily used passageway for employees, it is too slippery to walk on.
10. Work in fact done properly
    PI. The plant manager who observed the floor admits that it was properly waxed. NI. JD admits that the floor was not properly waxed.
11. Work outside job description
    PI. Waxing of floors is not included in the janitors' job description. NI. Waxing of floors included in janitors' job description.

Mitigation
1. Provocation by supervisor
   PI. FF says, "You incompetent idiot, do this floor again." NI. FF says, "Do this floor again."
2. Employee's past record of obedience, and in general
   PI. Good work record; no past disciplinary record. NI. Poor work record; past record of numerous disciplinary offenses.
3. Seniority
   PI. JD had been working for the employer for 20 years. NI. JD had been employed by the company for 6 months.

10

4. Position as employee representative
   PI. JD is an employee representative. NI. JD holds no position as an employee representative.

Enforceability
1. Clarity of order
   PI. FF says, "Would you mind waxing the floor again?" NI. FF says, "Do this floor again."
2. Past tolerance of disobedience by employee
   PI. On two previous occasions when JD refused to rewax floors, he was not warned or punished. NI. On a previous occasion JD refused to rewax a floor and was warned that failure to do this again would result in discipline.
3. Past tolerance of disobedience by other employees
   PI. JD had observed other janitors refuse to obey orders without being disciplined. NI. JD was aware that other employees who had disobeyed orders were terminated.

II. SOBRIETY

Scenario

RR, a laborer on the loading dock of B Trucking Company, is observed by his supervisor, JB, reaching into the pocket of a coat that is hanging near his workplace. JB observes RR bring something to his mouth, appear to swallow, and then replace it in the coat. JB approaches RR and asks, "What are you drinking?" RR reaches into the pocket of the coat and hands JB a bottle that contains an alcoholic beverage. JB forms the opinion that RR's breath smells strongly of alcoholic spirits and that his eyes are unfocused.

Factors and Variations

Seriousness
1. Degree of intoxication
   PI. There is clear proof that RR is not intoxicated. NI. There is clear proof that RR is highly intoxicated.
2. Intoxicant
   PI. The bottle contains wine. NI. The container holds "crack," a form of cocaine.
3. Potential for harm to employer's property

11

PI. RR loads light boxes of paper that are not easily damaged if dropped. NI. RR loads boxes of crystal glasses that are highly breakable and valuable.
4. Potential for harm to other employees
PI. RR loads light boxes of paper that are unlikely to cause injury to RR or other employees if dropped. NI. RR loads heavy boxes of crystal that would cause serious injury to RR or other employees if dropped on them.
5. Potential for damage to employer's reputation
PI. The loading dock is located in an area well removed from public view. NI. The loading dock is in an area where customers pass nearby on a regular basis.
6. Harm to employer's property
PI. No harm results from RR's intoxication. NI. RR drops a case of crystal, causing $1,000 worth of damage.
7. Harm to other employees
PI. No harm results from RR's intoxication. NI. RR drops a case of crystal, breaking the foot of a fellow employee.
8. Loss of business
PI. No member of the public observes that RR is intoxicated. NI. A valued customer observes RR's intoxication and cancels a large order.

Mitigation
1. Alcoholism or drug addiction
PI. RR produces evidence that he is an alcoholic and has just begun treatment. NI. No additional facts.
2. Nature of industry
PI. The employer is engaged in the beer-brewing industry, where there is a custom that permits drinking on the job. NI. No additional facts.

Enforceability
1. Consistency of enforcement
PI. Other employees have often consumed alcoholic beverages on the job and been intoxicated at work, with no action being taken. NI. Other employees who have consumed alcoholic beverages at work or been intoxicated at work have been terminated.
2. Sobriety of supervisors
PI. RR has observed supervisors and managers consum-

ing alcoholic beverages at work and being intoxicated at work. NI. No additional facts.
3. Existence of formal rule
PI. No rule on this subject. NI. Company rule states that drinking and intoxication on the job will be punished by severe disciplinary sanctions, including termination.

III. SECURITY OF EMPLOYER'S PROPERTY

Scenario

PR, a clerk employed by C Gourmet Foods Company, is observed by two supervisors taking company products out of a packing box, concealing them on his person, and walking out the door with them. He is apprehended after he exits the store, and admits taking the products.

Factors and Variations

Seriousness
1. Value of goods stolen
PI. Goods stolen were of a value of $1.00. NI. Goods stolen were of a value of $1,000.
2. Seriousness of theft problem to employer
PI. No previous problems with theft at C. NI. Serious losses incurred from employee theft.
3. Knowledge of other employees
PI. No knowledge of incident by other employees. NI. Incident observed by five other employees.
4. Whether goods abandoned
PI. Products were taken from a trash bin, where they had been thrown by mistake. NI. Products were on shelf.

Mitigation
1. Needs of employee
PI. PR desperate for money for highly specialized medical treatment for his child. NI. No additional facts.
2. Low probability of reoccurrence
PI. No previous record of dishonesty. NI. Previous arrest and conviction for petty theft.
3. Kleptomania
PI. Proof of kleptomania induced by job-related stress. NI. No additional facts.

13

4. Seniority
   Pl. Employed by C for 20 years. NI. Employed by C for 6 months.
5. Custom of free goods
   Pl. Proof of employer permitting employees to leave premises with small amounts of goods. NI. No additional facts.

Enforceability
1. Past tolerance of employee theft
   Pl. Previous incident of another employee stealing goods of same value and not disciplined. NI. No additional facts.

IV. PEACEFUL WORKPLACE

Scenario

MM is a clerk in D Department Store. NN is another clerk in the same department store; he is physically larger than MM. While MM is moving some heavy equipment from one area to another NN says, "I'm surprised that you did not ask a real man like me to handle this job." MM, angered, strikes NN on the jaw, knocking him down. NN gets up and walks away.

Factors and Variations

Seriousness
1. Who is aggressor
   Pl. NN gives MM a hard push when making his initial comment. NI. NN says, "May I help you with this?"
2. Injury inflicted
   Pl. No injury to NN. NI. NN suffers a broken jaw.
3. Use of weapon
   Pl. MM strikes NN with open hand. NI. MM strikes NN with an iron bar.
4. Damage to employer's property
   Pl. No damage to employer's property. NI. MM falls into a display case, breaking it and some merchandise; there is a total cost of damage of $1,000.
5. Potential for damage to employer's property
   Pl. Incident takes place in open area of store where there is no danger to property of employer. NI. Incident takes

place immediately next to highly valuable and breakable merchandise.

6. Potential for injury to employees
   PI. Incident takes place in broad, clear aisle. NI. Incident takes place in vicinity of packing machinery that is dangerous to employee safety.
7. Interference with production
   PI. Both employees state that they are still able to work well together. NI. Both employees admit that they will have difficulty working together in the future, although their jobs require this.
8. Presence of other employees
   PI. No other employees were present. NI. Five other employees observed the incident.
9. Damage to employer's business
   PI. No customers present. NI. One major customer present, who immediately advised the employer that he was terminating his business with D because of this incident.
10. Merits of employee's position in dispute
    PI. MM's job includes moving the equipment and NN's does not. NI. NN's job includes moving the equipment and MM's does not.

Mitigation
1. Peaceableness of employee's history
   PI. MM has no previous history of violence. NI. MM has previously engaged in a fight on the job in which he was the aggressor.
2. Peaceableness of relationship between involved employees
   PI. MM and NN previously had a friendly relationship. NI. MM and NN have previously had altercations, including an occasion where they shoved each other.
3. Status as an employee representative
   PI. MM is an employee representative. NI. No additional facts.
4. Seniority
   PI. MM has been employed here for 20 years. NI. MM has been employed here for 6 months.

Enforceability
1. Tolerance of previous violence by employee

PI. MM had struck NN at work during a previous altercation and was not punished. NI. When MM pushed NN during a previous altercation at work, he was warned that he
would be disciplined if he again engaged in this type of
behavior.

2. Tolerance of previous violence by other employees
PI. Other employees had engaged in similar fights in the
past without discipline being imposed. NI. When other
employees engaged in fights in the past they were
terminated.

V. OFF-DUTY CONDUCT

Scenario

TT, head salesclerk for E Toy Store, participates in a white
supremacist demonstration. He is arrested for disorderly behavior, and a photograph of him handcuffed to a post and snarling
at police is printed in the local newspaper, along with his name
and the name of his employer.

Factors and Variations

Seriousness
1. Conviction of crime
PI. TT acquitted of crime. NI. TT convicted of crime.
2. Heinousness of offense
PI. TT charged with disorderly conduct. NI. TT charged
with physically attacking police.
3. Effect on employer's reputation
PI. Name of employer not given in newspaper. NI. Picture,
name of employee, and employer name prominently fea-
tured on front page of newspaper in city of 5,000
residents.
4. Effect on employer's sales
PI. No evidence of effects on employer's sales. NI. Two
regular customers notified employer that they would no
longer shop there because of incident.
5. Effect on authority of supervisors
PI. All supervisors white. NI. TT's supervisor is black.
6. Willingness of other employees to work with employee
PI. All five other employees state that they remain willing

16

to work with TT. NI. Two of the five other employees, who are black, state that they could no longer work with TT.

Mitigation
1. Seniority
PI. TT has been employed by E for 20 years. NI. TT has been employed by E for 6 months.
2. Provocation
PI. TT was engaged in a peaceful demonstration until he was attacked by members of a counterdemonstration group. NI. TT instigated violent actions during the demonstration.

Enforceability
1. Tolerance of similar behavior by other employees
PI. On a previous occasion one of E's employees who is black was arrested on the same charge, and had this publicized in the same way, but was not disciplined. NI. Black employee arrested on same charge with same publicity terminated.
2. Tolerance of similar behavior by this employee
PI. TT was arrested for a similar event previously and not disciplined. NI. TT was arrested for a similar event previously and was warned that he would be disciplined for future occurrences.
3. Tolerance of similar behavior by supervisors
PI. TT's supervisor was a participant in the same demonstration. NI. No additional facts.

VI. ATTENDANCE

Scenario

JJ is a nurse's aide at F Nursing Home. Because of an illness her attendance at work has been erratic for two years. During that period she has missed 30 percent of her scheduled working days. During the last month she has missed 20 percent of her scheduled working days. All of these absences were excused. She then misses three days of work, without notifying her employer, because she decides to extend her holiday.

17

Factors and Variations

Seriousness
1. Number of absences
   PI. JJ missed 10 percent of scheduled shifts over two years and 5 percent in the last month. NI. JJ missed 40 percent of scheduled working days over two years and 30 percent in last month.
2. Length of unexcused absence
   PI. JJ missed one day without calling in in order to stay over on holiday. NI. JJ missed five days without calling in in order to stay over on holiday.
3. Reasons for absences
   PI. Reason for excused absences was an illness that is totally disabling for the period that she has it. NI. JJ simply claimed not to feel well and received physician's excuses on this basis.
4. Whether absences excused or unexcused
   PI. All absences excused. NI. No absences excused.
5. Trend
   PI. During two months preceding last absence, she had not been absent. NI. During two months preceding last absence, she missed 50 percent of her scheduled working days.
6. Predictions of future attendance
   PI. A physician appointed by F to examine JJ states that he predicts that she will be able to attend work regularly in the future. NI. JJ's physician says that it is not likely that she will be able to attend work regularly in the future.

Mitigation
1. Seniority
   PI. JJ has been employed by F for 20 years. NI. JJ has been employed by F for 6 months.
2. Financial needs of employee
   PI. JJ has three children, of which she is the sole support. NI. No additional facts.
3. Performance record
   PI. JJ has an excellent record of performance. NI. JJ has a below average performance record.
4. Discipline record

18

PI. JJ has no previous discipline record. NI. JJ has been disciplined on three previous occasions for offenses other than attendance.
5. Lack of unexcused absences
PI. Last absence was caused by illness and excused. JJ called in. NI. No additional facts.

Enforceability
1. Tolerance of absences by other employees
PI. On other occasions employees with records the same as JJ's have not been disciplined. NI. F has consistently terminated employees with the same record as JJ.
2. Lack of counseling or warnings for absenteeism
PI. JJ had never been warned that her absences might lead to discipline. NI. JJ was counseled, and then warned, that her absences might lead to termination if they continued.
3. Specificity of rules
PI. F had no written policy on absenteeism. NI. F had an absenteeism policy which stated that employees with records such as JJ's would be terminated.

VII. PERFORMANCE

Scenario

HH is a warehouseman for G Distributing Company. G has instituted a program that determines levels of productivity for warehousemen. This program meets accepted professional standards for such programs. Over a period of two months HH fails to produce at the prescribed levels, consistently falling 10 percent below the standard. He is warned that he will be terminated if he fails to improve his productivity within two weeks. HH claims that the standards of the new system are impossible to meet. He proves that prior to the institution of the new system he was given above-average evaluations by his supervisor for producing at his current level, covering a period of ten years.

Factors and Variations

Seriousness
1. Degree performance is below standard

PI. HH's performance is 2 percent below the standard. NI. HH's performance is 40 percent below standard.

2. Period of low performance

PI. HH fails to meet the standard for a period of one week. NI. HH fails to meet the standard for a period of six months.

3. Trend of performance

PI. During the last two weeks HH's performance has improved so that it is only 5 percent below standard. NI. During the last two weeks HH's performance has not changed.

4. Degree production is affected

PI. There is no proof that HH's low production has hurt the overall production of his unit. NI. HH's low production has caused the overall production of his unit to be 2 percent lower than it would be if he were meeting the standard.

5. Hazard to safety or property

PI. There is no proof that there is any impact upon safety of employees or property caused by HH's low production. NI. Because HH does not keep up with the machine-paced work that precedes his work, occasional bottlenecks occur that create dangerously cluttered aisles for vehicles.

6. Costs of low performance

PI. There is no proof that HH's low production results in any costs to the employer. NI. It is reliably estimated that HH's low production costs G $200 per week.

7. Influence on productivity of other employees

PI. There is no proof that HH's behavior has any influence on other employees. NI. Two other employees have complained that they are required to keep to high standards and HH is not.

8. Ineptitude

PI. HH apparently possesses the ability to perform the work required of him. NI. HH does not have the degree of manual dexterity required to perform efficiently some of the tasks required of him.

9. Inability to adapt to new machinery

PI. No new machinery has been introduced. NI. At the same time the new production standard was adopted, new machinery was introduced which HH appears to be unable to learn to operate.

Mitigation
1. Seniority
   PI. HH has worked for G for 20 years. NI. HH has worked for G for 6 months.
2. Past performance
   PI. HH has always been an above average performer in this and previous jobs for the employer. NI. HH has generally performed at or below average.

Enforceability
1. Reasonableness of standard
   PI. All of the other employees in HH's unit are failing to meet the new standard to about the same degree as HH. NI. All of the other employees in HH's unit are meeting the new standard.
   PI. G's company physician states that HH and several other warehousemen have suffered from extreme fatigue since the adoption of the new standard and attributes this to their working harder than before. NI. No proof of physical detriment to warehousemen from the adoption of the new standard.
2. Warning of consequences of low performance
   PI. HH not warned of possible disciplinary consequences of failing to meet the standard. NI. HH warned after the first week and again after two months that he would be disciplined if he failed to meet the standard.
3. Lack of enforcement of standard as to other employees
   PI. Two other warehousemen with the same level of production as HH have not been disciplined. NI. Two other warehousemen with the same level of production as HH have been terminated.

VIII. LOYALTY

Scenario

JS, a teller for H Bank, during an appearance on a television consumer information program states that her employer regularly fails to advise customers when they make mistakes in favor of the bank, but promptly corrects mistakes made in favor of the customers.

Factors and Variations

Seriousness
1. Effect on employer's reputation
   Pl. TV show at 3:00 A.M., small audience. Nl. TV show during highest viewing time, large audience.
2. Effect on employer's trade
   Pl. No evidence of loss of customers by employer. Nl. Ten large depositors canceled accounts the next day, citing JS's statement as their reason.
3. Truthfulness
   Pl. Statement truthful. Nl. Statement not true.
4. Reasonable grounds to believe facts true
   Pl. JS had been told that this was true by the head of the accounts department. Nl. JS's source was a rumor among clerical employees.
5. Justification for breach of loyalty
   Pl. JS believed that customers deserved to know of this practice. Nl. JS merely thought that it would be fun to annoy her employer.
6. Illegality of employer behavior
   Pl. Bank's practice illegal. Nl. Bank's practice not illegal.
7. Industry
   Pl. JS is a credit department employee of a clothing store. Nl. No additional facts.
8. Level of employee's job
   Pl. JS is a janitor. Nl. JS is chief teller.

Mitigation
1. Mistreatment of employee by employer
   Pl. JS had been harassed sexually by her supervisor. Nl. No additional facts.
2. Seniority
   Pl. JS had been working for H for 20 years. Nl. JS had been working for H for 6 months.
3. Status as employee representative
   Pl. JS is an employee representative on H's board of directors and came to this knowledge in this capacity. Nl. No additional facts.

Enforceability
1. Reasonableness of rule

22

PI. H has rule prohibiting any revelations of bank business, legal or illegal, to any outside person or agency under any circumstances. NI. H has rule requiring employees to consult with management before revealing damaging information to the public, giving H a chance to change policies that are wrong or to explain them to the employee.

2. Existence of formal rule prohibiting behavior
   PI. H has no rule with regard to employees making public information about H or its business. NI. H has a written rule prohibiting employees making public information about the bank or its business.
3. Communication of rule to employee.
   PI. H has not communicated to JS any rule prohibiting statements about the bank or its business to outsiders. NI. H communicated to JS its rule prohibiting statements about the bank or its business to outsiders.

IX. RESTRICT COLLECTIVE ACTION

Scenario

JJ, a machinist at I Manufacturing Company, becomes angry because he believes that his supervisor is treating him and other employees in a disrespectful manner. In protest, he persuades the other employees in his work group to leave work together in the middle of their scheduled work shift and not return until the next day.

Factors and Variations

Seriousness
1. Length of refusal to work
   PI. Walkout lasted for one hour. NI. Walkout lasted for one week.
2. Level of antagonism
   PI. JJ states to supervisor that there are no hard feelings involved. NI. JJ tells supervisor that he and other employees hate the supervisor and screams at him that the employees will "fix" him.
3. Presence of violence or destruction of property
   PI. No violence. NI. JJ threatens and then pushes out the door an employee who refuses to join in the walkout.

23

PI. No destruction of property. NI. JJ strikes a machine causing $200 in damages.
4. Effect on production
PI. Production is not reduced. NI. One-half day's production is lost for JJ's unit, costing the employer $10,000 in lost production.
5. Proportion of employees involved
PI. One percent of the employees are affected by the walkout. NI. All of the production employees in the plant are involved in the walkout.
6. Position of leadership of collective action
PI. JJ, instead of being the leader of the walkout, merely walks out when others do. NI. JJ is the leader and argues vigorously with other workers to persuade them to walk out.

Mitigation
1. Seniority
PI. JJ has worked for I for 20 years. NI. JJ has worked for I for 6 months.
2. Provocation
PI. JJ's supervisor has in fact abused and insulted employees over a period of 6 months. NI. JJ's supervisor has treated employees with respect.
PI. JJ's supervisor has regularly demanded that employees perform work in ways that are contrary to agreed-upon work rules. NI. JJ's supervisor has required workers only to do work that is appropriate for them.

Enforceability
1. Lack of existence of rule against strikes
PI. There is no rule, either by law or contract, prohibiting strikes. NI. A lawful collective bargaining agreement provision prohibits strikes during its term.

X. AVOID CONFLICT OF INTEREST

Scenario

IB, a systems analyst for J Company, has access to private computer systems of his employer. IB accepts a string of freelance, relatively routine programming jobs for K Company, a competitor of his employer, performing the work at his home.

Factors and Variations

Seriousness
1. Existence of formal rule
PI. J has no rule on employees working for competitors.
NI. J has a rule that prohibits employees from working for competitors.
2. Connection between types of work performed both places
PI. IB's jobs for K involve the writing of advertising copy.
NI. IB's jobs for K involve creating systems similar to those on which he works for J.
3. Revelation of trade secrets
PI. No proof that IB has revealed to K anything relating to J. NI. IB admits to revealing to K the details of private systems used by J.
4. Use of training and skills acquired in employer's employ
PI. IB's jobs for K involve different skills than those used in his employment with J. NI. IB's jobs for K require him to use system design skills that he learned as a part of his training at K.
5. Acquisition of ownership interest in competitor
PI. IB has no stock ownership in K. NI. IB owns a 50 percent share of K.
6. Negative effects on employer's business
PI. IB's work for K has no effect on J's business. NI. IB's work directly competes with J's business, taking substantial business away from J.
7. Valuable private information known to employee
PI. IB has access only to routine, nearly valueless information about J's business. NI. IB has access to highly secret and valuable information about J's systems.
8. Known to other employees
PI. IB's work for K is not known to other employees. NI. IB's work for K is widely known among J's employees.
9. Continuing nature of other job
PI. IB's work for K has ended. NI. IB's work for K is continuing.

Mitigation
1. Seniority

Pl. IB has worked for K for 20 years. NI. IB has worked for K for 6 months.

2. Financial needs of employee

Pl. IB has a strong need for money, arising from a serious illness of one of his children. NI. No additional facts.

Enforceability

1. Lack of clarity of rule

Pl. J has a rule which states, "No employee shall have a conflict of interest." NI. J has a rule which states, "No employee may perform any work for a competitor of J."

2. Reasonableness of rule

Pl. J's rule states, "No employee can engage in any activity that might possibly harm the interests of J, either while employed by J or after termination of employment with J." NI. J's rule states, "While in J's employ, employees will engage in work for competitor of J only with the permission of their supervisors. Permission will not be unreasonably withheld."

3. Tolerance of violation of rule by other employees

Pl. On three previous occasions within the last year, employees have been found to be performing work for a competitor and have not been disciplined. NI. On three previous occasions in the past year, employees have been terminated when found to be working for a competitor.

4. Toleration of violation of this rule by this employee

Pl. On one previous occasion IB was discovered to be working for a competitor and was not warned or disciplined. NI. On one previous occasion when IB was discovered to be working for a competitor by his supervisor, he was warned that any future occurrence would result in discipline.

NOTES

1. Hoyt N. Wheeler, "Labour Market Flexibility and New Employment Patterns," *Proceedings, 9th World Congress, International Industrial Relations Association,* 1989, 1–20.

2. W. Dercksen, "Labour Market Flexibility in Termi-

nation of Employment," *Proceedings, 9th World Congress, International Industrial Relations Association,* 1989, 30–45.

3. Lawrence Stessin, *Employee Discipline* (Washington: BNA, 1960); Walter E. Baer, *Discipline and Discharge under the Labor Agreement* (New York: American Management Association, 1972); Dallas L. Jones, *Arbitration and Industrial Discipline* (Ann Arbor: Bureau of Industrial Relations, University of Michigan, 1961).

4. Roger I. Abrams and Dennis R. Nolan, "Toward a Theory of 'Just Cause' in Employee Discipline Cases," *Duke Law Journal* 85 (1985): 594–623.

5. Fred K. Foulkes, *Personnel Policies in Large Nonunion Companies* (Englewood Cliffs, NJ: Prentice-Hall, 1980).

6. The following articles all appeared in the *European Industrial Relations Review:* "Termination of Contract: Italy," Oct. 1988: 16–20; "Termination of Contract: Austria," Oct. 1986: 19–21; "Termination of Contract: Switzerland," Sept. 1986: 26–28; "Termination of Contract: Greece," July 1986: 18–20; "Termination of Contract: Finland," Jan. 1987: 20–22; "Termination of Contract: Iceland," Jan. 1988: 22–24; "Termination of Contract: Norway," May 1986: 21–23; "Termination of Contract: Sweden," April 1986: 21–24; "Termination of Contract: Portugal," Mar. 1986; "Termination of Contract: Spain," Jan. 1986: 18–21; "Termination of Contract: Belgium," Oct. 1985: 24–27; "Termination of Contract: United Kingdom," July 1985: 19–22; "Termination of Contract: France," June 1985: 17–20; "Termination of Contract: West Germany," May 1985: 16–19; "Termination of Contract: Denmark," June 1986: 22–24; "Termination of Contract: Malta," Nov. 1986: 16–19.

7. M. E. Bandaret, "Discipline at the Workplace: A Comparative Study of Law and Practice," *International Labour Review* 125 (May–June 1986): 261–78.

8. "Termination of Employment on the Initiative of the Employer," *Comparative Labor Law* 5 (Summer 1982): 221–347.

9. "The Role of Neutrals in the Resolution of Shop Floor Disputes," *Comparative Labor Law Journal* 9 (Fall 1987): 1–211.

AUSTRALIA[1]

Brian Brooks

To understand the Australian system of handling employer–employee relations it is necessary to consider its constitutional and historical background.[2] The tyranny of distance has shaped Australian attitudes and institutions since formal British settlement in the 1780s. For over a century the six colonies that were established on the continent were closer to England than to each other. By the middle 1880s the six colonies were moving closer together, and at a series of constitutional conventions in the 1890s two significant political decisions were taken. One conscious political decision was to federate rather than to unite. The second was to adopt a policy of massive government intervention into the relations of employer and employee. These decisions are embodied in the Constitution. In most features of its political, social, and economic life the Commonwealth of Australia looks to the Westminster model for its examples. But, for reasons that still remain obscure, the founding fathers of the Constitution elected to pursue a quite distinctive and novel path in one important area of national life—the handling of industrial relations and, more specifically, the handling of industrial disputation between employer and employee.

OVERVIEW OF THE SYSTEM

In contrast to the noninterventionist nineteenth-century British philosophy, the Australian model adopted in federal legislation in 1904 is one of massive intervention into the relations of employer and employee by way of permanent industrial tribunals. Broadly speaking, the characteristic that sets the Australian system apart from virtually every other industrialized country is that of compulsory settlement of industrial disputation. Authority and responsibility in the area of industrial law and industrial relations are not confined exclusively to the federal government. Each of the six state governments also has legislative competence to deal with industrial relations and industrial law within its own jurisdiction. Pursuant to their power, each of the state jurisdictions has enacted laws that regulate industrial relations. It follows from this that there is not a single Australian system of industrial law but a complex web of industrial relations systems comprising the federal and the six states, and that there is an equally complex interrelationship of labor laws affecting employer and employee involving the labor legislation of the federal government and the labor and industrial legislation of each of the six states.

Reduced to its simplest, what all this complexity comes to is this: The parties engaged in disputes concerning the relations of employer and employee have a choice of jurisdictions. Trite though this may seem, it is a reality that creates quite astonishingly intricate legal and industrial problems. What is also clear is that the regulation of labor relations in the Commonwealth of Australia does not take place within either a simple employer-employee model or an equally simple management–union model but within a complex network of relationships. Labor relations in Australia is a multistage process. Arguments, and their resolution, occur at the workplace, before state and federal industrial tribunals, in the civil, criminal, and equity courts, and before the High Court of Australia.[3] The arbitration system was imposed on top of the existing common law and legislation that had evolved in England and in the six Australian colonies in the nineteenth century. The outcome is a crazy-quilt effect which provides a strange contrast to the largely unregulated industrial bargaining that exists in most Western industrial societies. In contrast to most industrialized countries, industrial relations in Australia is industrial law.

Discussion about employer–employee relations in Australia has traditionally been focused upon the operation of the arbitration system and the functioning of the industrial tribunals. Historically there has been little attention paid to the day-to-day conduct of labor relations at the workplace. There are many reasons advanced for this imbalance. Some commentators have captured the received wisdom when they identify the inclination of many managers to dump their industrial relations problems as speedily as possible on the doorstep of industrial tribunals which, paradoxically, are not designed to cope effectively at this level.[4] It is equally true that access to permanent industrial tribunals to regulate workplace labor problems has appealed to trade unions as well as management. There is, for example, an absence of a tradition of a strong shop-floor delegate structure amongst Australian trade unions. Nor has there been a tradition of works committees, and Australian trade unions have never shown great interest in developing worker-participation schemes. The reality is that the arbitration system makes the individual trade union member highly dependent upon his or her union. Moreover, the High Court of Australia has allowed the industrial tribunals jurisdiction over the most fundamental of workplace issues, including questions of discipline of employees. Very recently the High Court has allowed the federal industrial tribunal to hear legal arguments from an applicant union that a member should be reinstated in employment following a dismissal.[5] Not surprisingly, therefore, Australian labor relations has not seen the development of workplace grievance procedures. Nor have personnel and labor relations managers been highly regarded in the past.

The Australian system of labor relations is highly legalistic and interventionist. Both the bargaining procedures and the bargaining structures are tightly regulated, and the employer–employee relationship is surrounded by a complex body of substantive law.

Australian industrial tribunals, at both the federal and the state level, exist to settle industrial disputes. An industrial dispute is defined as a dispute concerning the relations of employer and employee. No serious condition of hostility need exist for there to be an industrial dispute. An industrial dispute in Australia is an artificial legal concept. The creation of a legal industrial dispute is the first step toward obtaining an award that is made in settlement of the dispute. The process begins with a party, which must be either a registered union of employers or employees or an individual employer, notifying the relevant tribunal of a dispute. The first function of the tribunal is to satisfy itself that the notification concerns industrial matters—in other words, that the dispute raises issues between employer and employee. Once so satisfied, the tribunal will declare that a dispute exists and will invariably order the parties into a compulsory conference with the hope that the parties themselves will settle the dispute. In this sense the first step is a form of institutionalized collective bargaining. If the parties do reach agreement, they will approach the tribunal to ratify the agreement. An agreement so ratified becomes an award of the tribunal. The award is a legally binding collective contract binding employer and employee. Should the parties not reach agreement at the conciliation stage, then the tribunal will hear arguments from the opposing parties and hand down an arbitrated award which, again, has binding legal force. At the compulsory conference stage proceedings are informal and resemble collective bargaining processes. At arbitration the procedure is more akin to that of a formal common law court; in other words, it is adversarial, with the parties commonly represented by lawyers who prove evidence, examine witnesses, and so forth.

SUBSTANTIVE AND PROCEDURAL RULES OF EMPLOYMENT OBLIGATION

The establishment of various state and federal industrial tribunals at the turn of the century marked a novel departure from the British tradition of nonintervention in the collective relations of employer and employee. It also alerts us to the reality that when the six colonies were first established on the continent, they brought with them legal concepts rooted in the British common law. As in Britain, so in Australia, throughout the nineteenth century the relations of employer and employee were seen a governed by the law of contract, and there was very little statutory control.

Another branch of judge-made law derived from the British system, and imported into the six colonies is the web of reciprocal rights and duties independent of contractual obligations and known compendiously as tort law. The principles of tort law are relevant to Australian labor relations. The general notion of a duty of care imposed on all those whose acts or omissions could foreseeably cause harm is directly relevant to the employer–employee relationship. Vicarious liability is central to the employment relationship. The criminal law is also imported into Australian labor relations. For example, the "might of the state" is applied in the arbitration system to secure the observance of rights and duties as prescribed in awards and orders of the various industrial tribunals. The legislation establishing the arbitration systems was superimposed upon this existing common law. In addition today there is a plethora of legislation governing labor relations at the workplace. Occupational health and safety, compensation for work-related injuries, prohibitions against various forms of discrimination (including dismissal), procedures for ensuring a measure of job security, and a host of other matters are on the statute books. Furthermore, every workplace has its customs and practices and usages which have grown up over time. This was acknowledged in the original federal arbitration act of 1904, which prescribed the matters which could be put before the industrial tribunal as including "any custom or usage of any industry whether general or in a particular locality."[6]

Notwithstanding the apparent breadth of this prescription, it is clear that not all workplace practices will be recognized in the Australian arbitration system as forming part of the rights and duties of the parties. The legal problem is clear: Will an industrial tribunal or a common law court recognize a factually established practice as a source of legal obligation? There is no short answer to encapsulate the approach of the industrial tribunals or the courts. What is clear is this: The applicant will first have to prove the practice as existing in fact and will secondly have to persuade the tribunal to imply this practice into the employment contract. Courts have from time to time implied terms to flesh out gaps in the contract, and do so from an examination of the conduct of the parties and the nature of their relationship. Today there is very little room for employer and employee to create binding obligations through their consensual practices. For this there are many reasons, including the operation of the arbitration system, the wide reach of a range of protective legislation, the increasing practice of issuing works rule books, and the trend toward reducing employment contracts to writing.

By way of summary it is safe to say that there is no general and widespread agreement as to the nature and sources of Australian labor law. The content of such law cuts across traditional compartments of law as well as drawing upon many diverse sources. As the present writer has noted elsewhere, "Legislation, the common law, equitable remedies, awards and industrial agreements, the pronouncements of many industrial tribunals, custom and practice and 'gentlemen's agreements,' terms presumptively implied under the common law, rules and terms incorporated or imposed by various pieces of protective industrial legislation, are all sources of industrial law."[7]

THE AUSTRALIAN LAW OF MASTER AND SERVANT

The individual relationship of master and servant is central to Australian labor relations and labor law. Unless this relationship exists, the rights and duties found in awards of the industrial tribunals will not apply. Access to trade union membership is dependent on the applicant being engaged as an employee and not, say, as an independent contractor. In other words, the self-employed cannot join an Australian trade union. Furthermore, as a general proposition, the wide range of protective employment legislation operates in favor of only those who work pursuant to an employment contract. And, as noted earlier, it is only matters pertaining to the relationship between employers and employees that give jurisdiction to industrial tribunals. Thus it can be argued that industrial relations in Australia is all about the proper administration of the employment contract.

When the early English colonists settled the Australian continent, they carried in their baggage such of the laws of England as were applicable to the circumstances of the colony. Among these applicable laws were those pertaining to the special relationship of master and servant. In the nineteenth century that relationship was seen as comparable to a family relationship. Thus a catalog of rights and duties residing in the master and servant relationship reads like the matters which the law would expect to govern the relationship of parent and child. An echo of this earlier age is found in the words of Lord Denning MR in a judgment delivered in 1982: "The employer must be good and considerate to his servants. Just as a servant must be good and faithful, so an employer must be good and considerate. Just as in the old days an employee could be guilty of misconduct justifying his dismissal, so in modern times an employer can be guilty of misconduct justifying the employee in leaving at once without notice."[8] But with the emergence of the welfare state, the encouraged growth of trade unions in Australia, the establishment of the system of compulsory arbitration, and the plethora of protective legislation regulating employment, it has been suggested that there is very little room for the operation of traditional master–servant law. One commentator suggests that those who operate largely within the framework of a compulsory arbitration system should not encourage "an inflated estimate of the common law" as a component of labor law.[9] Yet despite extensive federal and state industrial legislation, many aspects of employment are governed by principles resting in the common law of master and servant. This is especially the case for those in the nonunionized sector of the work force. Australia has a very high degree of unionization, and almost 90 percent of employees have their terms and conditions of employment regulated by industrial awards or agreements. But this still leaves about 10 percent of Australian employees whose employment lies outside the reach of industrial tribunals. These employees are described as being award free. For these employees, especially absent a written contract of employment, the terms implied by the common law form the basis of their relationship with their employer. Moreover, even where an industrial tribunal has regulated the employment relationship through an award, there will remain areas where the award has to be fleshed out by resort to the common law. The clearest illustration of this is in the area of discipline and termination of the employment relationship.

The law as to the manner in which obligations under a contract of employment may be discharged has been clearly stated by Lord Reid in *Ridge v. Baldwin* 1964 in these words: "The law regarding master and servant is not in doubt. There cannot be specific performance of a contract of service, and the master can terminate the contract with his servant at any time and for any reason or for none. But if he does so in a manner not warranted by the contract he must pay damages for breach of contract."[10] The question is obvious: When is there a termination which is "not warranted by the contract"?

Another way to put this question is to ask what are the legal limitations placed on employers to terminate the engagement of their employees. In Australia the answer is found in an examination of five interrelated matters. The first is the common law aspects of the employer's right to dismiss. The second concerns restrictions imposed by industrial tribunals. The third comes from restrictions imposed directly through industrial arbitration legislation. The fourth involves special employment protection, or job security, legislation. And the fifth requires an examination of the effect of certain antidiscrimination legislation.

THE COMMON LAW

Until comparatively recently the common law operated on the presumption that where an employment contract is entered into for an indefinite period, it is taken to be a contract for a yearly hiring. In short, the contract renews itself on each anniversary. Generally today the contract of employment, or the award which is incorporated into the contract, will express a measured period of notice which must be given by either party to terminate the contract legally. In employment which is regulated by an award or industrial agreement the required period of notice is usually specified in a clause in the award or agreement. The relevant clause is entitled "the contract of employment clause" and it usually specifies that employment shall be by the week and that it may be terminated by the giving of a week's notice by either employer or employee.

Where there is no expressed term, the legal position becomes complex. Put shortly, the law will imply a term of "reasonable notice," and termination short of the proper notice period will be a breach of contract by the employer. What is reasonable notice will vary with the circumstances, including the status, grade, or level of the employee's appointment, the nature of the work, the amount of remuneration, the length of service of the employee, what the employee might have given up to take the employment, prospective pension rights, and so forth. In light of this it is not surprising that Australian courts have explained that the purpose of providing in a contract for a period of notice of termination is to enable the party receiving the notice to make other arrangements.[11]

Generally, it is safe to say, no reasons need be given for the termination. As Lord Reid said in *Ridge v. Baldwin* in 1964: "The question in a pure case of master and servant does not at all depend on whether the master has heard the servant in his own defence: it depends on whether the facts emerging at the trial prove a breach of contract."[12] It follows that where continuance in the job is subject to "the satisfaction of the employer" there is no objective test, no requirement that the employer must have had reasonable grounds for saying that he or she is no longer satisfied with the employee.[13] There is one category of employee entitled to be given reasons for termination, and this is hinted at in Lord Reid's formulation where reference is to the "pure case of master and servant." Australian law recognizes a class of employees who are characterized as "the holder of an office." It is no easy matter to define who holds an "office" so as to be entitled to reasons for termination. All we need note here is that the "holder of an office" is entitled to be given reasons for termination, to be given an opportunity to answer any allegations, and to have the case for or against termination determined without bias. All this is embraced in the concept of "natural justice," and the employer who terminates the holder of an office without displaying natural justice is in breach of contract. Public servants are in a different position again.[14] At common law the rule, which originated with military officers, was that employees of the Crown were dismissable at will. The position in Australia has changed, and there is for most public servants detailed legislation which indicates that the old common law no longer applies.

Leaving aside the holder of an office and the public servant, and concentrating on the employer and employee in the private sector, we find that termination is not confined to the contractual period of notice. The common law of master and servant allowed the employer to terminate the relationship instantly—that is, to dismiss the employee "on the spot" and without notice. This right continues to exist in Australia even where the employment contract contains an express term as to notice. All awards emanating from the industrial tribunal preserve the common law right by reserving to the employer the right to dismiss instantly for such stated matters as misconduct, inefficiency, malingering, insubordination, neglect, and dishonesty. These concepts are never defined in the industrial award, and to discover what they mean we must look to the grounds that historically the common law allowed as reasons justifying instant termination. Furthermore, even should the award of agreement be silent on the right to dismiss instantly, the employer remains so entitled for the simple reason that the core common law obligation resting on the employee is personal service, and this entails, among other things, obedience, diligence, honesty, care, and fidelity. Any conduct that is inconsistent with the fulfillment of these implied terms will justify dismissal. Such behavior will be misconduct.

There is no legal measure for ascertaining misconduct sufficient to justify dismissal. The power to dismiss instantly was once based on the superior status of the master, and has a history closely linked with the concept of punishment for misbehavior.

It is clear today, however, that Australian courts approach the issue of instant dismissal by applying ordinary contractual principles, in particular the general principles of repudiation. By drawing on analogies with conditions and warranties in commercial contracts the courts require that conduct justifying instant dismissal be such as to strike at the fundamental basis of the employer–employee relationship.

Given that adherence to contract principles governs the legal approach to instant termination, it is possible to break the enquiry into two steps. The first is to ask whether the employee's conduct amounts to a breach of the employment contract and, second, if so, does that breach amount to a repudiation of the contract. By maintaining a distinction between a fundamental breach and a less serious breach the courts have allowed for a flexible approach to termination and have made it clear that not every act of misconduct by an employee will justify instant dismissal. Instant dismissal is a very strong measure; it amounts to the employer taking the law into his or her own hands. Not surprisingly, then, the Australian courts place the onus on the employer, on the balance of probabilities, to bring his or her conduct within the common law entitlement to dismiss instantly.

INDUSTRIAL TRIBUNALS

As noted earlier, Australia is a society that has tried to ensure order and stability in employment relationships by legislation. The creation of the system of industrial arbitration was seen as opening up "a new province for law and order"[15] and today the great majority of Australian employees have their employment contract regulated by awards and agreements emanating from legislatively created industrial tribunals. The awards detail how the employment relationship may be terminated. Often this is merely a reiteration of common law principles. Increasingly, however, the industrial tribunals, and the legislation pursuant to which they function, are introducing concepts unknown to the common law and are restricting the common law freedom of employer and employee. There are several illustrations.

Perhaps the most contentious illustration is found in the legislative power of the industrial tribunals to award preference in employment to trade union members. Given that it is government policy to encourage trade unions, it follows that there will be trade union security provisions. Preference is one such provision. It is invariably the case that when an award is made there will be a clause that provides that in engaging and in dismissing labor, preference should be given financial members of a trade union. In short, a paying union member will be employed ahead of a nonunionist, and when there is a mass dismissal the nonunionist will be dismissed ahead of union members. Preference is obviously important when redundancies occur, that is, when the job disappears. Mass dismissals at a time of historically high unemployment and high inflation is a contemporary phenomenon. Australian industrial tribunals are authorized to deal with redundancy, especially that occasioned by technological change, and have made awards that clearly interfere with an employer's right to dismiss.

The clearest example is the outcome of the Australian Council of Trade Unions test case argued before the federal industrial tribunal between 1982 and 1984. The case is reported as the *Termination, Change and Redundancy Case* 1984, and its name indicates the substantial issues argued. In that decision the federal tribunal established guidelines for insertion in federal awards. In summary, the provisions now inserted in federal awards include: a model unfair dismissal clause which prohibits termination of employment on harsh, unjust, unreasonable, or discriminatory grounds; employers of more than fifteen people are required to consult with their employees as soon as a decision has been taken about technological changes that are likely to affect employees; the traditional notice period of one week is extended on a scale peaking at four weeks' notice for employees with five or more years continuous service; an employee terminated on the ground of redundancy receives special payments on a sliding scale based on years of service.

INDUSTRIAL ARBITRATION LEGISLATION

There are several limitations on an employer's right to terminate imposed by industrial legislation. The most striking example is found in the prohibitions on victimization for trade union activities. These prohibitions are found in federal and state arbitration acts. The effect of these provisions is that an employee is protected from arbitrary dismissal on the ground that he or she is active in union affairs. The union delegate or shop steward is not entitled to protection from disciplinary action merely because he or she is an official or member of a trade union. Any employee, including an active trade union member, is vulnerable to dismissal with proper notice or to instant dismissal for misconduct, malingering, neglect, and the other usual reasons. But the arbitration legislation prohibits dismissal merely because of trade union activities, and the onus is upon the employer to prove that he or she was not victimizing the trade union activist but was dismissing the employee for reasons unconnected with trade unionism.[16] The distinctive feature of the protection against victimization is that, unlike the common law courts, the industrial tribunals in Australia are empowered to order the reinstatement of the victimized employee. Moreover, the remedy of reinstatement is available to all employees who are members of trade unions and whose employment has been disadvantageously altered by the employer. No firm guidelines exist as to when such an order will be made: "The objective in these cases is always industrial justice and to this end weight must be given in varying degrees according to the requirements of each case to the importance but not the inviolability of the right of the employer to manage his business, the nature and quality of the work in question, the circumstances surrounding the dismissal and the likely practical outcome if an order of reinstatement is made."[17]

JOB SECURITY LEGISLATION

There is no consistent or coherent attention to job security in Australia. There are constitutional limitations on the legislative power of the federal government, and while no such constraints inhibit the six state governments, few have enacted legislation. One that has is the state of New South Wales, the most populous and most industrialized state. In 1982 that state government enacted the Employment Protection Act. The act requires an employer to give seven days' notice to the New South Wales industrial tribunal of his or her intention to dismiss an employee. This notification must contain comprehensive information about the intention to dismiss. The industrial tribunal has jurisdiction to inquire into the circumstances of the dismissal and has wide powers to make orders respecting the dismissal.

ANTIDISCRIMINATION LEGISLATION

One of the most rapidly developing areas of the law in Australia is legislation prohibiting discrimination. The legislation, among other things, makes it unlawful to discriminate against an employee by dismissing the employee because of sex, race, marital status, and physical or mental handicap.[18]

THE PARTICULAR OBLIGATIONS OF EMPLOYMENT

The scenarios are clearly based on an American model and do not allow for the unique system of compulsory conciliation and arbitration of disputes between employer and employee which operates in Australia. Nor do the scenarios appear to allow for the fact that a trade union presence will make a considerable difference to the issues considered. In Australia the simple fact is that there will be a trade union presence. Furthermore, it is difficult to refrain from asking what, in practice, law will have to do with these scenarios? The distinction between theory and practice is great when the contract of employment is at issue. As a trade union official recently remarked when interviewed in connection with this project, "There are the legalities and there are the realities." The law may weave itself in and out of the issue depending on such factors as union participation, the strength of the parties and the individuals involved, the relationship between supervisor and employee, and the relationship between the supervisor and his or her immediate superior. What the employer may do according to law and what he or she does in fact might be quite different.

Furthermore, the scenarios make some large assumptions. For example, the survey assumes a rigidly hierarchical work organization and an arguably outdated view of work ethics (encompassing e.g., "moral turpitude"). Gender segmentation of the labor market is not fully addressed; only two of the miscreant employees are styled female. In addition, notions of the "typical employee" are increasingly tenuous as part-time, casual, and intermittent employment arrangements increase.[19] It follows that the conventional view of "master and servant" (itself an inappropriate terminology) premised on standard hours and conditions is also becoming less relevant in Australia. It is possible, for instance, to transform overnight an employee under a contract of employment into a subcontractor free of an employment contract notwithstanding the fact that the same work is being performed. Overall, as will be shown below, the employment environment in Australia is one in which the practice and the law is less defined and therefore less certain. With those caveats entered, let us turn to a brief examination of the issues.

SUBORDINATION

Case Scenario

JD, a janitor at the A Manufacturing Company, is assigned the task of waxing office hallways. He completes one hallway. His supervisor, FF, inspects the hallway and says to JD, "Do this floor again." JD replies "No," and walks away.

Analysis

The common law has long recognized the right of the employer to terminate summarily for willful disobedience to lawful orders. In England the then Master of the Rolls, Lord Evershed, said that for disobedience to be willful it required "a deliberate flouting of the essential contractual conditions."[20] In Australia the then Chief Justice observed that if willfulness meant merely intentional or deliberate, then willful disobedience would not be sufficient in itself to justify summary dismissal. The disobedience must amount to a repudiation of the contract.[21] Thus when a secretary left a meeting against the direct orders of the managing director, but at the direction of her immediate superior, it was held that she had not acted in a manner sufficiently disobedient to warrant instant dismissal.[22]

In Australia if the employee unreasonably refuses to work as directed, the employer has a range of options. In ascending order of severity they are to: formally warn the employee; withhold wages for the period of refusal; stand down the employee (this is an option available when the employer has no work available because of factors beyond the employer's control, such as strikes and stoppages, and is dependent upon the employer making application to the industrial tribunal to insert a stand down clause in the relevant award); dismiss the employee. All of the options are subject to various constraints. For example, the warning may be required to be given in writing and given in the presence of the relevant trade union official; the "no work no pay" option is still of uncertain legal validity[23] and is unlikely to be upheld if the work in question is but a small proportion of the total work to be done; the stand down option is only applicable in the event of collective industrial action and has to be awarded by an industrial tribunal;[24] the termination must comply with common law principles and any operative award terms.

Seriousness. The likely response would be an informal warning, but a refusal amounting to an intention to repudiate the contract would lead to instant dismissal. A mild threat to the supervisor would lead to a warning. A serious threat would result, at the very least, in a warning, and a repeat of the order. This would be followed by instant dismissal if the threat were repeated. This would be even more likely if other employees were present. The employee's belief that the order was unjustified does not warrant insubordination, but an order to do the job in a demeaning manner, say with a toothbrush, would not be within the terms of the job which would justify refusal.

Mitigation. If the supervisor goes beyond the context of the supervisor–employee relationship, as by calling the employee an incompetent idiot, than the employee has grounds for complaint. A poor disciplinary record would increase the penalty. Longer service with the company, while no excuse for insubordination, may mitigate the behavior. In Australia the employee who is also a union representative has extensive legal rights that protect against victimization. Of greater immediate concern to the supervisor would be the reaction of the union and how this might impact the company.

Enforceability. If the supervisor asks a question in the first instance, this implies that the employee has a right to an opinion or to a reply without being in breach of contract. The statement "Do this floor again" is a direct order, allowing the employee no such luxury and making it clear that the employee must obey. Past tolerance would mitigate the severity of the penalty and probably lead to an informal warning rather than a disciplinary warning. The employer certainly could not single out this particular employee for special treatment.

SOBRIETY

Case Scenario

RR, a laborer on the loading dock of B Trucking Company, is observed by his supervisor, JB, reaching into the pocket of a coat that is hanging near his workplace. JB observes RR bring something to his mouth, appear to swallow, and then replace it in the coat. JB approaches RR and asks, "What are you drinking?" RR reaches into the pocket of the coat and hands JB a bottle that contains an alcoholic beverage. JB forms the opinion that RR's breath smells strongly of alcoholic spirits and that his eyes are unfocused.

Analysis

In practice the reason given for many dismissals is drunkenness. Two situations can be described. One is where the drunkenness occurs at work through drinking on the job and/or arriving at work drunk. These situations can justify instant dismissal, as the misconduct and disobedience amount to a repudiatory breach of the contract. The other situation is one of a pattern of alcoholism which may manifest itself in deterioration in physical and mental health and overall performance, even though it is not possible to identify either drunkenness or drinking at the workplace. Many companies now treat alcoholism as an illness and try to treat it as they would any other illness. This means taking into account relevant factors, psychological as well as physical, counseling, the giving of warnings, and an indication of the consequences of further deterioration. As in most cases of misconduct, more than one act would be required to warrant instant dismissal. The case law makes it very clear that this is especially the case with drunkenness, with Lord James of Hereford giving the leading exposition: "when the alleged misconduct consists of drunkenness there must be considerable difficulty in determining the extent or conditions of intoxication which will establish a justification for dismissal. The intoxication may be habitual and gross, and directly interfere with the business of the employer or with the ability of the servant to render due service. But it may be an isolated act committed under circumstances of festivity and in no way connected with or affecting the employer's business. In such a case the question whether the misconduct proved establishes the right to dismiss the servant must depend upon facts—and it is a question of fact."[25]

Seriousness. Whether the drunkenness would be sufficient to justify instant dismissal would depend on work rules (the most important variable), the degree of intoxication, and other circumstances—if, say, the bottle contained only wine. If it contained "crack" which the employee consumed and the supervisor knew, or was told, of the contents, then dismissal would be instant, and it is likely that the police would be called. Whatever the intoxicant/drug, the greater the possibility for harm to property, other employees, and the employer's reputation, then the greater the likelihood of instant dismissal and the less the likelihood of the union supporting an action for reinstatement.

Mitigation. Admission of alcoholism and treatment would affect the outcome, depending on company policy as described above.

Enforceability. Consistency would be maintained. The sobriety or otherwise of supervisors would not make a difference. The existence of formal rules is the variable.

SECURITY OF EMPLOYER'S PROPERTY

Case Scenario

PR, a clerk employed by C Gourmet Foods Company, is observed by two supervisors taking company products out of a packing box, concealing them on his person, and walking out of the door with them. He is apprehended after he exits the store, and he admits taking the products.

Analysis

It is well established at common law that businesses are entitled to preserve their operations from disloyal interference or sabotage from their own employees. The obligation of fidelity is an implied term in every contract of employment.[26] As with drinking on the job, so with theft from the employer, this is misconduct inconsistent with the fulfillment of the conditions of service and will justify instant dismissal. The duty of fidelity may vary with the class of the employee and the type of work he or she does.

Seriousness. Theft is a breach of contract and a crime. In legal theory there is no difference between stealing $1 and stealing $1,000. But in industrial relations practice it is unlikely that the theft of $1 would lead to more than a warning. At the most it might lead to dismissal with proper notice. The dismissal with notice option would be pursued if the problem was perceived as serious, if customers were disadvantaged, or if other employees knew. If goods were taken from a trash can and not from a packing case, then this would lessen the severity of the offence.

Mitigation. Theft is an affront to the company as well as a breach of contract. Most managers, however, would investigate the clerk's story and seek advice from their Human Resources Department. A low probability of recurrence would not affect the outcome because of the extreme difficulty in detecting such recurrence. A previous conviction would cancel any mitigating circumstances and result in dismissal. A senior employee would be unlikely to be instantly dismissed.

Enforceability. Pilfering from business operations has in many instances become "an accepted fact of life," and many businesses budget for the theft of tools and equipment. Management is reluctant to involve the police, yet at the same time loath to be seen by other employees as tolerating theft. The most likely outcome is that the offender is warned and other employees advised of the company's action.

PEACEFUL WORKPLACE

Case Scenario

MM is a clerk in D Department Store. NN is another clerk in the same department store; he is physically larger than MM. While MM is moving some heavy equipment from one area to another, NN says, "I'm surprised that you did not ask a real man like me to handle this job." MM, angered, strikes NN on the jaw, knocking him down. NN gets up and walks away.

Analysis

Along with drinking at work and stealing, fighting constitutes the classic justification for instant dismissal. The particular facts are important, as there are gradations of involvement in fighting, and it has been held that a protective reaction to being attacked is insufficient to warrant dismissal.

Seriousness. If one party is entirely blameless, then in practice he would not be dismissed. But if both are involved, it is likely that both would be dismissed. In some circumstances, as in a mild scuffle, only the aggressor would be warned or perhaps dismissed. Fighting needs to be distinguished from horseplay, which in practice is usually tolerated or only mildly castigated if in a safe environment and out of the view of other workers and customers. But fighting resulting in a serious physical injury, especially if inflicted by an instrument such as an iron bar, would result in instant dismissal and the likelihood that the police would be called. Damage to the employer's property, especially if in the presence of other employees, would result in instant dismissal of all employees involved in the fight. The same action would be taken if production were hindered and customers were disadvantaged.

Mitigation. Unless one employee were acting to defend himself against unprovoked attack, both would be dismissed. The fact that the aggressor was a trade union representative and/or a senior employee would not affect the outcome.

Enforceability. The most likely outcome is that both employees would be suspended for a period without pay.

OFF-DUTY CONDUCT

Case Scenario

TT, head salesclerk for E Toy Store, participates in a white supremacist demonstration. He is arrested for disorderly behavior, and a photograph of him handcuffed to a post and snarling at police is printed in the local newspaper, along with his name and the name of his employer.

Analysis

The common law has frequently been called on to consider what implications, if any, need to be read into the employment contract with regard to the employee's use of his or her spare time. This inquiry is also relevant to the scenario on loyalty. In each it is the implied obligation of fidelity that is in issue. What is clear is the proposition expressed by Lord Justice Greer that "during the subsistence of the contract of service and during his master's time the servant has to look after, not his own interests, but those of his master."[27] What this means is that an employee impliedly agrees to perform his or her duties faithfully and will not do anything that may injure or undermine the trade or business of the employer. It may be that there is emerging a legally recognized mutual obligation of cooperation between employer and employee. Certainly Lord Denning has observed that one thing an employee must not do "is willfully obstruct his employer as he goes about his business."[28] How wide this goes, and whether it reaches to off-duty conduct, depends on whether the conduct is inconsistent with the fulfillment of the express or implied conditions of the employment contract. In short, there will have to be some connection with the employment obligations to make the off-duty conduct relevant to questions of dismissal. After all, employees have a right to their own beliefs and to freedom of speech and to engage in whatever activities they choose in their own time, given that the legalities of those activities are a matter for the state to address. There is an ethic in many Australian industries that employers and employees are "square at every payday" and that each owes the other nothing outside the workplace.

Seriousness. If this were an isolated action of the employee, the arrest would not unduly concern the employer. The concern would be the effect on the business reputation. The facts would then be critical in determining the likely response of the employer. The size of the town, the newspaper's circulation, the policy of the employer about discrimination, the relevance of antidiscrimination and equal opportunity legislation, and the ethos of the townspeople would all impact on how this action affected sales. If TT is an outstanding salesperson with a good work history, he may well be retained, albeit with a caution. This would be so even if the media had revealed the employer's name. In Australia if TT were dismissed and was a union member, the employer may face a statutorily based action for unfair dismissal and reinstatement.

Mitigation. If TT is a senior employee with a good service record, it is likely he would not lose his job. The onus, in Australia, would be on TT to show that the demonstration was initially peaceful and that he did not instigate violence but was provoked.

Enforceability. It would depend on whether there had been a precedent and on company policy generally. Realistically the company would apply the same policy irrespective of the color of the employee or whether the employee was a supervisor or not and would follow precedent. A sense of fairness and good industrial relations go together.

ATTENDANCE

Case Scenario

JJ is a nurse's aide at F Nursing Home. Because of an illness, her attendance at work has been erratic for two years. During that period she has missed 30 percent of her scheduled working days. During the last month she has missed 20 percent of her scheduled working days. All of these absences were excused. She then misses three days of work, without notifying her employer, because she decides to extend her holiday.

Analysis

Where an employee consistently fails to be present for work there may be grounds for instant dismissal. But while a series of absences may justify instant dismissal, it is only in the most unusual of circumstances that a single act of absence would be sufficient. The most likely response to JJ's pattern of absence would be termination by notice. Typically in Australia awards provide that three days' unnotified absence from work constitutes abandonment and entitles the employer to treat the contract as ended by the employee. Whether award-regulated or governed by common law, a failure by the employer to terminate an employment contract in the face of repeated absences raises the issue of condonation by the employer.

Seriousness. In a less serious example there would be insufficient absences to justify termination, especially if there were improvement. But combined with the three days' unnotified absence, JJ would be vulnerable to dismissal unless seen as a very valuable worker, in which case a formal warning might result. In the case of more serious absenteeism no mitigation would be available to JJ, and it is unlikely that an Australian industrial tribunal would order reinstatement. The tribunal would not be swayed by a doctor's prediction that attendance will improve, and, of course, a prediction of inability to attend regularly would confirm the dismissal.

Mitigation. Length of service, JJ's financial position, and the fact that JJ is a worker with a performance record of high quality and quantity may affect the outcome and may result in a formal final warning. The opposite would occur if JJ had a prior poor discipline record and a history of unexcused absences.

Enforceability. Unexcused absences are treated as willful misconduct. Chronic excused absences still result in the employee being treated as unable to perform the job. In both cases termination will result, and because of the fundamental obligation to attend and the regulation of absences in awards, an absence of specific company rules would make no difference. It may be that where the employee is the sole breadwinner for, say, three children and is a particularly good worker, the job will be redesigned to suit the employee's needs. For example, casual or part-time work may be offered. But it is important to appreciate that unreasonable absences from work will invariably be considered justification for dismissal as far as Australian tribunals are concerned.

PERFORMANCE

Case Scenario

HH is a warehouseman for G Distributing Company. G has instituted a program that determines levels of productivity for warehousemen. This program meets accepted professional standards for such programs. Over a period of two months HH fails to produce at the prescribed levels, consistently falling 10 percent below the standard. He is warned that he will be terminated if he fails to improve his productivity within two weeks. He fails to do so. HH claims that the standards of the new system are impossible to meet. He proves that prior to the institution of the new system he was given above-average evaluations by his supervisor for producing at his current level, covering a period of ten years.

Analysis

Instant dismissal for poor performance is rare in Australia. This is for the simple reason that the incompetence or neglect must amount to a fundamental breach of the employment contract. Clearly, there are many degrees of incompetence in performance, ranging from forgetting some trivial matter to omitting the performance of an essential matter. The seriousness of the consequences likely to result from poor performance will have some bearing on whether the act can be characterized as of a trivial or substantial nature. Termination with proper notice is the most likely response. In practice most employers are more likely to adopt a series of warnings with specific performance objectives developed for the next review. It would be impossible in the Australian context for an employer unilaterally to institute productivity increases that a competent worker cannot meet, particularly if the employer demanded more productivity without more pay. The reality is that the union would negotiate the implementation of the program with the employer.[29] All the factors and variations in the scenario would be canvassed in the negotiations, and if agreement could not be reached, then an industrial tribunal would be invoked to conciliate and/or arbitrate. The tribunal would take a "hands-on" approach to such a dispute and would reject any employer assertion of a managerial prerogative to effect changes. The seniority and past performance of the worker, and other workers being expected to conform, would be central to the award of the tribunal.

Seriousness. Assuming that there is a award covering the performance standards, it is unlikely that a 2 percent below par performance by a worker with 10 years service would justify dismissal and a tribunal would order reemployment. A 40 percent lower performance would result in HH being placed on immediate short-term objectives, and if there were no improvement after several reviews he would be terminated with proper notice. One week of low performance would be ignored in practice. The degree of harm to production would be irrelevant, as would other factors given. The only test in Australia would be whether or not HH had committed a breach of his employment contract. Ninety years ago an English judge put the matter in these terms: "Some trivial acts of forgetfulness might not even justify a complaint or remark; but to forget to do a thing which, if not done, may cause considerable damage to the master, or to his property, or to fellow servants, may be a serious neglect of duty."[30]

Mitigation. As always, length of service and past performance will significantly affect the outcome.

Enforceability. The reasonableness of the standard is the critical variable and, as shown above, will have been set by agreement between the employer, the trade union, and the industrial tribunal. Certainly the company could not terminate HH if he had not been given a fair chance to meet the agreed standards, including warnings and performance reviews.

LOYALTY

Case Scenario

JS, a teller for H Bank, during an appearance on a television consumer information program states that her employer regularly fails to advise customers when they make mistakes in favor of the bank, but promptly corrects mistakes made in favor of the customers.

Analysis

Good faith on the part of the employee is a basic condition of employment. It is a portmanteau duty which covers many aspects of day-to-day employment. Frequently it is expressed as a duty of fidelity, and it rests on attention being given to all the delicate factors which make up the necessary mutual trust and confidence between employer and employee. At common law the overriding duty on the employee is to advance the employer's best interests at all times and not to do anything that may injure or undermine the trade or business of the employer. It is important to emphasize that, in the words of an Australian judge, "Where a person is by virtue of his employment charged with the duty of furthering his employer's interest, he is also charged with the duty of not using information obtained by him as their employee to their detriment."[31] In short, an employee is under a duty not to use information about the employer's trade secrets in a manner that is hostile to the employer's interests. Yet there is a limit to the duty of confidentiality, and the law has recognized a point where a duty to disclose collides with the duty of fidelity. The question is: Does the public interest justify disclosure of information obtained in the course of employment? Lord Denning has recognized an exception to the duty of confidentiality: "The exception should extend to crimes, frauds and misdeeds, both those actually committed as well as those in contemplation provided always—and this is essential—that the disclosure is justified in the public interest."[32] Modern cases focus on the nature of the information and assess whether or not it is confidential.

Seriousness. It is likely that the information would be found to be confidential, not because of any inherent complexity, but because of its sensitive nature. However, as the disclosure about the practice was to people who deal with that practice, namely a television consumer information program, it is likely that the "public interest" exception would protect the employee against dismissal. It is likely that the employee would be dismissed, in fact, but a tribunal would order reinstatement.

Mitigation. The knowledge of the senior management, the truth of the statement, the illegality of the employer's behavior, the status of the employee, whether or not the employee was ventilating some unrelated grievance, and whether or not the statement was related to some peripheral business with, say, a clothing store would be irrelevant if the disclosure harms the employer's interests. If the employee has disclosed confidential information, that is sufficient to warrant dismissal.

Enforceability. It is not necessary to have a rule; the situation is covered by the common law. The only issue is whether the employee could bring herself within the public interest exception to the duty not to disclose confidential information.

RESTRICT COLLECTIVE ACTION

Case Scenario

JJ, a machinist at I Manufacturing Company, becomes angry because he believes that his supervisor is treating him and other employees in a disrespectful manner. In protest, he persuades the other employees in his work group to leave work together in the middle of their scheduled work shift and not return until the next day.

Analysis

There is no right to strike in Australia.[33] Indeed, as discussed earlier, the system of compulsory conciliation and arbitration of industrial disputes is seen as having removed the need for parties to take direct industrial action. Consequently, there is an arsenal of legal weapons that can be brought to bear on the facts given in the scenario. These range from penalties in industrial legislation, to common law tort actions, to remedies for breach of the employment contract. Prima facie on the facts of the scenario there is a breach of an award, a tortious inducing of breach of contract by JJ, and a breach of JJ's own employment contract. Yet while there is this range of sanctions available, the reality in Australia is that legal action against JJ or the other employees would be unlikely.

Seriousness. A wildcat action such as this is uncommon in Australia. Usually a walkout will be governed by the advice of the trade union representative at the workplace, and full-time industrial organizers will be immediately involved. The likely response from management will depend on the history of relations in the plant. What has occurred might be an isolated action or it might be a skirmish in an ongoing dispute. If the latter, it will be referred immediately to an industrial tribunal for conciliation and/or arbitration. Whether or not a tribunal is notified will depend on such factors as the level of antagonism between the employees and the supervisor, the level of the disruption, and the capacity of the dispute to spread. If it is no more than a transient workplace personal dispute, then it will be resolved without resort to state instruments and will be resolved by direct negotiations between union and management representatives.

Mitigation. In law there will be no mitigating circumstances, whatever the legal remedy sought. In reality the matter will be handled at the workplace or in a compulsory conference chaired by an industrial tribunal member where the factors mentioned above will be relevant, including JJ's seniority and the conduct of the supervisor.

Enforceability. The employer has a range of legal remedies. It is highly unlikely, on the facts given, that such remedies would be sought.

AVOID CONFLICT OF INTEREST

Case Scenario

IB, a systems analyst for J Company, has access to private computer systems of his employer. IB accepts a string of free-lance, relatively routine programming jobs for K Company, a competitor of his employer, performing work at his home.

Analysis

In the leading case, which appears to be directly in point, the English Court of Appeal held that the obligation of the employee to act in good faith existed for as long as the contract existed and that even in his spare time an employee owes the duty of fidelity.[34] In that case the employee was a skilled technical worker who took a moonlighting job working for a rival of the employer. Even though no confidential information was used, the employee was restrained by injunction from performing the moonlighting. In another case Denning J (as he then was) observed that "it is a principle of law that if a servant, in violation of his duty of honesty and good faith, takes advantage of his service to make a profit for himself, in this sense, that the assets of which he has control, or the facilities which he enjoys, or the position which he occupies, are the real cause of his obtaining the money . . . then he is accountable for it to his employer. It matters not that the master has not lost any profit, nor suffered any damage."[35]

Seriousness. In summary: IB has breached the fundamental

obligation of good faith; is vulnerable to instant dismissal; can be required to render accounts of secret profits; will be restrained from working for a rival if his employer wishes to retain his services. In the state of New South Wales if the employee acquires a share ownership in a competing business, there is precedent for saying that a court will declare, in favor of the employer, an equitable lien over those shares.[36] It should also be noted that in addition to the employee who is in breach of good faith, a third party who procures or participates in the employee's conduct knowing it to be in breach of the employee's obligation to his employer is also liable to account for gains made.[37]

Mitigation. The court may refuse to enforce a rule that prohibits free-lancing where that poses no threat to the business or where there is a rule which has been applied capriciously and has perhaps been waived in respect to other workers. Any restraints imposed by the rules will be measured against the test of reasonableness (as between the parties and in the public interest) and will be tested against the proposition that people should not be unreasonably restrained from free trade.

Enforceability. Not unexpectedly, given the free and unrestrained competition which, at least in theory, underpins our market economy, the law does not look favorably upon rules which have the effect of restraining trade or limiting agreements. Nevertheless the law recognizes that the employer has property rights in the business which the law will protect. It will protect the employer from unfair competition from existing employees. The scenario illustrates one of those situations. The remedies available to IB's employer are outlined above.

CONCLUSIONS

The purpose of this paper is to examine the law of dismissal in Australia from the perspective of the employer whose power to dismiss an employee remains an overriding aspect of contracts between master and servant. The law is examined from the employer's viewpoint. The analysis describes, according to the law, what the employer may do in respect to termination of the employment contract. In real terms the legal powers available to an employer are far greater than any legal remedy which may be exercised by the employee. This reality is obscured by the language of the law, and the real power imbalance is masked by the legal fiction that the employment contract is struck between parties of equal bargaining strength. Furthermore, the language of the law puts the power of the employer to terminate on the same footing as that of the employee. The reality, of course, is that the employer's power to dismiss greatly outweighs the so-called reciprocal right of the employee to leave employment. Dismissal, especially instant dismissal, is a punitive device that strikes at the employee's financial stability and well-being. This is especially true where less than perfect labor mobility exists, and in such circumstances the unskilled and other disadvantaged groups are peculiarly vulnerable. In the absence of some form of reinstatement action being available to the employee, the employer retains a sanction that has, at least in Australia's present economic environment, serious consequences for employees.

It is fair to say that the common law, received from England and applied in Australia, provides the employee with very little protection from dismissal. The employer is free to dismiss an employee for any reason, or for none, provided he or she does so in accordance with the terms, express or implied, in the employment contract. In reality this usually means one week's notice to terminate in Australia. For some employees even less than one week is legally proper notice. For the employer faced with an employee who has repudiated the essential terms of employment, instant termination, without notice, is available. As far as the common law is concerned, little has changed over the past century.

The concept of an employment contract being an individual arrangement between employer and employee is incongruous when set against the quite fundamental changes in the employment relationship that have been brought about by industrial arbitration legislation and other protective industrial legislation. The reality today is that the employment relationship in Australia is dominated by collective relationships. Yet the industrial legislation has not interfered with the employer's right to dismiss to any great extent. Only where a preference clause in an award is operative, where redundancy is legislatively regulated, where the legislation prohibits victimization of trade union activists, or where the award prescribes termination procedures and obligations is the managerial common law right to terminate in any way restricted.

Of course there is the broad requirement that the employer respect the operation of the relevant industrial arbitration system, state or federal, but overall the employer in Australia has considerable freedom to terminate contracts of employment. This is because the common law governing employment remains the foundation on which Australian statute law is built. The core of the employment relationship is the employer's right to command and the employee's obligation to obey. The limits to the right to command and the duty to obey are imprecise, for the whole process of command–obey is constantly being renegotiated on a day-to-day basis, as the scenarios discussed in this paper demonstrate. The employment relationship is a dynamic concept, difficult to fix and define in inflexible legal rules.

This was recognized by the first president of the South Australian Industrial Court in these words

> A judge of an Industrial Court is driven by practical necessities towards the goal of a body of coherent principles: he is forever looking both behind him and before him. If he failed in this respect his Court would not be a Court of industrial justice, but a tribunal of caprice. Instead of conducing to industrial stability he would be an instrument for the creation of industrial unrest. He must aim at uniformity, consistency, certainty—an accordance between justice and the legitimate expectancy of the parties. If he were to take upon himself the part of a universal providence he would produce uncertainty, inconsistency and chaos; he would be false to the very nature of the eternally enduring elements of law in the best sense of the term. But the code of law which he slowly and laboriously evolves, and which he interprets and applies in particular cases, is not a cast-iron code; it is a code adopted from time to time in accordance with the advancing needs of progressive society.[38]

NOTES

1. This paper would not have been possible without the diligent fieldwork and research of Paul Barnes, Tom Blackett, Richard Cheney, Barry Cotter, Tim Cumberland, Patricia Hewitson, Brian Mills, and Rodney Young. To them, jointly and severally, I express my gratitude and thanks.

2. There is a wide range of standard textbooks of authority, but for the purposes of this paper those which treat the history from an industrial relations perspective are considered most relevant. Amongst this group can be listed: W. B. Creighton, W. J. Ford, and R. J. Mitchell, *Labour Law: Materials and Commentary* (Sydney: Law Book Company, 1983); N. Gunningham, *Industrial Law and the Constitution* (Sydney: The Federation Press, 1988); J. J. Macken, *Australian Industrial Laws: The Constitutional Basis*, 2nd ed. (Sydney: Law Book Company, 1980); R. C. McCallum and M. J. Pittard, *Australian Labour Law: Cases and Materials*, 2nd ed. (Sydney: Butterworths, 1990).

3. W. B. Creighton and A. Stewart, *Labour Law: An Introduction* (Sydney: The Federation Press, 1990).

4. D. Plowman, S. Deery, and C. Fisher, *Australian Industrial Relations*, rev. ed. (Sydney: McGraw-Hill, 1981), ch. 12.

5. *Re Ranger Uranium Mines Pty. Ltd; Ex parte Federated Miscellaneous Workers Union of Australia* (1987) 163 CLR 656; *Re Federated Storemen and Packers Union of Australia; Ex parte Wooldumpers (Victoria) Ltd* (1989) 63 ALJR 286.

6. Conciliation and Arbitration Act 1904 (Cwlth) sec. 4(1).

7. B. Brooks, *Contract of Employment: Principles of Australian Employment Law*, 3rd ed. (Sydney: CCH Australia, 1986), p. 1.

8. *Woods v. W. M. Car Services (Peterborough)* (1982) IRLR 413 at p. 415. See similar sentiments in the English Court of Appeal in *Bliss v. South East Thames Regional Health Authority* (1987) ICR 700 at p. 714. The notion that the employer must act reasonably, and that a failure so to act amounts to constructive dismissal for which the employee can obtain remedies, has been recognized by Australian tribunals for some time: *Perks v. Willert* (1974) 12 ALR 408; *Silberschneider v. MRSA Earthmoving Pty Ltd* (1988) 30 AILR para. 65.

9. D. L. Mathieson, *Industrial Law in New Zealand* (Wellington: Sweet and Maxwell, 1970), p. 2.

10. *Ridge v. Baldwin* (1964) AC 40 at p. 65.

11. For a detailed analysis see R. Clark, *Private Sector Employment: The Law of Dismissal* (Sydney: Industrial Relations Research Centre, University of New South Wales, 1984).

12. *Ridge v. Baldwin* (1964) AC 40 at p. 65.

13. *Hogan v. Tumut Shire Council* (1954) S.R.(N.S.W.)284.

14. G. J. McGarry, *Aspect of Public Sector Employment Law* (Sydney: Law Book Company, 1988).

15. H. B. Higgins, *A New Province for Law and Order* (London: Constable, 1922). Higgins was the person responsible for having the labor power included in the Constitution. He subsequently became the attorney general responsible for introducing the legislation pursuant to the labor head of power and later became the president of the Court of Conciliation and Arbitration, a post he held for fourteen years.

16. *General Motors–Holdens Pty. Ltd v. Bowling* (1976) 51 ALJR 235.

17. *Re Loty and Holloway and the Australian Workers' Union* (1971) AR (NSW) 95.

18. In 1990 the following antidiscrimination legislation was in force in Australia: Sex Discrimination Act 1984 (Cwlth); Racial Discrimination Act 1975 (Cwlth); Human Rights and Equal Opportunity Commission Act 1986 (Cwlth); Anti-Discrimination Act 1977 (NSW); Equal Opportunity Act 1984 (Vic.); Equal Opportunity Act 1984 (SA); Equal Opportunity Act 1984 (WA).

19. B. T. Brooks, "Aspects of Casual and Part-Time Employment," *Journal of Industrial Relations* 27 (1985): 158; B. T. Brooks, *Working Towards 2000: The Future Organisation of Work* (Sydney: CCH Australia, 1990).

20. *Laws v. London Chronicle* (1959) 1 WLR 698 at 700.

21. *Adami v. Maison De Luxe Ltd* (1924) 35 CLR 143.

22. *Laws v. London Chronicle*, supra.

23. McCallum and Pittard, *Australian Labour Law*, pp. 87–100.

24. In the federal jurisdiction the procedure is governed by the Industrial Relations Act 1988 sect. 126.

25. *Clouston and Co. Ltd v. Corry* (1906) AC 122 at p. 129.

26. *Hivac Ltd v. Park Royal Scientific Instruments* (1946) 1 ch. 169 at p. 172 per Lord Greene MR.

27. Ibid.

28. *Secretary of State for Employment v. Associated Society of Locomotive Engineers and Firemen (No. 2)* (1972) 2 QB 455 at p. 491.

29. See the kinds of negotiation accepted in Australia as illustrated by *Federated Clerks Union v. Victorian Employers Federation* (1984) 154 CLR 472.

30. *Baster v. London and County Printing Works* (1899) 1 QB 901 at p. 903 per Darling J.

31. *Prebble v. Reeves* (1910) VLR 88 at p. 108 per Hood J.

For a full survey of the cases see *Ansell Rubber Company v. Allied Rubber Industries* (1967) VR 37.

32. *Initial Services v. Putterill* (1967) 3 All ER 145 at p. 148.

33. E. I. Sykes, *Strike Law in Australia*, 2nd ed. (Sydney: Law Book Company, 1982); Creighton and Stewart, *Labour Law: An Introduction*, ch. 9.

34. *Hivac Ltd v. Park Royal Scientific Instruments* (1946) ch. 169.

35. *Reading v. Attorney-General* (1951) AC 507 at p. 51.

36. *Timber Engineering Company v. Andreson* (1980) 2 NSWLR 488.

37. *Granosite Pty. Ltd v. Wieland* (1982) AILR 503.

38. W. Jethro Brown, "Industrial Arbitration Courts," *The Law Quarterly Review* 186 (April 1918): 195.

BELGIUM

Chris Engels

Belgian labor law deals exclusively with workers who perform their jobs in a position of subordination. Independent contractors do not fall within its scope. In general, Belgian labor law is of an imperative nature. Parties cannot, either by individual contract or by collective bargaining agreement, deviate from the statutory standards. Where the law only sets minimum standards, deviation for the "better," beneficial to the employee, is allowed.[1]

OVERVIEW OF THE SYSTEM

The primary sources of Belgian labor law are parliamentary acts and royal decrees. These legislative acts grant the Belgian employee fairly extensive protection. They are supplemented by detailed social security regulations dealing with situations in which the employee is "prevented" from working.[2]

Trade union freedom is guaranteed, and the degree of unionization is high—up to 70 percent. Interaction between trade union organizations and employers' associations is frequent and institutionalized at the different levels of the Belgian economy. Collective bargaining takes place at each of the different levels: in the enterprise, at branch or industry level, and on a national level. Employees enjoy an almost complete freedom to engage in industrial warfare. Although Belgian legal doctrine has recently shown an increased interest in the problem of strikes and lockouts, Belgian employees and trade unions are not exactly strike prone.[3]

By establishing an employment relationship the parties to the contract of employment receive certain rights and benefits (wages, social security benefits, right to allocate labor, etc.), but at the same time take up certain obligations. One of the main features of establishing a contract of employment is that the employer gains authority over the employee. The employer's authority and the employee's subordination are two sides of the same coin. The employer may give directions to its employees concerning actual job performance, techniques to be used, duration and time of work, and may as a consequence reprimand and punish employees not living up to its directions and instructions. However, the employer's authority is not unlimited. Nor is the employee's duty to obey his or her employer's orders.[4]

SUBSTANTIVE AND PROCEDURAL RULES OF EMPLOYMENT OBLIGATION

CURRENT STATUTORY PROVISIONS

The Belgian parliamentary act respecting contracts of employment requires both the employer and the employee to show respect and consideration for each other. Both "shall ensure and show respect for each other's property and decency during the performance of the contract."[5] Section 17 of act imposes on the employee a number of more specific duties to:

1. carry out his work carefully, honestly, and conscientiously at the agreed place and time and in accordance with the agreed conditions;
2. act in accordance with the orders and instructions given to him by the employer or his agents in connection with the performance of the contract;
3. refrain both during the contract and after its termination from revealing manufacturing or business secrets or any personal or confidential matter coming to his knowledge in the performance of his duties, or engaging or cooperating in any form of disloyal competition;
4. abstain from anything that might prejudice his own safety or the safety of his work mates, the employer, or any other person;

5. return to the employer any tools or unused raw materials that have been entrusted to him, in good condition.[6]

The employee is obliged to perform the duties and the work the parties to the contract of employment have agreed upon. The employer, on its behalf, must provide the employee with work in accordance with the agreed conditions and at the agreed time and place.[7] If the contract of employment does not specify what particular job the employee has to perform, the employee must carry out the orders given within the framework of the goals and organization of the enterprise.[8] If the contract of employment, however, describes in detail the employee's job, the employer may not unilaterally decide to change the job content. Any such order given by the employer may be disregarded by the employee without being subject to any kind of penalty or sanction. Moreover, substantial unilateral modification of any of the essential parts of the contract of employment—not just the content of the job itself, but also elements such as wages, working time, etc.—may be regarded by the employee as a breach of contract and may subject the employer to payment of damages.

Failure by the employee to perform duties, or failure to do so properly, may lead to disciplinary sanctions and/or dismissal. Sanctions may be of a "moral" nature, such as an oral or written warning, or of a pecuniary nature, such as fines. Temporary suspension of the contract of employment, whereby the employee is prohibited to work or even to enter the premises of the enterprise, may be the result of disciplinary action against an employee.[9] Even a dismissal, with or without taking a period of notice into account, can be imposed as a disciplinary sanction.

Other disciplinary sanctions are not aimed at terminating the employment relationship as such, but may be intended to bring about important changes to the conditions under which the employee is performing: reduction in salary, downgrading in the hierarchical structure of the enterprise, etc. As already noted, the employer is not allowed under Belgian labor law to unilaterally change the essential parts of the employment relationship. The employer is only granted what is called a *ius variandi*. Minor changes to nonessential parts of the contract may be made. This right is seen as a necessity for the survival of the employer's business; minor changes have to be made on a day-to-day basis, due to the ever-changing circumstances in which the company is operating. Major unilateral changes are not allowed. The parliamentary act respecting contracts of employment further provides that any stipulation whereby an employer reserves itself the right to unilaterally modify the terms of a contract of employment shall be null and void.[10] One may question whether disciplinary sanctions provided for in the work rules of some companies whereby the employee's salary is, for example, decreased by half or whereby he or she is transferred from a skilled to a semiskilled or unskilled position do not run contrary to the provisions of the above mentioned parliamentary act. The Belgian Court of Cassation (Belgium's highest court) held in 1974 that a provision of this kind did not violate the act respecting contracts of employment that was in force at that time which did not include a provision similar to section 25 of the present act.[11] A recent Court of Cassation case, however, suggests the opposite.[12] The court held that a stipulation whereby the employer reserves to itself the right to impose a disciplinary sanction that would make the employee lose his or her security of employment clearly falls within the scope of section 25 of the act respecting contracts of employment, and that it therefore should be considered null and void. While the ultimate reach of the 1988 decision may not yet be completely clear, it is at least evident now that certain disciplinary sanctions provided for in work rules or in individual contracts of employment will be regarded as too far reaching, contrary to section 25 of the act respecting contracts of employment, and thus null and void.[13]

A further restriction of the employer's disciplinary power is that it may only impose sanctions that are laid down in the work rules.[14] Section 6 of the parliamentary act of April 8, 1965, concerning the institution of work rules, states that the work rules shall indicate "sanctions, amounts of fines and uses to which they shall be put, together with offences in respect of which they are imposed."[15]

The worker who incurs a disciplinary sanction has to be notified of it no later than the first working day following the day on which the offence was noted.[16] The one-day term for notification starts only on the day following the one during which the employer acquires knowledge of the offences that occurred. The fact that a lower-ranking foreman was aware of the offence but did not inform the employer about it during the one-day period following the offence does not mean that the employer cannot validly impose any sanctions.[17] In principle it is the employer or its representative that has to have knowledge of the facts before the one-day notification period starts running. The hierarchical structure of the enterprise, however, cannot be abused by artificially prolonging the short period during which the employer must notify the employee of disciplinary sanction.

If the disciplinary sanction is not communicated in due time to the employee, it will not be valid.[18] The notification of the disciplinary sanction has to be in writing.[19] The employer also has a duty to enter details concerning any sanction(s) imposed in a register containing, among other things, the date, the grounds, and the nature of the sanction.[20] These entries have to be made before the date of the next payment of remuneration. Failure to do so might lead to criminal actions against the employer, without, however, at the same time affecting the validity of the disciplinary sanction.[21]

In case the employer imposes a fine, it must also enter into the register the amount of the fine to be deducted from the employee's salary. The total fine to be deducted cannot exceed one-fifth of the employee's daily remuneration.[22] The employer is not allowed to use the money from the fines that it imposes for its own benefit. "All amounts deducted shall be set aside for the employees' welfare."[23] In case a works council is operating in the enterprise, the employer has to obtain the council's agreement with regard to the purpose for which the money shall be spent.[24]

It should be noted here that in many enterprises work rules no longer contain references to fines as disciplinary sanctions.[25] Disciplinary sanctions in general seem to be applied less frequently nowadays as compared to a couple of decades ago. Sanctions, if applied, are applied more frequently to blue-collar than to white-collar workers.[26] A 1986 survey covering 2,250 blue-collar workers in eight companies reveals that 117 of them got written warnings without any further ramifications during the survey year. Eight workers were suspended for a period of one to three days. Two workers were expelled for drunkenness. Sanctions were only imposed after at least two oral warnings for similar offences.[27] The survey thus shows that disciplinary sanctions are only imposed for repeated offences. A very limited number of sanctions with "real" (read: material) repercussions for the employees were imposed.

The almost complete absence of any case law dealing with disciplinary sanctions and procedures further illustrates the limited use of disciplinary actions by Belgian employers. This statement, however, does not hold for dismissals for serious reasons.

Even though one could theoretically raise the question as to whether dismissal for serious reasons can be regarded as a disciplinary sanction under Belgian labor law, the fact is that employers quite often use dismissals for serious reasons to sanction offences by employees.

The parliamentary act concerning the institution of work rules requires work rules to indicate the serious grounds for termination of the contract of employment without notice by either party.[28] Most work rules enumerate a number of offences that could, in general, be considered serious enough for termination of the contract of employment without notice, such as a number of unjustified absences, fraud, theft, drunkenness on the job, violation of safety regulations, etc.

The fact that a violation of safety regulations is mentioned in the work rules as a serious offence does not mean that an actual dismissal without notice for a particular violation of a safety rule will be regarded as justified by the labor courts when the discharged employee decides to take his case to court. Termination of the contract of employment remains at all times subject to judicial control. This holds as well for enumerated serious reasons in the individual contract of employment[29] as for those in the work rules.[30]

Mentioning certain offences in the work rules and/or in the individual contract of employment is not, however, without any significance. Quite often courts will take the enumeration of serious offences into account as being the expression of the parties' intent to attach considerable importance to those rules, the violation of which they consider serious enough to justify a dismissal without notice.[31]

The concept of dismissal for serious reasons is itself statutorily defined.[32] Any serious fault making it immediately and finally impossible for the employer and the employee to cooperate at work shall be deemed to constitute a serious reason. This basically means that three requirements have to be met in order to classify an offence as a serious reason for dismissal:

1. The dismissal without notice shall not be justified unless the dismissed party was seriously at fault.
2. The further professional cooperation between employer and employee thereby became impossible,
3. in an immediate and final manner.[33]

The fault justifying a dismissal for just cause can be a breach of a statutory or contractual duty. It is thus not required that the employee's offence be of a contractual nature.[34] A breach of a duty imposed by work rules[35] or by a collective bargaining agreement[36] may under the appropriate circumstances be considered a serious reason. The same holds true for violations of a statutory duty or legal obligation.[37] Fraud[38] or a deliberate intention on behalf of the employee to harm the employer[39] is not required in order to find a dismissal for serious reasons to be justified.

Violation of any duty, not by fault but by, for example, an act of God, can never justify a dismissal for serious reasons. Shortcomings by employees can only be justified as serious reasons for dismissal when the employee's conduct or inaction[40] can be regarded as constituting a fault.[41]

Violation of a statutory duty by the employee may lead, as already mentioned, to a justified dismissal for serious reasons. The employer, however, in its turn, also has a duty to respect the law. It may not demand from its employees that they violate the law. For example, an employer may not sanction its employee for a refusal to drive a truck that is not insured, in violation of the legal obligation to insure all vehicles used for road transport.[42] Furthermore, the employer may not give directions that would endanger the employees' lives or go contrary to public order or morality.[43]

In principle, only faults attributable to the employee justify imposing a disciplinary sanction upon the employee. Courts do, however, occasionally accept faults committed by third parties—not parties to the individual contract of employment, but, for example, directed by the employee—as a justification for the dismissal of an employee.[44] An explicit mandate is not always required.[45]

The fault justifying a dismissal without compensation or period of notice has to be a serious fault. Not just any fault will do. One can give only very general guidelines concerning the degree of seriousness required to justify a summary dismissal. One has to look at the particular facts and circumstances of every case individually. Is it the employee's first fault, or is it one of a series? How long has the employee worked for the same company without committing any offences? What is the function of the employee; is he or she working at the assembly line or is he or she a supervising manager?[46]

A serious fault that would justify a dismissal for serious reasons has to make further cooperation between the employer and the employee impossible. It has to be a fault that destroys the mutual trust and confidence of the parties to the contract of employment. The impossibility of future cooperation is of a psychological nature. When determining whether cooperation between employer and employee has become impossible, labor courts will not, however, take the purely subjective viewpoint of any of the parties to the conflict, but will determine if the facts rationally, taking normal human relationships into account, make further employment, even during the term of notice, impossible.[47]

The fact that a serious fault or offence is committed by a particular employee resulting in an absolute impossibility for his or her immediate supervisor to work together with the employee does not necessarily mean that professional cooperation between the employee and the employer has become impossible.[45] The employer might not have an absolute duty to provide the offending employee with a different position or with a position not requiring cooperation with the supervisor with whom the employee has clashed, but when such a job is readily available in the enterprise, labor courts might consider the serious fault that was committed not to be of such a nature as to furnish a sufficient justification for summary dismissal.

The second requirement, emphasizing the fact that the fault or offence committed by the employee has to render any further professional cooperation between the parties to the contract of employment impossible, raises the question whether offences committed during the employee's time off may justify a dismissal for serious reasons or any other disciplinary sanction. In general, one can say that events in the private life of the employee are of no concern to the employer, and can thus justify neither a summary dismissal nor any other disciplinary sanction.[49] However, this principle is not without its exceptions. Labor courts on various occasions have accepted actions in the employee's private life as a justification for summary dismissal when these contradicted explicit or implicit contractual obligations of the employee, or when the circumstances under which they were committed, their consequences, or their notoriety deeply influenced and made impossible any cooperation between the parties to the contract of employment.[50]

Cooperation between the parties to the contract of employment has to be rendered immediately and definitively impossible by the offences committed by the employee in order to justify a dismissal for serious reasons. When further cooperation during the normal term of notice would work out to be possible, the summary dismissal has to be regarded as unjustified. Further employment for a few days after the moment the employer obtained sufficient knowledge of the offences committed excludes the existence of serious reasons for terminating the contract of employment.[51]

The requirement that the offences committed have to render any further cooperation impossible is also reflected in the procedural requirements that have to be satisfied in order to dismiss an employee without any compensation or term of notice. The parliamentary act of July 3, 1978, requires the employer who wants to terminate an employee's contract of employment without taking a term of notice into account to act within a period of three working days following the day during which the employer obtained knowledge about the facts it wants to invoke as justification for the disciplinary sanction taken.[52] This does not mean that the employer has to make a decision based on a simple suspicion about offences presumedly committed by an employee. The employer may investigate the matter until it has reasonable certainty about the offences.[53] Reasonable certainty, however, is not necessarily the same thing as complete and absolute proof.

Questions can be raised as to whether the rights of the party under investigation are respected. The system of industrial justice in Belgium, as set out above, is not characterized by formal guarantees of the rights of the employee up for possible disciplinary sanctions.[54] There is no statutory obligation for the employer to hear the employee it wants to sanction. However, work rules in a number of enterprises, especially the larger ones, do provide employees with this right.[55] Some labor courts mention the fact that there is no legal requirement for the employer to hear the employee it wants to discharge, but at the same time emphasize that the employer has some kind of moral duty to do so before imposing the hardest sanction.[56] If the interrogation or the hearing of the employee allowed the employer to gain better knowledge about the actuality and/or the seriousness of the employee's offence, it is more likely than not that the dismissal will not be regarded by the labor courts as being untimely, even when it took place more than three working days after the employer first heard about the offence but still within a three-day period after the completion of the investigatory process in which the employee was heard.[57]

The parliamentary act of April 8, 1965, concerning the institution of work rules requires work rules to mention "possibilities of redress open to employees having grievances or wishing to make observations or objections with regard to sanctions"—not only dismissal for serious reasons, but any sanction imposed or likely to be imposed.[58] The employee will have to present complaints through the usual hierarchical channels in the enterprise. If the employee so requests, he or she may be supported by the trade union delegate. The trade union delegate has a right to be heard in the event of any conflict or dispute of a personal nature that cannot be settled through the normal channels.[59]

The employer has to dismiss the employee within a three-day (working days) period after acquiring reasonably certain knowledge about the serious offences the employee committed. The parliamentary act respecting contracts of employment also requires the employer to notify the employee of the reasons it invokes to terminate the employment relationship summarily. The only justifications the employer may invoke for termination of the contract of employment without notice are those of which the employee was notified. "To be valid, such notification shall be made either by registered letter or by writ served by court bailiff. The notification may also be made by handing of a document in writing to the other party."[60] When the employee signs a copy of the document drafted by the employer, the signature is valid only as an acknowledgment of the receipt of the notification.[61] Other forms of notification are null and void, and will thus have no effect. The notification has to be done within a period of three working days following the day on which the employer terminated the contract of employment. The act respecting contracts of employment requires the employer who terminates the contract of employment for a serious reason, in case it comes to a conflict brought before court, to provide the court with proof that such reasons exist, and that it has terminated the contract and notified the employee of the reasons for doing so in a timely manner.[62]

It should also be mentioned that Belgian labor law requires the employer to follow a different and special procedure for dismissing trade union representatives for serious reasons. When dealing with a trade union representative the serious reasons for dismissal have to be recognized by the labor court prior to the dismissal itself. Unjustified dismissal combined with a refusal to reinstate the trade union representative subjects the employer to the payment of a rather high pecuniary compensation.[63]

Labor courts only come into play in the scheme of industrial justice when the sanctioned employee is dissatisfied with the disciplinary sanction, believes that it was unjustified, and takes steps to go to court. An employee who is convinced that the offences committed were not serious enough to warrant a summary dismissal, or did not make the professional cooperation with the employer immediately and definitely impossible, can take the case to court. Even if the labor court agrees with the employee's view, it cannot, however, force the employer to reinstate the employee. Compensation is the only satisfaction courts can grant.[64] The dismissal is thus always considered as the end of the employment relationship, even when it was unjustified. As far as other disciplinary sanctions are concerned, labor courts can determine whether the employee committed the offences and whether the sanction imposed was commensurate with the offences. If disproportionate, the employee can demand that the sanction be lifted. The employee may also ask for compensation. However, the labor court cannot impose upon the employee the sanction it deems appropriate.[65]

DEVELOPMENT OF BELGIAN STATUTORY LAW

As mentioned earlier, the disciplinary power of the employer over the employee is based on the employer's authority over the employee. Thus, in order to determine whether the above described disciplinary apparatus comes into play or not, one has to determine first whether the worker concerned is a subordinate employee or not.

When describing the scope of labor law in general, one necessarily has to define the concept of subordination.[66] This concept is the prime condition for triggering the application of protective labor law in general. The subordinate worker who negotiates an employment contract with an employer is covered by labor law; the independent contractor is not. Besides the contract of employment characterized by the employee's subordination, various contracts exist that, to a large degree, are similar to the contract of employment. These contracts also deal with workers rendering services in return for a price to be paid by their contract partners. The only way to distinguish these kinds of contracts from a contract of employment is to look at the way in which performance is delivered: in a *subordinate* position or as an *independent* contractor.

There is no statutory definition of the concept of subordination in Belgian labor law. In the early days a distinction was drawn between subordinate workers based on the "intensity" of the subordination to which the worker was subjected. Different statutes applied to the different categories of workers. Not all subordinate workers were considered to be employees covered by labor law to the full extent. This distinction, however, is now history.[67] At the turn of the century the statutory definition of a contract of employment referred, as far as subordination is concerned, to a combination of three concepts: authority, control, and command. Only when the employer could effectively exercise command, control, and authority over the worker would the latter really be considered an employee having a contract of employment *sensu strictu.* The parliamentary act respecting contracts of employment now only refers to the employer's authority.[68]

The change of language in the statutory definition of a contract of employment reflects an evolution in the legal thinking on subordination. The employer's command and control powers are no longer seen as independent requirements to be satisfied in order for a relationship of subordination to exist. They are seen only as means by which the employer can express its authority over its employees. While in the early days it was thought to be impossible for a medical doctor, for example, to work as a subordinate employee, due to the fact that the doctor, as far as the technical aspects of the job are concerned, always kept and was legally guaranteed a certain degree of independence, attitudes have now changed. Technical independence does not preclude performance as a subordinate employee. The determination by the employer of the external circumstances (working hours, place of work, equipment to be used, choice of assisting personnel, etc.) in which the worker has to perform can be sufficient to establish subordination. The fact that the employer in practice leaves its workers an almost unfettered freedom in the performance of their jobs does not in itself preclude the existence of an employer-employee relationship. This is always conditioned, however, on the actual existence of a possibility for the employer to step in and direct or control the performance if it wants to do so. The fact that the employer is lacking the technical skills to intervene in an efficient and productive manner is of no consequence. There is no legal requirement conditioning the employer's authority on its ability to give economically and technically sound commands. Jumping ahead to the scenario on insubordination, one has to mention here that even when the employee is convinced, based on his superior knowledge and skills, that he or she did perform a particular task properly but the employer or one of its representatives demands that the employee do the job all over again, in the end the employer may legally do so.

Subordination and economic dependence of the employee upon the employer used to be two sides of the same coin. Although labor courts in principle denounce taking the economic dependence of a given worker into account in order to determine whether an employer–employee relationship exists, the fact is that they often consider it—albeit indirectly—to be one of the indicia pointing in the direction of subordination. By opening up the opportunity for what were previously considered to be the skilled "liberal" professions—for example, medical doctors and architects—to perform as employees, the link between economic dependence and subordination became blurred.[69] A new "coin" got introduced in the "monetary system" of labor relations—subordination as one side of the coin and economic independence as its flip side. This evolution might influence the functioning of the disciplinary sanction apparatus, inasmuch as the employer, knowing that an employee is not completely economically dependent upon the employer, but as a skilled employee is of vital importance to the company, might feel restrained from disciplining the employee too harshly.

Belgian labor law now grants protection to employees who enjoy freedom and independence to a much greater degree than it did to the employees it initially intended to protect. While this evolution may restrain the employer from imposing too severe a sanction, it may also influence the system of industrial justice in a different way. The employer–employee relationship is based on mutual trust and cooperation. Independence and confidence go hand in hand. The employee that is granted more independence supposedly enjoys the employer's full confidence. Labor courts therefore seem willing to accept that violations of this increased confidence may be punished with more severe sanctions, such as a summary dismissal for serious reasons.[70]

TERMINATION WITH NOTICE

Contracts of employment are not terminable at will under Belgian labor law. A summary discharge, without paying compensation or taking a term of notice into account, is only allowed for serious reasons. Absent serious reason, and without reference to the general ways in which obligations may be extinguished, engagements arising out of contracts of employment can be terminated by the expiry of the term or by the completion of the work for which the contract was concluded, by the will of either party, by the worker's death, or by force majeure.[71] Where a contract of employment has been concluded for an unspecified period, either of the parties may terminate it by giving notice.[72] To be valid the termination of the contract must be communicated to the other party in writing.

The length of the term of notice is statutorily defined for blue-collar workers.[73] For white-collar workers the length of the term of notice is dependent upon three elements: the amount of remuneration, the length of the employee's service with the same employer, and the identity (employer or employee) of the party terminating the employment relationship.[74] If one party terminates the contract of employment without serving the prescribed term of notice, the other party can claim damages, in principle equal to the remuneration corresponding to the length of the term of notice that should have been served or to that part of the term of notice not yet expired.

The employer has no statutory duty to communicate its reasons for giving notice to an employee. The employer is not obliged to explicitly justify the employee's dismissal at the time of termination.[75] Termination of the contract of employment can thus easily be used as a disciplinary sanction against an offending employee. Some kind of explicit justification may, however, be required from the employer when the dismissed employee claims that his dismissal is abusive and is related neither to his conduct or aptitude nor to the functional requirements of the enterprise that employed him.[76] It is the employer who carries the burden of proof of the existence of the reason justifying the dismissal.[77] Only in exceptional circumstances will the employer not be able to come forward with a reason related to the employee's conduct or aptitude, or to the functional requirements of the enterprise itself. The employer has to satisfy this burden of proof only when the employee claims the dismissal to

73

be abusive. When no such claims are made, no justification has to be proffered. Additional financial compensation is the only remedy available for the abusively dismissed employee. Reinstatement cannot be granted by the labor courts.

THE PARTICULAR OBLIGATIONS OF EMPLOYMENT

Case law dealing with disciplinary sanctions in general and with their appropriateness in a particular setting is almost completely absent. The statutory regulations on industrial justice tend to be of a formal nature, describing a procedure to be followed in order legally to discipline the offending employee. The statutes dealing with a problem do not list the sanctions that an employer can impose.

Case law is available only on dismissal for serious reasons, this being the most severe sanction an employee can incur. This certainly does not come as a surprise. It is a well-known fact that an employee will prefer not to sue his or her employer so long as the employment relationship lasts. Most likely the sanctioned employee's situation in the enterprise will not be improved by instituting a lawsuit against his employer. It will be more advantageous to the employee not to do so. However, when the employer terminates the employment contract, the employee has nothing to expect anymore from his former employer except possibly financial compensation for an unjust dismissal. The only way to obtain this compensation is by filing suit.

For the above mentioned reasons, the central part of the analysis of the scenarios will be dedicated to the question of whether the pattern of facts would justify a summary dismissal for serious reasons. If a given fault is serious enough to justify a summary termination of the contract of employment, it is obvious that less severe sanctions would be equally justified. If dismissal for a serious reason is considered not to be justified for a given offence, the employer may impose the sanctions that the work rules indicate, taking into account the general principles described above.

Some offences by employees may not be sufficiently serious to justify a dismissal for serious reason if they were committed only once. A series of the same or similar offences may, however, become sufficiently grave to warrant a summary discharge. Repetition may thus be an aggravating circumstance. However, the employer has some duty to warn the employee that the offence committed might lead to disciplinary sanctions, and ultimately to the employee's dismissal, if it happens again. When the employer does not take any action at all, and does not inform the employee of the possible consequences of his or her shortcomings, the employer cannot rely on the repetitive character of the offences to justify a dismissal without notice.[78] The employee's long and loyal service to the company may be a mitigating circumstance, especially if he or she never before incurred any disciplinary sanctions.[79]

The fact that other employees previously committed the same or similar offences as the employee up for disciplinary sanctions, yet were not dismissed for serious reason, is likely to prove that cooperation between the employer and the offending employee did not become immediately impossible by virtue of the offence. Further employment during the term of notice is therefore not excluded. Summary dismissal of the offending employee will, at least generally speaking, be considered unjustified. Dismissing one employee out of a group of offenders engaged in the same serious offence, just to set an example for the other employees, is not warranted. Other disciplinary sanctions may be imposed.

SUBORDINATION

Case Scenario

JD, a janitor at the A Manufacturing Company, is assigned the task of waxing office hallways. He completes one hallway. His supervisor, FF, inspects the hallway and says to JD, "Do this floor again." JD replies "No," and walks away.

Analysis

An employee has a duty to obey the lawful orders of his employer. A refusal to do so may lead to termination of his contract of employment for serious reasons,[80] especially when refusal to obey the order is expressed in the presence of other employees.[81]

Seriousness. The fact that the employee believes the order to be foolish or unnecessary will not excuse disobedience. Even when the employee thinks he did a good job waxing the floor the first time, he still has to obey the employer's orders. A politely uttered opinion, of course, does not constitute a serious reason for dismissal, at least if the employee after expressing his opinion fulfills the task the supervisor required him to do. When the refusal to perform is combined with an insulting or threatening attitude toward the supervisor, a summary dismissal will most certainly be considered justified.[82] The employee's reasonable belief that doing the job over might be a threat to his own health may justify his refusal. The same holds true when waxing the floor a second time could be a hazard to other employees' safety or health, since the employer may not give commands or instructions that endanger the lives of its employees.[83]

When the order clearly falls outside the employee's job description, he may refuse to obey it.[84] As already explained, unilateral modification of the job content by the employer constitutes a breach of contract.

Mitigation. An insulting attitude taken by the supervisor might be a reason for complaint, but does not in itself justify the employee's refusal to obey the order. The fact that the employee never previously refused any of the orders given to him might be a mitigating factor, but does not necessarily exclude disciplinary sanctions. The same is true for an employee's twenty-year seniority with the company.[85]

The fact that the offending employee is a trade union representative grants him protection against employer antiunion activity, but does not allow him to disobey legitimate orders. However, a different procedure has to be followed for his dismissal.

Enforceability. When other employees who disobeyed similar orders got away with it and remained undisciplined, labor courts are likely to find the employee's dismissal unjustified. The fact that the other employees remained in service shows that the professional cooperation between an employee committing an offence of this kind and his employer does not become immediately impossible. Picking out one employee to set an example is not allowed. Other disciplinary sanctions, such as termination of the contract of employment with notice, are available.

SOBRIETY

Case Scenario

RR, a laborer on the loading dock of B Trucking Company, is observed by his supervisor, JB, reaching into the pocket of a coat that is hanging near his workplace. JB observes RR bring something to his mouth, appear to swallow, and then replace it in the coat. JB approaches RR and asks, "What are you drinking?" RR reaches into the pocket of the coat and hands JB a bottle that contains an alcoholic beverage. JB forms the opinion that RR's breath smells strongly of alcoholic spirits and that his eyes are unfocused.

Analysis

Drunkenness on the job is often successfully invoked by employers as a serious reason for dismissal.[86] Even when the employee is off duty, it is sometimes accepted as a reason for summary dismissal.[87] The existence of formal company rules indicating that drunkenness on the job would be severely sanctioned would be an aggravating factor. Absence of prior similar offences would be a mitigating circumstance,[88] without excluding, however, the possibility of a justified dismissal. It should always be kept in mind here that employees are statutorily forbidden to bring alcoholic beverages to their place of work.[89]

Seriousness. Most of the cases accept drunkenness as a serious reason, without even considering the absence or presence of factors such as harm to the employer's property, harm to other employees, damage to the employer's reputation, or loss of business. The presence of such factors would most likely be considered as aggravating circumstances.

Mitigation. One has to take into account that the employee's shortcomings will only justify a summary dismissal when they constitute a fault attributable to the employee. Applying this principle, some labor courts have held that in cases of alcohol addiction the drunkenness of the employee should be considered as a disease and should thus suspend the execution of the contract of employment rather than being invoked as a serious reason for its termination.[90] Using drugs on the job would mean that the employee is engaging in a criminal offence.[91] This factor will probably be considered as an aggravating circumstance. Drug addiction might, however, more easily be seen as a disease. No significant cases have yet come up.

Enforceability. The fact that other people (supervisors or fellow employees) have shown up drunk at work and were not dismissed would show that drunkenness does not immediately make the professional cooperation between employer and employee impossible. The requirements for the existence of a serious reason would not be met.

When it is a custom in a given industry that employees consume alcoholic beverages on the job, then the employee cannot be sanctioned for "respecting" this custom. Consumption is not, however, the same as drunkenness.

SECURITY OF EMPLOYER'S PROPERTY

Case Scenario

PR, a clerk employed by C Gourmet Foods Company, is observed by two supervisors taking company products out of a packing box, concealing them on his person, and walking out the door with them. He is apprehended after he exits the store, and admits taking the products.

Analysis

The employment relationship is built on mutual trust between employer and employee. Theft by an employee of goods or materials belonging to the employer will destroy the cornerstone on which their cooperation is built.[92]

Seriousness. The value of the stolen goods in unimportant, and might only work as an aggravating factor.[93] The same holds for the fact that an employer has had previous problems with theft by employees and has difficulties in establishing a mechanism of control to prevent reoccurrence.[94] Knowledge of the theft by other employees is also an aggravating factor and would allow the employer to impose more severe sanctions. Courts take into account that a lax stand taken by the employer would undermine its authority over its employees.

The fact that the goods were taken out of a trash bin—and the employee had reason to believe that the goods were of no value anymore to the company—would render the offense less serious. The same holds for a clearly established custom in the industry of allowing employees to take some goods home.[95] Strict company rules against this kind of practice might lead to a different solution.

Mitigation. When the employee is suffering from a mental illness that makes him completely unaccountable for the shortcomings committed, there will be no fault on his part, and thus the requirements for the existence of a serious reason for summary dismissal will not be fulfilled. A condition of depression leading to kleptomania was held not to be of such a nature as to deprive the employer of its right to dismiss the employee summarily. Only upon proof of the fact that the mental condition of the employee completely prevented him from controlling his actions would the court have been willing to hold the employee not accountable.[96]

PEACEFUL WORKPLACE

Case Scenario

MM is a clerk in D Department Store. NN is another clerk in the same department store; he is physically larger than MM. While MM is moving some heavy equipment from one area to another NN says, "I'm surprised that you did not ask a real man to handle this job." MM, angered, strikes NN on the jaw, knocking him down. NN gets up and walks away.

Analysis

Seriousness. When an employee insults a co-worker, the insulting party is subject to disciplinary sanctions. A dismissal for serious reasons seems to be too severe a sanction. The circumstances in which the insult was uttered would be of importance. And so would both employees' functions in the company, their records of previous offences, etc.

The insulted employee may not, however, take the law into his own hands. Acts of violence committed against another employee spoil the atmosphere of cooperation and are often regarded as sufficiently serious reasons for summary dismissal of the aggressor,[97] especially when weapons such as knives or iron bars are used to assault fellow workers.[98] Damage, or potential damage, to the employer's property or business, the infliction of severe injury, the presence of other employees, or a previous record of offences would be considered aggravating factors.

Mitigation. The absence of any of the above-mentioned circumstances might be mitigating factors, without, however, excluding the possibility of a justified dismissal of the aggressor. The same holds true for the fact of both employees involved in the conflict declaring that their future cooperation was not jeopardized by the event. However, one of the requirements for finding a serious reason for summary dismissal is that the cooperation between employer and employee, not employee and employee, becomes impossible. When both engage in the fight, both can be dismissed for serious reasons. When both are equally guilty, the employer might have the option to dismiss both or not to do so. Dismissing one, while imposing a lesser sanction on the other employee, would not be justified.

Enforceability. A prior warning for similar offences would be an aggravating factor. So would a company history of dismissing employees engaging in fights at the workplace.

OFF-DUTY CONDUCT

Case Scenario

TT, head salesclerk for E Toy Store, participates in a white supremacist demonstration. He is arrested for disorderly behavior, and a photograph of him handcuffed to a post and snarling at police is printed in the local newspaper, along with his name and the name of his employer.

Analysis

The general principles governing off-duty conduct and the imposition of disciplinary sanctions have been set out above. Events in the private life of the employee may justify a dismissal for serious reasons if they disrupt production in the enterprise and create serious tensions between the employees and management. The fact that the offences committed might cause serious damage to the employer has been on various occasions taken into account to justify a summary dismissal.[99]

Seriousness. Criminal convictions are not necessarily sufficient reason for the summary termination of the contract of employment.[100] They can become a serious reason when the facts upon which the conviction is based show that the employee may be dangerous to his co-workers.[101] The fact of being taken into custody can never of itself justify a summary dismissal. A 1983 amendment to the act respecting contracts of employment provides that the performance of the contract of employment may only be suspended—suspension, not termination—for the time a worker is subject to measures depriving him of his freedom for preventive purposes.[102] This does not, however, prevent the facts for which the employee was taken in custody from justifying a dismissal for serious reasons. The same is true for an acquittal.[103]

Of course, the employee has a right to have his own opinion—even about racial inequality or equality—and is allowed to express it in his free time. But when the way in which he does that interferes substantially with the functioning of the enterprise, he may be asked to bear the consequences of his action.

The fact that cooperation between the offending employee and his immediate supervisor would be rendered impossible by the employee's offence does not transform an offence that the employer considered not to be serious enough for summary termination into a serious reason for dismissal. Placing the offending employee under a different supervisor might solve the problem. Disciplinary sanctions short of dismissal remain available.

Enforceability. When fellow employees of a different color have engaged in similar action, publicized in the same way, and were not punished for it, a summary dismissal is not warranted, since this shows that, at least for the term of notice, cooperation between employer and employee is not absolutely impossible.

ATTENDANCE

Case Scenario

JJ is a nurse's aide at the F Nursing Home. Because of an illness, her attendance at work has been erratic for two years. During that period she has missed 30 percent of her scheduled working days. During the last month she has missed 20 percent of her scheduled working days. All these absences were excused. She then misses three days of work, without notifying her employer, because she decides to extend her holiday.

Analysis

Seriousness. The act respecting contracts of employment provides that the contract of employment shall be suspended if a worker is unable to work on account of illness or an accident. The employee has to notify the employer immediately of incapacity to work. If a provision to that effect is made by collective bargaining agreement or is in the work rules or, in the absence of any such provision, if the employer so requires, a worker shall provide a medical certificate. Except in cases of force majeure she shall send it to the employer or hand it in within two working days, reckoned from the date of the incapacity or the date on which she receives the employer's request to produce a medical certificate. Other time limits may be specified in collective bargaining agreements or work rules. If the worker fails to produce the medical certificates within the prescribed period of time, she loses her right to guaranteed remuneration, as provided for in the act respecting contracts of employment.[104] It is the statute itself that determines the disciplinary sanction the employer can legally impose for failure to provide it with medical certificates for an absence because of sickness or accident.[105]

Unjustified absences can justify a dismissal for serious reasons.[106] Circumstances that have been taken into account as aggravating factors are intent to harm the functioning of the enterprise,[107] limited seniority of the employee,[108] prior warnings given for similar offences,[109] and the fact that the absence immediately followed the employee's holiday period.[110] One unjustified absence will normally not be considered a sufficient justification for summary dismissal. A series of unjustified absences will.

Mitigation. A good performance record and the lack of prior disciplinary sanctions would be mitigating circumstances. So would the fact that the unjustified absences were separated by a considerable period.

Enforceability. The absence of a written policy concerning unjustified absences does not preclude the employer from imposing the most severe disciplinary sanction. A clear written policy, strictly enforced, would be an aggravating factor.

PERFORMANCE

Case Scenario

HH is a warehouseman for G Distributing Company. G has instituted a program that determines levels of productivity for warehousemen. This program meets accepted professional standards for such programs. Over a period of two months HH fails to produce at the prescribed levels, consistently falling 10 percent below the standard. He is warned that he will be terminated if he fails to improve his productivity within two weeks. HH claims that the standards of the new system are impossible to meet. He proves that prior to the institution of the new system he was given above-average evaluations by his supervisor for producing at his current level, covering a period of ten years.

Analysis

Low performance by an employee is not in itself a serious reason for summary dismissal.[111] Only the surrounding circumstances could raise the employee's shortcoming to the level of serious reason for dismissal. When the low productivity is a consequence of the employee's incompetence to reach a certain level of productivity despite his best efforts, it will not warrant termination of the contact of employment for serious reason. When, however, the low productivity is caused by intent to harm the employer's enterprise, it can justify a summary dismissal.[112] When the employee is able to perform at a higher level of production, a level both parties to the contract of employment agreed upon when they entered into the contract of employment, but deliberately stays under it, his attitude can be equated with insubordination.

The employer can always terminate the employee's contract of employment by giving him notice. If the worker is performing clearly under the average standard, the dismissal is most certainly not abusive, since it is obviously related to the employee's skills and aptitude.[113]

If the introduction of a new program transforms the employee from an above average to a well below average performer, probably more is involved than just a new way of measuring employees' performance. If the job is changed significantly and unilaterally by the employer, the employee can invoke a breach of contract by the employer and claim financial compensation.

The introduction of new technologies is the subject of a collective bargaining agreement that was concluded at the national level on December 13, 1983.[114] If an employer has decided upon an investment in a new technology and if this has major collective consequences with regard to employment, the organization of work, or working conditions, the employer must, at least three months before the start of the installation of the new technology, supply written information to the works council or the trade union representatives committee concerning the nature of the social consequences that this entails.[115] The employer must also consult with the works council, the health and safety committee, and the trade union representatives committee, depending upon their competence, on the social consequences of the introduction of new technology. This consultation concerns the prospects regarding number of jobs, the employment structure, and the social measures planned regarding employment; organization of work and working conditions, and the qualifications of the employees and eventual measures regarding training and retraining of the employees.[116] If the employer does not respect these procedures, it cannot unilaterally terminate a contract of employment except for reasons unconnected with the introduction of the new technology. The burden of proof rests on the employer. For dismissal following a three-month period after the new technology has been put into operation, the burden shifts to the employee.[117] If the employer is not able to meet its burden, the employee will be granted an additional compensation in addition to the normal compensation, equal to a lump sum of three months' gross salary.

LOYALTY

Case Scenario

JS, a teller for H Bank, during an appearance on a television consumer information program states that her employer regularly fails to advise customers when they make mistakes in favor of the bank, but promptly corrects mistakes made in favor of the customers.

Analysis

An employee has a duty not to reveal any manufacturing or business secrets learned in the course of the performance of his or her job. If the employee communicates information of this nature, she can be discharged for serious reasons. She may at the same time incur penal sanctions.[118]

The act respecting contracts of employment also imposes upon the employee a duty not to reveal any information of a personal or confidential nature.[119] Revealing information of a confidential nature, not accessible to the public at large and of vital commercial importance to the employer, might justify a dismissal for serious reasons.[120] A clerk working in a bank who does not respect the bank's secrecy rules, and makes public the names of the customers, can be dismissed for a serious reason.[121]

Seriousness. The negative impact the employee's revelations might have on the employer's business or its reputation would probably be considered an aggravating factor. So would

84

the employee's knowledge about the untruthfulness of the information. The position and job of the employee in the company would also be of importance. An employee who is granted the employer's utmost confidence and who has access to information of a most confidential nature can more easily be summarily dismissed if she commits an infraction of her duty of secrecy. The nature of the industry involved—banking, for example—might also lead to heightened scrutiny of the employee's behavior.

Mitigation. The fact that the employee divulged the information in reaction to previous misconduct by a supervisor or by the employer would not change the serious nature of the offence. The status of an employee representative to the works council gives the employee access to information otherwise not accessible. Penal sanctions apply to any member of the works council who improperly makes public information concerning the enterprise that is confidential and obtained through works council membership.[122]

Enforceability. The existence of a formal and written rule communicated to the employee may only highlight the importance of the duty imposed upon the employee in a general way by the act respecting contracts of employment. The central problem in dealing with the situation wherein an employee makes public information on the employer's failure to correct mistakes that are in favor of the customers is how to classify the information. Assuming that the employer has a legal duty to correct its mistakes, either in favor of the customers or in its own favor, it is hard to see how this information can be seen as confidential in the sense of the act respecting contracts of employment. If the employer's attitude is clearly illegal, and the employee tried to convince management to take a different stand, and dismissal for serious reason does not seem to be warranted. The employee's duty of loyalty toward the employer might require her first to address the problem internally in the company before going public with it.

RESTRICT COLLECTIVE ACTION

Case Scenario

JJ, a machinist at I Manufacturing Company, becomes angry because he believes that his supervisor is treating him and other employees in a disrespectful manner. In protest, he persuades the other employees in his work group to leave work together in the middle of their scheduled work shift and not return until the next day.

Analysis

The Belgian Court of Cassation has held that a strike—the walkout described in the scenario would be considered a strike—in itself does not terminate the employment relationship. It only leads to an automatic suspension of the execution of the contract of employment for the duration of the strike. The court recognized the liberty (read: right) of each individual employee to engage in collective action.[123] The right to engage in industrial warfare is a right that belongs to the individual employee, as an employee, and not as a trade union member. The absence of any trade union involvement does not make the strike action illegal, and has no influence on the disciplinary sanctions the employer can legally impose on the striking employees. The Belgian Court of Cassation treats all kinds of strike actions equally, whether the strike is spontaneous, organized by a trade union, a sympathy strike, a strike to get a salary increase, or a political strike.[124] As long as the action undertaken is collective, the number of participating employees does not make a difference. The organizer of the strike and the followers should be treated the same way. Neither capacity influences the sanctions that can be imposed.[125] Since a strike action suspends the execution of the contract of employment, the strike itself can never justify a dismissal for serious reasons,[126] nor any other disciplinary sanction. The duration of the strike and the economic loss the strike might cause to the employer are irrelevant in determining whether the participating employees can be sanctioned.

Events surrounding the strike may, however, lead to disciplinary sanctions, including summary dismissal. Events such as theft, deliberate destruction of machinery, and violence may lead to the dismissal for serious reasons of employees committing these offences.[127]

Strike action tends to heat up the feelings on both sides of the conflict. Insults might be uttered. The fact that such events are a regular part of strike actions is sometimes considered a mitigating factor. Insulting a supervisor during a strike might not be as serious an offence as insulting him during a regular meeting.[128]

Parties to collective bargaining agreements quite often include a peace obligation in the terms of their agreement. A peace obligation is an obligation to abstain from industrial warfare for the term of the contract.[129] The peace obligation is considered an obligatory part of the collective bargaining agreement and binds thus only the parties to it, these being trade union organizations on the one hand and an employer or an employers' association on the other hand. The individual employee, who is the holder of the right to strike, is not bound by this kind of obligation, and can thus not be sanctioned for its breach.

AVOID CONFLICT OF INTEREST

Case Scenario

IB, a systems analyst for J Company, has access to private computer systems of his employer. IB accepts a string of freelance, relatively routine programming jobs for K Company, a competitor of his employer, performing the work at his home.

Analysis

The concept of good faith underlies the employment relationship. It prevents an employee from becoming a competitor of his own employer during the execution of the contract of employment. Direct competition with the employer is a serious reason justifying instant dismissal without notice.[130] The act respecting contracts of employment explicitly imposes upon the employee the duty to "refrain both during the contract and after its termination, from . . . engaging or cooperating in any form of disloyal conduct."[131]

Seriousness. The competition the employee engages in does not have to be deceptive in order to warrant a summary discharge;[132] but if it is, its disloyal nature will surely be taken into account as an aggravating factor.[133] The same holds true for explicit company rules in this regard. If an employee is granted considerable leeway in the performance of his job, his activities will become subject to a heightened level of scrutiny.[134] The nature of the job the employee is performing and his place in the hierarchy of the company will thus be of importance. Revealing professional secrets can furthermore be sanctioned with penal sanctions such as imprisonment, fines, and indemnification.

If the employee takes up a second job with a different

employer, in no way competing with the first employer's activity, and if this activity in no way interferes with the quality or quantity of his performance for his first employer, courts are likely to find summary discharge unjustified.[135]

Summary dismissal will only be justified if the employee is actually competing with his own employer. The mere fact that an employee, in his time off and without any interference with his on-the-job performance, is preparing the start of his own business after the expiration of the contract of employment cannot justify a dismissal for serious reasons.[136] Some courts, however, have accepted as justified the summary dismissal of an employee because of his personal participation in the establishment of a private limited company.[137] Buying stock would not of itself be a sufficient reason for instant dismissal, unless, of course, the employee acquires an amount of shares that would allow him to influence the company's policies and goals. In the latter case he would be "participating"—albeit perhaps only indirectly—in the management of the company and would become a direct competitor with his own employer.

After the termination of the contract of employment the employee regains his complete freedom of labor. He can set up a competing business or start working for his employer's direct competitors. Under Belgian labor law, however, the employee can waive this right by subscribing to a covenant of noncompetition.[138] The act respecting contracts of employment requires the employer to indemnify the employee for subscribing to a covenant of noncompetition. The minimum amount payable by way of compensation must be equal to half the employee's gross remuneration for the period for which the covenant effectively applies.[139] Violation of the covenant of noncompetition is sanctioned by a financial compensation.[140] In order to obtain this compensation, the employer has to sue its former employee and bring its case before the labor courts.

CONCLUSIONS

The system of workplace, or industrial, justice set out above describes the sanctions an employer can legally impose on an employee who has committed an offence. It describes when the employer is justified in striking the employee with the most severe sanction that can be imposed, namely summary dismissal for serious reasons. The employee then loses the job without any term of notice or compensation. This sanction also has consequences in the field of social security. The employee is, among other things, deprived of unemployment benefits. In practice, the employee will also meet considerable difficulties in trying to find a new job. It surely does not make an applicant for a job highly desirable if, when asked for the reason why he or she left his former employer, the answer is "dismissal for serious reasons."

The employee can fight the dismissal in court. But courts, even labor courts, have a considerable backlog. The final result, especially when one of the parties appeals the case, may take several years. Success is even then not guaranteed. The fact that the factual circumstances of each case are of great importance in determining whether the dismissal was justified allows, on the one hand, taking the particulars of each case into account, and avoidance of the application of strict and impersonal legal rules; but, on the other hand, it diminishes the predictability of the final outcome of the case.

Assuming that the employee finally prevails in the action against the employer, labor courts have no power to reinstate an employee who was summarily dismissed without term of notice. Financial compensation will be the only remedy available. The fact that the employee can get only financial relief underlines once more that a distinction has to be drawn between the employer's *right* and its *power* to sanction an employee on disciplinary grounds. The employer who is willing to pay for it can dismiss, or impose any disciplinary sanction on, any employee, however small and irrelevant an offence the employee committed. Industrial warfare by an organized group of employees may then well be the only available and effective avenue for relief.

NOTES

1. See Roger Blanpain and Chris Engels (assistance), "Monograph Belgium," *International Encyclopedia for Labour Law and Industrial Relations [ELL]* (The Netherlands: Kluwer Law and Taxation Publishers), looseleaf, 30, no. 23. The hierarchy of sources in Belgian labor law is determined by sec. 51 of the act respecting Collective Industrial Agreements and Joint Committees, 5 Dec. 1968, in *International Encyclopedia for Labour Law and Industrial Relations [Legislation] Belgium [ELL [Leg.] Bel.)]* (Kluwer Law and Taxation), looseleaf, Act No. 8.

2. See Blanpain and Engels, "Monograph Belgium," *ELL* 45, no. 41.

3. See, e.g., Roger Blanpain, "Probleemstelling en begripsomschrijving (Formulation and definition)," *Werkstaking— Lock-out en arbeidsrecht en sociale zekerheid [Strike and Lock-out—Labor Law and Social Security]* (Antwerp: Kluwer Rechtswetenschappen, 1988).

4. While this paper will sometimes refer to the employee as "he," this should not be seen as an expression of male bigotry. Whenever "he" is used to refer to the employee, "he" stands for "she," and "his" for "her" also. Absolute sexual equality!

5. Act respecting Contracts of Employment, 3 July 1978, Sec. 16, *ELL [Leg.] Bel.*, Act No. 24.

6. Act respecting Contracts of Employment, 3 July 1978, Sec. 17, *ELL [Leg.] Bel.*, Act No. 24.

7. Act respecting Contracts of Employment, 3 July 1978, Sec. 20, *ELL [Leg.] Bel.*, Act No. 24.

8. See Blanpain and Engels, "Monograph Belgium," *ELL* 81, no. 81.

9. See, e.g., Labor Court Liège 23 Nov. 1983, *Tijd schrift voor Sociaal Recht [T.S.R.]*, 248 (1985).

10. See Act respecting Contracts of Employment, 3 July 1978, Sec. 25, *ELL [Leg.] Bel.*, Act No. 24.

11. See Court of Cassation 4 Dec. 1974, *Arresten van het Hof van Cassatie [Arr. Cass.]*, 426 (1976), 49.

12. See Court of Cassation 10 Oct. 1988, *TSR*, 388 (1988). For an extensive discussion of and comments on this case, see: Chris Engels, "De vastheid van betrekking in het katholiek onderwijs opnieuw in vraag gesteld, enkele bedenkingen bij het cassatiearrest van 10 oktober 1988 [Security of Employment in the Catholic Educational System: In Jeopardy again]," *Rechtskundig Week blad [RW]* (1988–89): 870–79.

13. See Engels, "Security of Employment,": 873.

14. Act to Institute Work Rules, 8 Apr. 1965, Sec. 16, *ELL [Leg.] Bel.*, Act No. 4.

15. Ibid.

16. Ibid., Sec. 17.

17. See, e.g., Labor Court Antwerp 18 Apr. 1985, *Journal des Tribunaux de Travail [JTT]* 158 (1987).

18. Act to Institute Work Rules, 8 Apr. 1965, Sec. 17, *ELL [Leg.] Bel.*, Act No. 4. See also Labor Court Liège 23 Nov. 1983, *TSR*, 248 (1985).

19. See, e.g., Labor Court Brussels 18 June 1979, *JTT*, 333 (1979).

20. Act to Institute Work Rules, 8 Apr. 1965, Sec. 17, *ELL* [*Leg.*] *Bel.*, Act No. 4.

21. See, e.g., Labor Tribunal Charleroi 29 Oct. 1968, *TSR*, 139 (1969).

22. Act to Institute Work Rules, 8 Apr. 1965, Sec. 18, *ELL* [*Leg.*] *Bel.*, Act No. 4.

23. Act to Institute Work Rules, 8 Apr. 1965, Sec. 19, *ELL* [*Leg.*] *Bel.*, Act No. 4.

24. Ibid.

25. See, e.g., Petit, "Arbeidsreglement [Work Rules]," *Arbeidsrecht* [*Labor Law*], Roger Blanpain, ed. (Brugge: Die Keure, loose leaf), 79, No. 83.

26. Ibid., 79, No. 83.51

27. See: Steyaert, "Tuchtrecht en Gezagsuitoefening in de onderneming [Disciplinary Actions and the Exercise of Authority in the Enterprise]," *Tijdschrift voor Privaatrecht* [*TPR*]; 487, No. 15 (1987).

28. Act to Institute Work Rules, 8 Apr. 1965, Sec. 6.4, *ELL* [*Leg.*] *Bel.*, Act No. 4.

29. Act respecting Contracts of Employment, 3 July 1978, Sec. 35, *ELL* [*Leg.*] *Bel.*, Act No. 24 : "Either of the parties may terminate a contract without notice or before the expiry of its term if there is a serious reason for doing so in the opinion of the judge."

30. Act to Institute Work Rules, 8 Apr. 1965, Sec. 6.4, *ELL* [*Leg.*] *Bel.*, Act No. 4 : "The work rules shall indicate . . . 4. periods of notice required, and serious grounds for termination of the contract by either party, without notice, subject to judicial opinion." See also Labor Court Brussels 6 Feb. 1984, *Orientations,* 203 (1984); Labor Court Liège 10 Mar. 1971, *Jurisprudence de Liège* [Jur. Liège], 236 (1970–71); Chris Engels, *Ontslag wegens dringende reden* [*Dismissal for Serious Reasons*] Brugge: Die Keure, 1988), 56–58, Nos. 314–24; Labor Court Brussels 8 Apr. 1986, *JTT*, 462 (1986).

31. See also Engels, *Dismissal for Serious Reasons,* 58, Nos. 325–28; Labor Court Brussels 8 Apr. 1986, *JTT,* 462 (1986); Labor Court Liège 15 June 1983, *TSR,* 104 (1983); Labor Court Liège 21 Nov. 1978, *Jur. Liège,* 178 (1978–79); Labor Court Brussels 12 July 1972, *RW* 1099 (1973–74).

32. See Act respecting Contracts of Employment, 3 July 1978, Sec. 35, *ELL* [*Leg.*] *Bel.*, Act No. 24.

33. See also Engels, *Dismissal for Serious Reasons,* 1–52, Nos. 1–295.

34. Court of Cassation 9 Mar. 1987, *JTT,* 128 (1987).

35. See, e.g., Labor Tribunal Dinant 21 June 1977, *Jur. Liège,* 215 (1977–78).

36. See, e.g., Labor Court Liège 17 Jan. 1984, *Revue du Notariat Belge,* 159 (1985); Labor Court Antwerp 22 Oct. 1975, *RW,* 1775 (1975–76).53

37. See, e.g., Labor Court Brussels, 19 Dec. 1985, *Sociaal-rechtelijke Kronieken* [*Soc. Kron.*], 267 (1986); Labor Court Liège 26 June 1979, *Mededelin gen V.B.O.,* 3381 (1980).

38. See, e.g., Labor Court Brussels 22 Apr. 1987, *Soc. Kron,* 306 (1988); Labor Court Brussels 17 Jan. 1978, *JTT,* 178 (1978).

39. See Engels, *Dismissal for Serious Reasons,* 15–16, Nos. 85–86.

40. See ibid., 14, Nos. 73–78.

41. See, e.g., Court of Cassation 23 Oct. 1989, *RW,* 1313 (1989–90); Engels, *Dismissal for Serious Reasons,* 13–14, Nos. 67–78; 17–19, Nos. 96–103.

42. See, e.g., Labor Tribunal Verviers 22 Nov. 1972, *JTT,* 157 (1973).

43. See, e.g., Labor Court Liège 5 June 1973, *Pasicrisie* [*Pas.*], 89 (1973).

44. See, e.g., Court of Cassation 22 Apr. 1985, *TSR,* 578 (1985).54

45. See Engels, *Dismissal for Serious Reasons,* 6–7, Nos. 25–27.

46. See ibid., 9–10, Nos. 43–53.

47. See, e.g., Labor Tribunal Antwerp 13 Jan. 1981, *Soc. Kron,* 38 (1982).

48. See, e.g., Court of Cassation 19 Dec. 1988, *Arr. Cass.,* 489 (1988–89).

49. See, e.g., Petit, "Arbeidsreglement (Work Rules)," 79, No. 82.

50. See Engels, *Dismissal for Serious Reasons,* 26–28, Nos. 147–160; Court of Cassation 9 Mar. 1987, *JTT,* 128 (1987).

51. See, e.g., Court of Cassation 12 Jan. 1981, *Arr. Cass.,* 514 (1980–81); Court of Cassation 14 Feb. 1973, *Arr. Cass.,* 594 (1973); Court of Cassation 8 Sept. 1971, *Arr. Cass.,* 26 (1972). See also Engels, *Dismissal for Serious Reasons,* 29–30, Nos. 161–70.

52. See Act respecting Contracts of Employment, 3 July 1978, Sec. 35, *ELL* [*Leg.*] *Bel.,* Act No. 24.55.

53. See Court of Cassation 14 May 1979, *Arr. Cass.,* 1092 (1978–79).

54. See, e.g., Petit, "Arbeidsreglement (Work Rules)," 80, No. 84; Steyaert, "Tuchtrecht en Gezagsuitoefening in de onderneming," *TPR,* 489, No. 18 (1987).

55. Ibid.

56. See, e.g., Labor Court Brussels 14 Aug. 1986, *Soc. Kron.,* 227 (1986); Labor Court Brussels 22 Dec. 1982, *TSR,* 523 (1983); Labor Court Brussels 2 June 1982, *Soc. Kron.,* 11 (1984).

57. See, e.g., Court of Cassation 16 June 1971, *Arr. Cass.,* 1045 (1971). See also Engels, *Dismissal for Serious Reasons,* 35–37, Nos. 198–211.

58. Act to Institute Work Rules, 8 Apr. 1965, Sec. 6.7, *ELL* [*Leg.*] *Bel.,* Act No. 4.

59. See National Collective Labor Agreement No. 5 regarding the Rules for Trade Union Delegates Representing Employees in Undertakings, 24 May 1971, Sec. 13, *ELL* [*Leg.*] *Bel.,* Act No. 10.56.

60. Act respecting Contracts of Employment, 3 July 1978, Sec. 35, *ELL* [*Leg.*] *Bel.,* Act No. 24.

61. Ibid.

62. Ibid.

63. See Act to Protect Employee Representatives and Non-Elected Candidates, 29 March 1991 (effective from 1 May 1991).

64. See Engels, *Dismissal for Serious Reasons,* 70–75, Nos. 392–420.

65. See Steyaert, "Tuchtrecht en Gezagsuitoefening in de onderneming," *TPR,* 501, No. 32 (1987).

66. For a general description of the concept of subordination in Belgian labor law see Chris Engels, "National Report : Belgium," *Employed or Self Employed,* special issue of *Bulletin of Comparative Labour Relations* (The Netherlands: Kluwer Law and Taxation Publishers), forthcoming. For a detailed analysis of the concept of subordination in Belgium labor law see Chris Engels, *Het ondergeschikt verband naar Belgisch arbeidsrecht* [*The Concept of Subordination according to Belgian Labor Law*] (Brugge: Die Keure, 1989).

67. See Engels, *Subordination,* 13–20.

68. See, e.g., Act respecting Contracts of Employment, 3 July 1978, Sec. 3, as amended by Parliamentary Act of 17 July 1985, *ELL* [*Leg.*] *Bel.,* Act No. 24.

69. One major exception to this tendency is the profession of lawyer. Lawyers "pretend," for no justified reason whatsoever, always to work as independent contractors. See, however, Engels, *Subordination,* 56–59.

70. See, e.g., Labor Court Brussels 29 June 1983, *JTT,* 483 (1984); Labor Court Brussels 22 Dec. 1982, *JTT,* 486 (1984); Labor Tribunal Brussels 2 June 1982, *JTT,* 488 (1984).

71. See Act repecting Contracts of Employment, 3 July 1978, Sec. 32, *ELL [Leg.] Bel.,* Act No. 24.

72. See Act respecting Contracts of Employment, 3 July 1978, Sec. 37, *ELL [Leg.] Bel.,* Act No. 24. Where a contract of employment has been concluded for a specified period or for a clearly specified piece of work, the party terminating it before its expiry and without a serious reason shall pay the other party compensation equal to the remuneration due until the expiry of the contract, provided that such compensation shall not exceed twice the remuneration corresponding to the period of notice that would have been required if the contract had been concluded for an unspecified period. See Act respecting Contracts of Employment, 3 July 1978, Sec. 40, *ELL [Leg.] Bel.,* Act No. 24.

73. See Act respecting Contracts of Employment, 3 July 1978, Sec. 59, *ELL [Leg.] Bel.,* Act No. 24.

74. See Blanpain and Engels, "Monograph Belgium," *ELL,* 123–25, Nos. 143–44.

75. See Blanpain and Engels, "Monograph Belgium" *ELL,* 116, No. 127.

76. Abusive dismissal is regulated by the parliamentary act respecting contracts of employment (see Act respecting Contracts of Employment, 3 July 1978, Sec. 63, *ELL [Leg.] Bel.,* Act No. 24). However, Sec. 63 only deals with blue-collar workers. With respect to white-collar workers, the theory of abuse of law was developed in order to limit the employer's discretionary power to dismiss.

77. See Act respecting Contracts of Employment, 3 July 1978, Sec. 63, *ELL [Leg.] Bel.,* Act No. 24.59

78. See, e.g., Labor Court Brussels 4 Apr. 1974, *TSR,* 520 (1974). See also Engels, *Dismissal for Serious Reasons,* 11, Nos. 54–56.

79. See, e.g., Labor Court Brussels 19 Sept. 1986, *Rechtspraak van de Arbeidsgerechten van Brussel,* 387 (1986); also Engels, *Dismissal for Serious Reasons,* 12–13, Nos. 62–64.

80. See, e.g., Court of Cassation 17 Oct. 1973, *TSR,* 110

(1974); also Engels, *Dismissal for Serious Reasons,* 96, Nos. 545–48; 117, Nos. 677–80.

81. See, e.g., Labor Tribunal Liège 29 May 1972, *Jur. Liège,* 117 (1972–73).

82. See, e.g., Labor Court Liège 22 June 1981, *Jur. Liège,* 22 (1982); Labor Court Brussels 25 June 1979, *RW,* 1053 (1979–80); Labor Court Brussels 19 Feb. 1979, *JTT,* 142 (1979).

83. See, e.g., Labor Court Liège 5 June 1973, *Pas.,* 89 (1973).

84. See, e.g., Engels, *Dismissal for Serious Reasons,* 117, No. 681.

85. See, e.g., Labor Tribunal 29 Nov. 1969, *JTT,* 8 (1970).60

86. See, e.g., Engels, *Dismissal for Serious Reasons,* 91–92, Nos. 517–24.

87. See, e.g., Labor Court Liège 16 Oct. 1981, *JTT,* 58 (1983).

88. See, e.g., Labor Tribunal Brugge 3 Nov. 1969, *TSR,* 82 (1970).

89. See Act respecting the General Regulation Concerning Labor Safety, Sec. 99.

90. See, e.g., Labor Court Antwerp 14 May 1987, *RW,* 1511 (1987–88).

91. The criminal conviction in itself is not necessarily a serious reason for dismissal; see, e.g., Labor Court Brussels 27 Apr. 1983, *TSR,* 336 (1969).

92. See, e.g., Labor Court Brussels 22 Sept. 1980, *JTT,* 94, (1981).

93. See, e.g., Labor Court Liège, 14 Mar. 1984, *TSR,* 483 (1984); Labor Court Brussels 22 Sept. 1980, *JTT,* 94 (1981). Some courts do, however, follow a different approach. See Engels, *Dismissal for Serious Reasons,* 89, n. 94.

94. See, e.g., Labor Court Brussels 9 Feb. 1973, *JTT,* 172 (1973).

95. See, e.g., Labor Tribunal Brussels 12 July 1977, *JTT,* 356 (1977).

96. See, e.g., Labor Tribunal Brussels 29 Feb. 1988, *JTT,* 164 (1988); also Labor Court Liège 17 Apr. 1984, *TSR,* 487 (1984).

97. See, e.g., Engels, *Dismissal for Serious Reasons,* 93–94, Nos. 531–35.

98. See, e.g., Labor Tribunal Brussels 3 Dec. 1979, *JTT,* 182 (1980).

99. See, e.g., Labor Tribunal Liège 26 Feb. 1980, *JTT,* 338 (1980); Labor Tribunal Liègc 6 Jan. 1972, *JTT,* 207 (1973).62.

100. See, e.g., Labor Tribunal Brussels 27 Apr. 1983, *TSR,* 373 (1983).

101. See, e.g., Labor Court Liège 28 June 1971, *Jur. Liège,* 146 (1971–72).

102. See Act respecting Contracts of Employment, 3 July 1978, Sec. 28, *ELL* [*Leg.*] *Bel.,* Act No. 24.

103. See, e.g., Labor Court Brussels 27 Apr. 1983, *TSR,* 373 (1983).

104. See Act respecting Contracts of Employment, 3 July 1978, Sec. 31, *ELL* [*Leg.*] *Bel.,* Act No. 24.

105. See Steyaert, "Tuchtrecht en Gezagsuitoefening in de onderneming," *TPR,,* 492, No. 22 (1987). Where the performance of a contract has been suspended for more than six months on account of incapacity or illness, the employer may terminate the contract by paying the wage earner compensation equal to the remuneration for either the period of notice or the residual period of notice (Act respecting Contracts of Employment, 3 July 1978, Sec 58, *ELL* [*Leg.*] *Bel.,* Act No. 24).

106. See, e.g, Labor Court Liège 3 Nov. 1982, *Jur. Liège,* 105 (1983), Engels, *Dismissal for Serious Reasons,* 76–79, Nos. 423–43.

107. See, e.g., Labor Tribunal Charleroi 5 Jan. 1964, *TSR,* 42 (1965), 63.

108. See, e.g., Labor Tribunal Mons 18 Sept. 1978, *JTT,* 167 (1979).

109. See, e.g., Labor Court Liège 30 Jan. 1981, *Jur. Liège,* 212 (1981); Labor Court Brussels 28 Oct. 1975, *TSR,* 255 (1975).

110. See, e.g., Labor Court Mons 15 June 1968, *TSR,* 329 (1968); Labor Court Brussels 18 Apr. 1968, *Journal des Tribunaux,* 427 (1969).

111. See, e.g., Engels, *Dismissal for Serious Reasons,* 101–02, Nos. 583–84; 104–05, Nos. 601–02.

112. See, e.g., Labor Court Brussels 3 Dec. 1980, *Med. VBO,* 1166 (1982); Labor Court Brussels 19 Mar. 1971, *JTT,* 4 (1972).

113. See Act respecting Contracts of Employment, 3 July 1978, Sec. 63, *ELL* [*Leg.*] *Bel.,* Act No. 24.

114. See National Collective Labor Agreement No. 39 Concerning Information and Consultation on the Social Consequences

of the Introduction of New Technologies, 13 Dec. 1983, *ELL* [*Leg.*] *Bel.*, Act No. 34.

115. Ibid., Sec. 2; Sec. 4.64

116. Ibid., Sec. 2.

117. Ibid., Sec. 6.

118. See Blanpain and Engels, "Monograph Belgium," *ELL,* 81–82, No. 82; also Act respecting Contracts of Employment, 3 July 1978, Sec. 17, *ELL* [*Leg.*] *Bel.*, Act No. 24.

119. See Act respecting Contracts of Employment, 3 July 1978, Sec. 17, *ELL* [*Leg.*] *Bel.*, Act No. 24.

120. See, e.g., Labor Court Brussels 20 Feb. 1980. *Med. VBO,* 1784 (1981); Labor Tribunal Charleroi 26 Jan. 1987, *TSR,* 136 (1987).

121. See, e.g., Labor Tribunal Charleroi 26 Jan. 1987, *TSR,* 136 (1987).

122. See Act to Make Provisions for the Organization of the Economic Life of the Country, 29 Sept. 1948, Sec. 30, *ELL* [*Leg.*] *Bel.*, Act No. 2; also Blanpain and Engels, "Monograph Belgium," *ELL,* 201–02, No. 286.

123. See Court of Cassation 21 Dec. 1981, *Arr. Cass.,* 541 (1981–82).

124. See, e.g., Chris Engels, "staking en lockout : gevol gen ten aanzien van de individuele arbeidsovereenkomst [The Consequences of Strikes and Lockouts on the Individual Contract of Employment]," *Werkstaking Lock-out en arbeidsrecht en sociale zekerheid* [*Strike and Lockout Labor Law and Social Security*] (Antwerp: Kluwer Rechtswetenschappen, 1988), 72.

125. Ibid., 78.

126. See, e.g., Engels, *Dismissal for Serious Reasons,* 108–10, Nos. 621–31.

127. See, e.g., Engels, "The Consequences of Strikes and Lockouts," 73.

128. Ibid., 81.

129. See Blanpain and Engels, "Monograph Belgium," *ELL,* 240, No. 359.

130. See, e.g., Chris Engels, "Daden van concurrentie tijdens de arbeidsovereenkomst als dringende reden voor ontslag [Competition during the Execution of the Contract of Employment as a Serious Reason for Dismissal]," *Oriëntatie,* 193–203 (1988).

131. Act respecting Contracts of Employment, 3 July 1978, Sec. 17, *ELL* [*Leg.*] *Bel.*, Act No. 24.

132. See, e.g., Labor Court Antwerp 13 Oct. 1975, *JTT,* 358 (1976).

133. See, e.g., Labor Court Brussels 23 May 1986, *Med. VBO,* 1737 (1987).

134. See, e.g., Labor Tribunal Brussels 2 June 1982, *JTT,* 488 (1984).

135. See, e.g., Labor Court Brussels 20 Nov. 1987, *JTT,* 161 (1988); Labor Tribunal Verviers 2 Mar. 1977, *JTT,* 261 (1977); also Engels, *Dismissal for Serious Reasons,* 86–87, Nos. 489–91.

136. See, e.g., Labor Court Mons 18 June 1987, *JTT,* 164 (1988); Labor Court Liège 16 Feb. 1983, *JTT,* 485 (1984); Labor Court Brussels 21 Nov. 1973, *TSR,* 231 (1974).

137. See, e.g., Labor Court Brussels 27 May 1977, *RW,* 2014 (1977–78); also Court of Cassation 5 May 1976, *Arr. Cass.,* 994 (1976).

138. For the conditions of validity of a covenant of noncompetition and for its scope, see Blanpain and Engels, "Monograph Belgium," *ELL,* 139–40, Nos. 168–69. See also Act respecting Contracts of Employment, 3 July 1978, Sec. 65, *ELL [Leg.] Bel.,* Act No. 24.

139. See Act respecting Contracts of Employment, 3 July 1978, Sec. 65, *ELL [Leg.] Bel.,* Act No. 24.

140. Ibid.

![3]

CANADA[1]

Roy J. Adams and Bernard Adell

By international standards there is a wide gap between the job rights of organized and unorganized employees in Canada. Organized employees, who make up less than half of the work force, usually have the substantive protection of collective agreement provisions prohibiting their dismissal (more often called discharge) without just cause. They also enjoy the procedural protection afforded by a specialized and relatively fast system of grievance arbitration which has the power to grant remedies tailored to the specific situation. Unorganized employees, in contrast, must rely on the weaker common law protection against dismissal without cause and on the ordinary courts, whose remedial powers are limited to awarding money damages and whose procedures are often relatively slow and expensive.[2]

However, the differences between the rights of the two classes of employee are gradually shrinking. For one thing, all employees are now protected by various substantive statutory regimes, principally in the areas of human rights, employment standards, and occupational health and safety (McPhillips and England; Adell). For another, the common law courts have gradually been narrowing the concept of cause for dismissal, thereby bringing it more into line with the concept of just cause applied in the organized sector (Failes; Eden).

After some general discussion of the Canadian law on dismissal, first with respect to unorganized employees and then with respect to organized employees, we will look at ten hypothetical disputes involving dismissal for misconduct in order to see how Canadian courts and arbitrators would resolve each of them. When we speak of what a *court* would do, we are referring to a common law wrongful dismissal action brought by an *unorganized* employee. When we speak of what an *arbitrator* would do, we are referring to the outcome of an *organized* employee's grievance, brought under a collective agreement, claiming that he or she has been dismissed or otherwise disciplined without just cause.

OVERVIEW OF THE SYSTEM

INDUSTRIAL JUSTICE AND THE UNORGANIZED EMPLOYEE

Under Common Law

Under the Canadian common law of employment (or "master and servant law," as it was called in the past) either party may terminate the employment relationship but must give "reasonable notice" before doing so,[3] unless the other party's conduct has given "cause" for termination. An employee who claims that he or she was dismissed without cause or without sufficient notice may sue the employer for damages for wrongful dismissal.[4] The concept of cause arises from the idea, fundamental to the common law, that employees owe their employers certain implicit obligations. Central among them are the duty to obey reasonable instructions, to act with good faith and fidelity, and to exercise skill and care (Christie). Violation of any of those duties may amount to cause for dismissal without notice.

In a wrongful dismissal action the legal burden of proving cause is on the employer. Traditionally, that burden was not very heavy. Any significant breach of the employee's obligations to the employer would suffice to justify dismissal. The employer was required neither to impose a lighter sanction for lesser acts of misconduct nor to give an employee any warning or any chance to do better. Nor would the courts take into consideration such factors as the length of service or prior record of the employee (Failes, p. 35).

Lately, however, the Canadian courts have been tightening up the meaning of cause, in both the substantive and procedural senses. Judgments in recent years have emphasized that an employee's misconduct must be serious substantively in order to ground dismissal, and there is also a trend toward requiring employers to warn employees that their conduct is unacceptable and that failure to improve will lead to dismissal.

The courts have traditionally taken a narrow, all-or-nothing view of the options open to an employer in dealing with employee misconduct. If an employee's conduct, in the court's view, provides cause for dismissal, the employer is free to dismiss the employee without notice but not to impose lesser discipline such as a fine or suspension without pay unless such a penalty has been foreseen and agreed upon by the parties.

Even more significantly, the courts have also taken a narrow view of what is an appropriate remedy in a wrongful dismissal case. No matter how wrongful the dismissal may have been, the courts will not order reinstatement as a remedy, but will only award damages equivalent to the wages which the employee would have earned during the notice period. On the other side of the coin, if an employee has been guilty of some misconduct, but not quite enough to provide cause for dismissal, most Canadian courts will nonetheless order the employer to pay the full amount of damages in lieu of notice, without any reduction for the employee's misconduct.[5]

Three Canadian jurisdictions (the federal jurisdiction, Quebec, and Nova Scotia) some years ago adopted statutory reforms extending "just cause" protection to the unorganized. This protection is not enforced by the courts, but by a process of administrative adjudication modeled on arbitration under collective agreements in the organized sector. For the most part, the substantive and procedural principles of just cause applied in that adjudicative process are very similar to those applied by arbitrators (Failes; Eden; Grosman, ch. 5). The remedies open to an employee through that process also parallel those available in arbitration, in that they include the power of reinstatement. Early research on the operation of these reforms suggested that workers found to have been unjustly dismissed were in most cases effectively reinstated in their jobs.[6] More recent research has, however, been less optimistic, and has indicated that it may be difficult to make reinstatement work in the unorganized sphere (Eden), perhaps because of the absence of a union in the workplace to oversee the reintegration of the worker.[7]

Under Statute Law

In every Canadian jurisdiction a range of human rights, employment standards, and occupational health and safety statutes prohibit employers from dismissing or taking other action against employees on certain specified grounds. For example, human rights legislation, which is having an ever-increasing impact on both unionized and nonunionized employment relationships, generally forbids discrimination against an employee on a wide range of grounds, including race, religion, ethnic origin, sex, age, marital status, and physical or mental handicap (McPhillips and England). Such statutes generally provide for the reinstatement of employees who have lost their jobs as a result of the employer's breach of their statutory rights.

INDUSTRIAL JUSTICE AND THE ORGANIZED EMPLOYEE

Collective bargaining in Canada has usually been conducted at enterprise level, and the predominance of relatively small and homogeneous bargaining units has led to detailed collective agreements well suited to enforcement by third-party adjudication. Rights and obligations under such agreements are enforced through multistep grievance procedures, culminating in binding arbitration by a jointly acceptable arbitrator. In some provinces arbitrators adjudicate certain complaints brought under employment standards and occupational health and safety legislation as well as disputes over the interpretation of collective agreements, and have the explicit power to apply provisions of other statutes that may be relevant to the matter at hand.

Canadian arbitrators have generally been willing to move away from traditional common law attitudes and take a broader view of both the substantive and procedural rights of employees with respect to discipline and discharge, even without explicit support in the language of the collective agreement. Nevertheless, arbitrators consider employees who are covered by such agreements to have the same basic obligations, discussed above, as their forebears had at common law and as unorganized employees still have. Conversely, arbitrators impose on employers a duty, parallel to that imposed by the courts at common law, not to discipline employees who meet those obligations and a further duty to administer discipline fairly.[8]

In some other respects the Canadian courts have drawn an opaque curtain between the common law regime and the collective bargaining regime. In a leading case the employer argued that employee participation in an illegal strike in breach of the collective agreement constituted a repudiation of the agreement and thus allowed the employer to disregard certain of its financial obligations to those employees under the agreement. Chief Justice Laskin rejected that argument in the Supreme Court of Canada, and said:

> The common law as it applies to individual employment contracts is no longer relevant to employer–employee relations governed by a collective agreement. . . . [Labor relations statutes could not] operate according to their terms if common law concepts like repudiation and fundamental breach could be invoked in relation to collective agreements which have not expired and where the duty to bargain collectively subsists.[9]

The tension between common law concepts and the collective bargaining regime has also appeared in the development of the remedial power of Canadian arbitrators. Arbitrators have been given a clear statutory power to reinstate employees in cases where the employer has not shown just cause for dismissal—a power which, as noted above, the courts still do not have when dealing with unorganized employees. Reinstatement is in fact ordered in the great majority of cases in which the dismissal of unionized employees is held to be unjust,[10] and research findings show that reinstatement works moderately well if gauged by the rate of survival of the employment relationship afterward.

As an adjunct to their power to reinstate, arbitrators now also have the explicit statutory power to tailor a disciplinary sanction to fit the particular case. They very often use that power to substitute lesser penalties, such as suspensions without pay, where they find the employee to have been guilty of some misconduct but where they see dismissal as being too harsh in the circumstances.

Arbitrators in Canada universally accept the idea of progressive discipline; that is, they will rarely allow dismissal unless the employer has made the particular employee clearly aware of the unacceptability of his or her conduct, through a course of warnings and perhaps suspensions as well, and has given the employee a chance to improve. Only for a few types of especially serious employment offences is an arbitrator likely to uphold a dismissal that is based on a single incident. Theft, aggravated insubordination, severe violence, and the leading of an illegal strike are the major examples. The courts, in wrongful dismissal actions, have traditionally been less tolerant of single acts of misconduct, but have moved a long way toward the arbitral position on progressive discipline in recent years.

An important element of the theory of progressive discipline in arbitral jurisprudence is the doctrine of the "culminating incident." This doctrine holds that an instance of employee misconduct not sufficient in itself to justify dismissal but sufficient to justify some disciplinary action will allow the employer to use the employee's prior record, in combination with the most recent incident itself, to establish cause for dismissal.

In assessing the appropriateness of the discipline imposed by an employer in a particular case, arbitrators have a well-established practice, now gradually being adopted by the courts as well, of looking at the overall employment relationship, at what the parties have invested in that relationship, and at whether there is any hope of salvaging it. Certain factors are often held to reduce the seriousness of an employee's misconduct and thereby to limit the degree of discipline which the employer may impose. Of those factors, long seniority and a good work record are perhaps the most important and the most often used. Along the same lines, with respect to most employment offences, arbitrators (and now courts as well) will give some weight to other evidence that the employee's offence is out of character, unpremeditated, or the result of unusual short-term pressures either on the job or in other parts of his or her life. In such circumstances arbitrators will use their power to reduce the severity of the penalty.

Proof of employer condonation of similar conduct by other employees in the past will always be a potent defence to disciplinary action, on the basis that an employer cannot discriminate between employees on irrelevant criteria. If an employer decides to crack down on a type of misconduct which was previously tolerated in the particular workplace, the employer must clearly notify employees beforehand.

The fact that an employee is a union officer will seldom affect the permissible level of discipline. Canadian arbitrators have generally held that the duty of union officers as such is not to the employer but to the union. Thus, they cannot be disciplined more severely than other employees for the same offence unless they have used their union positions to incite misconduct among others (Brown and Beatty, pp. 9:14–15).

One of the most important current issues in Canadian arbitral jurisprudence on unjust dismissal is the extent to which arbitrators may enforce such statutes as human rights codes, employment standards acts, and occupational health and safety acts—statutes which confer substantive rights and obligations on employers and employees but which have their own specialized enforcement processes (Adell). Some years ago the Supreme Court of Canada held that arbitrators have the power (and indeed the duty) to strike down provisions of collective agreements that are inconsistent with such statutes.[11] More recently arbitrators have begun to enforce statutory rights and obligations more directly.[12] That is particularly true of the antidiscrimination provisions of human rights codes, which prohibit not only direct or intentional discrimination but also indirect or unintentional discrimination.[13] Those provisions may oblige the employer to make changes in work schedules, processes, or machinery in order to accommodate the needs of a disabled employee, for example, or an employee who refuses to work on a certain day for religious reasons. The only limitation on such changes is that they need not be so costly or awkward as to cause undue hardship to the employer.[14]

THE PARTICULAR OBLIGATIONS OF EMPLOYMENT

SUBORDINATION

Case Scenario

JD, a janitor in a manufacturing plant, waxes an office hallway. His supervisor, FF, inspects the hallway and says to JD, "Do this floor again." JD replies "No," and walks away.

Analysis

Under the principle that the employer must be allowed to direct and control operations with a view to efficient production (Brown and Beatty, p. 7:107), willful disobedience of an order to do work is considered by courts and arbitrators to violate an essential element of the employment relationship. JD's refusal to obey a reasonable order is serious misconduct, but whether it is serious enough to justify dismissal will depend on various circumstances discussed below.[15]

Seriousness. JD's conduct will be treated as less serious if he merely walks away without saying anything or if he politely declines to carry out the order. On the other hand, if his refusal to obey is accompanied by highly insolent language or (even worse) by a threat to harm FF, such an overt challenge to a supervisor's authority is very likely to constitute cause for dismissal.[16] Similarly, if the refusal takes place in front of other employees, it may be seen as more of an affront to the supervisor's authority (Palmer, pp. 268–69).

If the act of insubordination is isolated and out of character for JD, a court or arbitrator is less likely to treat it as cause for dismissal than if he has done the same sort of thing in the past. That is especially true if he has many years of service.

Generally, under the "obey now, grieve later" principle, an employee must follow a supervisor's instructions even if he or she thinks they are foolish or incompetent, and even if they are contrary to a company rule. However, although a refusal to obey in such circumstances might be misconduct, it might well not be considered serious enough to provide cause for dismissal. Thus, if JD can show that he did in fact wax the floor properly in the first place and that FF was simply mistaken, his dismissal will probably not be upheld by a court or arbitrator.

Collective agreement provisions often impose more or less strict limits on an employer's right to change employee duties, but the "obey now, grieve later" principle may require the employee to enforce those limits through the grievance procedure rather than by refusing to obey an employer order (Brown and Beatty, p. 7:112, nn. 5, 6). As for unorganized employees, the employer may have more leeway to change their assigned duties in accordance with the needs of the enterprise. However, if the newly assigned duties are beyond the reasonable limits of the job, or if they involve a demotion, an unorganized employee may treat the employer's action as a "constructive dismissal" and may demand notice or pay in lieu of notice—at the cost of having to leave the job. Courts and arbitrators may find some degree of culpability in an employee's refusal to do work not explicitly or implicitly agreed upon as part of his or her duties, but such a refusal will not usually be enough to ground a dismissal (Brown and Beatty, p. 7:108).

An order to carry out a task in an unnecessarily demeaning

fashion is an unreasonable order and will not have to be complied with.[17] The "obey now, grieve later" principle will not apply, because it is not considered fair to require the employee to submit to such an indignity and to seek redress only after the fact. So if FF orders JD to clean the floor with a toothbrush, he almost certainly can refuse.

What if JD thinks that his health or safety will be threatened if he carries out FF's order? The old common law rule was not concerned with what the employee thought but with whether the work was in fact unsafe. If the work was later proven to have been safe, the employee's refusal to do it may have constituted cause for dismissal (Christie, p. 241). However, in recent decades a somewhat stronger employee right to refuse unsafe work has been recognized by statute across Canada, in terms that vary slightly from jurisdiction to jurisdiction.[18] Generally an employee may refuse to do work if he or she believes, on reasonable grounds, that the work is dangerous to himself or herself or to another worker. If the employee has such a belief, the employer may not take any reprisals against him or her, even if it later turns out that the work was in fact safe.

If an otherwise minor act of insubordination causes real disruption—for example, if the hallway is heavily used and is too slippery to walk on until it is rewaxed—the employer will be allowed to treat it more severely, especially if the employee should have realized it would have that effect.

Mitigation. If abusive remarks by FF provoked JD into the act of disobedience, and if it was a single, uncomplicated act, a court will be reluctant to uphold a dismissal. If JD is a senior employee with a good record, he probably cannot be dismissed for this incident alone. He will be entitled to a warning and at least one more chance.[19] However, if he has a poor record, even a minor act of insubordination might well be considered to be a culminating incident and thus to be adequate cause for dismissal.[20]

If JD is an employee representative in a nonunionized workplace, that fact cannot add to the seriousness of his act of insubordination unless he has used his position as a representative to incite other employees to behave similarly. If he has been active in campaigning for unionization by lawful means, labor relations legislation forbids disciplinary action against him unless the employer can prove that the discipline had nothing at all to do with his union activity.

Enforceability. If FF gives a vague or tentative order, leaving the impression that JD can choose whether or not to comply, noncompliance will not ground dismissal. If the employer has in the past condoned similar conduct by JD or other employees, the employer will not be able to dismiss JD without first giving him a clear warning that its attitude toward such conduct has changed. Without such a warning a court or arbitrator will consider him insufficiently aware that he is doing anything wrong.

SOBRIETY

Case Scenario

RR, a laborer on the loading dock of a trucking company, is seen by his supervisor, JB, reaching into a coat that is hanging near his workplace. JB then observes RR bring something to his mouth, appear to swallow, and put it back in the coat. JB approaches RR and asks, "What are you drinking?" RR reaches into the coat and hands JB a bottle containing an alcoholic drink. JB notices that RR's breath smells strongly of alcohol and that his eyes are unfocused.

Analysis

Canadian employment law has not taken as clear a stand on alcohol use or abuse as on such matters as insubordination and theft. How courts and arbitrators will treat a dismissal for drinking on the job or for intoxication will depend heavily on contextual factors, including the type of workplace and the previous attitude of the employer toward such conduct.[21] The loading dock of a trucking company will probably not be considered an overly sensitive area with respect to drinking. That fact points away from a finding of cause for dismissal on the facts at hand. So does RR's frankness when confronted by JB.

Two other points should be noted. First, although the scenario at hand does not refer to any absences from work, alcohol or drug abuse often leads to excessive absenteeism, thereby bringing into play considerations discussed below under attendance. Second, as noted above, Canadian human rights legislation now imposes stringent limitations on an employer's right to discipline an employee because of a physical or mental disability. Alcoholism and drug addiction are generally considered to

108

be disabilities,[22] so an employer must carefully consider that legislation before imposing any discipline.

Seriousness. If the dismissal is for intoxication rather than for the act of drinking itself, the employer will have to prove that RR's condition was such as to interfere with his ability to do his job properly or safely. Proof of actual harm is not needed; proof of a real danger of harm to other people or to the employer's property or reputation is enough. If actual harm does result, though, the misconduct will be treated more seriously.

It probably does not matter what sort of alcoholic drink the employee has consumed. In most Canadian workplaces no distinction would be made between wine or beer on the one hand and strong liquor on the other. As for illegal drugs, one writer, in comparing arbitrators' attitudes toward alcohol and marijuana, suggests colloquially that "the noon-hour beer is viewed with more tolerance than the noon-hour joint" (Young, p. 149). However, it is not clear that courts or arbitrators will treat the possession or use of such drugs more severely because of its illegality alone,[23] unless the particular job is one where that sort of illegal behavior in itself indicates unsuitability. What is centrally important, in the case of both drugs and alcohol, is the actual or potential effect on job performance or safety.[24] As in the case of allegations of theft, courts and arbitrators tend to impose a somewhat higher standard of proof on the employer when possession or use of illegal drugs is alleged, because of the greater stigma attached to workplace misconduct that also amounts to a crime.[25]

Mitigation. Courts and arbitrators now generally see alcoholism, and perhaps drug addition too, as illnesses rather than as straightforwardly culpable conduct. Thus, if RR can show that he has a problem of that sort, cause for dismissal might not be found unless the employer has given him a chance to rehabilitate himself before dismissing him,[26] especially if he is a long-service employee with an otherwise good record. That is particularly true in the arbitral forum.

With respect to drinking on the job, even more than in most of the scenarios discussed in this study a great deal depends on the nature of the industry and the general attitude toward such conduct in that industry, as well as on the past attitude of the particular employer toward it.

Enforceability. A clear company rule against any drinking in the workplace, if communicated to employees, will be an important factor supporting a dismissal. Conversely, the absence of an explicit rule will make it harder to dismiss an employee for drinking on the job, though perhaps not for being intoxicated. Arbitrators and courts are often willing to presume that employees realize the unacceptability of conduct which affects their capacity to do the job, even if there is no express employer rule against it.

Employer condonation of similar conduct in the past, whether by RR or by other employees, will probably preclude RR's discharge.[27] If managerial employees are permitted to drink in the plant, the company may have difficulty in arguing that it should be allowed to treat ordinary employees differently.

SECURITY OF EMPLOYER'S PROPERTY

Case Scenario

PR, a clerk employed by C Gourmet Foods Company, is observed by two supervisors taking company products out of a packing box, concealing them on his person, and walking out the door with them. He is apprehended after he leaves the store, and admits taking the products.

Analysis

Except for serious violence against the person, stealing from the employer (or from customers or suppliers) tends to be seen as more unambiguously immoral than anything else an employee might do, and as being more likely to destroy the trust necessary to the employment relationship. Many employers call in the police in cases of theft by employees and encourage the police to bring criminal charges.

A finding of theft in a wrongful dismissal proceeding or arbitration proceeding does not in itself give the employee a criminal record, but it carries a strong stigma nonetheless. Thus, courts and arbitrators generally require employers to provide "clear and convincing" evidence of theft—a standard of proof lower than that in criminal cases (proof "beyond a reasonable doubt") but higher than the usual standard in civil cases (proof "on a balance of probabilities"). This means that an employer cannot lightly accuse an employee of such conduct, but must have very solid evidence of it.[28]

Seriousness. Variations in the seriousness of the act in ques-

110

tion tend to be less important with respect to theft than with respect to other types of employee misconduct. Courts and arbitrators often treat any act of fraud (including theft) as indicating a character flaw inconsistent with the trust an employer is entitled to place in an employee.[29]

On that reasoning, the value of what is taken by the employee is seen as irrelevant, at least in principle.[30] Even the taking of scrap has been held to ground severe discipline where the employee knew that the employer, if asked, would not have consented. However, if the goods taken are of very little value and the employer has not made it quite clearly known that employees are not allowed to take such items, the fraudulent intent required for theft may be found not to be proven.[31]

Mitigation. Until quite recently Canadian courts and arbitrators gave little weight in theft cases to some of the mitigating factors, such as a long record of good service, which are so important with respect to other types of employee misconduct. However, that very strict approach has been departed from recently, especially where there has been only one act of relatively minor theft and where all of the circumstances, including the employee's record, indicate that it is unlikely to recur. Similarly, if the employee is passing through a time of unusual financial hardship, the employer may be expected to show some tolerance for a minor instance of theft, but probably not for more than that.

If PR can prove that he is a kleptomaniac, his conduct might be seen as essentially nonculpable. Thus, as with an alcoholic employee, the employer will have to keep him on, probably under suspension without pay or in a position where he has no access to easily stolen items, while he undergoes psychiatric treatment. He can be dismissed only if it becomes clear that such treatment has failed. Canadian human rights statutes also support that conclusion. As mentioned above, those statutes prohibit dismissal or other discrimination against an employee because of a physical or mental handicap, unless the employer would suffer "undue hardship" from retaining the employee. Although there does not year appear to be any jurisprudence on the point, kleptomania may well be a mental handicap for the purposes of that legislation, and what is an undue hardship will no doubt vary with the employee's access to cash or other easily stolen items.

Enforceability. As in most of the other scenarios, condonation by the employer would bar a dismissal, whether the condonation is done formally through an express rule or informally through toleration of otherwise disciplinable conduct. Thus, if there is an informal practice of permitting employees to take small quantities of goods, PR would have to exceed the tolerated limits before he could be dismissed. To end such a practice the employer would have to give clear advance notice.

PEACEFUL WORKPLACE

Case Scenario

MM is a clerk in D Department Store. NN is another clerk in the same store; he is physically larger than MM. While MM is moving some heavy equipment from one area to another, NN says to him, "I'm surprised you didn't ask a real man like me to handle this job." MM, angered, strikes NN on the jaw, knocking him down. NN gets up and walks away.

Analysis

Canadian civil and criminal law places great importance on the physical integrity of the individual. Assault is both a tort (or delict) and a crime. If NN sues MM for assault or initiates a criminal prosecution against him, MM may face heavy damages, a large fine, or possibly (if he has prior criminal record) a jail sentence. In tort law and criminal law NN's disparaging remark would not be nearly enough to give MM the defence of provocation.

Employment law may treat MM somewhat less severely than tort law or criminal law. On the basic facts of this scenario it is quite unlikely that a dismissal would be upheld in the courts, and even less likely that it would be upheld at arbitration. NN's disparaging remark would probably be given some weight in MM's favor, though it would still be only a minor factor.

Seriousness. The seriousness of the incident depends very much on what the evidence shows about MM's propensity or lack of propensity for violence.[32] If the incident resulted from an isolated outburst of temper that was out of character for him, the courts will treat it quite differently than if he had acted similarly in the past. If he used a dangerous weapon such as a iron bar, unless he was defending himself against the danger of severe bodily harm, that in itself would show that he could not be trusted in a workplace where he would be in contact with others.

If the attack resulted in injury or in substantial damage or disruption to the employer, a dismissal would be more likely to be sustained, especially if MM intended such consequences or could readily have foreseen them. As for the merits of the dispute between MM and NN, they will probably be given very little or no weight, whichever way they may point.

Mitigation. If MM's actions were the result of a momentary flare-up, his personal circumstances of the moment may be quite important as a mitigating factor. Thus, if he was under unusual stress because of family or health problems or the like, his assault on NN may be treated as uncharacteristic and therefore as less likely to recur. And, as in most of the scenarios, lengthy seniority will weigh significantly in MM's favor, particularly before an arbitrator, unless his record discloses numerous earlier instances of discipline.

Enforceability. In this scenario the nature of the workplace and the employer's previous attitude toward fighting may blend together as factors affecting the allowable severity of discipline. A fist fight would no doubt be considered less tolerable in a department store than on a construction site, but slightly more tolerable if MM and NN were moving equipment in a back area of the store than if they were serving customers. Past condonation of fighting would pose an obstacle to disciplinary action, unless the employer had made it clear that such conduct would no longer be tolerated.

OFF-DUTY CONDUCT

Case Scenario

TT, head salesclerk for E Toy Store, participates in a white supremacist demonstration. He is arrested for disorderly behavior. A photograph of him handcuffed to a post and snarling at police is printed in the local newspaper, with his name and the name of his employer.

Analysis

Off-duty conduct is not cause for discharge unless it "prejudices either the employer or the employee's ability to carry out the job functions" (Levitt, p. 102). It is not clear whether the

113

events described in the basic version of this scenario would directly affect TT's ability to sell toys or to carry out the other specific duties of head salesclerk. That could be enough to convince a court or arbitrator that a dismissal should not be upheld.[33]

Many Canadian courts and arbitrators today would not confine themselves to a consideration of the financial loss or employee strife caused by TT's actions, but would give a good deal of weight to the inconsistency between those actions and the prevailing moral consensus against blatantly racist conduct. However, even if the immorality and social undesirability of TT's actions was in fact the main reason why they were upholding TT's dismissal, few courts or arbitrators would be venturesome enough to admit that fact in the written decision. Most would feel compelled to express their reasons mainly in terms of the harmful financial and employment relations consequences which TT's actions would have for the employer.

Freedom of speech considerations are of course relevant in the other direction; an employer cannot lightly use its economic power to censor an employee's off-duty political expression. It would not be surprising, however, if an employer were given more leeway to discipline an employee whose off-duty actions showed contempt for racial equality than one who had engaged in similar off-duty actions in favor of racial equality. Again, a court or arbitrator would probably explain the distinction by suggesting that the employer would be more likely to suffer opprobrium from an employee's participation in a racist demonstration than in an antiracist one—even if that might in fact be untrue in the particular local community.

Seriousness. As TT's duties appear to involve extensive contact with the public, including children, and some authority over co-workers, a serious criminal conviction will make it more likely that a dismissal will be sustained, whether or not the conviction is widely publicized.[34] An acquittal will certainly make it harder to sustain a dismissal but will by no means preclude it, as an employer's burden of proof of cause for dismissal is somewhat lighter than the Crown's burden of proof in a criminal prosecution. Also, particularly in arbitration proceedings but in a civil action for wrongful dismissal as well, the rules of evidence are less stringent than in a criminal court.

Mitigation. If TT is a long-service employee with a good

work record, that will certainly count in his favor. So will proof that he has never before engaged in violent conduct.

If TT had been demonstrating peacefully until he was attacked by others, that may reduce the blameworthiness of his conduct sufficiently to tip the balance against discharge. Conversely, if he personally instigated the violence, that will not only increase the gravity of the offence in the eyes of others, but may also be taken to say something about his fitness to deal with the public and with co-workers as a toy salesperson.

Enforceability. Condonation of similar behavior would once again be a clear bar to dismissal, whether that behavior was engaged in by supervisors or by ordinary employees. However, for the reasons discussed above, it should not too readily be assumed that toleration of similar acts committed without similar motives will be treated by courts or arbitrators as condonation of what TT did.

ATTENDANCE

Case Scenario

JJ is a nurse's aide at F nursing home. Because of an illness her attendance at work has been erratic for two years. During that period she has missed 30 percent of her scheduled working days. During the last month she has missed 20 percent. All of those absences were excused. She then misses three days of work, without notifying her employer, because she decided to extend her holiday.

Analysis

Innocent absenteeism—that is, absenteeism for illness or other reasons beyond the employee's control—is not cause for dismissal unless it is severe enough and persistent enough to preclude him or her from functioning effectively as an employee, either currently or in the foreseeable future. In the language of the courts in wrongful dismissal cases, becoming unable to function as an employee frustrates the contract of employment. In the language of arbitrators in the organized sector, it precludes a viable employment relationship.

JJ's absence rate of 30 percent over two years might not be enough to show long-term inability to function as an employee,

115

especially since that rate had lately declined a bit. On the other hand, no employer will be expected to tolerate so much absenteeism indefinitely. JJ's medical prognosis will therefore be important.

The last three days' absence, which presumably led to JJ's dismissal, was not innocent but culpable. Three days of unnotified culpable absence is quite a serious act of misconduct. Many collective agreements expressly provide that an unreported absence for more than a certain number of working days—often in the range of three to ten days—will be construed as abandonment of the job and will result in loss of seniority, which means that the employee loses many important job rights and may be exposed to immediate termination. However, unless there is a specific provision of that sort in the collective agreement, it is unlikely that an arbitrator will hold a three-day absence to be enough in itself to ground dismissal of an employee with a few years' seniority and an otherwise clear record. The same will probably be true in a wrongful dismissal action in the courts.[35]

Would those three days of culpable absence be made more serious by JJ's extensive innocent absenteeism, on the reasoning that an employee who has frequently missed work because of illness should take extra care to be there whenever she can? Probably not. It would be very hard to argue that absences for illness can be transformed into culpable absences by the occurrence of other culpable absences. However, if the culpable absences are themselves frequent, that fact may cast doubt on the employee's evidence that the other absences were due to illness.

This scenario is a particularly good one for illustrating the greater remedial flexibility of arbitrators as compared to courts. If JJ is an unorganized employee, and a court finds her absenteeism to fall short of providing cause for dismissal, all the court can do is award her money damages equivalent to her wages for the full period of notice which she ought to have received upon dismissal. The court would not order her to be reinstated in her job, nor would it reduce the amount of damages because of her three days' culpable absence. In contrast, if JJ is an organized employee covered by a collective agreement, and an arbitrator finds insufficient cause for dismissal, the arbitrator will probably order her reinstated in her job, subject to a lesser penalty in the form of a suspension as punishment for her three days' culpable absence. The length of the suspension will depend largely on the length and quality of JJ's record of service with F nursing home.

Seriousness. JJ's three-day culpable absence may be more serious if it occurred at the end of a holiday, because absences that extend weekends and holidays are a particular problem in many enterprises. It will certainly be more serious if the employer has a specific rule that emphasizes the unacceptability of absences at those times.

With respect to the absences due to illness, they will be more likely to support a dismissal if they have been increasing in frequency, if the medical evidence indicates that they are likely to continue far into the future, or if the nature of the job makes it especially hard for the enterprise to function normally when the employee is absent.

Mitigation. Lengthy seniority and a good work record will be important mitigating factors with respect to the culpable absence. With respect to the innocent absences, a few years of service will probably carry little weight. However, a very long record of good service may persuade a court or arbitrator that the employer owes the employee extreme patience. That may be especially true if the illness was caused at least in part by the job, as often happens with long-service employees.[36]

Enforceability. Condonation in the form of toleration of similar absences by other employees or by JJ herself will preclude dismissal. Proof of extensive efforts by the employer to help JJ overcome her health problems may help to convince a court or arbitrator that the employer has already "walked the last mile" with her.

PERFORMANCE

Case Scenario

HH is a warehouse worker for G Distributing Company. G has instituted a program that determines levels of productivity for warehouse workers. This program meets accepted professional standards for such programs. Over a period of two months HH fails to produce at the prescribed levels, consistently falling 10 percent below the standard. He is warned that he will be terminated if he fails to improve his productivity within two weeks. He fails to do so. HH claims that the standards of the new system are

117

impossible to meet. He proves that over the ten-year period before the new system was introduced, he was given above-average evaluations by his supervisor for producing at his current level.

Analysis

In many cases it may be extremely difficult to tell whether an employee's poor performance is culpable or innocent—that is, whether it is caused by negligence or laziness, which means it is culpable, or by physical or intellectual limitations, which means it is innocent. As one writer puts it, "There is often a very thin line between failing to do work of which one is capable and being unable to do the work" (Palmer, p. 416). However, as in the case of absenteeism discussed above, determining which side of the line a particular case of poor work performance falls on is important in determining the permissible employer response.

Let us look first at culpable poor performance—the situation where the employee is allegedly not trying to do well. Here a disciplinary approach is not only appropriate but is in fact required if the employer wants to terminate the employee. Thus, if the employee is unionized, the usual dictates of progressive discipline will apply: the employee must be clearly warned that poor performance is putting his or her job in jeopardy, the employee must be given a reasonable chance to improve, and a culminating incident must occur before dismissal is allowed. And to justify a dismissal the shortcomings in the employee's performance must be serious. Unless he or she has a very short or unsatisfactory record of service, minor instances of inattentiveness or lack of effort are unlikely to justify dismissal, especially if the employee is covered by a collective agreement but probably nowadays for unorganized employees as well.

A termination for innocent (or nonculpable) poor performance is quite different in nature. It is not disciplinary but is more analogous in some ways to a termination for temporary or permanent lack of work—or, as such a termination is often called in collective agreements, a lay-off. The legal rules governing terminations of that sort differ considerably between the organized and unorganized sectors.

In organized relationships most collective agreements provide for a probationary period at the beginning of the employment relationship—a period commonly one to three months in length for unskilled or semiskilled workers and often longer for more specialized jobs. During that time the employer has an unfettered right to dismiss for incompetence or for any other legitimate reason.[37] Once an employee survives the probationary period and acquires seniority rights under the collective agreement, the employer is more or less presumed to have recognized that the employee has the basic competence to do the job. It is seldom easy to prove that the employee has lost that competence; employers have a low success rate in arbitration cases involving dismissal for nonculpable poor performance (McPhillips and Shetzer).

What, precisely, must an employer prove in such a case? A leading treatise on arbitral jurisprudence says:

> In the context of . . . non-disciplinary, deficient work performance, the employer may exercise its power of termination, as in cases of innocent absenteeism, only where it has established that the employee's shortcomings are such as to undermine the employment relationship and when it is also established that the situation is not likely to improve. Generally, . . . the employer must establish the level of job performance it required, that such a standard was communicated to the employee, that it gave suitable instruction and supervision to enable the employee to meet the standard, that the employee was incapable of meeting the standard of that job or other positions presumably within her competence, and that it warned the employee that failure to meet the standard would result in her dismissal. (Brown and Beatty, pp. 7:96–97)

Unless the collective agreement says otherwise, an employer has the right to change the specified skill requirements of a job in accordance with changes in technology, work organization, and the like. Also, though perhaps less clearly, the employer can introduce reasonable increases in the job's output requirements, as long as the collective agreement, once again, says nothing to the contrary. On the basic facts of the scenario at hand, G Distributing Company appears to have had the right to act as it did in that respect.

However, if an employee simply cannot meet new skill or production requirements, the employer cannot proceed by way of a straightforward dismissal. First, in order to establish the right to move the employee out of the particular job, the employer must be able to prove the various facts mentioned in the passage quoted above. Next, as a recent paper puts it,

> The employer should also be able to demonstrate it has exhausted other possible solutions, such as:
>
> 1. Transferring the employee to a job which he is able to perform if one is available and if that can be done consistent with other provisions of the collective agreement;
>
> 2. Demoting him to a job which he is able to perform if one is available and if that can be done consistent with other provisions of the collective agreement, or
>
> 3. Placing him on layoff if no such job is available. (McPhillips and Shetzer)

A lay-off involves releasing an employee from the employer's work force, either temporarily or indefinitely, not because the employee has misbehaved but simply because the employer has no work for that employee to do. Most lay-offs result from a decline in the amount of work to be done, but they can be due instead to the nonculpable inability of an employee to do the work which the employer has available. Unlike an employee who has been dismissed for cause, an employee who is on lay-off usually has the right, under the applicable collective agreement, to be recalled to work if a job opens up which he or she can do—at least if such a job opens up during a certain period (commonly one to two years) after the beginning of the lay-off.

The concept of a lay-off can be useful to unionized employers in cases of nonculpable poor performance because it gives them a way, in the last resort, of dispensing with the services of employees who cannot do any job which the particular employer needs done. And because lay-offs generally entail the right of recall if suitable work becomes available, they can also be useful to unionized employees in such cases.

In contrast to collective agreements, the common law, which governs unorganized employment relationships, traditionally has not recognized the concept of lay-off. Perhaps that is because unorganized employers have always had the right to terminate unwanted employees by giving them notice or pay in lieu of notice. Thus, if a once-competent employee in an unorganized workplace simply cannot adapt to changing circumstances or otherwise suffers a decline in his or her performance level, the employer can buy its way out of the employment relationship in a way which an employer covered by a collective agreement cannot.[38]

In line with what we have just said, Canadian courts have tended to treat dismissal for cause as being reserved for situations of culpable incompetence, and have required employers to give notice in order to terminate for innocent incompetence. In deciding whether culpable incompetence has been proven, the courts tend to be quite protective of employees in cases where the employee has not measured up to the employer's expectations. For example, one court recently observed:

> In every hiring "the employee is taken to some extent for better or for worse." . . . He cannot be dismissed summarily because he does not live up to expectations. The threshold test is incompetence. It must be proved to be serious or gross incompetence because in law the conduct of the employee must amount to a repudiation by him of his contract of employment. The law also appears to require that the employee be warned that his job is in jeopardy and be given a reasonable chance to improve.[39]

At common law, if the employer raises performance standards so sharply as to change the essential character of the job, the employee can treat the employer's action as a "constructive dismissal" and can claim pay in lieu of notice—but at the cost of having to give up the job. Less drastic increases in performance expectations are generally permissible, for both unorganized and organized employees, unless there is a contractual or collective agreement provision to the contrary.[40] However, the employer cannot impose discipline for failure to meet the new standards unless employees have been clearly notified of them and given an ample opportunity to adapt to them.

More facts are needed to establish whether HH's failure to meet the new standards is innocent or culpable. Unless the employer can prove that HH is not making a reasonable effort to meet those standards, a court or arbitrator will treat his failure as innocent. But whether his shortcomings are innocent or culpable, a court or arbitrator will probably find him entitled to much more than two or three months to try to overcome them, because he has at least ten years' service and received favorable evaluations for such a long time before the employer raised the standards.

Seriousness. The extent of the shortfall in HH's productivity will no doubt be relevant to what the employer can do about it, because termination for either innocent or culpable poor performance requires proof that the employment relationship is no longer viable. Thus, a 40 percent deficiency will more easily support disciplinary action or a nondisciplinary transfer, demotion, or lay-off than a 5 or 10 percent shortfall. For the same reason, evidence that HH's slow work is causing financial or safety problems will also be relevant, especially if he is made well aware of that fact. If his performance has begun to improve but is not yet adequate, dismissal or a nondisciplinary move may be held unwarranted, especially in light of the fact that he has had only a fairly short period of unsatisfactory performance after a long period with good evaluations.

Mitigation. As already noted, HH's long service and above-average performance under the old standards will militate quite strongly against a finding of cause for dismissal.[41]

Enforceability. If all or most—or even a substantial minority—of the employees who met the old standards are falling about as far short of meeting the new ones as HH is, then, unless there is evidence that they are simply not making a reasonable effort, the new standards will probably be held to violate the implicit understanding between the parties as to the required level of performance and thus to be unenforceable. Similarly, if other employees who have managed to meet the new standards have suffered illness or excessive fatigue as a result, a court or arbitrator will refuse to hold HH to those standards.

The question is harder if HH, while trying to measure up to the new standards, is alone or almost alone among his co-workers in being unable to do so. Under those circumstances the fact that he did his job well enough under the old system may force the employer to keep him on, especially if he is a long-service employee.

Condonation by the employer of failure to meet the new standards, on the part of HH or other employees, will preclude disciplinary action, at least until the employees have been clearly told that such failure would no longer be tolerated and have been given a reasonable chance to improve their performance.

LOYALTY

Case Scenario

During an appearance on a television consumer informa-tion program JS, a teller for H Bank, states that her employer regularly fails to advise customers when they make mistakes in favor of the bank, but promptly corrects mistakes made in favor of customers.

Analysis

"Whistleblowing" is the name given to employee disclosure to the outside world of alleged employer wrongdoing. It often furthers important social interests, and it represents an exercise of freedom of expression. But it sits very uneasily with the employee's "duty of good faith and fidelity" to the employer, recognized both at common law and under collective bargaining.

A recent writer on whistleblowing says:

> The common law in Canada does not impose a com-plete blanket on public disclosure or criticism by employees to the detriment of employers. . . . [How-ever] this author cannot find a Canadian employ-ment case in which an employee who has blown the whistle escaped discipline of some form unless the employee's act was protected by statute (McKenna, pp. 156, 180n).[42]

Such statutory protections, found mainly in human rights and labor relations legislation, only prohibit reprisals for bringing legal proceedings for alleged violations of those statutes themselves or for testifying in such proceedings.[43] No common law or statutory principle gives broad, general protection to employees against dis-cipline for public criticism of the employer.

Neither courts nor arbitrators,[44] it appears, will be likely to protect an employee against dismissal for public statements crit-icizing the employer unless two conditions are satisfied. First, there must be "an overriding public interest in the disclosure." There probably was such a public interest in JS's disclosure, as the bank's alleged actions would be fraudulent and criminal. Sec-ond, the employee must first have exhausted any internal chan-nels of complaint available within the employer's organization (McKenna, p. 163). We do not know if JS did that.

Seriousness. The extent to which JS "went public" with her allegations will be important. Airing them on a television program will no doubt be considered as going very public, whatever the time of day. Concrete evidence of resulting financial loss to the employer may add to the seriousness of the conduct, but courts and arbitrators will probably be willing to presume such loss if it is not actually proven.[45]

If JS had no reason to believe what she said, that will add markedly to its seriousness. However, if she did have reason to think it was true, that will not detract greatly from its seriousness, unless perhaps she had made concerted and unsuccessful attempts to have the matter corrected through channels within the bank.

In Canada some types of enterprises, such as newspapers and educational and health service institutions, are expected to tolerate even very strong employee criticism, private and public, of their policies and practices. It is less clear that such organizations must put up with employee criticism which squarely impugns their financial integrity. Because banks are particularly vulnerable to that sort of criticism, JS's conduct will undoubtedly be looked upon more seriously as a result.

The higher the job level of the employee who makes the allegations, the greater the likely damage to the bank. However, if conduct like JS's is not excusable on any other grounds, the mere fact that she is in a low-level position will probably not be held to excuse it.

Mitigation. Once again, the employer will find it harder to show cause for dismissal on these facts if JS has a long record of good service. Her loyalty in the past will be weighed against this instance of disloyalty.

Being a union representative, or at least a union activist, may sometimes give an employee more latitude to criticize the employer. Explicit provisions in Canadian labor relations statutes protect employees against discrimination for union activity, whether their workplace is organized or unorganized and whether or not they are union officers or employee representatives. In accordance with the prevailing view of the union–employer relationship as an adversarial one in which open criticism is to be expected, those statutory provisions allow any employee to claim redress (including reinstatement) from a labor relations board against disciplinary action for comments made about the employer in the context of an organizing campaign or in furtherance of collective bargaining goals. That statutory protection probably extends not only to comments on matters directly related to terms of employment, but also to criticism of the employer on a wider range of issues, such as the social desirability of investment practices. However, it is less likely to shelter blunt allegations of fraudulent behavior of the sort that JJ has made.

The same principles are likely to apply if a union activist or union representative's complaint of unjust dismissal is taken to arbitration under a collective agreement rather than to a labor relations board. In deciding what is just cause for dismissal in such cases, some arbitrators have held that "because the union and the employer are combatants, . . . critical public comment is part of the adversarial relationship" (McKenna, p. 160).

Enforceability. The absence of an employer rule against public criticism by employees is not likely to have much weight, as courts and arbitrators will presume that employees know it is unacceptable to accuse their employer of fraud and theft. However, as always, employer condonation of such conduct by employees in the past will virtually compel a finding that dismissal is unjustified.

RESTRICT COLLECTIVE ACTION

Case Scenario

JJ, a machinist at I Manufacturing Company, becomes angry because he believes his supervisor is treating him and other employees without respect. In protest, he persuades the other employees in his work group to leave work together in the middle of their scheduled work shift and not return until the next day.

Analysis

Canadian labor relations legislation absolutely prohibits collective employee (or employer) action except at certain very specific times in the collective bargaining cycle and after certain very specific procedural prerequisites have been met. Those prerequisites are as follows: The union must gather written proof that a majority of the employees in the particular workplace want that union to bargain collectively for them; the union must be certified by the labor relations board as bargaining agent for those employees; the union and employer must attempt to negotiate a collective agreement and must participate in compulsory conciliation or mediation; a further "cooling off" period must expire; and in some provinces a further ballot must be held among the employees involved, and a majority of them must vote in favor of a strike.

If all of those steps have been taken, unionized employees may legally strike during the negotiation or renegotiation of a collective agreement. However—and for the purposes of our study, this is the most important restriction—strikes are almost totally prohibited whenever a collective agreement is in force.

Thus, with certain narrow exceptions not relevant here, organized employees may not strike legally while a collective agreement is in force, and unorganized employees covered by the labor relations statutes may never strike legally at all.[46] These legislative prohibitions against striking are treated as a matter of public order which cannot be waived by collective agreement or contract.

Conduct that violates the statutory restrictions on collective action is considered a very serious offence for both organized and unorganized employees. Among unorganized employees illegal strike action is uncommon enough that most treatises on wrongful dismissal law do not even discuss it as cause for dismissal. One treatise on individual employment law which does mention it says only the following:

> [A] strike by non-unionized employees will always be illegal and will, presumably, constitute a breach of their work obligations sufficiently serious to entitle the employer to dismiss them summarily, provided the [employer's] motivation for doing so is their intentional absence from work and not any apprehended union affiliation. (Christie, p. 273)

Participation by employees in a collective work stoppage or slowdown is treated by arbitrators and courts as roughly equivalent to an act of open insubordination. It may well be held to be cause for dismissal unless the particular employee had only a minor part in it or can point to a mitigating factor such as a long record of good service. An employee who actually leads a strike, rather than merely following the leadership of others, will almost certainly be subject to dismissal unless he or she has an unusually strong record of service or unless the employer has been guilty of severe provocation in the form of seriously illegal or highly abusive conduct.

AVOID CONFLICT OF INTEREST

Case Scenario

IB, a systems analyst for J Company, has access to private computer systems of his employer. He accepts a string of free-lance, relatively routine programming jobs for K Company, a competitor of his employer, and does the work at his home.

Analysis

There is a large body of case law on conflict of interest in the unorganized sector, but not as much in the organized sector. A writer on wrongful dismissal law puts the thrust of the case law in these terms: "Conflict of interest, along with theft and dishonesty, are the three situations which, if established, invariably will be held to constitute cause for discharge" (Levitt, p. 73).

Most conflict of interest cases do not arise over simple "moonlighting" in the form of fee-for-service work for a competitor of the employer, but involve a deeper relationship between the employee and the competitor—for example, as a shareholder or partner (Harris, pp. 3:144–54). If only fee-for-service work is involved, the nature of the work is important. Thus, if IB's moonlighting for K Company consists of routine tasks that can be done by many programmers, and if IB had no reason to think that his work would give K Company a competitive advantage over J Company, a court or arbitrator might not find cause for dismissal.

Seriousness. The existence or nonexistence of a relevant employer rule is more important in this scenario than in most of the others. J Company can undoubtedly make a valid rule prohibiting its systems analysts from moonlighting for any other enterprises that do similar work, and can probably dismiss IB if he knowingly violates that rule. In the absence of any such rule a court or arbitrator has to look more closely at the exact circumstances. The most important factual question is not whether IB did the same sort of work for K Company as for J Company but whether, in his work for K Company, he used any information or techniques not widely known outside J Company or otherwise helped to enhance K Company's competitive position vis-à-vis J Company.

There is a division of opinion among Canadian courts on whether an *actual* conflict of interest, or only a *potential* conflict, must be proven in order to justify dismissal. One well-known statement of the rule is the following: "In conflict of interest situations, the rule of Caesar's wife applies. It must not only be pure, it must be seen to be pure."[47]

So strict an approach is more likely to be taken where the employee has attained a high position with the employer. In that case the courts may treat the employee as a fiduciary, with the result that "he then owes a clear duty to his company to use all his energy, ability and imagination in the best interest of the company."[48] If IB is a lower-level employee who does not occupy a position of particular trust with J Company, a court may look for proof of actual and not merely potential conflict of interest before upholding a dismissal.

In the organized sector fewer employees are in fiduciary positions than in the unorganized sector, although that may be changing as the focus of union organizing shifts from blue-collar to white-collar employment. Arbitrators' decisions in conflict of interest cases are based on more or less the same factors as court decisions.

Mitigation. A long record of good service will again be a mitigating factor unless the employee, as well as being very senior, has acquired a position of trust giving him or her access to trade secrets or other confidential information. In that case the higher standards of propriety which the law imposes on fiduciaries may outweigh the latitude usually enjoyed by long-service employees.

Enforceability. As discussed above, the existence of an employer rule against working for other companies will be important, at least in cases where it might not otherwise be obvious to the employee that such conduct is unacceptable. As always, the employer will be in difficulty if it has previously tolerated conduct similar to that for which IB has now been taken severely to task.

CONCLUSIONS

We began by calling attention to the gap between the employment rights given by Canadian law to employees who are covered by collective bargaining and to those who are not. The various scenarios considered in this paper show that the gap has been narrowing with respect to the substantive principles used by adjudicators to decide whether employers have established cause for dismissal. Even in that respect, however, the fact that unorganized employees are still covered by a separate and usually less generous set of principles than their organized counterparts shows that the gap remains wide by international standards. It appears wider yet when it is remembered that organized employees have access to the remedy of reinstatement and to a specialized arbitration process, while unorganized employees in most parts of Canada have to make do with monetary remedies alone and have to pursue dismissal claims in the ordinary courts. Extending to unorganized employees the same standard of industrial justice accorded to those covered by collective bargaining is one of the challenges now facing Canadian legislators.

NOTES

1. We are very grateful to Hilary Warder for her research assistance and to Geoffrey England for comments on an earlier draft of this paper.

2. In a common law wrongful dismissal action, the plaintiff employee has full carriage of the proceedings. No one has the legal right to force him or her to settle or abandon the action prior to final adjudication by the court. In contrast, most collective agreements provide that only the union, and not the complainant employee, can decide whether a grievance (even one as important to the employee as an unjust dismissal claim) will be taken to arbitration or will be settled or abandoned at an earlier stage. To some employees this may make the prospect of a wrongful dismissal action more appealing than the prospect of an unjust dismissal claim under a collective agreement. However, two factors point in the other direction. (1) To pursue a wrongful dismissal claim in the courts, the employee must hire and pay for his or her own lawyer, whereas unions provide counsel in arbitrations under collective agreements. (2) In deciding how far or how vigorously to pursue a particular grievance, a union is under a statutory "duty of fair representation," which (in its most common formulation) requires that the union not make that decision in a way that is "arbitrary, discriminatory, or in bad faith." Although this duty has been interpreted quite nar-

rowly by labor relations boards, it has had an impact on union grievance processing, particularly with respect to unjust dismissal claims. Some major unions have gone so far as to develop a policy of taking any such claim to arbitration if the dismissed employee insists.

3. In theory, reasonable notice means the length of time it should take the employer or employee to make a comparable employment contract with someone else. *Bardal v. Globe and Mail* (1960) 24 DLR (2d) 140 (Ont. High Ct.).

4. Wrongful dismissal suits have become increasingly common in recent years, and have led to a substantial increase in the amount of notice, or pay in lieu of notice, which an employer must give when terminating without cause. A 1988 survey found that notice periods ordered by Canadian courts in recent years ranged from an average of 4.3 months for relatively junior clerical and technical employees to an average of 20.9 months for long-service senior executives. Barry Fisher and Lori Ashley Goodfield, "A Computerized Analysis of Notice Periods in Wrongful Dismissal Actions," in *Leading Edge Issues in Employment Law and Wrongful Dismissal* (Toronto: Canadian Bar Association, 1988). See also S. L. McShane and D. C. McPhillips, "Predicting Reasonable Notice in Canadian Wrongful Dismissal Cases," *Industrial and Labor Relations Review* 41 (Oct. 1987): 108–17.

5. A few courts have tried to develop a concept of "near cause," or "the third alternative," under which an employee guilty of misconduct insufficient to ground dismissal would have to accept lower damages than a wholly innocent employee. *Wilcox and Marshall v. GWG* [1984] 4 WWR 70 (Alta. QB). Most courts have rejected this innovation. *Jim Pattison Industries Ltd. v. Page* (1984) 10 DLR (4th) 430 (Sask. CA).

6. Geoffrey England, "Unjust Dismissal in the Federal Jurisdiction: The First Three Years," (1982) 12 Manitoba L.J. 9, at pp. 25–29.

7. In the federal jurisdiction from April 1989 to March 1990, dismissals were held to be unjust in 30 cases, but reinstatement was granted in only 11 of those cases. (1990) 14 Arbitration Services Reporter (no. 5), Table 2.

8. In most Canadian jurisdictions it is not clear whether an employer can discipline or discharge without just cause if the agreement says nothing on the point. Early arbitral jurisprudence refused to read in a requirement of just cause if the collective agreement was silent on the matter, but more recently some

arbitrators have been willing to do so in certain circumstances. See, e.g., *K-Line Maintenance & Construction Ltd.* (1989) 35 LAC (3d) 358 (Cromwell). In the few cases where no management rights clause is included in the agreement, arbitrators nonetheless generally consider management to have a right to discipline, on the basis of the prevailing labor relations milieu or the conduct of the parties.

9. *McGavin Toastmaster Ltd. v. Ainscough* (1975) 54 DLR (3d) 1, at pp. 6–7 (SCC).

10. For the results of empirical research on the effectiveness of the reinstatement remedy with respect to unionized employees, see Adams; Ponak; and, for the most detailed analysis, Barnacle. Of the 240 employees in Barnacle's sample who were reinstated by arbitrators in Ontario between 1983 and 1986, 210 actually went back to the job, and 118 were still with the same employer at the time of the survey in late 1988 and early 1989 (Barnacle, pp. 149–50). Arbitrators occasionally refuse to order reinstatement if they are of the view that the particular employment relationship is no longer viable (Young, ch. 22).

11. *McLeod v. Egan* [1975] 1 SCR 150 (SCC).

12. The judicial and arbitral authorities are discussed in *Rothmans, Benson & Hedges Inc.* (1990) 10 LAC (4th) 18 (R. M. Brown).

13. See, e.g., Ontario Human Rights Code, 1981, S.O. 1981, c. 53, ss. 4(1), 10, 16(1) and 16(1a), as amended by S.O. 1986, c. 16, ss. 18(5), 18(8), 18(9), and 18(10).

14. On the meaning of "undue hardship" under the Ontario Human Rights Code, see Ontario Human Rights Commission, "Guidelines for Assessing Accommodation Requirements for Persons with Disabilities," 1989, pp. 7ff.

15. It would be more precise to say that "the employer may have grounds for *summary* dismissal." However, in order to avoid tedious repetition in the cases below, where we use the words "dismissal" or "discharge" without a qualifier we are using the terms to refer to summary dismissal—that is, dismissal without notice. As noted above, Canadian common law, which is effective for working people outside of the collective bargaining system, permits either party to end the employment relationship at any time with appropriate notice.

16. *Laird v. Saskatchewan Roughrider Football Club* (1982) 18 Sask. R. 33 (Sask. Q.B.); *Camco, Inc.* (1988) 34 LAC (3d) 12 (Barton); *Raven Lumber Ltd.* (1986) 23 LAC (3d) 357 (Munroe).

17. *Parks v. H.H. Marshall Ltd.* (1984) 62 NSR (2d) 172 (NSSC).

18. The relevant statutory provisions in each Canadian jurisdiction are summarized in Peter Barnacle, *Labour Legislation and Public Policy: Reference Tables,* Queen's Industrial Relations Centre, Kingston, pp. 213–15.

19. *Laird v. Saskatchewan Roughrider Football Club* (1982) 18 Sask. R. 33 (Sask. Q.B.); *Welmet Industries* (1980) 28 LAC (2d) 84 (Rayner); *Oxford Warehousing* (1980) 25 LAC (2d) 111 (Burkett).

20. In what are often called "sunset clauses," many collective agreements provide that recorded instances of misconduct are struck from an employee's record after a certain period—for example, two or three years, or sometimes as little as one year. Such clauses greatly enhance the mitigating effect of long service.

21. *Johnston v. Algoma Steel Corp.* (1989) 24 CCEL 1 (Ont. HC—Granger J.); *Brewers' Warehousing* (1984) 16 LAC (3d) 84 (MacDowell); *Resthaven Memorial Gardens* (1981) 2 LAC (3d) 146 (Brown).

22. With respect to drug addiction as a handicap, see *Stelco Inc.* (1990) 9 LAC (4th) 129 (Brent).

23. *Canada Post Corporation (Marini grievance)* (1987) 26 LAC (3d) 403, at p. 429 (Swan).

24. Ibid.

25. *Billingsley v. Saint John Shipbuilding Ltd.* (1988) 23 CCEL 300 (NBQB); *Toronto Abbattoirs,* LAN Apr. 1987 (M. G. Picher).

26. *Cox v. Canadian National Railway Company* (1988) 84 NSR (2d) 271 (NSSC); *Cominco* (1987) 30 LAC (3d) 46 (Hope).

27. *Hardie v. Trans-Canada Resources Ltd.* (1976) 71 DLR (3d) 668 (Alta. C.A.); *Brewers' Warehousing Co.* (1958) 8 LAC 302 (Curtis).

28. If the employee has been convicted of the theft in question by a criminal court and is dismissed by the employer, the conviction may be used by the employer in a subsequent wrongful dismissal or arbitration proceeding as prima facie evidence that the employee committed the theft. *Re Del Core and Ontario College of Pharmacists* (1985) 51 OR (2d) 1 (Ont. C.A.); *Re Greater Niagara Transit Commission and Amalgamated Transit Union* (1988) 61 OR (2nd) 565 (Ont. Div. Ct.). However, an acquittal on the criminal charge will not provide any evidence of innocence in a subsequent wrongful dismissal or arbitration pro-

ceeding, largely because the standard of proof is higher in the criminal courts. *Re Gillen and College of Physicians and Surgeons of Ontario* (1989) 68 OR (2d) 278 (Ont. Div. Ct.).

29. *Neigum v. Wilkie Co-Operative Association Ltd.* (1987) 55 Sask. Rep. 210 (Sask. QB); *Phillips Cables Ltd.* (1974) 6 LAC (2d) 35 (Adams).

30. *Beyea v. Irving Oil Ltd.* (1985) 8 CCEL 128 (NBQB); *Langley Memorial Hospital* (1985) 18 LAC (3d) 123 (Thompson).

31. *Air Canada* (1981) 2 LAC (3d) 442 (Shime).

32. *Gurvit v. Richmond Plywood Corporations Ltd.* (1979) 10 BCLR 141 (BCSC); *Seaspan International* (1985) 18 LAC (3d) 220 (Germaine).

33. See *Rhodes v. Zehrmart* (1986) 15 CCEL 236 (Ont. Div. Ct.); cp. *Pliniussen v. University of Western Ontario* (1983) 2 CCEL 1 (Ont. Cty. Ct.); *Cape Breton County Correctional Centre* (1978) 19 LAC (2d) 325 (Ferguson); *Bell Canada* (1979) 21 LAC (2d) 154 (Beck).

34. *City of Calgary* (1981) 4 LAC (3d) 50 (Beattie).

35. *Beal v. Grant* (1984) 52 NBR (2d) 163 (NBCA).

36. *Yeager v. R. J. Hastings Agencies Ltd.* (1984) 5 CCEL 266 (BCSC).

37. That is, a reason not related to union activity or to a statutorily prohibited ground of discrimination.

38. If a particular event happens which renders a formerly competent employee wholly unable to do the job, the employer may not have to give notice or pay in lieu of notice in order to terminate the employment relationship but may be able to rely on the doctrine of frustration of contract, which is mentioned above in the context of innocent absenteeism.

39. *Stewart v. Intercity Packers Ltd.* (1989) 24 CCEL 135, at p. 138 (BDSC, per Catliff LJSC).

40. *Larose v. T. Eaton Co.* (1980) 3 CCEL 51 (Ont. Co. Ct.). For organized employees, see *Province of Newfoundland* (1982) 3 LAC (3d) 329 (Woolridge) with respect to culpable behavior, and *Western Marine Ltd.* (1983) 12 LAC (3d) 260 (Albertini) with respect to nonculpable incompetence.

41. *McHugh v. City Motors (Nfld.) Ltd.* (1988) 22 CCEL 187 (Nfld. S.C., T.D.).

42. See also *Ministry of Attorney-General, Corrections Branch* (1982) 3 LAC (3d) 141, at p. 155 (J. M. Weiler).

43. It is interesting to note that the Ontario Environmental

Protection Act has a similar provision, which prohibits dismissal or other discrimination against an employee for complying with any one of a number of environmental protection statutes or for trying to enforce one of those statutes. RSO 1980, c. 141, s. 134b, enacted by SO 1983, c. 52, s. 22. This provision, which is enforced by the Ontario Labour Relations Board, appears to have been used only once since it was enacted.

44. *Simon Fraser University* (1985) 18 LAC (3d) 361 (Bird); *Treasury Board* (1982) 5 LAC (3d) 193 (Kates); *Province of British Columbia* (1981) 3 LAC (3d) 140 (Weiler).

45. *MacDonald v. Canada Games Park Commission* (1986) 58 Nfld and PEI Rep. 29 (Nfld. Dist. Ct.) and arbitration cases at n. 29.

46. Canadian labor relations statutes exclude certain employees. Agricultural workers and managers, for example, are common exclusions. For such employees the right to strike is not regulated by statute, nor is it clearly established (or extinguished) at common law.

47. *Bursey v. Acadia Motors Ltd.* (1979) 28 NBR (2d) 361, at p. 369 (NBQB), varied on other grounds (1981) 35 NBR (2d) 587 (NBCA); cp. *Wilcox v. GWG Ltd.* (1984) 4 CCEL 125 (Alta. Q.B.).

48. *Helbig v. Oxford Warehousing Ltd.* (1985) 51 OR (2d) 421, at p. 430 (Ont. HC).

REFERENCES

Adams, George W. *Grievance Arbitration of Discharge Cases: A Study of the Concepts of Industrial Discipline and Their Results.* Kingston: Queen's Industrial Relations Centre, 1978.

Adell, Bernard. "The Rights of Disabled Workers at Arbitration and Under Human Rights Legislation," *Canadian Labour Law Journal* 1 (1991).

Barnacle, Peter J. *Arbitration of Discharge Grievances in Ontario: Outcome and Reinstatement Experience.* Kingston: Queen's Industrial Relations Centre, 1991.

Brown, Donald J. M., and David M. Beatty. *Canadian Labour Arbitration.* 3rd ed. Aurora: Canada Law Book, 1988 (updated to 1990).

Christie, Innis. *Employment Law in Canada.* Toronto: Butterworths, 1980.

Craig, Alton W. J. *The System of Industrial Relations in Canada.* 3rd ed. Scarborough: Prentice-Hall Canada, 1990.

Eden, Genevieve. *Unjust Dismissal in the Canadian Federal Jurisdiction.* Ph.D. Diss., University of Toronto, 1990.

Failes, Michael D. *Statutory Protection from Unjust Dismissal for Unorganized Workers in Canada.* LL.M. Thesis, Queen's University, 1986.

Grosman, M. Norman. *Federal Employment Law in Canada.* Toronto: Carswell, 1990.

Harris, David. *Wrongful Dismissal.* rev. ed. Toronto: DeBoo, 1990.

Krashinsky, Stephen, and Jeffrey Sack. *Discharge and Discipline.* Toronto: Lancaster House, 1989.

Labour Law Casebook Group. *Labour Law: Cases, Materials and Commentary.* 5th ed. Kingston: Queen's Industrial Relations Centre, 1991.

Levitt, Howard A. *The Law of Dismissal in Canada.* Aurora: Canada Law Book, 1985.

McKenna, Ian. "Whistleblowing and Criticism of Employers by Employees: The Case for Reform in Canada." I. McKenna, ed. *Labour Relations into the 1990's.* Don Mills: CCH Canadian, 1989.

McPhillips, David, and Geoffrey England. "Employment Legislation in Canada." J. Anderson, M. Gunderson, and A. Ponak, eds., *Union-Management Relations in Canada.* 2nd ed. Don Mills: Addison-Wesley, 1989.

McPhillips, David, and Larry Shetzer. "Culpable and Non-Culpable Incompetence: A Canadian Arbitral Perspective." Paper presented at the annual meeting of the Canadian Industrial Relations Association, Victoria, 1990.

Palmer, Earl E. *Collective Agreement Arbitration in Canada.* 2nd ed. Toronto: Butterworths, 1983.

Ponak, Allen. "Discharge Arbitration and Reinstatement in Alberta." (1987) 42 Arb. J. 39.

Young, Bruce. *Beyond Discharge.* Toronto: Canada Labour Views, 1984.

4

FRANCE[1]

Jacques Rojot

A good understanding of the functioning of industrial justice in France must be grounded in the general French law of employment. Industrial justice applies to the relationship between employer and employee, as it is within this relationship that the obligations and rights of employment exist. The system and its substantive rules are rather complex. They will be set out at some length in this chapter, and then applied to the particular obligations focused upon in our study.

OVERVIEW OF THE SYSTEM

In France the legal categories of employer and employee, as well as the nature of the relationship between them, are defined by a contract of employment that determines the parties' reciprocal rights and duties. It must be noted that this contract of employment need not be in the form of a written document specifying terms and conditions. It is assumed to come into existence as soon as an employment relationship materializes and is deemed to have an implicit legal content made up of statutory labor law, administrative regulations, shop rules, custom, and all applicable collective agreements (for their duration). Of course, the parties may explicitly add to that implicit content, so long as this either improves the lot of the employee or is allowed explicitly by statute.

136

As statutory law does not give a definition of the contract of employment, it has fallen to the courts to provide one. As it stands now, this rests upon three criteria: (1) the performance of a task or activity (2) done for payment and (3) in a condition of subordination. These three conditions define an employee as distinguished from a self-employed person, who would fulfill only the first two. The condition of subordination is therefore the fundamental element characterizing a contract of employment. This has both a practical and a theoretical consequence. On the theoretical level the subordinate position defines the role of the employee vis-à-vis the employer. Practically, the condition of employee presents many advantages compared to that of the self-employed. These include social security coverage, permanent employment, etc. However, the chronic financial deficit of the social security system has driven the national administration to try to collect the funds financing the system from as many individuals as possible. These payments are wage-based and are more extensive on wages paid to employees than on payments made to the self-employed. Therefore, the statutory definitions of subordination, although overlapping somewhat, have tended to be somewhat broader in social security law than in labor law.[2]

Two alternative justifications of the superordinate powers of employers have been suggested. These have very different consequences. One approach, institutional theory, bases the powers of the employer upon the role and responsibilities of a leader of a community, in this case an enterprise. Under this theory every institution needs to be managed and directed. Therefore, a leader, the employer, is granted the powers necessary to that end. The limits of these powers arise from their very reason for existing. Their nature is functional. They are granted for the survival of the enterprise. Therefore, they can be exerted only toward that end. The exercise of these powers by the employer toward a different goal is thus ill founded and must be curtailed by the courts.[3] This theory has recently enjoyed something of a renewal because of the attention being paid to employee involvement programs, cultural engineering, quality circles, financial participation, and other managerial practices that put emphasis on the community of interest between employer and employee. These programs attempt to actively involve employees in acting globally in the "interest of the enterprise" (as defined by management).

The other fundamental theory underlying employer superordinate powers is more traditional. It remains the most influential and is still the basis of most court decisions. Besides, it is the only true legal foundation, that is, the only one based in the legal texts.[4] It rests upon liberal classical economics and political liberalism of the nineteenth century and combines property law with the law of contracts.

On the one hand, the right of property gives the employer ownership of the land, plant, equipment, etc., used in productive activities. This right is absolute.[5] Section 544 of the Civil Code specifically mandates that real estate as well as chattels belong to the employer, who may "enjoy their use in the most absolute way." Of course, this gives the employer no direct rights over the persons of individuals who, besides, are forbidden from entering into contracts of employment for a life term for fear of the reintroduction of serfdom or slavery. This has the side effect of allowing termination by either party of such a contract when it is for an indeterminate duration. On the other hand, however, in order to put his property into operation for productive purposes, the employer hires employees through contracts of employment, and Section 1134 of the labor code says, in effect, that the contract is the law of the parties. Originally, in the absence of statutory labor provisions, the contract clearly reflected the social and economic inequality of the parties. Now, hiring, wages, and dismissal are well regulated. However, once the relevant legal requirements are met, the contract principle remains. From this grounding, two distinct types of power come to the employer—the power to manage the enterprise and the power to discipline employees.

EMPLOYER POWER TO MANAGE THE ENTERPRISE

The power to manage the enterprise is roughly equivalent to U.S. managerial rights. In the nineteenth century employer/owners of plants and equipment could use them fully as they saw fit. The growth of labor law has since created multiple legal limits, often improved upon by collective agreements. These limits cover minimum wages, duration of work, overtime, vacations and holidays, Sunday work restrictions, the employment of children, women and migrant workers, and the requirement that work be assigned that is relevant to the skill level of the employee. However, the prevailing principle remains that since the employer receives the profit from the operations of the business that he or she owns, and also solely runs the risks of the business cycle, the employer should be able freely to fix enterprise objectives and policies and strategies, as well as the tactics and the means to reach and perform them. The slow movement away from employer/owners toward professional managers at the head of enterprises has not affected this principle.

The limits on employer financial and economic decisions as well as on the organization of the enterprise and of work are few, even taking into account those contained in collective agreements. Certainly works councils exist and are given extensive powers with regard to information, consultation, and even concertation (a relatively strong, in-depth, form of consultation), but they stop short of codetermination. The employer is almost never legally obliged to follow the advice of a works council. The only major exception to that rule was dismissal for economic reasons between 1974 and 1986. Even during that period, when the employer was required to obtain administrative authorization from the Ministry of Labor prior to dismissals for economic reasons, the highest administrative court held that the role of the labor inspectors was limited to verifying the facts alleged by the employer to constitute grounds for the dismissals. Because of the doctrine of the employer being the sole judge of what is good for the business, the inspectors had no right to interfere with or weigh managerial options in the face of, for example, declining orders.

Except for a few very minor points (choice of vacation period or appointment of the enterprise physician, for instance) the works council has only advisory power. This situation changes only in case of bankruptcy, when employer powers of all kinds are severely curtailed. This is, of course, merely the legal principle, not necessarily the practice. In the day-to-day life of an enterprise an employer may find it expedient to entertain a good relationship with the works council and, therefore, to bow to its opinions from time to time. However, there is no legal compulsion for the employer to do so, and the situation varies with the de facto power relationship between employer and council.

The supreme civil court has consistently held that the employees, and for that matter the judiciary, have no right to interfere with managerial decisions, which are within the sole competence of the employer. The employer is deemed the sole judge of what is good for the enterprise and where the business is headed. This is the case however catastrophic or ill advised the decisions. This applies even to a decision to close a viable, or even thriving, business. Therefore, logically, decisions of a less momentous nature are subject to extensive managerial prerogatives. By "employer" is meant the employer himself or herself in the case of an employer/owner business or, in the more common case of a corporate employer, the owners' direct representative—the chief executive officer.

There are, however, two minor kinds of limits to these prerogatives. First, there are the obvious ones of business law and criminal law. Second, courts have decided that even though the employer is sole judge in matters of management, these powers must be carried out "in the interest of the enterprise." This is understood in a more limited sense than that used in institutional theory, meaning only that the action must be within the scope of the management of the enterprise and only within that scope. The employer has the right to make perfectly wrong, unjustified, or erroneous decisions, even flying in the face of simple economic facts, but the decisions must be taken with the goal of running the business. The employer cannot, under the guise of business reasons, hide decisions motivated by other causes. Such would be the case, for instance, if a dismissal for economic reasons were engineered in order to get rid of militant union activists, and only of them, or if a plant closure were done in retaliation against a successful strike. If proof of such a misuse of managerial power can be proved to a judge, sanctions will be applied. Such proof has traditionally been difficult. However, an act of August 2, 1989, although not formally reversing the burden of proof (what in the United States would be called the burden of coming forward with the evidence), which remains upon the employee, provides that in case of doubt such doubt is resolved in favor of a dismissed employee.

EMPLOYER POWER TO DISCIPLINE EMPLOYEES

The second set of powers of the employer consists of disciplinary powers. They flow from the same source as the general powers to manage the enterprise. Traditionally they have notably included the rights to hire, terminate, decide on working time, set conditions of work, allocate tasks, and sanction inappropriate behavior.

Just as has been the case with the general power to freely

manage the enterprise, employer disciplinary powers have come to be bounded by multiple regulations—on working time, wages, and dismissal (only for real and serious cause). Nevertheless, the principle of the disciplinary powers of the employer remains, including sanctioning inappropriate employee behavior. However, this power has been the subject of somewhat more severe limits than has been the case with the general power to manage the enterprise. An act of August 4, 1982, curtailed this power in two different ways—the reasons for which an employee can be disciplined and the procedures to be followed.

Flowing from the same sources as the managerial powers, prior to 1982 the disciplinary powers of the employer had few limits insofar as they related to sanctioning employee behavior believed to be inappropriate. Traditionally, the principal tool for carrying out the employer's disciplinary powers, although by no means the only one, was the shop rules. These rules (*reglement interieur*) were unilaterally announced by the employer. Upon hiring, these rules were deemed to become implicitly a part of the contract of employment. Therefore, the employee was considered as having accepted them and submitted to the applicable sanctions contained in these rules. Employers had come to include various types of regulations in the shop rules, including not only items relating to conditions of work, but also all kinds of duties pertaining to the personal conduct of employees. Included, for example, were rules forbidding two employees from marrying; providing that employees agree in advance to submit to unconditional body searches upon leaving work; and imposing the obligation to maintain the plant and equipment in working condition in the event of a strike. Sanctions for the nonobservance of these rules were also unilaterally established by the employer. Except for rare instances of misuse of disciplinary powers toward other ends, as discussed above, the courts generally held that sanctions (often including dismissal), when provided for in shop rules, were enforceable by employers.

In addition, the employer in the exercise of its disciplinary power was not limited to application of the shop rules. The employer was bound to apply the rules only in the sense that it could not impose a punishment more severe than that provided for in the rules. The employer could, however, always impose a lesser sanction. Also, cases of misconduct not covered in the shop rules can still, post-1982, be sanctioned by employers under their general disciplinary powers. Furthermore, courts have con-

141

sistently held that the contract of employment inherently includes mutual obligations that can give rise to the exercise of disciplinary powers.

The situation has been greatly affected by the wave of reform in labor law that occurred between 1982 and 1985. An act of August 4, 1982, overhauled the law applicable to shop rules and the procedures for handling discipline. This statute set up a disciplinary procedure that employers are required to follow. The date of August 4 to publish this act was not selected by accident. It was a reminder, and an echo, of the night of August 4 during the French Revolution, when the nobility was stripped of the privileges that it enjoyed under the kings. It is highly indicative of the spirit of the government at the time that such a parallel was drawn to the limitations of the employers' privileges.

The first thing that the act of August 4 did was to restrict the domain of the shop rules and exclude negotiable subjects from them. The employer could no longer include anything that it wished. Shop rules were to exclusively concern matters relating to health and safety and discipline. All other topics previously included under the shop rules were excluded. Such was the case, for instance, with rules relative to hiring, pay, trial periods, and age of retirement. The reason for this limit was the decision of the government to promote collective bargaining as the predominant tool for regulating French industrial relations. To be properly understood, the act of August 4 should be considered in conjunction with the act of November 13, 1982, which introduced a duty for employers to negotiate with unions at both enterprise and sectoral levels.

If there was to be a duty to negotiate, it made sense to have the maximum number of topics to negotiate over. To that end, everything except health, safety, and discipline—subjects that were considered not to lend themselves to negotiation—were removed from the employer's unilateral control (via the shop rules). Hours of work, scheduling vacations, etc., are now subject to negotiation and cannot be included in the shop rules.

The second thing that the act of August 4 did was to restrict the extent of employers' disciplinary powers. Now the shop rules cannot contain provisions limiting civil rights or individual freedoms, unless justified by the nature of the task or its goals. For instance, a general interdiction from leaving one's job site during working hours without authorization, frequently found in shop rules, must now expressly exclude employee delegates and instances where the absence is protected by law—during strikes, for example. A provision for random drug testing at any time for all employees is now unlawful, although it is permissible to test where there is reason to believe that an employee is under the influence of drugs.

Third, shop rules cannot contain provisions that are contrary to rules that come from a higher level authority.[6] This includes not only statutes but also collective bargaining agreements. Therefore, provisions in collective bargaining agreements relative to discipline supersede shop rules.

Fourth, while the shop rules were in the past freely and informally drawn up by the employer alone, their creation and elaboration are now subject to a compulsory procedure. It should be noted that these procedures are mandatory only in enterprises employing more than twenty employees. This follows the tradition of establishing legal "floors," which is common in French law. In enterprises covered by this requirement a draft of the shop rules must be submitted for advice to the health and safety committee with regard to provisions within its competence. Then, as to all of the provisions, the rules must be submitted for information, followed by consultation, to the enterprise committee. This falls short of codetermination, as the only right of the committee is to give advice which the employer is not bound to follow.

The advice from the committees and a draft of shop rules, together with the minutes of the committee meetings, must be submitted to a labor inspector, who is a civil servant from the Ministry of Labor charged with the implementation of the labor law. If the labor inspector remains silent, the shop rules automatically become applicable one month after their submission to this official. During this one-month period, or at any time in the future, the labor inspector may demand the withdrawal or modification of provisions that he or she deems unlawful. This decision is effective immediately, and the employer must withdraw or modify the provisions concerned. However, after withdrawal the employer may appeal from the labor inspector's decision, eventually to the administrative court, which judges state actions.

Finally, it has been noted that the labor courts may also have a role to play.[7] An employee to whom a sanction has been applied by virtue of a provision of the shop rules may challenge the lawfulness of this provision before the labor court in order to have that sanction lifted by the court. This court cannot void a provision or withdraw it from the shop rules, because this is within the exclusive competence of the administrative court. It can, however, nullify the sanction by deciding not to enforce the provision.

As noted above, the law of August 4, 1982, also established for the first time a procedure that the employer is required to follow in disciplinary matters. This procedure does not apply to dismissals, either for cause or for economic reasons, as they are the subject of different statutory provisions. The law on disciplinary procedures starts with a definition of what is an employer-imposed sanction. French law previously had no such definition. The law now states that a sanction is any measure, other than an oral observation, taken by an employer in the wake of an act on the part of the employee that the employer considers to be a wrongdoing, whether or not the measure immediately affects the employee's presence in the enterprise, job, career, or remuneration. It should be noted that for some time the imposition of a fine deducted from wages has been unlawful.

In the case of a sanction, except for the most minor one (an oral warning), the employer must call the employee to a meeting by a letter. The letter must indicate that the employer is considering the application of a sanction against the employee, the time and place of the meeting, and that the employee may bring along another employee. The letter must be sent no more than two months after the alleged wrongdoing. A delay of at least twenty-four hours but no more than one month may elapse between the notification of the sanction and the meeting. The sanction, when decided upon, must be communicated in writing to the employee, along with the wrongdoing on which it is based.

The employee can request from the labor court the nullification, but not the modification, of the sanction. Nullification can occur in three cases: (1) the wrongdoing did not take place; (2) the compulsory procedure was not followed; (3) the sanction is manifestly disproportionate to the wrongdoing. In the latter two cases nothing prevents the employer from reimposing a sanction. It has been argued that this fact, along with the obvious effects upon future promotions, explains why there are in practice few suits on these two grounds on the part of employees.

It should also be noted that the act of August 4, 1982, although giving a definition of a sanction, fails to provide a definition of a wrongdoing. Section L.122-40 of the act simply mandates that sanctions can only be consequences of employee behaviors that are considered by the employer to be wrongdoings. The power to determine what constitutes a wrongdoing remains with the employer.

Clearly, violation of one of the shop rules, the validity of which has been tacitly approved and not challenged in court, constitutes a wrongdoing. The employer is free to apply the sanction established in the shop rules or a milder one, but not a more severe one. If the wrongdoing has been defined in the shop rules, but no sanction established, the employer is free to apply any sanction that it wishes. In any case the courts may still redress a sanction judged to be manifestly disproportionate to the wrongdoing.

The employer retains its general disciplinary powers with respect to behaviors that are not defined as wrongdoings in the shop rules, and may sanction such behaviors. However, it cannot apply a sanction not provided for violation of any shop rule. With regard to the justifiable limits on individual freedoms and the nature of a wrongdoing, courts test employer sanctions for proportionality to the offense. In the absence of a statutory definition of a wrongdoing, however, the question of defining what constitutes a wrongdoing remains. The courts have most often simply noted that such and such a behavior constitutes a wrongdoing, without giving any consistent or generally applicable definition. An instruction (*circulaire*) from the Ministry of Labor of March 15, 1983, attempts to define a wrongdoing. However, this instruction merely indicates the position of the administration and will not necessarily be applied by the courts. According to the ministry's instruction, wrongdoing may be either a positive behavior or the abstention from a behavior that would normally be expected.

A wrongdoing, active or passive, is generally seen as being limited to the scope of the contractual relationship. This would normally exclude behavior of the employee outside the hours and place of work. However, it is understood that the contract of employment includes certain duties on the part of the employee that carry over from the time and place of employment. In that sense, it has been argued, limits of a contractual nature to which employees implicitly agree in their contracts of employment come to limit their public freedoms.[8] The duties involved here

145

are those of discretion, loyalty, professional secrecy, and non-competition. The border between private life and performance of work is therefore not totally clear.

This situation can be summarized by advancing two sets of propositions. On the one hand, the principle is that the subordination of the employee is limited to the performance of work, and that the employer cannot intrude on his or her private life. For instance, an interdiction made by an airline prohibiting stewardesses from marrying is unlawful. However, obligations issuing from the duty to perform the contract of employment in good faith may apply in private life, by way of an exception to this rule. For instance, the marriage of an employee in a confidential position to a person employed by a competitor who also has a decision-making position may constitute grounds for dismissal. Disloyalty may be found in a manager bad-mouthing the company to fellow employees or questioning its financial soundness in public. On the other hand, the public freedoms of the employee are not suspended during the employment relationship. However, restrictions may be imposed on employee freedom only if they are justified by, and appropriate to, an employer's goals. For instance, an employee cannot insist on following his or her religious convictions by declining certain schedules of work. Also, the employer may impose a uniform upon salespersons who are required to be easily identifiable by members of the public. The employer may also forbid the wearing of a transparent blouse by a braless female employee, but cannot, except for very specific health and safety or production reasons (such as the necessity for a sterile atmosphere), forbid young female employees to wear heavy makeup, outsized glasses, and a frizzy hairdo "in the present condition of juvenile lifestyles."

Although the employer is limited to the scope of the employment relationship in carrying out its general disciplinary powers, it is not only disciplinary wrongdoings that can be sanctioned. This is because there are other categories of wrongdoing. For instance, it is possible for the employer to be the victim of a civil wrong, which may or may not also constitute a criminal offense. This could be entirely outside the employment relationship. Such would be the case, for instance, with an employee threatening the employer at home, outside of the working time and place. The employer cannot in this case use its disciplinary powers. However, it can legitimately consider the civil wrongdoing as a

146

basis for dismissal, in addition to possibly suing the employee for civil damages or bringing criminal charges. This behavior on the part of the employee is considered to constitute circumstances that may affect the employment relationship. The employer may thus, on the basis of a loss of confidence in the employee that is based on objective facts, dismiss the employee or change his or her assignment for real and serious cause that makes it impossible to continue the relationship as is.

An interesting if highly theoretical problem concerns the question of whether a contractual wrongdoing should be distinguished from one that is disciplinary or civil. If a disciplinary wrongdoing principally concerns the duties to be performed by the employee fulfilling the employment contract, this same wrongdoing could be considered to be simple nonperformance of the contract, having no reference to discipline. This would be the case, for instance, with negligent performance or occasional tardiness. The distinction, although abstract, is capable of having far-reaching consequences. This is true because if the wrongdoing is purely contractual, the employer theoretically does not have to follow statutory disciplinary procedures. However, the courts have generally abstained from categorizing an instance of wrongdoing as either contractual or disciplinary, and simply require that the statutory procedures be followed.

Finally, dismissals must be considered separately, for they are the subject of special regulations. The act of August 4, 1982, expressly provides that its provisions do not concern either the procedures or the merits of dismissal cases. Dismissals for cause are to be distinguished from dismissals for economic reasons as to their consequences for the employee in terms of unemployment compensation, application of a social plan, etc. Since the 1986 removal of the requirement of administrative authorization prior to an economic dismissal, there is in principle no longer any involvement of the administrative courts in dismissals. However, a role for the labor inspector still remains, and may in the future bring about a reversal of the exclusion of the administrative courts. Now, dismissals for economic reasons are treated in much the same way as other dismissals, and are subject to much the same procedural requirements.

Since an act of 1973 dismissals for cause have to meet certain conditions in order to be lawful. Before that act, dismissals were considered within the managerial rights of employers who, as mentioned above, were the sole judges of the interests of the enterprise. Besides, contracts of indeterminate duration, such as the contract of employment, could always be terminated unilaterally. However, as is the case with other managerial rights, the right to dismiss could be abused. The law provided for the possibility of damages in the case of a breach of a contract of employment by such abuse. Nevertheless, an employee considering himself or herself unfairly dismissed had to prove both that (1) the dismissal was not for the reason given by the employer (one that was allegedly in the interests of the enterprise) and (2) it was for another, abusive, reason. Now, as before, an employee who believes that he or she was unlawfully dismissed must challenge the dismissal in the labor court. The change under the act of 1973 is that the employer not only has to follow prescribed procedures but also must dismiss for lawful cause, and not merely avoid an abusive dismissal. Accordingly, dismissals have to be for "real and serious cause." Finally, the act provides that the burden of proof falls equally on the employer and the employee, not solely on the employee.

Nevertheless, the act failed to give a definition of "real and serious cause." Here also the courts have filled in the void left in the statutory law. During a parliamentary debate on the act, the Minister of Labor gave the following indications: (1) a cause is real if it is of an objective nature, which would exclude employer prejudice and personal convenience; (2) a real cause might be, for instance, a wrongdoing, incompetence, or reorganization of the enterprise; (3) a serious cause must have a degree of gravity that to some extent prevents the further continuation of the employment relationship without damage to the enterprise. Supreme Court decisions now allow us to have a clearer picture of what constitutes real and serious cause.

The two conditions, real and serious, are cumulative. A cause for dismissal must be both real and serious at the same time. It is deemed real if it exists. There must be reasons for the dismissal. It cannot take place on a whim. It also must be for the reasons alleged, and not under the guise of another reason. Therefore, the judge must now establish successively the actual existence of the alleged facts that constitute the cause for dismissal at the time the dismissal occurred, its accuracy as the true reason for the dismissal, and the objective character of the cause for termination. It is in this sense that the procedure to be followed plays an important role. Since an act of 1989, the employer is required to communicate to the employee in writing the reasons for the dismissal. The employer is subsequently bound to the reasons for dismissal invoked at that time and cannot change them later.

The cause must also be serious. The judges must, therefore, decide whether it sufficiently hampers the satisfactory functioning of the enterprise. It does not have to be linked to a prejudice suffered by the employer. It is evaluated *in concreto,* which means that its seriousness is judged according to the degree of wrongdoing that it constitutes and to the person of the employee in terms of age, seniority, circumstances, etc.

As is the case for disciplinary sanctions other than dismissal, the real and serious cause for a dismissal can be a particularly severe disciplinary wrongdoing, or can find its roots in a civil wrongdoing or a contractual violation. In the case of dismissal, causes other than wrongdoings may constitute real and serious reasons for employer action. These are causes that would not apply to lesser sanctions because this would be meaningless, as they arise from acts that are not voluntary or intentional on the part of the employee. First among these causes are professional incompetence or insufficient results from performance that do not stem from the voluntary lack of or faulty execution of the contract of employment. The judge in such a cause has only to consider if (1) the professional incompetence alleged has been proved (here the reality of the cause implies also that it is serious); (2) independent of professional competence, the results of the employee's work are insufficient; and, (3) the employer is not fraudulently using its powers to serve other ends.

A second set of such causes rests with the person of the employee. A relatively frequent situation is the employer losing confidence in the employee. This may occur as a consequence of an action in which the employer and employee are both involved, such as civil or criminal wrongdoing by the employee toward the employer. However, this is not the only type of such a case. A loss of confidence may follow from circumstances foreign to the employment relationship and also to any other relationship between the employer and the employee. Thus, an employee convicted by a criminal court may be dismissed for cause if it is a cause that throws doubt on the trustworthiness or mental stability required for the job. Labor courts use this notion of loss of confidence restrictively as to lower-level employees but enlarge it considerably when it concerns managers or confidential employees. Nevertheless, since a Supreme Court decision of

149

November 1990 such dismissals must rest on objective facts that justify the loss of confidence and can no longer be based solely on the employer's arguments. Since an act of July 25, 1990, an employee cannot be dismissed for reasons of sickness or health per se. It remains true, however, that objective consequences of ill health such as absences may justify dismissal on the grounds that the employee is unable to perform his or her tasks. Finally, economic circumstances, whether structural or conjectural, constitute real and serious cause for dismissal.

As is the case with discipline, whether a dismissal is based upon wrongdoing or upon other reasons seems academic and confusing in application. Many facts can constitute at the same time wrongdoing, faulty execution of the contract of employment, professional incompetence, and insufficient results of performance. Also, some wrongdoings may also be material cause for a loss of confidence. Granted that many court decisions fail to categorize causes for dismissal, correct categorization is still of both theoretical and practical interest.

In the case of dismissal another factor is important. Traditionally, the Supreme Court has been reluctant to order a dismissed employee reinstated, whatever the provisions of the successive statutes terming certain dismissals as "abusive" or "unlawful." The basis for this was its interpretation of two sections of the civil code. Section 1780, to prevent serfdom, mandates that a contract of employment of indeterminate duration can always be broken at the initiative of one of the parties. Section 1142 provides that an obligation to act or to refrain from acting can be enforced only by the awarding of damages, and not by a judge's injunction to act.[9] As a result, for a long period reinstatement was denied to employees however wrongfully they had been dismissed. Even after employee representatives were granted certain protections against dismissal, until 1974 they could nevertheless have their contracts of employment terminated through judicial processes. The present situation is relatively complex and still not fully clarified for all cases. Several cases must be distinguished.

Employee representatives now have a clear status on this point. They can be dismissed lawfully for a real and serious cause only after a special procedure involving formal authorization by the enterprise's works council and the labor inspector. If the authorization is not granted, the dismissal is void and the employee representative can sue the employer and obtain an injunction ordering his or her reinstatement. Damages may also be assessed along with lost wages.

The situation regarding other employees is much less simple. Traditionally the Supreme Court has denied them reinstatement, granting them only damages for improper dismissal. Under the act of 1973 reinstatement was purely voluntary on the employer's part. However, laws of amnesty passed after the presidential elections of 1981 and 1988 have given rights of reinstatement, under certain conditions, to employees who were validly dismissed.

There are now some possible grounds for reinstatement of ordinary employees who have been improperly terminated. The new Section L 122-45 of the labor code, modified by an act of 1985, provides that an employee cannot be sanctioned or dismissed because of origin, sex, family situation, belonging to an ethnic group, nationality, race, political opinions, activities on behalf of unions and mutual help societies, normal exercise of the right to strike, or religious convictions. Any contrary action is void. This section has been further modified by an act of 1990 stating that dismissals because of disease or life-style (*moeurs*) are also void. Other sections of the code that have been newly modified void the dismissal of employees in specific cases (occupational disease, national service, being a city councilor, refusal of overtime, exercise of right of free expression). In cases where an employee has been dismissed after a suit for sexual discrimination, Section 123-5 explicitly provides that the reinstatement is "by full right." Improper cause of dismissal must be proved by the employee. However, the difficulty of the employee's case may be alleviated by a provision of the act of 1989 which states that doubt should be resolved in favor of the employee.

At the time of this writing there are no published court decisions on this subject, and the Supreme Court has not taken a position on the question of whether the "void" character of some of these dismissals warrants a remedy of reinstatement. The Supreme Court has avoided ruling on this when given an opportunity to do so. Thus, the matter of reinstatement of employees is still in limbo. It is expected that there will be developments in the law on this soon.

A last point of a general nature should be made. This is that the courts, in the absence of a statutory definition of wrongdoings, have set up a scale of gravity of those wrongdoings that are capable of leading to dismissal. The lowest step on this scale is light, or minor, wrongdoing, which does not justify dismissal but, at most, the strongest disciplinary sanction short of dismissal. It is a wrongdoing that is "real" but not sufficiently "serious" to constitute cause for dismissal. The disciplinary procedure provided for in the act of August 4, 1982, has to be followed, except in the case of the mildest sanction, oral warning. In other cases the employee who believes that a sanction is too severe can demand its nullification in the labor courts, as discussed above. Examples of such a wrongdoing would be a single instance of being late or an oral dispute with another employee where there is no heavy verbal abuse present, refusal to perform a task for which the employee is not trained, and voicing disagreement with a superior on a technical matter.

The next step up the scale is serious wrongdoing—wrongdoing that constitutes a real and serious cause. This is wrongdoing that prevents the continuation of the employment relationship. The employee is lawfully dismissed but has a right to a period of notice, severance pay, and accumulated vacation pay. However, here, as in all cases of dismissal, the employee in principle, but with qualifications to be discussed below, cannot be reinstated. The dismissal cannot be nullified. It is simply unlawful, giving rise to damages. Separate damages are due if the procedure for dismissal has not been followed. The burden of proof as to the reality and seriousness of the offense is shared by the employer and the employee. The judge makes up his or her mind on the basis of the elements of proof brought forward by both parties. Doubt is resolved in favor of the employee. Examples of real and serious wrongdoings are repeated minor offenses, opening confidential mail addressed to a superior, a vocal incident with another employee in front of members of the public, insulting a superior in front of other employees, returning from vacation two days late without notice, rough horseplay with another employee without injuries resulting, and simple intemperance without negative consequences.

One step above serious is the grave wrongdoing. It is a wrongdoing that not only prevents continuation of the employment relationship in the future, but necessitates the immediate termination of the relationship and requires that the employee immediately leave the premises of the enterprise. Here the employee has no right to a period of notice or to severance pay, but does receive accumulated vacation pay. Of course, the statutory procedures must be followed and the burden of proof is shared, but the burden of proof as to the gravity of the offense falls upon the employer. Examples of grave wrongdoing are insubordination in front of other employees, thefts against the employer or fellow employees, physical violence against the employer, serious fighting with another employee which results in injuries, accepting money from suppliers, sexual abuse of an employee, and being drunk while working on dangerous machines or when the employee is a vehicle driver. In general it is not necessary that a wrongdoing be the cause of prejudice to the employer to qualify as grave, but wrongdoings that do cause such prejudice are grave.

The final step in the graduation of wrongdoings is heavy. This is wrongdoing of a particularly grave nature, both as to its consequences for the enterprise and as to the unacceptable nature of the behavior. It is characterized by the willful character of the wrongdoing, performed intentionally in order to harm the employer. Here also the burden of proving the heavy character of the offense rests on the employer, and doubt is resolved in favor of the employee. In such a case dismissal takes place immediately, without rights to notice or severance pay. Also, the right to accumulated vacation pay is lost. This last consequence is exceptional because this right is normally considered as already acquired by the employee. There is an element of private sanction here; the wrongdoing has caused harm to the employer and the loss of vacation pay provides some reparation. In addition, the employer can sue the employee for damages. Cases of heavy wrongdoing include a manager inciting fellow employees to leave an enterprise and follow him to work for a competitor, violence or destruction of property during a strike, serious theft, and unlawful strikes.

It should be emphasized that the examples given here must be understood as what they are—examples only. They do reflect decisions of the Supreme Court. However, at the level of the lower courts wide variations exist around the central tendencies set by these rulings. In French law the situation is such that a case of a given wrongdoing in a given court might be considered minor, whereas in another court exactly the same act might be considered grave, and in the same court on another day real and serious. This is so for a number of reasons. First, the courts must consider the behavior of an employee in order to qualify the wrongdoing *in concreto*. This means that they take into account such factors as age, seniority, and past record. Second, many decisions of the lower courts are not appealed even when they can be, that is, when they involve more than a certain minimum monetary amount. When they entail an amount below that limit, they can be appealed to the Supreme Court only as to matters of law. Third, and more importantly, the courts, under the potential control of the courts of appeal, have a sovereign right to "qualify" the facts. This means that a court decides sovereignly if a behavior, in given circumstances by an individual, constitutes a wrongdoing, and which type of wrongdoing. These are considered questions of fact, not of law.

The supreme civil high court deals only with questions of law, never of fact. When a case reaches the Supreme Court, the facts are considered established and cannot be challenged. The Supreme Court is competent only to decide if the application of the law to the facts, which are themselves beyond debate, was correctly carried out by the lower courts. Therefore, there is in theory no harmonization at the national level of what facts in what circumstances constitute wrongdoings of various types. Wide variations of interpretation can and do exist. This situation is alleviated by the doctrine that the facts, even if considered established by the lower court, can be subjected to categorization. That is, a factual situation, sovereignly established, is to be identified with a legal notion that is established but often, as was noted above in several instances, not precisely defined by statutory law. This operation of qualification, as distinct from the establishment of the facts, is a matter of law. It is, therefore, subject to the control of the Supreme Court. However, in recent years the position of the Supreme Court on this has been somewhat erratic.[10] It may currently be moving back toward expanding and fully using its power to control categorizations by lower courts.[11]

THE PARTICULAR OBLIGATIONS OF EMPLOYMENT

SUBORDINATION

Case Scenario

JD, a janitor at the A Manufacturing Company, is assigned the task of waxing office hallways. He completes one hallway. His supervisor, FF, inspects the hallway and says to JD, "Do this floor again." JD replies "No," and walks away.

Analysis

This is a clear case of insubordination. Generally insubordination, ill will, and obstruction are cause for termination. They may well justify a simple dismissal for real and serious cause, with notice and severance and vacation pay. However, as is set out below, circumstances may affect the outcome.

Seriousness. The presence of other employees, abusive language, or physical contact with the supervisor would likely result in a categorization of grave wrongdoing. Belief that the order is contrary to rules or foolish or incompetent is normally not an excuse.

However, a real threat to health and safety would excuse and explain the refusal. Employees have a right to withdraw in certain circumstances of seriousness of such conditions. An order falling outside the job description but easy to perform might justify a lesser sanction than dismissal. It would constitute an excuse if it demanded special training or if it were demeaning. An unlawful order does not have to be followed. Neither does an order that is immoral, such as a bodily search of a woman by a man.

Ordering work that is largely outside the job description is considered a breach of contract on the part of the employer. The employee has the option of accepting and doing it or considering himself dismissed and possibly suing for damages beyond notice and severance pay. This would particularly be the case if the order were beneath the dignity of the employee.

Mitigation. Seniority could play a part. A good record of work in the simplest case—JD simply walks away, saying nothing—without added seriousness might result in a lesser disciplinary penalty for an employee with twenty years' seniority. On the other hand, an employee with only six months' service might be lawfully dismissed for the same conduct.

The type of work performed is also important. Less is expected from employees performing simple tasks involving unskilled labor. Also, the ability to understand language might be important. A foreign guestworker, for instance, might argue that he or she did not understand. The use of profane language by such workers has even been accepted by some courts because in their working environment—construction, for example—they know and have been exposed to no other. The status of employee representative often but not always seems to warrant a lesser sanction than would be appropriate for ordinary employees.

Enforceability. In this case, as in the following ones, the employer would proceed to dismissal, following the compulsory procedure described above. Past tolerance would perhaps be a reason for not upholding the sanction if there were a clear case of selective enforcement of discipline against an employee who was singled out for another reason such as union activities. In that case the employer's actions would amount to discrimination and might be criminally punishable.

SOBRIETY

Case Scenario

RR, a laborer on the loading dock of B Trucking Company, is observed by his supervisor, JB, reaching into the pocket of a coat that is hanging near his workplace. JB observes RR bring something to his mouth, appear to swallow, and then replace it in the coat. JB approaches RR and asks, "What are you drinking?" RR reaches into the pocket of the coat and hands JB a bottle that contains an alcoholic beverage. JB forms the opinion that RR's breath smells strongly of alcoholic spirits and that his eyes are unfocused.

Analysis

Use of alcohol on the job is forbidden by law and is generally forbidden by shop rules. It is a real and serious cause for dismissal. Intoxication is also cause for dismissal.

Seriousness. Drinking on the job may well constitute a grave or heavy wrongdoing if it leads to consequences of a serious nature—for example, accident, dangerous environment, scandal.

Mitigation. Alcoholism is no excuse. A custom that allows drinking beer on the job in a place of work such as a brewery would be unlawful.

SECURITY OF EMPLOYER'S PROPERTY

Case Scenario

PR, a clerk employed by C Gourmet Foods Company, is observed by two supervisors taking company products out of a packing box, concealing them on his person, and walking out the door with them. He is apprehended after he exits the store, and admits taking the products.

Analysis

This is a clear-cut case of theft. It is grounds for dismissal for a real and serious cause, and very likely grave cause for summary dismissal without severance pay or notice.

Seriousness. The value of the goods stolen is generally irrelevant as an excuse, even if the object of the theft were of only token value. For instance, a cleaning lady was found to be properly dismissed for real and serious cause for keeping, while cleaning an airplane, a small bottle of orange juice of the kind given free to passengers. Most likely it becomes a grave or heavy offense if the object has value. This would justify instant dismissal with the consequences outlined above for such cases. No other seriousness-related factors would likely affect the outcome.

Mitigation. Mitigating factors would, in all likelihood, be irrelevant. Only the custom of free goods consumed on the premises, as is customary in some industries such as chocolate manufacturing, would be germane. However, even here certain procedures have to be followed, and simply helping oneself as described in the scenario would be theft.

PEACEFUL WORKPLACE

Case Scenario

MM is a clerk in D Department Store. NN is another clerk in the same department store; he is physically larger than MM. While MM is moving some heavy equipment from one area to another NN says, "I'm surprised that you did not ask a real man like me to handle this job." MM, angered, strikes NN on the jaw, knocking him down. NN gets up and walks away.

Analysis

Violence is almost always a real and serious cause for dismissal.

Seriousness. Provocation is no excuse. Two employees fighting would both be dismissed. If injuries result, it is a grave or

157

heavy wrongdoing. Other elements adding to the seriousness could potentially lead to this same result.

Mitigation. Mitigating factors are unlikely to change the outcome.

OFF-DUTY CONDUCT

Case Scenario

TT, head salesclerk for E Toy Store, participates in a white supremacist demonstration. He is arrested for disorderly behavior, and a photograph of him handcuffed to a post and snarling at police is printed in the local newspaper, along with his name and the name of his employer.

Analysis

Political freedom is specifically protected by the law. In principle, a political demonstration is not related to the employment relationship and the employer has no disciplinary powers. It might well be discrimination under Section 122-45 of the labor code to sanction the employee for his political beliefs.

Seriousness. Conviction of a crime, if it occurred, is in principle also unrelated to the employment relationship. However, during imprisonment the employee cannot perform his work, and this is grounds for dismissal for real and serious cause. In the case in the scenario termination would probably be upheld on the basis of loss of confidence based upon facts arising outside the contract of employment. A man inclined to commit acts of violence and anger cannot be left in contact with children in a toy store.

ATTENDANCE

Case Scenario

JJ is a nurse's aide at F Nursing Home. Because of an illness her attendance at work has been erratic for two years. During that period she has missed 30 percent of her scheduled working days. During the last month she has missed 20 percent of her scheduled working days. All of these absences were excused. She then misses three days of work, without notifying her employer, because she decides to extend her holiday.

Analysis

Two different issues are involved: sickness and absenteeism. In the past, long-term sickness, if not connected with an occupational disease, was either a real and serious cause for dismissal or an act of God, not truly determined by the employer but of which the employer merely takes note, which deprives the employee, who is not really dismissed, of the elements of pay that are attached to severance. Repeated absences that "disorganize the enterprise" would probably fall under the first. Short-term sickness was not cause for dismissal. Very recently, in the wake of laws forbidding discrimination based on some kinds of sickness—AIDS, for example—a statutory act has made it unlawful and discriminatory to dismiss because of sickness. However, employees unable to perform because of too many absences caused by an illness might still be terminated for real and serious reason based on their failure to perform, particularly where this interferes with the work of other employees.

Absenteeism is another issue. Employees have a duty to warn the employer of an absence. Generally, however, a single act of absence will not justify dismissal.

Seriousness. A string of absences with appropriate warnings, if they harm the functioning of the enterprise, would be cause for dismissal. If the shop rules provide that an absence of several days without notification before or after a holiday were real and serious cause for dismissal, the employer could enforce this rule, but might face a challenge in a suit by the employee for damages.

PERFORMANCE

Case Scenario

HH is a warehouseman for G Distributing Company. G has instituted a program that determines levels of productivity for warehousemen. This program meets accepted professional standards for such programs. Over a period of two months HH fails to produce at the prescribed levels, consistently falling 10 percent below the standard. He is warned that he will be terminated if he fails to improve his productivity within two weeks. He fails to do so. HH claims that the standards of the new system are impossible to meet. He proves that prior to the institution of the new system he was given above-average evaluations by his supervisor for producing at his current level, covering a period of ten years.

159

Analysis

As discussed above, insufficiency of production is nonperformance of the contractual obligation and justifies a nondisciplinary dismissal. However, dismissal because of significant changes in job content not accepted by the employee is considered a dismissal that entitles the employee to the benefits usually attached to severance.

Seriousness. Low production may be willful. There could then be disciplinary sanctions for a serious or grave offense, with the consequences outlined above.

Enforceability. The fact that performance deemed satisfactory in the past suddenly becomes unsatisfactory may be highly suspect, particularly if the employee is an employee representative or union activist. This might raise doubts as to the selective nature of the enforcement of discipline and perhaps misuse or abuse of disciplinary powers.

LOYALTY

Case Scenario

JS, a teller for H Bank, during an appearance on a television consumer information program states that her employer regularly fails to advise customers when they make mistakes in favor of the bank, but promptly corrects mistakes in favor of the customers.

Analysis

This is a matter of the duty of loyalty due the employer. It is relatively strong in France. For instance, a bank teller has been held properly terminated for real and serious reason because she advised customers that the terms and conditions of deposit were better across the street in a competing bank.

The outcome will depend largely on the mitigating factors and the seriousness of the conduct. From the scenario itself it is difficult to decide the case. Also, such a behavior is much more severely treated if engaged in by a confidential employee or manager.

Seriousness. Seriousness depends largely upon the accuracy of the facts alleged by the employee. If they are inaccurate, it is a grave offense and immediate dismissal without severance pay is warranted. If they are accurate, it then becomes a question of whether or not the employer's act is lawful. If it is merely bad practice, and not unlawful, termination will likely be upheld. If the practice is unlawful, termination is much less likely to be justifiable. If JJ did this simply to annoy her employer, this would amount to willful misconduct. If the statement is false, JJ might additionally be sued by her employer.

Mitigation. Mitigating factors are unlikely to apply. If JS has learned of the practice in her role as employee representative, this is a matter of added seriousness because she would be violating the duty of secrecy imposed upon such officials. This might amount to a criminal offense if the bank's practice is lawful.

RESTRICT COLLECTIVE ACTION

Case Scenario

JJ, a machinist at I Manufacturing Company, becomes angry because he believes that his supervisor is treating him and other employees in a disrespectful manner. In protest, he persuades the other employees in his work group to leave work together in the middle of their scheduled work shift and not return until the next day.

Analysis

In France the right to strike is recognized in the preamble to the Constitution "in the framework of the laws which regulate it." It is in principle, therefore, granted not only to private sector employees but also to civil servants. The law provides that normally the act of striking does not break the individual contracts of employment of the employees taking part in the strike. Their contracts are merely suspended for the duration of the strike. Therefore, the employer must keep the strikers in its employment. It cannot impose *any* sanctions upon employees for participating in a strike, much less dismiss them.

Even in the absence of laws regulating the right to strike in the private sector the courts have nevertheless held that, like all rights, it is susceptible to abuse. Several successive partial cessations of work and a rotating strike, combined together, would amount to such an abuse. Also, certain behavior on the part of employees, such as working to rule, do not, properly speaking, constitute strikes, because they are not work stoppages and therefore are plainly not protected by the law.

With the exception of the public sector, where strikes are regulated by an act of July 31, 1963, and therefore subject to a requirement of three days' advance warning, there is no required period of notice for a strike. Also, there is no requirement that demands be explicitly presented to the employer before going on strike. Employees may freely choose the timing and duration of a strike. Finally, a strike does not have to be authorized by a union or a majority of the employees in order to be lawful.

However, a strike must have occupational or professional aims. The use of the right to strike for goals other than these—for example, for political ends—constitutes an abuse of the right to strike. Finally, in conjunction with a strike, unlawful behavior may take place, such as violent picketing or damage to the employer's property. The fact that this behavior occurs during a strike does not excuse it, making it a potential cause for dismissal.

Seriousness and Mitigation. None of the factors pertaining to seriousness or mitigation apply.

AVOID CONFLICT OF INTEREST

Case Scenario

IB, a systems analyst for J Company, has access to private computer systems of his employer. IB accepts a string of free-lance, relatively routine programming jobs for K Company, a competitor of his employer, performing work at his home.

Analysis

An employee in principle owes all his or her efforts to the employer during working time but is free to rest or work during free time. But, as discussed above in the general comments, a duty of noncompetition with the employer stems implicitly from the contractual obligations. Therefore, the case rests on factors relating to seriousness.

Seriousness. If IB is using J Company's hardware in his home or its proprietary software on his own equipment, he can be dismissed for a real and serious cause. It may even be a grave or heavy wrongdoing in the latter case. If IB is using his own software and hardware in his home, but is performing tasks that might constitute business for J Company, this is real and serious cause for dismissal. It becomes grave if he got in contact with K Company through his work at J Company and attracted the business to himself. If IB is performing work for K of the same nature that he performs for J, but the product of that work is not sold to J Company's customers, he is committing no wrongdoing unless through his work he provides K Company with proprietary knowledge belonging to J Company. If this is not the case, there is no cause for dismissal, unless shop rules forbid working for a competitor or performing work of the same nature outside of the place of work, or the contract of employment of IB contains a covenant of non-competition. In the latter case the issue is nondisciplinary and contractual.

CONCLUSIONS

In France, as elsewhere, the particular shapes that the institutions, practices, and customs of industrial justice have taken are the result of a long and complex process. Larger political, social, and economic forces have been at play. However, their object, the productive system, is the same as in other countries. Therefore, although they are unique in some respects, they also present some striking similarities to those in other countries, reflecting both the broader characteristics of French society and the omnipresent problem to which they apply.

Justice as to the obligations of the workplace is the object of strategies of lawmakers who aim to mold it to conform to their ideological goals. The pursuit of these goals, however, is subject to the whims of political majorities and alliances, and their translation into statutes is often far from clear. The interpretations of the statutes by members of the judiciary, themselves reflections of the larger society (perhaps with some time lag), add another layer of uncertainty.

The general result of these dynamics is growing complexity and uncertainty as to the outcome of a particular case, even a simple one. This uncertainty may be the chief characteristic of the French system of industrial justice.

NOTES

1. The author would like to express his appreciation to Prof. Jean Emmanuel Ray, University of Paris I, for his assistance in the work involved in this paper.

2. G. H. Cammerlynck, G. Lyon-Caen, and J. Pelisser, *Droit du travail* (Paris: Dalloz, 1984), p. 175.

3. P. Durand, *Traite de droit du travail* (Paris: Dalloz, 1947), p. 422.

4. J. E. Ray, *Droit du travail, droit vivant* (Paris: Editions Liaisons, 1991).

5. Ibid.

6. M. Despax and J. Rojot, *Labour Law and Industrial Relations in France* (Deventer: Kluwer, 1987), p. 38.

7. Ray, *Droit du travail, droit vivant,* ch. 1.

8. J. Savatier, "La liberte dans le travail," *Droit Social* Jan. 1990: 49.

9. F. Meyers, *Ownership of Jobs: A Comparative Study* (Los Angeles: Institute of Industrial Relations, UCLA, 1964).

10. J. Bore, "Le controle par la Cour de Cassation de la cause reele et serieuse du licenciement," *Droit Social* Mar. 1986: 176.

11. Ray, *Droit du travail, droit vivant.*

5

GERMANY

Werner K. Blenk and Hans Peter Viethen

This paper attempts to set out essential procedural and substantive rules pertaining to the obligations of employment and the consequences that may ensue from their violation. The first part provides a general overview of the actors and procedures involved in administering industrial justice, and the second part applies the legal frame thus described to imaginary situations. Although the main emphasis of the chapter is, in accordance with the plan of the study, to describe the law from the employers' viewpoint—that is, to discuss the range of sanctions available to employers—in order to complete the picture some reference is also made to the avenues open to employees in their search for workplace, or industrial, justice.[1]

OVERVIEW OF THE SYSTEM

The population of the Federal Republic of Germany stands at present (the third quarter of 1990) at about 78,770,000 (after reunification with the German Democratic Republic). About 36,400,000 persons participate in the labor market of the Federal Republic, some 2,440,000 of which are presently unemployed. About 40 percent of the workers are organized in unions in the old Länder (constituent states of the Federal Republic of Germany). The bulk of labor laws and industrial relations practices of the Federal Republic of Germany is now also applicable in the former territory of the German Democratic Republic.

Employers' and workers' organizations have fairly centralized structures. The largest union by far is the Deutsche Gewerkschaftsbund (DGB); it consists of seventeen individual unions that are predominantly organized on industrial lines. These operate country wide and represent the real focus of trade union power. The DGB unions organize both blue- and white-collar employees in both the private and public sectors. They are "unitary" in the sense that they accept members regardless of political, religious, or ideological considerations and are independent of political parties, although not necessarily without political preferences. The DGB unions are in competition mainly with the *Deutsche Angestellten Gewerkschaft* (DAG, German Union of Salaried Employees), which organizes white-collar employees, and the *Deutsche Beamtenbund* (DBB, German Confederation of Civil Servants), which organizes predominantly civil servants. In absolute numbers the DGB unions have more members than the other unions together.

At the national level the employers are represented by economic associations—in particular the *Bundesverband der Deutschen Industrie* (BDI, Federation of German Industry). There is also an association dealing with social policy issues, the *Bundesverband der Deutschen Arbeitgeberverbände* (BDA, Federal Association of German Employers' Associations), which consists of forty-seven individual associations. Its main functions are to formulate policies and strategies on industrial relations and labor law matters, to produce cohesion among employers, and to represent their interests in all public forums. Collective bargaining is carried out by its constituent members. The BDA encompasses in its membership about 80 percent of the eligible firms.[2]

Industrial justice in the Federal Republic of Germany is delivered by these actors as well as by public authorities at various levels of centralization, often on the basis of legal rules and procedures that both determine the function and relationship of these actors vis-à-vis each other and spell out the main obligations of employment as well as the penalties to be meted out in case of violation. However, important areas such as the recognition of unions, dispute settlement, industrial action, and the like are not, or only rudimentarily, regulated by statutory law—thus attributing important roles to other regulatory agencies such as labor courts and to the parties themselves. In many instances the law has a supportive function: it provides a frame—which is very detailed at the level of the enterprise—within which the social partners define their own relations as well as the conditions of employment of the majority of employees. Nevertheless, important areas of substantive labor law, such as pensions and employment protection, are regulated by statute, thus relieving the collective bargaining process of intricate and often controversial issues.

Trade unions and employers' associations interact with each other and with the public authorities through various procedures and institutions, in particular through collective bargaining, through the codetermination machinery, and—of particular relevance for workplace, or industrial, justice—through the labor courts.

COLLECTIVE BARGAINING

Collective agreements are negotiated on industry lines either at the national level or regionally. The various DGB and competing non-DGB unions engage separately in bargaining. However, as a rule the agreements negotiated by the various unions are similar as regards their results, despite formally separate negotiations. A few strong DGB unions set the pattern, and the other unions follow. Collective agreements are concluded on wages as well as other important aspects such as job classification and work organization. In many instances they lay down minimum conditions which are often topped up in individual labor contracts and/or elaborated upon in plant agreements. Plant agreements have gained increased importance in past years. Given the wide geographical scope of collective agreements and their application to a great number of highly diverse enterprises in terms of profitability and manpower, they cannot fix uniform conditions in detail. With the appearance of new bargaining items, such as the reduction of working time, which require adaptation to individual circumstances, the trend toward supplementary negotiations at the level of the enterprise between the works councils and management, based on the Works Constitution Act (*Betriebsverfassungsgesetz* [BetrVG]), has been strengthened. In many instances collective agreements

167

lay down ground rules and delegate their transformation to the level of the enterprise, where tailor-made rules fill out the lacunae left by collective agreements.

Collective agreements are legally binding on the parties which have concluded them and on their members. In certain circumstances they can be declared generally applicable by the Federal Minister of Labor and Social Affairs (Secs. 4, 5 of the *Tarifvertragsgesetz* [TVG; Collective Agreement Act, 1969]). Irrespective of the legal situation, there is a widespread practice, followed by most employers, of applying collective agreements also to those workers not formally covered by them. Thus collective agreements concern, in one way or another, the vast majority of West German employees.

CODETERMINATION

Under the Works Constitution Act, 1972, the employees are represented by works councils, which are elected every four years in all enterprises that normally have five or more permanent employees (Sec. 1, BetrVG). In reality, the rule is not always complied with, and there are many enterprises that come under the Works Constitution Act that do not have works councils.[3]

In principle all employees have voting rights in the works councils, irrespective of union membership. This means that works councilors are the representatives of all workers, not of the unions. In practice, however, about 75 percent of all staff councilors are union members, many of them belonging to the DGB unions. The works councils have a wide range of consultation and codetermination rights which are laid down in the Works Constitution Act, 1972. While consultation rights do not affect the decision-making prerogatives of the employer, codetermination implies that the employer cannot take a valid decision without the consent of the works council. Rights of codetermination concern predominantly social matters, which include, as will be explained later, disciplinary issues (Sec. 87, BetrVG), certain personnel matters (Secs. 94, 95, 98, 99, 102, BetrVG), and a few economic matters (Sec. 112, BetrVG, e.g. social plan in case of redundancy).

Works councils play a crucial role in establishing and maintaining industrial justice in the enterprise. Under the law the works council and the employer have to work together "in a spirit of mutual trust and cooperation" (Sec. 2.1, BetrVG).

According to Section 74.2, BetrVG, "Acts of industrial warfare between the employer and the works council are unlawful." In general the main purpose of the law is to stimulate cooperation at the level of the enterprise and to avoid confrontation wherever possible. In practice it would appear that the relationship between management and the works council is somewhat ambivalent in nature;[4] the rights of the works council may make management more difficult since they restrict management prerogatives. On the other hand, the consent of the works council may help legitimize decisions. To the extent works councils cooperate in unpopular decisions, such as work force reductions, their involvement may ease the application of such decisions. Whether one or the other aspect prevails depends on a number of variables, including the size of the enterprise, the personal influence of the owner, the presence of unions, the subject area in dispute, and the like.

A main instrument which works councils and management use on matters coming under co-determination is the *Betriebsvereinbarung* (plant agreement). A plant agreement is established through negotiations between the works council and management, and it takes the form of a written contract. Plant agreements create norms that are binding and directly applicable to all members of the enterprise. For example, the *Betriebsbussen* (penalty codes) which play an important role in the administration of industrial justice, and which will be described later, have to be cast in the form of a plant agreement. Plant agreements cannot deal with remuneration and other conditions of employment that have been fixed or are normally fixed by collective agreement (Sec. 77.3, BetrVG).

Since, under the Works Constitution Act, strikes and industrial action are forbidden at the level of the enterprise, it was necessary to establish conflict resolution machinery for collective interest disputes at this level. In this respect the Works Constitution Act provides for a conciliation committee (*Einigungsstelle*) whose main function is to settle differences of opinion between the employer and the works councils (Sec. 76, BetrVG) on a number of important issues listed in the law, including "social matters" (Sec. 87.1.i, (2), BetrVG) coming under co-determination. This means that those disciplinary matters that are considered social matters come under co-determination and are decided by the conciliation committee.

The conciliation committee is composed of assessors

169

appointed in equal numbers by the employer and the works council and of an independent chairman accepted by both sides. In an important number of cases the conciliation committee adopts its decisions, which are binding, by a majority vote. In many instances the chairman is a labor court judge. The chairman's voice will often be decisive, since the worker and employers' participants are appointed in equal numbers. In these circumstances there is some pressure for the two sides to negotiate with convincing arguments, since each party can defeat the other by making the chairman vote in its favor. This also creates some pressure for compromise. In practice, there is not much recourse to the conciliation committee. The enterprises try to solve their conflicts with their employees without involving external elements whose presence would be regarded as indicating a failure of good cooperation.

There is a much less elaborate framework for the resolution of individual disputes between the worker and management at the level of the enterprise because the interests of individual workers are frequently taken care of by the works council and their position in the enterprise is very much determined in terms of rights which are, if necessary, interpreted by the courts. It would appear that most of the grievances are settled informally between the employer and the worker. Nevertheless, since 1972 there is a grievance procedure available under the Works Constitution Act (Secs. 84–86). According to Section 84, BetrVG every employee is entitled to make a complaint to the competent authorities in the establishment if the employee feels that he or she has been discriminated against or treated unfairly or otherwise put at a disadvantage by the employer or by other employees. The employee may either complain directly to the employer or call on a member of the works council for assistance or mediation. If the employee chooses to address himself or herself to the works council, and if there are differences of opinion between the works council and the employer, then the works council may appeal to the conciliation committee. It is important at this point to decide whether it is a legal or an interest dispute. In the case of a legal dispute the conciliation committee can only formulate a recommendation, and the worker, if unsatisfied, has to go to the labor courts. If it is an interest dispute then the award of the conciliation committee "takes the place of an agreement between the employer and the works council" (Sec. 85.2,

BetrVG). In other words, the conciliation committee makes a binding decision on the matter.

Thus, in summary, the German system of industrial relations is characterized by collective bargaining at sectoral levels where conflicts may, under certain conditions, be subjected to a test of strength in strikes or lock-outs. At the enterprise level, the process of bargaining between the works council and management which leads to plant agreements that have been called "mini collective agreements," and the conciliation committee, which disposes of disputes through binding decisions, are functionally comparable institutions. These institutions cover a wide range of collective interest disputes.

LABOR COURTS

Another vital forum through which employers and employees interact on matters of workplace justice are the labor courts.[5] They are in fact the main mechanism for solving individual and collective disputes. Generally speaking, they deal with legal, or rights, disputes, whereas interest disputes should in principle be solved by the parties involved. However, a great number of disputes in the Federal Republic are legal in nature. This is so because the position of the worker is determined by a dense network of laws, collective and plant agreements that contain legal entitlements couched in terms of "rights." Their violation leads to a "legal" dispute. In addition, the question of whether the parties and, in particular, the conciliation committee have exceeded their range of discretion is also considered a legal question, which, as a result, establishes a residual legal control over the autonomous rule making by the parties.[6] On top of the competences laid down in the *Arbeitsgerichtsgesetz* (ArbGG, Labor Court Act, 1979) and other laws, the labor courts are heavily involved in rule making on such fundamental questions as industrial action. There has been a reluctance in the Federal Republic to legislate on controversial issues of labor policy. This has tended to leave the task of rule making to the judges. In these circumstances, and seen together with the preference of the industrial relations actors to seek legal clarification in case of doubt, the role of the labor courts cannot be underestimated. They are the most important actors in the provision of industrial justice.

The labor court system was started in 1926, when labor courts were constituted as a special branch of the judiciary. There are three levels: labor courts of first instance, appellate labor courts, and the Federal Labor Court. The labor courts are composed of panels which consist of a professional judge as chairman and two lay judges, one from the employer and one from the worker side. Professional and lay judges have an equal vote. However, the professional judges, being legal experts, exercise a dominant influence on the proceedings as well as on the findings of the court. The parties to a dispute may at the first and second levels either take their case in their own hands or choose to be represented by counsel—either by an attorney or by a representative of the unions or the employers' association. In the Federal Labor Court the parties have to be represented by an attorney.

The Labor Court Act provides for two procedures: A pretrial and a trial. The pretrial procedure takes the form of conciliation where the professional judge facilitates a free exchange of views among the parties and between the parties and himself with a view to producing an amicable early settlement. An important number of routine cases are solved this way. However, if the case touches on more fundamental questions, the parties tend to press for a judgment in a formal trial, which comes after conciliation.

The trial itself is carried out under rules of procedure that are based on general civil procedure, with certain adaptations required by the special nature of labor matters. There is, for example, less formality, the risk of facing high costs is small, and the rules are shaped in such a fashion as to accelerate the administration of justice. In labor matters more than elsewhere justice delayed may amount to justice denied. In principle the parties are themselves called upon to present the facts on which they base their claims or defence. As a general rule the court will only take into account those facts that have been advanced by the parties and have been proved by them. It will normally not investigate independently. The court is free to evaluate the proofs offered by the parties, and in doing so it will take into account all circumstances of the case. It may be added here that the discussion in the second part of this chapter of the sanctions to be meted out in case of a violation of employment obligations is to a certain extent incomplete due to the paucity of information in the fact patterns.

SUBSTANTIVE RULES OF EMPLOYMENT OBLIGATION

THE OBLIGATIONS OF EMPLOYMENT

Before entering into the question of how violations are sanctioned, it might be useful to describe briefly the main obligations of employment as laid down in laws and collective and plant agreements, as interpreted by the court and synthesized by legal scholars, which have a considerable influence on the development of labor law in the Federal Republic of Germany. The employment relationship is usually based on a contract between the employer and the employee. Since the nineteenth century the guiding principle in the law of contract has been "freedom of contract." It is based on the assumption that both parties to a contract, including an employment contract, are free to enter into a contractual arrangement, to abstain from it, or to terminate it. It is rooted in a philosophical tradition that sees persons as being able freely to determine their fate on the basis of their intellect and their capacity to make rational decisions. This conceptual basis leads to a formal idea of freedom and neglects the sociological reality that there is a grave imbalance of power between the employer and the employee. In its practical application the freedom of contract doctrine has served as a thin disguise for the exploitation of workers. Much of the labor law in the Federal Republic of Germany can be seen as an attempt to remedy the basic failure of the concept of freedom of contract in the field of labor. Thus, over the decades numerous constraints have been developed in the name of social justice concerning the conclusion, the content, and the termination of labor contracts, without however openly abandoning freedom of contract as a basic principle of labor law.[7] At present there is a school of thought that believes that constraints have been pushed too far. The protagonists press for more "flexibility" in the name of economic efficiency. Parallel to this movement new employment patterns are developing, such as fixed-term employment and subcontracting, which remove employment relationships to some extent from the ambit of traditional labor law.

According to Section 611 of the Civil Code a "service contract" is characterized by the fact that one party promises to perform services and the other party is obliged to pay the agreed remuneration. The resulting duties are conditional on each other and reciprocal in nature. Labor law academics and the judiciary have filled these abstract notions by developing a doctrinal frame of rights and duties of both workers and employers. For purposes of clarity, a distinction is made between "principal duties" and "ancillary duties," the violation of which may entail certain sanctions.

The principal obligation of the worker is to carry out the work agreed upon in the contract. Within these contractual limits the employer has the right to specify the nature of the work to be carried out. The employer has the right to give orders which the worker has to obey (duty of subordination). The right to give orders usually concerns the duties of the worker but also orderliness in the enterprise. It may also cover a transfer within the enterprise. The duty of subordination finds its limit where it would involve a transfer to a lower paid activity. The latter can only be achieved by mutual agreement or by a certain kind of dismissal whereby the employer dismisses the employee, while at the same time offering the employee another job (*Aenderungskündigung*).

Along with the principal obligation to carry out the work specified in the contract, the worker has a number of ancillary duties which either flow directly from the law or have been developed by the labor courts. The scope and content of these ancillary duties, which include the prohibition to disclose employer secrets and the prohibition to damage property belonging to the employer, depend on the circumstances of the individual case. They will therefore be exemplified in the second part of this chapter.

The principal duty of the employer is to pay the remuneration stipulated in the contract or, in the case of workers coming under a collective agreement, the remuneration stipulated therein. Furthermore, the Federal Labor Court has ruled that the employer has the duty to provide the worker with work assignments. Hence the worker has not only the duty to work, he also has a right to work. This is particularly important during the period of notice, where a suspension of the worker is only admissable if prevailing interests of the employer command such action. Moreover, the employer has numerous ancillary duties which, just like the corresponding duties of the worker, are designed to promote the proper execution of the contract. They concern, for example, the protection of the workers' health (Sec. 618, Civil Code), the provision of appropriate working conditions, and the duty of equal treatment.

To provide for equality of opportunity and treatment is an increasingly important obligation of the employer. According to Sec. 75. I, BetrVG the employer and the works council have to ensure that there is no discrimination against persons on account of their race, creed, nationality, origin, political or trade union activity or convictions, or sex. This provision identifies a few considerations which under no circumstances justify different treatment. Thus, the above elements can under no circumstances play a role in the process of sanctioning a worker. In addition to the prohibition of discrimination on certain grounds, the courts have adjusted the general principle of equality, which is a cornerstone of the basic law, that is, of the German Constitution, to the labor law environment. According to the Federal Labor Court, it is a violation of the principle of equality to exclude an individual worker from general regulations that are generally applicable and have a positive effect. However, there is no general right of all workers to receive the preferential treatment the employer may accord to certain individual workers on an individual basis.[8] In addition, the principle of equality does not apply as regards hiring and firing: There is no right to be hired because one is essentially in a similar position as another person who has been hired and there is no right not to be dismissed because somebody similar has been retained.

VIOLATIONS OF THE OBLIGATIONS OF EMPLOYMENT

If the employer or the worker violates the principal or ancillary duties, then they may face certain legal consequences. Disregarding at this point the institutions and procedures involved, the following sanctions may, in principle, be used against a worker who does not fulfill his or her obligation to work at all or does not fulfill it properly or violates ancillary duties: damages, dismissal, enterprise sanctions (*Betriebsbussen*), and contractual penalties (*Vertragsstrafen*).

Damages

Under general private law which, in principle, is applicable to the employment relationship, a person is responsible for any damage he or she causes either intentionally or by negligence to a third party. Since the 1920s it has been recognized that the strict application of these rules to the employment relationship would lead to unacceptable and unjust results. Under the present conditions of production workers often are responsible for assets the value of which by far exceeds their financial possibilities. Under these circumstances the worker will normally not be in a position to fully compensate the employer for damage the worker has caused. This is the main rationale behind the trend to transfer the risk of damage largely to the employer. Doctrinally, this has been achieved by subdividing work into two categories: work that might easily lead to damage and work that is neutral in this respect. As regards the latter category, which is becoming less important, the general rules apply; that is, the worker is liable for intentional damage and any form of negligence. Work of the first category concerns activities with an inherent risk of error even if the worker is generally a reliable person. The cause for the increased risk may, for example, lie in the nature of the material used (e.g., glass) or the work circumstances (e.g., intense heat; road traffic). As regards this category the courts differentiate according to the degree of negligence. Light negligence does not entail workers' liability. In "normal" or "average" negligence the liability for damages is split between the worker and the employer, taking into account all circumstances of each individual case. In the case of gross negligence and intentionally caused damages the worker remains fully liable. Thus, in the end the worker is liable to the employer or a third party (be it a person external to the enterprise or a work colleague) in proportion to the degree of negligence the worker displays in executing his or her duties. This solution would appear to reconcile requirements of social justice and economic efficiency; it restricts the worker's liability considerably without canceling it altogether, which might encourage carelessness. In practice, however, the lower courts have problems in applying these rules developed by the Federal Court, since differentiating between risky and nonrisky work is often difficult.

Dismissal

Depending on the case, dismissal is another possible reaction of the employer to the violation of employment obligations.[9] The law differentiates between "extraordinary" and "ordinary" dismissals. According to Section 626 of the Civil Code an extraordinary dismissal—that is, a dismissal without notice—can be pronounced if there are reasons which, in view of all circumstances of the case and in evaluating the interests of both parties, make it intolerable for either of the parties to respect the normal notice period. All other dismissals are called "ordinary." Instant dismissal is the means of last resort and, according to the case law of the Federal Labor Court, may only be pronounced in the most extraordinary situation. It may be based not only on the conduct or capacity of the worker but also on other circumstances—for example, of an economic nature—which have nothing to do with the worker.

Unilateral termination of the labor contract with no need to indicate reasons was viewed in the nineteenth century as an acceptable practice. Under the freedom of contract doctrine referred to earlier, nobody was to be held in a contractual relationship which he or she did not wish to continue. In case of grave misconduct the employment relationship could be terminated without notice. In all other cases it was necessary to respect the notice periods agreed upon in the contract. Due to the inferior bargaining position of the workers these periods were invariably very short. In the early decades of this century it became slowly recognized that limiting the powers of the employer, powers which could reduce the worker to a mere factor of production, was a social necessity. As early as 1920 the Works Councils Act established the general principle that dismissals had to be socially justified. After the Second World War this line of thinking was pursued, and in 1969 a Dismissal Protection Act (KSchG) was promulgated which is still the centerpiece of employment protection in Germany. In a nutshell, this act requires that ordinary dismissals, which are at the center of dismissal protection, be socially justified. This act is not applicable to small enterprises with five or less than five employees, and it concerns only workers who have completed at least six months with the same employer (Secs. 1, 23, KSchG). The first restriction confirms a feature of German labor law that can also be found in other countries: Small enterprises operate in a zone of diluted law. The second limitation institutes a kind of statutory probation period in the sense that during the first six months dismissal can be pronounced without reason.

Section 1.1, KSchG states that dismissals are illegal if they are socially unjustified. Obviously everything depends on the definition of this term. Section 1 clarifies the concept to a certain extent by stipulating that dismissals are socially unjustified if they are not justified by the "person or the conduct of the worker or by pressing reasons connected with the enterprise." This

177

clumsy wording indicates where the burden of proof lies: The party who claims the exception—that is, that the dismissal is justified—has to prove it. In general terms, reasons connected with the person of the worker are those which incapacitate the worker (for example, a serious illness) for a considerable period to perform his or her duties. Dismissal for reasons related to the conduct of the worker concerns misconduct that is not grave enough to justify instant dismissal (in the latter case the test of social justification is, of course, not applied). The second part of this chapter will apply these general rules to specific situations.

A third category that may justify dismissals, but is less important in this context, is the economic situation of the enterprise. Essentially the employer may dismiss workers if it can no longer retain them in employment for economic reasons. If the employer has to dismiss more than one worker for economic reasons, a selection has to be made which must, in the words of the law, respect "social aspects" such as age, duration of employment, and marital status (Sec. 1.3, KSchG). Over the years an important body of case law has been built up by the Federal Labor Court around the rather imprecise term "social justification." As a general tendency, it would appear that the Federal Court has increased the requirements for justifying dismissal. This trend and the uncertainty flowing from the imprecise wording of the law are severely criticized by employers. In addition, there is increased protection for members of the works council.

These are the basic rules of dismissal protection. But who determines whether a dismissal is socially justified or not? According to Section 4, KSchG this is the task of the labor court. The principle is that the dismissal is valid if the worker does not go to the labor court within three weeks of the dismissal. If the court has duly taken charge of the case and declares the dismissal to be illegal, the employment relationship is considered to have never been broken. The practical consequence is that the employer has to pay back wages for the whole period in question, irrespective of whether the employee actually worked or not.

The labor courts are not the only institution involved in dismissal cases. The works councils also have an important role to play. Only the very basic features of what is a very complicated system can be described here. As a basic rule, the works council has to be consulted before every dismissal, be it ordinary or extraordinary. According to Section 102 of the Works Constitution Act, 1972, any notice of dismissal that is given without consulting the works council is null and void. The works council has to be presented with all the information necessary to examine the case. Further procedure depends on the nature of the dismissal.

As regards extraordinary dismissals, the works council has three days to object. An objection does not affect the validity of the dismissal. However, the employee may have a better position in subsequent labor court proceedings when he or she can point out that the works council is on the employee's side. The influence of the works council on ordinary dismissals is more substantial. In this case the council has one week to react. If it does nothing—and this happens in a number of cases because the council is unable to reply—then it is deemed to have given its consent to the dismissal (Sec. 102.2, Works Constitution Act). If it raises objections, this does not prevent the employer from dismissing the employee. However, it is bound to keep the employee in employment at the latter's request after expiry of the term of notice until a final decision is given by the court (Sec. 102.5, BetrVG). If dissatisfied with this situation, the employer may apply for an interim decision releasing it from the obligation to provide continued employment. The employer will succeed (a) if the action brought by the employee is not likely to succeed, (b) if the continuation of the employment relationship would impose an unreasonable financial burden on the employer, or (c) if the objection raised by the works council is manifestly unfounded.

To make things even more complicated, the works council cannot object by referring to any reason that it might think fit. Section 102.3 of the Works Constitution Act describes in detail which elements may give rise to an objection. The council may object in the following cases: (a) if the employer, in selecting the employee to be dismissed, disregarded or did not take sufficient account of social considerations; (b) if the dismissal would amount to nonobservance of a guideline agreed on between the works council and the employer on the selection of employees for dismissal; (c) if the employee whose dismissal has been envisaged could be kept on in another job in the same establishment or in another establishment of the same company; (d) if the employee could be kept on after a reasonable amount of retraining or further training; or (e) if the employee could be kept on after a change in the terms of his contract and the employee has indicated agreement to such change. Considering the grounds for objection, the right of the works coun-

179

cil to make an objection does not play a major role in practice. The most common reasons for dismissal, such as violation of the labor contract, disappearance of the job, and the like, do not give rise to a right to object.

The objection of the works council represents an additional strategic advantage for the worker: According to Section 102.4 of the Works Constitution Act, the employer has to append a copy of the works council's point of view to the notice of dismissal if it gives notice of dismissal even though the works council has lodged objections. This helps the worker to fight the dismissal. This may help explain why the frequency of lawsuits is significantly higher when the works councils object.[10]

The decision of the court will depend on the question of whether or not it declares the dismissal socially unjustified. If it finds the dismissal socially justified, it will refuse the claim of the worker. This implies that the contract of employment is terminated. If the court declares the dismissal unjustified, it will state that the employment relationship has not been affected by the dismissal. In this case the employer has to pay back wages even if it did not actually employ the worker during the legal proceedings. However, account will be taken of any other income the worker had during this period, including unemployment benefits.

Experience shows that the controversies surrounding many dismissal cases tend to erode any possibility for future cooperation between the worker and the employer. Hence, according to Section 9, KSchG the court may dissolve the employment relationship even if the dismissal was socially unjustified. This can be done on either the worker's or the employer's request. The party that is pressing for dissolution has to show that a continuation of the contract would be unreasonable. In case the court dissolves the contract it has to grant compensation, the amount of which should usually not exceed twelve monthly salaries. In practice it would appear that dismissal protection suits are often entertained to obtain compensation, while continued employment, which in the conception of the law is the main remedy, takes only a secondary role.[11]

Enterprise Penalties

Damages and dismissals are handled by the labor courts. However, with a view to strengthening the cohesion and cooperation in the enterprise it appears desirable for conflicts to be solved at the level where they arise—that is, in the enterprise. For this purpose there are *Betriebsbussen,* or "enterprise sanctions," which are jointly elaborated and administered by the employer and the works councils. They provide a flexible instrument for minor infringements, for which damages or dismissal might be too severe.

Enterprise sanctions are social matters. These come, as has been explained earlier, under codetermination. They are part of Section 87.I of the Works Constitution Act, which provides that the works council has a right to codetermination in "matters relating to the order of the establishment and the conduct of the employees in the establishment." However, according to the—controversial—case law of the Federal Labor Court, this right of codetermination is limited in two respects. First, it only concerns orders that are to be applied generally; second, it does not apply to employer "production-oriented" instructions, or to orders concerning the performance and competence of the worker. In exercising the right of codetermination the works council and management elaborate "penalty codes." Technically these codes are cast in the form of plant agreements. If the works council and the employer do not agree on the content of a penalty code or on its implementation in an individual case, the conciliation committee will decide with binding effect. Enterprises without works councils cannot issue a penalty code unless it is contained in a collective agreement.

The Federal Labor Court has laid down rules that specify in some detail the procedures to be observed in meting out enterprise sanctions.[12] First, any penalty code has to be published and posted at an appropriate place in the enterprise. Second, behavior that entails sanctions has to be specified in detail in the code (e.g., smoking, theft, etc.). Third, since sanctions smack of penal law—that is, of an issue of public policy—the labor courts exercise, in principle, an important supervisory function in reviewing the factual and legal aspects of penalty codes. In particular, courts may examine whether the worker has indeed committed the violation he or she is accused of and whether the sanction is proportional to the violation. In practice, however, the influence of the courts is modest because they will not be invoked. Often workers will be interested in keeping the matter confidential unless dismissal is involved.[13] Fourth, reprimands and fines are the only sanctions that can lawfully be applied. Fifth, the procedure under which sanctions are pronounced has to correspond to the rule of law. In particular, the accused worker must be given a hearing and have the right to legal assistance. Finally, the moneys generated by the fines have to be used for the benefit of employees; they cannot lawfully accrue to the employer. Transfer and dismissal cannot be agreed between the employer and the works council as sanctions under a penalty code. They are considered employer prerogatives that are not negotiable.

Contractual Penalty

Finally, the parties to an employment contract may agree contractually on a penalty in case one party violates the contract (Sec. 339, Civil Code). A contractual penalty is, according to the Federal Labor Court, not a means to preserve order in the enterprise (such as an enterprise sanction); it is rather an instrument to encourage the proper fulfillment of contractual obligations. The main consequence of this view is that the scope for judicial control is more limited than in the case of enterprise penalties. Courts can only exercise a minimum amount of control, mainly in the sense that excessive penalties can be reduced to an appropriate level (Sec. 343, Civil Code).

THE PARTICULAR OBLIGATIONS OF EMPLOYMENT

This second main section of this chapter will examine the question of how German labor courts would treat particular instances of employee misconduct. However, as court judgments are strongly influenced by the factual circumstances of each particular case, it is often difficult to predict the outcomes. In general, labor courts base their decisions on all circumstances of the case rather than on a single factor. Owing to their complexity, it would be impossible to describe the various sanctions laid down in penalty codes or in individual employment contracts (contractual penalties). Therefore the discussion of the various scenarios will draw primarily on the law of damages. The real outcome of many of these scenarios involving dismissal might also be influenced by the consultation of the works council. Irrespective of the legal procedure mentioned above, the works council often succeeds in avoiding dismissals. In these cases the employer may impose a lesser penalty on the employee and no legal action will take place.

SUBORDINATION

Case Scenario

JD, a janitor at the A Manufacturing Company, is assigned the task of waxing office hallways. He completes one hallway. His supervisor, FF, inspects the hallway and says to JD, "Do this floor again." JD replies "No", and walks away.

Analysis

This is a case of the employee violating his duty to obey referred to earlier. It includes the duty to perform work in accordance with the contract and the duty to follow reasonable instructions given by the employer. Basically, the employment contract—and laws, collective bargaining agreements, shop agreements, standard company practice—indicate the type of work that the employee is expected to perform. Within this framework the employer can, on the basis of his authority to give instructions, charge the employee with all the tasks arising in this context. The employee has to carry out instructions and, if appropriate, repeat any tasks upon being instructed to do so. Refusal of the employee to perform the work incumbent upon him as per his contract, despite a previous formal warning, can entitle the employer to dismiss him with notice. Instant dismissal is generally also justified in cases of stubborn refusal to work.

Seriousness. Which reaction of the employer in respect to a violation of the duty to obey would be acceptable depends on the circumstances of the particular case. If this is the first instance of refusal to work, a formal warning would be the appropriate reaction. If JD has already failed to obey reasonable instructions given by the employer in the past and has already been formally warned on this count, termination with notice is in order. If JD not only refuses to work but also insults or even physically attacks his superior, or if he stubbornly ignores repeated instructions, instant dismissal is also possible. There is no serious violation of the duty to obey and thus no reason for dismissal if, on the basis of contradictory shop rules, the employee could have assumed that his refusal to wax the floor again was not a breach of contract. The same is true if the employee could reasonably have expected that repeating the task would represent a danger to his own health and safety or to that of other employees. In case of danger to health and safety, JD would have the right to refuse performance, as also in the case of an order that violates his human dignity. The same is true if the task of waxing floors is not part of his job description.

Mitigation. Provocation by the superior, such as calling the employee an incompetent idiot, may excuse the employee's behavior. When considering the question as to whether the employee can be dismissed on grounds of conduct in a specific case, he must be given credit for long service with the company, in particular when he has worked well and no complaints have been made concerning his conduct.

Enforceability. If the supervisor *asks* the employee whether he will wax the floor again, the employee can claim that he did not regard this as an order that he was expected to obey. However, this is not the case if this is the supervisor's normal way of giving instructions and the employee is aware of this. In contrast, the order "Do this floor again" is a clear, direct instruction which the employee has to obey. If in the past the employer has tolerated the fact that JD or other janitors have refused to wax the floor a second time, JD could again assume that the employer would not consider his behavior to be a breach of contract and grounds for dismissal.

SOBRIETY

Case Scenario

RR, a laborer on the loading dock of B Trucking Company, is observed by his supervisor, JB, reaching into the pocket of a coat that is hanging near his workplace. JB observes RR bring something to his mouth, appear to swallow, and then return it to the coat. JB approaches RR and asks, "What are you drinking?" RR reaches into the pocket of the coat and hands JB a bottle that contains an alcoholic beverage. JB forms the opinion that RR's breath smells strongly of alcoholic spirits and that his eyes are not focusing.

Analysis

This is a clear case of drinking on the job. The consumption of alcohol at work has an effect on perception and reaction speed, on the assessment of reality and one's self, on stamina and reliability, on the willingness to take risks, and on aggressiveness. An inebriated employee is generally not in a position to do proper work of high quality, and at the same time he may endanger himself and others. Up to 25 percent of all industrial accidents in Germany are associated with the consumption of alcohol or are induced by alcohol.

Assuming that RR is really slightly intoxicated, the employer can give him a formal warning based on a violation of his employment contract. The sanctions that an employer is authorized to take in cases of alcohol consumption at work are dependent on several factors. While, in the case of alcohol dependency, dismissal with notice based on reasons connected with the person of the worker is in order in accordance with the same principles that are applicable for other illnesses, it may also be possible, following a previous formal warning and depending on the circumstances of the particular case, to consider instant dismissal on grounds of conduct in the event of drunkenness at work or violation of a company ban on alcohol.

Another sanction is the cancellation of the continued wage payments which are otherwise granted in the event of illness if the inability to work was caused by drunkenness or an accident resulting from drunkenness. In addition, an inebriated employee who causes an accident at work or on his way home essentially has no claims against anyone for the personal injury or property damage he sustains.

Seriousness. The existence of a company ban on alcohol, the degree of intoxication, and the possible impact are decisive factors as regards the justification for dismissing RR. If there is no company ban on alcohol, the mere drinking of alcohol is not enough to justify dismissal. If, however, as a result of a high degree of intoxication the employee repeatedly neglects the duties set forth in his employment contract—for example, by producing poor quality work or insufficient quantities, by being unpunctual or absent without excuse—dismissal with notice on grounds of conduct may be considered following a formal warning. If a company ban on alcohol exists, repeated violation of this ban may justify termination of the employment contract with notice after a previous formal warning. A single violation of a company ban on alcohol may also be sufficient grounds for dismissal if the drunkenness results in serious property damage or injury to the employer or other employees, or if the company image is damaged. In the case of employees who represent a particular risk for other employees or the employer's property in the event of drunkenness (e.g., fork-lift truck drivers, crane operators), just a single minor violation of an alcohol ban, even if nothing happened, may justify dismissal with notice.

Mitigation. Depending on the degree and severity of the illness, its anticipated progress, and further disruptions and financial burdens to be expected in the company, alcoholism or drug addiction may, like any other chronic or recurrent disease, justify dismissal with notice for reasons connected with the person of the employee. When assessing the future development of the illness, any treatment undergone by the employee to combat his alcoholism would have to be taken into account in his favor. The fact that alcohol at work is standard in a given sector (e.g., breweries or the building industry) must also be considered in favor of the employee.

Enforceability. The employer cannot use the consumption of alcohol as grounds for dismissal if it has tolerated this among other employees in the past and the employee was thus able to assume that the employer would not consider his drinking at work as grounds for dismissal. The existence of a formal ruling—a company ban on alcohol—is in many cases the decisive variable.

SECURITY OF EMPLOYER'S PROPERTY

Case Scenario

PR, a clerk employed by C Gourmet Food Company, is observed by two supervisors taking company products out of a packing box, concealing them on his person, and walking out the door with them. He is apprehended after he exits the store, and he admits taking the products.

Analysis

This is clear case of theft at work. Theft or embezzlement on the employer's premises generally justifies dismissal with notice on grounds of conduct or, depending on the severity of the violation of duty, instant dismissal.

Seriousness. According to established case law, the value of the stolen goods is irrelevant, since the theft of goods belonging to the employer, even when of little value, can destroy confidence between the parties. There is thus no difference between stealing something worth $1 and something worth $1,000.

Whether or not the theft of the employer's property is justification for instant dismissal depends on the specific circumstances of the individual case. The aspects to be kept in mind here are the value and nature of the stolen goods, the position of the employee within the company, and the particular circumstances in the company (e.g., several thefts in the past). If the stolen object were lying in a rubbish bin as if worthless, the employee would be able to assume that his appropriation of it would not be taken as grounds for dismissal.

Mitigation. When weighing the interests of the worker and the employer, as is necessary before pronouncing a dismissal, it must be taken into account in the employee's favor if he stole in desperation and for true need, if he cannot be accused of any dishonorable conduct in the past, or if he has considerable seniority in the company. If the employer permits employees to take a small number of items for their own use when leaving the premises, PR cannot be seen as having violated his duties.

Enforceability. If the employer tolerated other employees taking away things of little value in the past, PR could reasonably assume that his conduct would also not be taken as grounds for dismissal.

PEACEFUL WORKPLACE

Case Scenario

MM is a clerk in D Department Store. NN is another clerk in the same department store; he is physically larger than MM. While MM is moving some heavy equipment from one area to another, NN says, "I'm surprised that you didn't ask a real man like me to handle this job." MM, angered, strikes NN on the jaw, knocking him down. NN gets up and walks away.

Analysis

This is a case of a dispute or, to be more accurate, a proper fight. In the event of a dispute between two employees, the employer is obliged to mediate between the two. Should this prove fruitless, or if an amicable settlement cannot be achieved, possible employer reactions include dismissal with notice on grounds of conduct and even instant dismissal.

Seriousness. In the event of a fight the employer can give notice on grounds of conduct to both the attacker who starts the physical violence and the person who provokes the fight. Depending on the circumstances, the physical attack may also be a just cause for instant dismissal. If the attacked person was seriously wounded, or if the attacker used a dangerous weapon, this would constitute a just cause for instant dismissal. Instant dismissal of all the employees actively involved in the conflict may be considered in the event of substantial damage to the employer's property, damage to the employer's business or reputation, or a major threat to the health of other workers. If an employee refuses to continue to work with another employee who was involved in a fight and demands that this person be given notice, the employer can exercise his right of dismissal, but only if it is objectively justified on the basis of the principles stated above (e.g., dismissal of the attacker). However, in the absence of such grounds (e.g., the employee merely defended himself reasonably against attack), the employer must attempt to persuade the other employee to give up his refusal to work with his co-worker in the future. Only if the employer fails in this attempt and serious disadvantages for the employer's business are to be expected may it give the employee involved in a fight notice of termination as demanded by the other employee.

Mitigation. The fact that MM has already been involved as the aggressor in a past fight at work would be grounds for instant dismissal. The fact that the employee has never used violence at work before, that he has been with the company for a long time, or that the employees involved in the fight previously used to be friends does not excuse the attacking employee. However, these circumstances must be considered when deciding whether dismissal with or without notice would be the appropriate reaction. The fact that the attacker is a member of the works council would not mitigate his behavior. However, a member of the works council can only be dismissed instantly for just cause, and the works council must give its approval to such a dismissal (Sec. 103, Works Constitution Act; Sec. 15.3, Dismissal Protection Act). However, if the works council refuses to give its consent, the labor court may supply the necessary consent.

Enforceability. The simple fact that the employer did not take any disciplinary action following similar fights involving the employee in question or other employees of the company cannot be interpreted as indicating that acts of violence are tolerated in the company. The attacker cannot assume on this basis that his attack will not be seen as grounds for dismissal.

188

OFF-DUTY CONDUCT

Case Scenario

TT, head salesclerk for E Toy Store, participates in a white supremacist demonstration. He is arrested for disorderly behavior, and a photograph of him handcuffed to a post and snarling at police is printed in the local newspaper, along with the name of his employer.

Analysis

Generally speaking, the employer cannot place any particular demands on the off-duty behavior of his employees. Private life and working life are two separate things. Off-duty behavior—particularly criminal acts or political activities—can only be justification for dismissal if it harms company interests and if a reasonable employer would be prompted to give notice after justly weighing all the circumstances of the individual case. In this context it must be proven that the objectionable behavior has a lasting and negative effect on the employment relationship.

Seriousness. If the employee were cleared of the charges, his conduct could not in principle be taken as grounds for dismissal. Nor is the mere fact that a court sentences the employee for a criminal act reason enough for dismissal. Dismissal may be considered if the criminal act impairs the employment relationship. This is the case if the arrest of the employee or the serving of a jail sentence disrupts company operations. The employment relationship can also be impaired by a criminal act if, following publication in a small-town newspaper stating the name of the employer, there are negative effects on the employer's reputation; for example, a number of customers avoid the store after the incident or black employees refuse to continue working with this salesclerk.

Mitigation. If the employee has been with the company for a long time or if he was attacked by a group of counter demonstrators, this must be taken into consideration in the employee's favor when weighing all the circumstances.

Enforceability. If the employer has not taken any disciplinary action in the past when this employee or other employees behaved in a comparable manner, the employee may assume that his conduct will not be taken as grounds for dismissal on this occasion. If the employer then changes his policy and the

189

employee is unaware of this, notice of dismissal cannot be given following the first infringement; at most a formal warning may be given as a reminder for the future.

ATTENDANCE

Case Scenario

JJ is a nurse's aide at F Nursing Home. Owing to an illness, her attendance at work has been erratic for two years. During that period she missed 30 percent of her scheduled working days. During the last month she has missed 20 percent of her scheduled working days. All of these absences were excused. She then misses three days of work, without notifying her employer, because she decides to extend her holiday.

Analysis

This is a clear case of unauthorized extension of leave. The obligation to perform the work stipulated in the contract is the main duty of the employee in the employment relationship. If the employee fails to perform this work, then the employer must issue a formal warning before considering either dismissal with notice on grounds of conduct or, depending on the seriousness and frequency of the violation of duty, even instant dismissal. The unauthorized extension of leave can thus be justification for termination. In addition, the employee is not entitled to payment for those extra days on which she has not worked. If the employer has suffered a financial loss as a result of the unauthorized absence, it can also demand compensation.

Seriousness. The length of the unexcused absence (five days or just one day) determines whether the employer can give notice or only issue a formal warning after the first instance of unauthorized leave. The case presented here involves a mixture of excused and unexcused absences. However, these must be considered separately under German law. The time during which JJ was absent owing to illness does not constitute a violation of the obligation to work and thus cannot justify a dismissal on grounds of conduct. Nor can it be considered when judging the unauthorized extension of the leave.

Chronic illness or frequent short-term illnesses may, however, justify dismissal with notice for reasons connected with the person of the worker. This is the case, for example, if there is a negative

190

prognosis for the future state of health of the worker or if the lost time already incurred or anticipated may lead to a substantial impairment of the company's interests, and a balanced consideration shows that the substantial impairment of the company's interests would result in an unacceptable burden on the employer.

Mitigation. Long service, family responsibilities, excellent performance, and no unexcused absences in the past are factors that must be credited to the employee when weighing the situation. In these cases the labor courts will not approve dismissal simply on the grounds of the unauthorized extension of leave.

Enforceability. If JJ has already been given a formal warning for unexcused absence from work on one occasion—in other words, if the unauthorized extension of leave is a repeated occurrence—dismissal with notice will usually be justified. However, if this sort of behavior on the part of JJ or other employees was tolerated in the past, JJ could assume that her conduct would not be taken as grounds for dismissal. Unauthorized extension of leave is a violation of the obligation to work and can lead to dismissal even if there are no rules in writing on the subject.

PERFORMANCE

Case Scenario

HH is a warehouseman for G Distributing Company. G has instituted a program that determines levels of productivity for warehousemen. This program meets accepted professional standards for such programs. Over a period of two months HH fails to produce at the prescribed levels, consistently falling 10 percent below the standard. He is warned that he will be terminated if he fails to improve his productivity within two weeks. He fails to do so. HH claims that the standards of the new system are impossible to meet. He proves that prior to the institution of the new system he was given above-average evaluations by his supervisor for producing at his current level, covering a period of ten years.

Analysis

Quantitatively insufficient and qualitatively poor performance on the part of an employee is a typical reason for dismissal with notice. If the inadequate performance results from unsuitability for the tasks assigned, it may be possible to consider dismissal with notice on grounds based on the person of the employee. On the other hand, if the employee has the necessary personal and technical qualifications, repeated inadequate performance is—after a formal warning has been given—a reason based on the conduct of the employee, which justifies dismissal with notice. In exceptional cases instant dismissal may be justified if the employee deliberately underuses his working capacity and fails to make reasonable use of his strength and capabilities, or if, as a result of inadequate performance, irreparable damage is suffered and similar inadequate performances are to be feared if the employment contract is allowed to continue.

In general, inadequate performance may lead to a dismissal if the performance of an employee is below average. The employer must present and, if necessary, prove this fact in a court case. Mere reference to the professional standards in a program for warehousemen is insufficient justification for dismissal. Furthermore, it must be borne in mind that the employer is not entitled to raise the productivity standards unilaterally if the previous standards were defined in the employment contract, a collective bargaining agreement, or a plant agreement. If the previous standards were defined in the employment contract and the employee does not agree with the new standards, the employer can only apply the new standards following effective notice of termination pending a change of contract (see the above discussion of labor courts). The employee has the right to have the social justification of the change examined in special proceedings before the labor courts (Art. 2, Dismissal Protection Act).

Seriousness. Assuming that the work performance of HH is below average, the following factors and variations are of importance. An insufficient performance of 2 percent less than the standard does not in itself justify dismissal. On the other hand, a performance which is 40 percent below standard makes dismissal a definite possibility. Below average performance over a period of just one week is also not serious enough for the employee to lose his job, while dismissal could be considered after a period of six months. If the performance has improved over the last two weeks, with the result that it is now only 5 percent below standard, then there are no grounds for dismissal. The impact of inadequate performance is important for the justification of a dismissal. Thus, inadequate performance is more serious if it affects the productivity of the entire unit, if it endangers the safety of other employees or the property of the employer, or if inadequate performance causes considerable costs.

192

If the employee does not have the ability—for example, the manual skills—for the work required or to adjust to a new machine, the last action open for consideration is dismissal with notice on grounds of the person of the employee. Before this step can be taken, however, the employer must examine whether the employee can acquire the necessary skill through familiarization or retraining within a reasonable period and at reasonable expense, and also whether the employee is willing and able to be retrained. Furthermore, before dismissing an employee in this way the employer must give him an opportunity to work at a different job if the employee has not already expressly rejected this possibility or the job is otherwise unacceptable to the employee.

Mitigation. As always, long service and good performance are factors that must be credited to the employee. If there is a decline in performance that has come about as a natural result of aging in the course of many years of service, and if the employee's performance is still of use, this must also be credited to the employee. The courts occasionally rule out the possibility of dismissal if the employer has tolerated inadequate performance for years.

Enforceability. The reasonableness of the new performance standard is the most critical variable in this scenario. If the labor court arrives at the conclusion that the new standards do not reflect the average performance, it will declare the dismissal based on inadequate performance to be invalid. If there is no other possible way of making a comparison in order to determine the average performance, the labor court will fall back on the experience of other company employees with the new standards. In this context it will examine whether other employees have also had problems with the new standards.

LOYALTY

Case Scenario

JS, a teller for H Bank, during an appearance on a television consumer information program states that her employer regularly fails to advise customers when they make mistakes in favor of the bank, but promptly corrects mistakes made in favor of the customers.

193

Analysis

This is a case of violation of the obligation of confidentiality on the part of JS. One of the important ancillary obligations of an employee is to maintain confidentiality of the employer's affairs. According to court decisions, this means that the employee must remain silent on company matters if she has agreed with the employer to do so, or if the employer has made it known that certain facts are confidential. Furthermore, the employee may not divulge any trade or company secrets to any persons outside the company, in particular to competitors. Also, the employee must maintain confidentiality as regards facts relating to the person or conduct of the employer or another employee if they could be harmed by such publicity or degraded in the public eye. A violation of the obligation of confidentiality justifies dismissal with notice on grounds of conduct, possibly after a formal warning. In serious cases there may also be just cause for instant dismissal.

Seriousness. If the employee makes a statement about the improper conduct of the employer on a television show, this will have an impact on the employer's reputation and its links with clients. This fact can justify dismissal of the employee with notice. If the employer suffers a loss due to this violation of the obligation of confidentiality, the employee must compensate the employer for it. If the employee acted with the intention of harming the employer, she is even punishable under criminal law (Art. 17, Act on Unfair Competition). Statements that harm the employer's reputation or business may not be made by the employee even if they can be proven to be true. She is of course also forbidden to express such views if they originate in hearsay, regardless of the source. If the statement regarding the employer's conduct were untrue and the employee were aware of this, there might even be just cause for instant dismissal.

The fact that the employee thought it only right to inform customers of the incorrect behavior of the employer is no justification for breaching the obligation of confidentiality. The employee is not entitled to act as the advocate of the public. Even if the bank's practices are illegal, the employee has no right to inform other people outside the company about them. She is only authorized to inform public authorities in cases where she is aware of serious crimes, which it would constitute an offence not to report, or if she has tried to persuade the employer to change its business practices by making complaints and suggestions. These principles apply equally in all sectors and regardless of the position of the employee in the company. However, the employee's statement concerning the employer's conduct is more serious in fields of work and professional groups where statements of this kind have a major impact on the employer's reputation or business, such as in banking.

Mitigation. Many years of service or poor treatment of the employee by the employer or a superior do not justify violation of the obligation to keep secret the employer's affairs although these aspects will be taken into account in the employee's favor by the labor courts when weighing all the circumstances of the case. Members of the works council are subject to a special statutory obligation to maintain secrecy according to Art. 79 of the Works Constitution Act, which states that members of the works council are bound to refrain from disclosing or exploiting trade or company secrets which become known to them in the capacity of members of the works council and which the employer has expressly defined as confidential. If a member of the works council violates this obligation, this generally constitutes grounds for instant dismissal.

Enforceability. In this scenario the existence or reasonableness of an express house rule, or its being made known to JS, is not necessary. The obligation of JS to maintain secrecy regarding the employer's conduct which, if publicized, could damage the reputation or business connections of the employer, arises automatically from the employment relationship as an unwritten ancillary obligation. This obligation can, however, be extended by agreement between employer and employee to cover other matters such as those relating to the personal situation of the employee in the company, i.e., her salary. If the employee breaches a contractually extended obligation to maintain secrecy on a matter as to which the employer has a legitimate interest there may be justification for dismissal with notice.

RESTRICT COLLECTIVE ACTION

Case Scenario

JJ, a machinist at I Manufacturing Company, becomes angry because he believes that his supervisor is treating him and other employees in a disrespectful manner. In protest, he persuades the other employees in his work group to leave work together in the middle of their scheduled work shift and not return until the next day.

Analysis

The collective refusal of a substantial number of employees to work can in principle be justified as a strike in Germany. However, a lawful strike must be based on objectives that can be the subject of a collective agreement. Furthermore, the strike must be organized and backed by a trade union with collective bargaining capacity. These conditions are not fulfilled in the case of JJ. On the contrary, this is a wildcat strike, which, in the opinion of the labor courts, is illegal. Consequently, incitement to join a wildcat strike and participation therein can be justification for dismissal with notice on grounds of conduct or, depending on the circumstances, for instant dismissal. As a rule, the employer has to give employees a formal warning.

Seriousness. Numerous factors can influence the seriousness of the case. A collective refusal to work for one hour is less serious than refusal to work for a week. Long-term refusal to work, violence against fellow workers who are unwilling to strike, acts of sabotage directed against the employer's property, and major production disruptions are causes which, in principle, justify instant dismissal. Furthermore, all the employees involved have to pay compensation to the employer for any damage suffered. If the employee were merely a "hanger-on," his behavior would be less serious than if he were the leader of the wildcat strike.

Mitigation. Although many years of service or provocation by the supervisor do not justify the collective refusal to work, they may be considered as mitigating circumstances. For example, the fact that the supervisor had insulted the employees over a period of six months would rule out dismissal as an employer option. If a shop agreement details the work that an employee is to perform and how it is to be done, neither the employer nor the supervisor can demand other work of the employee. The refusal by employees to do such other work does not constitute justification for dismissal.

Enforceability. Unlawful strikes are prohibited per se, not only because of contractual agreement.

AVOID CONFLICT OF INTEREST

Case Scenario

IB, a systems analyst for J Company, has access to the private computer systems of his employer. Working at home, IB accepts a string of free-lance, relatively routine programming jobs for K Company, a competitor of his employer.

Analysis

The case of IB deals with what is commonly known as moonlighting. In principle, the employee is allowed to do this, but he has no right to enter into competition with his employer. This means that the employee is not allowed to work in the same branch of industry as his employer without explicit permission, neither for his own profit nor for the profit of someone else. This rule is statutory for clerks (Art. 60, Trade Act), but the Federal Labor Court regards it as a general legal principle applicable to all employees. IB has violated this general principle. An employee's failure to fulfill this duty thus may be sufficient reason for instant dismissal; at any rate it suffices for dismissal with notice. If the employee's misconduct has negative effects on the employer's business, the employee is responsible for damage. Instead of compensation for damage the employer may take over the business and the work of his employee (Art. 61, Trade Act) and the employee has to hand over his profits to the employer.

Seriousness. If the employee works for a competitor, he violates his duty of noncompetition. This is true even when no formal rule to this effect exists in the enterprise, when there is no connection between the types of work performed, irrespective of whether or not he is making use of training and skills acquired with his principal employer, and when no trade secrets have been disclosed. If, however, these factors come together, the violation is clearly a grave one, justifying in principle instant dismissal. A violation also occurs when the employee is a shareholder of the K Company. A breach of the employee's duties takes place even when his misconduct has no effect on the employer's business or when the employee has access only to routine information about the employer's business.

Mitigation. Seniority as well as the financial needs of the employee cannot justify the misconduct but will significantly affect the outcome.

Enforceability. Even if the general company rule is unclear and unreasonable, the labor courts hold that moonlighting is forbidden if the employer has a justified interest to avoid competition. If the employer tolerated the violation of this general rule in the past, the employees concerned can reasonably assume that their moonlighting would not be taken as grounds for dismissal.

CONCLUSIONS

The system of industrial justice in the Federal Republic of Germany, as set out above, describes the sanctions the employer can legally impose on an employee who violates his or her principal or ancillary duties. It describes the legal consequences, namely enterprise sanctions, contractual penalties, damages, and especially dismissals, to be used against an employee who does not fulfill his or her obligation to work at all or does not fulfill it properly or violates ancillary duties.

The main mechanism for solving the disputes about these legal consequences is the labor courts. Violations of the principal or ancillary duties by employees lead to legal disputes because the position of the employee is determined by laws, collective agreements, plant agreements, and the labor contract, all of which contain legal entitlements and obligations of both employees and employers. When one seeks legal clarification of an entitlement or obligation in case of doubt, the labor courts are the most important actors in the provision of industrial justice.

Depending on the case, the violation of an employment obligation may lead to dismissal of the employee. Dismissal strikes at the employee's financial stability and well-being. Therefore, the main purpose of this paper is to examine the German law of dismissal in different scenarios that relate to the obligations of subordination, sobriety, collective action, etc. The German law differentiates between "extraordinary" and "ordinary" dismissals. An extraordinary dismissal—that is, a dismissal without notice—can be pronounced if there are reasons which, in view of all the circumstances of the case and an evaluation of the interests of both parties, make it intolerable for either of the parties to respect the normal notice period. This means grave misconduct relative to the employment relationship, and may be pronounced only in a most extraordinary situation. All other dismissals are called "ordinary." In case of an ordinary dismissal the notice periods agreed upon in the contract are to be respected. Furthermore, the German Dismissal Protection Act requires that the ordinary dismissal of an employee has to be "socially justified." This requirement is fulfilled if the dismissal is justified "by the person or the conduct of the employee or by pressing reasons connected with the enterprise." If an ordinary dismissal of an employee is socially unjustified, the dismissal is illegal. The determination as to whether a dismissal is socially justified is the task of the labor courts. Their decisions depend on the sum total of all of the factual circumstances of each particular case, not on a single factor. Thus it is often difficult to predict the outcome.

NOTES

1. For further information see W. Streeck, "Industrial Relations in West Germany: Agenda for Change," Discussion Paper IIM/LMP 87–95, Wissenschaftszentrum Berlin, 1987; Halbach/Mertens/Schwedes/Wlotzke, *Uebersicht über das Recht de Arbeit, Der Bundesminister für Arbeit* (Bonn, 1989); Schaub, *Arbeitsrechts-Handbuch*, 6th ed. (Munich, 1987); Viethen/Schwedes, *Arbeitsrecht in der betrieblichen Praxis 1990/91* (Munich, 1990).

2. See R. Bunn, "Employers' Associations in the Federal Republic of Germany," *Employers' Associations and Industrial Relations: A Comparative Study*, ed. P. Windmuller and A. Gladstone (Oxford, 1984), 174.

3. For general information see Fitting/Auffarth/Kaiser/Heither, *Betriebsverfassungsgesetz, Handkommentar*, 16th ed. (Munich, 1990).

4. See W. Müller-Jentsch, *Soziologie der Industriellen Beziehungen* (Frankfurt/New York, 1986), p. 225.

5. See, e.g., Werner Blenk, ed., *European Labour Courts— Current Issues*, Labour Management Relations Series, ILO (Geneva, 1989).

6. See Gnade/Kehrmann/Schneider/Blanke/Klebe, *Betriebsverfassungsgesetz, Basiskommentar* (Cologne, 1989), p. 72.

7. See M. Weiss, *Labour Law and Labour Relations in the Federal Republic of Germany* (Kluwer, Deventer, 1987), p. 45.

8. See Federal Labor Court Judgment of 3.4.57, in "Der Betrieb" 1957, p. 612.

9. For further information see Viethen/Schwedes, *Arbeitsrecht*, p. 235.

10. See Weiss, *Labour Law*, p. 88 with further references.

11. See, e.g., H. Brox, *Arbeitsrecht*, 9th ed. (Stuttgart, 1989), p. 112.

12. See Federal Labor Court Judgment of 12.9.67, in "Der Betrieb" 1968, p. 41.

13. See M. Weiss, "The Rule of Neutrals in the Resolution of Shopfloor Disputes, Federal Republic of Germany," *Comparative Labour Law Journal* 9, (Fall 1987): 91.

6

ISRAEL

Mordehai Mironi

It is of the utmost importance that the reader be aware at the outset of four unique aspects of the Israeli industrial relations system.

1. Over 85 percent of the Israeli labor force is unionized and covered by a network of collective bargaining agreements. The vast majority of workers are organized within one comprehensive union—the Histadrut (the General Federation of Israeli workers).

2. There are three major categories of employers in Israel: the public sector, the union-owned or Histadrut enterprises, and the private sector. The employers in the private sector are highly organized within several nationwide or industrywide associations and tend to coordinate their activities primarily in the area of labor relations.

3. The main source of employment rights and duties is the network of collective bargaining agreements which consists of national industrywide, multiemployer, and plant agreements. In addition, the Israeli legislature has enacted a broad spectrum of labor statutes that stipulate minimal labor standards for hours of work, paid vacation, sick leave, and severance pay. Two separate statutes regulate the collective bargaining process as well as the process to be followed in the settlement of interest disputes in both the private and public sectors.

4. As compared with other systems, Israel's labor law is still

in its infant stage. For many years Israel enjoyed an industrial relations system which, although completely autonomous and informal, managed to be very active and dynamic; in this system courts and lawyers were considered persona non grata. Thus, for example, although employers, unions, and individual employees could still, before 1969, bring suits before the regular courts, in practice this rarely occurred. Practically speaking, the informal, nonstatutory machinery negotiated by the parties to collective labor relations provided a procedure in which the processing of rights disputes was made possible. The establishment of a specialized labor court system in 1969 introduced formal state machinery and marked not only the beginning of a period in which the law has played an ever-increasing role in industrial and labor relations, but also the birth of a new field of law and legal practice.

In the field of industrial justice it appears as though the parties are still having difficulty in adjusting to the new role that the law and the legal institutions play in the day-to-day employment relationship. Consequently, the legal framework that governs industrial justice in Israel tends to be meager in scope and simpler or thinner than that found in other countries.

OVERVIEW OF THE SYSTEM

Broadly speaking, there are three distinctive models of industrial justice in Israel: (1) the public sector and union-owned enterprises; (2) the nonunionized enterprises in the private sector; (3) the unionized enterprises in the private sector. The differences between these three models are both substantive and procedural. All employees in Israel are covered by several substantive statutory and judge-made regimes that provide protection in certain aspects of industrial justice. The principal protections afforded are (a) the employer's duty to act in good faith, (b) the protection of particular categories of employees under labor legislation, (c) the employer's duty to grant severance pay, and (d) the employer's duty to give notice prior to dismissal.

THE DUTY TO ACT IN GOOD FAITH

The Law of Contracts (General Part) 1973, s39, provides that contractual obligations are to be implemented "in an acceptable manner and in good faith." In the High Court of Justice, Justice Sussman remarked that a dismissed employee might be able to persuade the labor courts that his employer is prohibited from dismissing him in a case where the dismissal is not in good faith and constitutes an abuse of the right of dismissal.[1] In practice, however, the labor courts have not yet developed adequate jurisprudence as to the meaning of good faith. The most that one can say is that the concept imposes very lenient restrictions on the contractual freedom to dismiss; much more lenient than the "just cause" requirement in Anglo-American and Continental systems. Hence, the concrete implications of Section 39 remain a matter for conjecture.

PROTECTION OF PARTICULAR CATEGORIES OF EMPLOYEES

Labor legislation provides special protection to certain categories of employees. The most important are the prohibitions against dismissing pregnant women[2] and soldiers who are returning from regular and reserve military service,[3] the protection bestowed upon members of safety committees[4] and the newly enacted antidiscrimination legislation[5] which prohibits any discrimination in dismissal on the basis of sex or parentage.

SEVERANCE PAY

Under Severance Pay Law 1963 employers are required to pay compensation in any case of dismissal involving an employee who has worked for a period of one year or longer. The compensation for loss of job amounts to one month's salary for every year of service.[6] The law stipulates that the cancellation or reduction of severance pay is permissible in those cases determined by the collective agreement to justify full or partial reduction of severance pay. However, when there is no collective agreement in the employment sector to which the employer and employee in question belong, the court retains the authority to determine if the dismissal justified the full or partial annulment of severance pay. Yet the court must be guided in its ruling by the General Collective Agreement binding the greatest number of employees.[7]

THE DUTY TO GIVE PRIOR NOTICE

In a series of widely acknowledged decisions, the labor courts have ruled that, on the basis of custom, the duty to give prior notice before resignation and dismissal still exists.[8] The length of the period ranges from two weeks to one month. The employer

203

may choose to pay salary in lieu of notice. Only in the most severe cases, such as theft, may the employer be relieved of this duty. Much like the case of the good faith and accepted manner requirements under Section 39 of Contract Law, and in contrast to the Canadian law, there is no case law defining the circumstances under which employers may dismiss an employee without notice. In the several cases that have dealt with this question, the court has ruled that employers are not obligated to give notice in cases where the contract (collective or individual) specifically provides for such punishment (on the grounds that contractual provisions supersede custom) and when the continuation of employment during the notice period is likely to increase the damage caused by the dismissed employee.

SUBSTANTIVE AND PROCEDURAL RULES OF EMPLOYMENT OBLIGATION

The description up to this point has portrayed the legal framework common to all three models of industrial justice. Following is a brief account of the substantive and procedural peculiarities of each specific model.

THE PUBLIC AND UNION-OWNED SECTOR

Basically the model of job security in the public sector and in union-owned enterprises is similar to that of the private unionized sector. The typical collective agreement, the Histadrut Employment Code, and the Takshir (Civil Service Employment Regulations), all incorporate a concept of tenure in their dismissal code that severely encroaches upon the employer' s freedom of dismissal, both substantively and procedurally. The norms regarding the dismissal of tenured employees are divided into three categories: regular or individual dismissal, disciplinary dismissal, and redundancy or collective dismissal. In the context of this volume only the first two are relevant. The public sector, the unionized private sector employers, and union-owned enterprises employ a common model regarding regular dismissal. They differ, however, in their treatment of employee discipline, including disciplinary dismissal.

Substantive limitations in cases of regular dismissal are based on the premise that there can be no dismissal of tenured employees without "adequate cause." The procedural limitations mostly refer to the requirement for prior consultation and,

204

more often, agreement with the relevant employees' organization. In cases where agreement cannot be reached, the matter is brought before a bipartite committee composed of an equal number of employee and employer representatives; the next step is arbitration.

The rights bestowed upon an employee in the dismissal code may be enforced either by the union or by the individual employee. Wrongful dismissal may provide the employee a right to damages or, in rare cases, to reinstatement. The Supreme Court still holds the view that no specific performance of employment contracts can be ordered and that the employee's remedy for wrongful dismissal lies in a declaratory judgment or in damages for breach of contract.[9] This well-established rule leaves only three possible avenues for the wrongfully dismissed employee who seeks reinstatement: (1) to demand that the union bring the case to arbitration, which is not customarily subject to substantive law; (2) to demand that the union, rather than the employee, bring the suit against the employer on the collective, rather than the individual, level on the grounds that the union does not seek to enforce a personal employment contract but to protect the collective framework of dismissal; (3) to obtain a declaratory judgment holding the dismissal to be illegal, and rely on tradition or on job action in order to make the employer act in accordance with it.

In the public sector and union-owned enterprises the third option is used much more frequently than it is in the private sector. The underlying reason for this is the long tradition of reinstatement in the first two sectors and the fact that union representatives in these sectors are relatively less hesitant to pull the lethal trigger of job action.

While regular dismissals are dealt with similarly in the public sector and the unionized private enterprises,[10] the two utilize different models for the enforcement of discipline.[11] This difference may also explain the relatively large volume of litigation in the public sector on the question of whether a particular dismissal was a regular or disciplinary dismissal.

In the public sector all disciplinary matters are regulated by the State Service (Discipline) Law 1963. This law attempts to meet the particular disciplinary requirements of the public sector, which take into consideration public interests as well as typical employer needs.

Section 17 of the State Service (Discipline) Law defines dis-

205

ciplinary violations in respect to an employee's duties as well as the behavior expected of a public servant on the job. Sections 25, 31, and 34 of the law outline disciplinary punishments and their implementation. The various punishments range from light (warning, reprimands) to moderate (demotion, partial wage loss) to severe (dismissal with loss of severance pay, disqualification for state service). The light punishments can be meted out by the minister or general manager of the ministry, while moderate punishments must be approved by disciplinary committees.

These disciplinary committees are designed and intended to reduce the workload of the disciplinary court (responsible for ruling upon only the most severe punishments). Each committee consists of three members, all of whom are appointed by the Minister of Justice. The President of the Court selects the three members who will form a specific committee, while strictly enforcing the rule that no member of the bench shall belong to the same office as the accused. The case is prosecuted by the Public Service Commissioner or any employee appointed by the relevant minister. The committees may avail themselves of sanctions up to a year's loss of seniority or demotion.

The disciplinary courts are empowered to impose the strongest of sanctions, including dismissal. The Minister of Justice is authorized by law to appoint the members of the disciplinary court; these appointments are made from four separate lists of candidates submitted by various organizations, including the State Service Employees Association, which represents the largest percentage of civil servants in the country. The separate three-judge benches are selected by the President of the Court, with the provision that one judge is chosen from the list submitted by the State Service Employees Association. Cases are prosecuted by the State Attorney. Appeals from the disciplinary courts are heard before a sole Supreme Court Justice, who is authorized to dismiss, overrule in full or in part, change verdicts, rescind verdicts, return the case to the lower court with instructions, or uphold the lower court's ruling.

THE PRIVATE NONUNIONIZED ENTERPRISES

The model of industrial justice in the private nonunionized sector represents a completely different approach, in regard both to job tenure and to the enforcement of disciplinary norms.

In accordance with common law tradition the National

Labor Court holds the following view regarding individual employment contracts: With the exception of a fixed-term employment contract, under which the employee has a legal right against premature dismissal, the employer is entitled to dismiss employees at any time for any reason, unless the dismissal is prohibited by special statutory provision or violates the duty to act in good faith.

Similarly, the treatment of discipline reveals the distinctive differences in approach. Only the large high-tech enterprises seem to have employee manuals that address the subject of discipline. Those few which do tend to confine themselves to stipulating detailed rules of conduct. They neither provide procedures for enforcement nor list corollary punishments for violation of the code. Consequently, they may legally utilize only the two extreme modes of punishment—warning and dismissal. In severe violations they may even attempt to refuse to grant severance pay or to give a notice of dismissal.

THE PRIVATE UNIONIZED SECTOR

As mentioned previously, the model that characterizes the private unionized sector differs from the public sector model in the manner that discipline is regulated and administered. In the private unionized sector almost all collective agreements regulate individual dismissal and disciplinary action. The one collective agreement encompassing the largest number of workers in the private sector was drawn up in 1962 between the Manufacturers' Association and the Histadrut. This collective agreement is generally referred to as the Labor Code.

The Labor Code defines in great detail employee obligations, grounds and procedures for dismissal, and the principal disciplinary violations, along with their respective punishments. These include violations such as absence, tardiness, and roll call violations; punishments such as employee placement in another job or on shifts; and obligations such as maintenance of tools and equipment, subordination, confidentiality, proper behavior, and restriction on additional employment (moonlighting) without approval.

The Labor Code includes a central code of disciplinary violations and punishments in which the violations are categorized according to severity. Each group of violations corresponds to a group of punishments. For example, absence without leave or reasonable cause, smoking in an area designated as nonsmoking, and tardiness all constitute one group. The corresponding group of punishments includes a written warning, with or without an announcement on the bulletin board, a pecuniary fine of up to half a day's salary, and suspension without pay of up to two days; these constitute the most lenient of punishments.

A more serious list of offenses includes insubordination, moonlighting without management approval, and causing a fight or brawl. The punishments to be meted out include a pecuniary fine (unlimited), suspension without pay (unlimited), dismissal with advance notice and severance pay, dismissal without advance notice but with severance pay. Repeated offenses lead to increased liability on the part of the worker. Thus it appears that the Manufacturers' Association and the Histadrut created a basic code for disciplinary punishment with several outstanding advantages. Employee obligations as well as definitions of disciplinary violations are set out in great detail. This, of course, affords a measure of stability when implementing disciplinary regulations. On the other hand, the code also maintains a certain degree of flexibility, in that certain violations are loosely defined, leaving a certain leeway for concretization through interpretation. The wide range of punishments correlating to every group of violations is also unique, and is usually not to be found in disciplinary arrangements based on individual agreements or employment manuals.

The basic premise of the unionized sector is that disciplinary action should be under the mutual control of both management and labor. Thus Israel differs from the United States, where employers can apply immediate disciplinary action and labor has only the right to a *post factum* appeal or review through the grievance procedure and arbitration, while the decision handed down by the arbitrator is an independent one.

The Labor Code virtually denies an employer the authority to act unilaterally against an employee who has violated Labor Code norms. Any sanction beyond giving a warning, or in severe cases imposing a forty-eight-hour suspension, must be decided upon by a joint labor–management conference or disciplinary committee. Consequently, the American concept of a grievance, in the sense of a *post factum* complaint by a worker against management, a complaint that is processed by the union, is foreign to labor relations practices in Israel.

In cases where management and labor disagree, the issue

can be referred to the dispute processing procedure, which may include one to three steps of discussion and negotiation between employee and management representatives, one or two steps or levels of bipartite committees, and finally arbitration. As the dispute progresses through the succeeding steps, the proceedings become increasingly formal and further removed from the locus of the dispute and its original protagonists. It is the bipartite committee stage where the vast majority of disciplinary cases are terminated. By tradition, only on rare occasions may the case be brought to arbitration.

The bipartite committee has always been praised as the most important component of the nonstatutory machinery of dispute processing, yet only scant information is available about its mode of operation. The proceedings tend to be nonadjudicative, informal and intimate, somewhat like a small-scale negotiation session. The National Labor Court has ruled that bipartite committees are not required to keep records of proceedings, and the decisions of such committees do not have to include reasoning and must never be made public.

Therefore, contrary to the United States, the private sector in Israel has neither produced rich jurisprudence that can serve as a guide in disciplinary matters, nor has it formed a set of uniform criteria for judging discipline. Seldom does the labor court see a suit brought by an employee about a disciplinary action, and the few that are brought before the court do not facilitate the formation of general standards of disciplinary punishment. Practically speaking, there is no judicial review of bipartite committees' decisions, and similarly absent is judicial review of arbitration awards, since they seldom carry any reasoning. Consequently, court decisions in the area of discipline generally concentrate on ascertaining whether the proper procedures and norms of natural justice were followed. Substantive rulings can be primarily found in litigation over the refusal of employers to grant severance pay to employees who were dismissed due to severe violations of their employment duties and obligations.

THE PARTICULAR OBLIGATIONS OF EMPLOYMENT

The following discussion will concentrate on the private unionized sector and the union-owned enterprises. The public sector model was previously described in order to provide the reader with a full continuum of the industrial justice models practiced in Israel. The private nonunionized enterprises are not significant insofar as industrial justice jurisprudence is concerned. In the area of severance pay and prior notice the nonunionized sector must follow in the unionized sector's steps; the duty to act in good faith has so far served only as a token protection.

The discussion of the ten scenarios draws primarily upon two sources: (1) the language of the Labor Code, especially when regulating discipline and dismissal, and (2) case law regarding the full or partial annulment of severance pay in cases of dismissal on the grounds of improper conduct. As noted above, the Labor Code, the agreement signed in 1962 between the Histadrut and the Manufacturers' Association, has emerged as the single most important contractual document in Israel's industrial and labor relations. Not only does it apply to the largest number of employees in the private sector; over the years it has also served as a model for many other industrywide and plant collective agreements in the private sector. The need to rely on case law regarding severance pay stems from the fact that most disciplinary matters are dealt with by the informal and autonomous procedure of bipartite committees. Only in rare cases will disciplinary action reach the arbitration stage. In any event, the common practice is that bipartite committees' decisions and arbitration awards are neither reasoned nor made public. Furthermore, the subject of employee discipline is rarely litigated on substantive grounds. Hence the jurisprudence regarding the annulment of severance pay is the only reliable source from which one may perceive the courts' attitude toward industrial justice.

The nature of the two sources to be utilized calls for a caveat. The language of the Labor Code serves only as a guideline for the administration of industrial justice. Employees may be subject to a lesser penalty than that prescribed by the Labor Code. In addition, the labor courts come into play only in the harshest cases of dismissal—that is, when employers or bipartite committees decide to deprive the dismissed employee of severance pay.

In practice, many cases of misconduct draw lesser penalties. In addition to this caveat one must keep in mind that the administration of industrial justice is inherently influenced by particular factual circumstances and individual differences. Consequently, any attempt to predict outcomes involves a large degree of extrapolation and speculation.

210

SUBORDINATION

Case Scenario

JD, a janitor at the A Manufacturing Company, is assigned the task of waxing office hallways. He completes one hallway. His supervisor, FF, inspects the hallway and says to JD, "Do this floor again." JD replies "No" and walks away.

Analysis

The duty to obey lawful and reasonable managerial orders is considered to be an inherent and essential element of the employment relationship. Hence insubordination will always be treated as a disciplinary offence which may ultimately lead to dismissal. The only question to be decided is the severity of the offence and the correlating punishment. A regular case of insubordination may be punished by a fine, a short-term layoff, or dismissal without notice but with severance pay. In contrast, an employee who is charged with a severe case of insubordination may be subject to a long-term layoff and lose his severance pay. The characterization of the particular act of insubordination will depend on several factors, among them the nature of the order and of the refusal, the circumstances and behavior of the employee during the incident, and the employee's reason for refusing to carry out the order.

Seriousness. JD's refusal to rewax the floor will be treated relatively lightly if he politely declines or just walks away. In contrast, if the instance of disobedience is accompanied by highly insolent language or a threat against the supervisor, it may be characterized as a severe offence. Such an overt challenge to management's authority, especially when it takes place in front of other employees, is considered to be sufficiently serious to warrant the deduction of a substantial portion of severance pay.

A very important factor in assessing the seriousness of insubordination is the employee's record—whether the incident is an isolated act of disobedience or reflects a repeated behavior pattern. However, previous incidents may be taken into account only if the employee was properly warned. There are several circumstances that may diminish the seriousness of the offence: among them, long period of seniority; the fact that the employee believed in good faith that the order was mistaken or the task was completely outside the reasonable limits of his job description; or the task could seriously endanger his health and safety; or the order required the employee to go about the task in an unnecessarily demeaning fashion (e.g., to clean the floor with a toothbrush). On the other hand, the employee's belief that the work was unnecessary is irrelevant since the basic premise of the employment relationship is that management is authorized to issue work instructions.

Mitigation. A single act of insubordination, where the employee was provoked by the supervisor and the employee had a long period of flawless service, usually calls for no more than an interview accompanied by a warning. Legally speaking, it is irrelevant whether the employee functions as an employee representative. In contrast to many other legal systems, Israeli law does not provide any particular protection against discrimination for employees involved in union activity.

Enforceability. Consistency in enforcing the disciplinary code and other employee obligations is a basic tenet of industrial justice. Hence the failure to have taken action against JD in similar incidents or against other employees who were involved in similar misconduct may militate against any punishment, certainly a severe one. The underlying explanation is that such behavior becomes the norm and replaces the formal code which has fallen into disuse. Should the employer wish to return to the old code and to be able to legally enforce it, the employer must communicate to the workers a clear warning that the policy toward such conduct has changed.

SOBRIETY

Case Scenario

RR, a laborer on the loading dock of B Trucking Company, is observed by his supervisor, JB, reaching into the pocket of a coat that is hanging near his workplace. JB observes RR bring something to his mouth, appear to swallow, and then replace it in the coat. JB approaches RR and asks, "What are you drinking?" RR reaches into the pocket of his coat and hands JB a bottle that contains an alcoholic beverage. JB forms the opinion that RR's breath smells strongly of alcoholic spirits and that his eyes are unfocused.

Analysis

Due to cultural differences, the problems of drinking on the job, intoxication, alcoholism, and drug abuse that occupy an

212

important part of the North American and some European industrial relations and arbitration literature is a "nonissue" in Israel. Until the last decade the volume of beer and wine consumption in Israel was negligible in comparison to other Western societies. Even though these industries have experienced a high growth rate in recent years, this has not yet produced the type of negative effect one may find elsewhere. The fact that our research has revealed not even one single case regarding sobriety on the job or even analogous misconduct make it impossible to respond to this obligation.

SECURITY OF EMPLOYER'S PROPERTY

Case Scenario

PR, a clerk employed by C Gourmet Foods Company, is observed by two supervisors taking company products out of a packing box, concealing them on his person, and walking out the door with them. He is apprehended after he exits the store, and admits taking the products.

Analysis

The offence of stealing from one's employer tends to be seen as one of the most serious cases of misconduct. The Israeli Criminal Law 1977 categorized thefts by a manager or by an employee as more serious than regular thefts, and accordingly attaches to them more serious punishments. In the world of work, theft is considered to be a breach of the fundamental duty of loyalty and is viewed as destroying that trust which is essential for employment relationship. It may often lead to a discharge without notice and a loss of severance pay. Due to the stigma associated with this offence, the labor courts tend to require clear and convincing evidence of it. This is a standard of proof lower than that required in criminal law—proof beyond a reasonable doubt—yet higher than the prevailing standard in civil cases—proof on balance of probabilities. Hence even though a mere suspicion may not suffice, an employee may be dismissed for theft even if acquitted of the same offence in a criminal court. On the other hand, since employment relationships cannot exist without a high degree of mutual trust, the labor courts have allowed dismissal in several instances, even though the employer failed to prove his allegation. However, under these circumstances the employer was ordered to pay full severance pay and wages in lieu of notice.

Seriousness. At least in principle, the value of what is taken by the employee, be it money, goods, or equipment, does not constitute an especially important factor in court. In a recent case of theft in a department store—an industry that is both sensitive and prone to theft problems—the labor court ruled that stealing a penny' s worth of goods is as serious an offence as the dishonest taking of valuable employer property.[12] Nevertheless, one can guess that it may carry weight in the earlier stages of the disciplinary process. A theft of trivial value may lead to a warning, and the value of the stolen goods is likely to be taken into account during the nonadjudicative deliberations of the bipartite disciplinary committee. The fact that the alleged stolen goods were abandoned might call for the employer to make it clearly known that employees are not allowed to take such items off of the premises.

Mitigation. Mitigating factors such as a long record of good service, financial hardship, job problems, and stress do carry weight in the decision whether to deprive the dismissed employee of notice and severance pay. Furthermore, the punishment of dismissal may be seen as too harsh when such mitigating circumstances do exist and the theft in question was of relatively minor value or when the employer falls short of proving the offence. The existence of a practice under which it is legitimate to take home a small quantity of goods or equipment might lead the court to decide that the fraudulent intent required for theft was not proven, providing that the employee act followed the common practice.

Enforceability. As in most other cases of misconduct, consistency in enforceability is vital. An employer who condoned incidents of theft might be required to show that the decision to depart from its previous policy was communicated to the work force. This approach may be more strongly applicable to minor cases of theft.

PEACEFUL WORKPLACE

Case Scenario

MM is a clerk in D Department Store. NN is another clerk in the same department store; he is physically larger than MM.

While MM is moving some heavy equipment from one area to another NN says, "I'm surprised that you did not ask a real man like me to handle this job." MM, angered, strikes NN on the jaw, knocking him down. NN gets up and walks away.

Analysis

Violence in the workplace is another type of offence that has both criminal and tort implications and is treated with a heavy hand in both the collective agreements and case law. Furthermore, the physical inviolability of an individual is perceived to be a basic human right. Thus violence may be punishable even in the absence of an explicit work rule. A peaceful workplace with harmonious or cooperative relationships among employees and supervisors is considered by the labor courts to be an essential ingredient of any successful work organization. Hence the courts have extended antiviolence rulings to cover verbal as well as physical violence. In the present case both MM and NN may be disciplined—MM for beating a fellow employee and NN for causing a fight. Under the Labor Code they may be subject to penalties ranging from a fine or short-term suspension to a summary dismissal (without notice but with severance pay). Given this framework, one can expect that if the incident is an isolated case of violence, MM might be suspended while NN might be ordered to pay a fine.

Seriousness. Sufficient provocation by NN might result in equal punishments for both employees. A serious injury to the veteran employee, involving the use of a dangerous weapon such as an iron bar, or causing damage to property and equipment would tend to increase the evident seriousness of the offence. Such accompanying circumstances would place the incident under the most severe category of offenses in the Labor Code. They would show that the employee is not to be trusted in a workplace that necessitates contact with other people to whom the enterprise has an obligation to provide a safe and peaceful environment. It is of interest to note that violence is one of the unique offenses in the Labor Code, where not only the act itself is taken into account when defining the offence but also the actual outcome of that act. In any case, violence under such circumstances may lead to summary dismissal and loss of severance pay.

The presence of other employees would not change the char-

215

acterization of the offence. But the presence of customers might in fact aggravate the situation, due to the likely harm to the firm's reputation. The labor courts have ruled that a teacher who insulted her superintendent in front of students and a salesman who cursed a fellow employee in front of customers deserved a more serious penalty due to the presence of a "sensitive audience" during the incident.

Mitigation. A record of fighting and violent behavior might certainly justify the immediate removal of MM from the organization; but even in the absence of similar incidents in the past, a clear-cut case of serious fighting without inflammatory provocation might also lead to dismissal. Here as well, lengthy seniority, a previous record of flawless behavior, and personal or family problems may serve as mitigating factors.

Enforceability. Evidence regarding consistency of treatment and the employer's tolerant attitude toward fighting might bear definite weight and would affect the allowable severity of discipline.

OFF-DUTY CONDUCT

Case Scenario

TT, head salesclerk for E Toy Store, participates in a white supremacist demonstration. He is arrested for disorderly behavior, and a photograph of him handcuffed to a post and snarling at the police is printed in the local newspaper, along with his name and the name of his employer.

Analysis

The basic approach in labor law is that off-duty conduct is part of the employee's private life, and his alone.[13] Thus off-duty conduct is not subject to the employer's control *unless* it adversely reflects on the employee's ability to carry out his job functions or on the employer's business. In both cases of adverse effects a dismissal is not likely to be a direct result of the action, but rather the implementation of the employer's conviction that the employee is not suitable for the job. This approach is particularly germane when employees in positions of trust are involved in off-duty improprieties, or when employees who must be looked up to as models (e.g., teachers) are engaged in immoral or highly controversial activity, incongruent with the values that

216

they allegedly represent. It also applies, as in the present case, when the offence might damage the employer's reputation in the eyes of the public or when off-duty behavior may cause unreasonable difficulties with either customers or co-workers. In any case, although TT may be dismissed, he is still entitled to full severance pay and notice.

Seriousness. With the exception of a long-term prison sentence (which is regarded as involuntary desertion) a criminal conviction is not crucial. The unsuitability of TT stems from the fact that his job involves extensive contact with the consumer public and that he must continue to work with co-workers who may resent him. Hence the publicity of his act is the most important factor. A clear acquittal and limited or lack of publicity may militate against dismissal and call for a temporary suspension as a cooling-off period. The principle of freedom of speech and the belief that in modern employment relationships an employer has no right to take a moral stand on the off-duty conduct of employees may lead the court to review the employer's decision with close scrutiny. On the other hand, evidence as to an adverse impact on sales or the deterioration of the work atmosphere at the shop would support the employer's position.

Mitigation. Long seniority and a record of high performance and good relationships with co-workers may count in TT's favor. A similarly positive effect can be obtained by evidence that he has never been involved in off-duty violence or that he was clearly provoked by others.

Enforceability. It is clear that if TT were previously arrested or warned with regard to a similar offence, a summary dismissal might be the natural response. However, given the underlying reason for the employer's decision—the likelihood of serious damage to the business—his act may merit a dismissal even for a first offence, despite no action having been taken against him in the past.

ATTENDANCE

Case Scenario

JJ is a nurse's aide at F Nursing Home. Due to an illness, her attendance at work has been erratic for the past two years. During that period she has missed 30 percent of her scheduled working days. During the last month she has missed 20 percent of her scheduled working days. All of these absences were excused. She then misses three days of work, without notifying her employer, because of her decision to extend her holiday.

Analysis

This particular scenario raises three separate subissues regarding employee absenteeism: (a) the attitude toward relatively long, albeit innocent, absenteeism; (b) the treatment of unexcused absenteeism; (c) the impact of (a) on (b)—that is, whether innocent and excused absenteeism may be taken into account when penalizing the unexcused absenteeism.

Absenteeism for illness or other causes beyond the employee's control is not considered to be a disciplinary offence. If, however, the irregular attendance is sufficiently severe and persistent and is unlikely to change in the foreseeable future, it may bring the employment relationship to an end. The termination of the contract under such circumstances does not come under the heading of disciplinary dismissal or dismissal on the grounds of incompetency. However, it is entirely possible that the court may rule that the employee is unable or incapable of functioning in accordance with the job requirement, hence the contractual purposes of the employment are frustrated.[14]

JJ's absence rate of 30 percent over a period of two years might not be regarded as evidence of her long-term inability to perform her job regularly, especially since under both the statute[15] and collective agreements employees are entitled to relatively long periods of sick pay, coupled with the fact that her absenteeism rate had lately declined. On the other hand, no employer can be expected to tolerate unreasonable absenteeism, even if medically certified. Therefore, JJ's medical prognosis might be highly important in order to establish grounds for either frustration of contractual purposes or dismissal due to incompetence. In addition to the medical prognosis, the employer may be required to prove that the nature of the enterprise or job makes it very difficult for the employee to function normally in light of her frequent absences, and that alternative jobs that might be more suitable for JJ were explored in good faith by the employer, but none was found.

The three-day unexcused absence constitutes a clear violation of the Labor Code. It is considered to be a minor offence and is thus punishable by a written warning, fine, or three-day suspension. Only a long unexcused absence, probably longer than several weeks, would be considered a severe offence justifying dismissal with partial annulment of severance pay. A longer period of continuous absenteeism has been recognized by the labor courts to be desertion, which is akin to resignation.[16] Consequently, the employees involved were not entitled to notice and severance pay.

The attitude toward the three-day absence of JJ will probably not be affected by her previous extensive absenteeism due to illness. That was medically excused absenteeism and it received employer approval. By taking it into account when judging the current incident of absence, the previous absence due to illness would thus be transformed into a culpable absence.

The story of JJ provides a good example in which the difference between unionized and nonunionized enterprises can be illustrated. In the unionized sector it would hardly be feasible to convince the employee representative to assent to dismissal for adequate cause, especially since the collective agreements tend to require a high tolerance level for tardiness and absenteeism as well as temporary inability to adequately perform one's job, due to illness. In the nonunionized sector a dismissal due to an absenteeism rate of less than 20 percent may pass the test of good faith; the same is probably true if the dismissal had been a result of the three-day culpable absence.

Seriousness. The seriousness of JJ's three-day unexcused absence may not be significantly increased by the fact that it occurred at the end of a public holiday. Yet the timing will probably affect her paycheck, as the deduction of the three-day period is certain, while the special holiday payment is in danger of being deducted. In Israel employees are usually paid for public holidays, yet many collective agreements and employee manuals rule that an employee who is absent on the days directly before or after a holiday is not entitled to holiday payments.

Mitigation. Seniority and a good record may play an important role when judging culpable absences. A very long record of good service may carry a lot of weight with regard to extensive absenteeism due to illness. Equitable considerations create certain standards, among which is the expectation that the employer must act with extreme patience with an employee who has made important contributions to the organization during a long period of flawless attendance and performance. This expectation is further reinforced if the illness was even partly attributed to the job itself.[17]

Enforceability. Tardiness and absenteeism are common disciplinary problems. Hence employers are expected to stipulate clear, precise policies and rules on the subject, and to consistently enforce them. Condonation in the form of tolerating similar absences by other employees may render illegitimate any disciplinary action against JJ.[18]

PERFORMANCE

Case Scenario

HH is a warehouseman for G Distributing Company. G has instituted a program that determines levels of productivity for warehousemen. This program meets accepted professional standards for such programs. Over a period of two months HH fails to produce at the prescribed levels, consistently falling 10 percent below the standard. He is warned that his employment will be terminated should he fail to improve his productivity within two weeks. HH claims that the standards of the new system are impossible to meet. He proves that prior to the institution of the new system he was given above-average evaluations by his supervisor for producing at his current level, covering a period of ten years.

Analysis

In light of HH's previous record of above-average performance spanning ten years, it is unlikely that the employer will be able to establish adequate cause for dismissal. The union will probably force the employer to review the standards of the new system or to provide the employee with adequate training, the opportunity for consultation when confronting difficulties, and an extended period to enable HH to adapt. If HH continues to perform below standard, the employer might be expected to place HH in a more suitable job.

Seriousness. The extent to which HH's performance falls short of the new standard is a significant factor. Evidence that his slow pace is causing production to lag or creates safety problems of an unreasonable magnitude may be relevant, especially if the employee is made well aware of that fact and under the circumstances an alternative job is not available. Any sign of improvement may preclude dismissal.

Mitigation. Again, long seniority and a record of above

220

average performance would mitigate strongly against justifying the employer's position.

Enforceability. If there is evidence that other employees who met the old standards try in good faith to meet the new standard yet fail, the employer may not enforce the new standard against HH. This also holds true if other employees suffered from excessive fatigue or illness as a result of their unreasonable efforts to meet the new standard. HH's predicament will be much harsher if other workers easily meet the new standard and surpass it. Under these circumstances he may have to rely on his decade of above average performance and demand an extended period for adaptation or a transfer to a more suitable job.

LOYALTY

Case Scenario

JS, a teller for H Bank, during an appearance on a television consumer information program states that her employer regularly fails to advise customers when they make mistakes in favor of the bank, but promptly corrects those mistakes made in favor of the customers.

Analysis

With the exception of the public service, where this subject is regulated by statute, the question of whistleblowing—that is, employee disclosure to the outside world (usually through the media) of alleged employer wrongdoing—has never been litigated. The dilemma is quite obvious: the employee endangers herself in order to further important social interests while exercising her freedom of expression. On the other hand, she inflicts damage on the employer's business by severely breaching her duties of loyalty and fidelity.

Given the court's uncompromising attitude toward employee loyalty, it is difficult to imagine how JS can escape discipline in some form. Furthermore, the employer might argue that JS could have expressed her criticism using internal procedures, or she could have drawn the attention of external agencies such as the Banks Controller without actively participating in the consumer information program.

It is interesting to note that, in the few instances of whistleblowing that took place in recent years, employee representatives and co-workers sided with management against the whistleblower due to their fear that the information about improprieties might threaten their own reputation or, in some extreme cases, even the very existence of their place of work. Hence the employer is likely to establish adequate cause and secure the consent of the employee representatives for dismissal. Moreover, since divulging business secrets is considered to be a severe offence under the Labor Code, JS may theoretically lose her right to notice and severance pay. In practice, however, the court might well express its sympathy with her courageous act and order the full payment of severance pay as well as salary in lieu of notice.

It is worth noting that under recent legislation public sector employees who blow the whistle on their employers have protection against the possibility of dismissal.[19] The state comptroller may intervene on their behalf and order that they be reinstated with all rights and privileges.

Seriousness. It is unclear whether factors such as the appearance being on a prime-time television program or presence of concrete evidence of public response and loss of business which may be attributed to JS's statement would add to the seriousness of the conduct. If JS's act is perceived to be an illegitimate breach of the duty of loyalty, then in any event it is sufficiently serious to justify the maximum penalty. The extent to which she "went public" would not affect the nature of the offence. Losses or negative public reaction can be presumed without producing actual proof. On the other hand, if the act of whistleblowing is legally protected, these factors become irrelevant. In contrast, factors such as malicious intent, negligence regarding the truthfulness of her allegations, or the knowledge that what she was saying was clearly false would most likely add to the severity of her act. The vulnerability of the industry to public criticism might carry substantial weight as well. Yet the fact that a bank was allegedly involved in fraudulent and criminal actions leaves it unclear whether it would count in her favor or not.

The hierarchical level of the employee in the organization definitely matters. The labor courts have ruled that managers and high echelon employees are to be judged by higher norms of behavior.[20] In addition, information disseminated by high-level managers may be perceived to be more credible by the public and is that much more likely to cause damage to the bank. Finally, one might expect that a manager would have easier access to management as well as the opportunity to exercise her influence over the decision makers, and thus may not need to go outside the organization.

Mitigation. Once again long seniority, a good performance record, and unquestioned loyalty in the past would probably be taken into account as mitigating factors. The fact that a worker in her capacity as employee representative might be accorded a certain degree of latitude to criticize the employer in the context of an organizing campaign or in the furtherance of the collective good might not extend to those acts of disloyalty that fall outside the reasonable scope of union activity.

Enforceability. The duties of loyalty and fidelity are an enshrined facet of the employment relationship. Consequently, publicly accusing one's employer of theft and fraud would be punishable even in the absence of a formal rule.

RESTRICT COLLECTIVE ACTION

Case Scenario

JJ, a machinist at I Manufacturing Company, becomes angry because he believes that his supervisor is treating him and other employees in a disrespectful manner. In protest, he persuades the other employees in his work group to leave work together in the middle of their scheduled work shift and not return until the next day.

Analysis

Israeli labor legislation[21] and case law bestow upon Israeli workers an almost unlimited liberty to strike. Strikers enjoy immunity in the sense that the participation in a strike is not considered to be a breach of the employment contract, and neither the employees nor their collective representative may be required to pay damages for causing breach of contract. Legally speaking, the strike is treated only in the collective sphere, hence the individual employment contract is suspended for the duration of the strike. More precisely, only the duty to work and to be subject to the employer's discipline are suspended, along with the employer's duty to pay wages and salary. Basically these rules are applicable to any strike—even those that take place while the collective agreement remains in force or those of nonunionized employees.

Strikes are always treated as a collective phenomenon. Furthermore, both legal and illegal strikes are similarly immune, at least in the private sector and Histadrut-owned enterprises. The only difference lies in the fact that illegal strikes may be prevented or stopped by injunction. Since 1972 there has been a marked change in the attitude toward illegal strikes. The legislature introduced the concept of an unprotected strike,[22] which is applicable to the public sector (in its broadest definition) and to enterprises that provide essential services. In an unprotected strike the workers and the union forfeit the immunities for strikes that are generally provided under Israeli law. A strike is considered to be illegal (in the private sector) or unprotected (in the public sector) if it meets at least one of the following criteria: (a) the collective failed to give a fifteen-day notice in advance; (b) the strike was not called according to the substantive and procedural requirements set in the union's constitution; and (c) it is a mid-term strike (i.e., when a collective agreement is in force) and is aimed at furtherance claims with regard to subjects already covered in the collective agreement. The current difference between the illegal strike and the unprotected strike is that only the latter is not immune from penalties. Hence unprotected strikers and their representatives may be charged with breach of contract and inducing breach of contract.

Given the fact that I is a private firm, JJ and the employees in his work group will be immune against disciplinary action, provided the court perceives their industrial action to be a strike. It is no wonder that the great bulk of Israeli case law focuses on the definition of strike. Generally speaking, the Courts have opted for a broad definition to encompass any kind of organized interference in the regular production process which has the ultimate goal of furthering collective, work-related objectives.[23]

In recent years, however, the Supreme Court has started to chip away at the cherished liberty to strike. Three examples which may have bearing on the given scenario are worth mentioning. In the first case, the court decided that a collective resignation did not constitute a strike since the workers had failed to communicate clear demands to the employer.[24] In the second case, the court stated that a "quickie" strike called by the head of the workers' committee was not a strike since the decision to strike had not followed the steps provided for in the union's constitution.[25] Although this disciplinary action took place in the public sector, the language of the court could be construed to justify the application of a similar rule to the private sector. In the third and most extreme case, the court decided that a union must pay compensatory damages to customers who had suffered monetary losses as a direct result of a strike called by the union in a negligent manner while breaching the duty of care owed to the employer's customers.[26] It is interesting to note that this breakthrough ruling in the law of strikes came about in the instance of a perfectly legal strike.

The strike called by JJ was short, hence injunction was not the proper remedy. Israeli courts will accept a strike held by a small group of employees. Thus the only questions are whether a work-related demand was communicated and whether JJ was authorized to initiate the short work stoppage. If the answers are in the affirmative, JJ and his fellow workers are immune against any disciplinary action.

AVOID CONFLICT OF INTEREST

Case Scenario

IB, a systems analyst for J Company, has access to the private computer systems of his employer. IB accepts a string of relatively routine programming jobs for K Company, a competitor of his employer, performing the work at his home.

Analysis

The fact that moonlighting is so prevalent in Israel is probably the reason why it is dealt with in the majority of collective agreements and employee manuals. The most common provision prohibits moonlighting without obtaining the employer's prior consent. The Labor Code distinguishes between moonlighting without permission, for which the maximum penalty is a summary dismissal with severance pay, and unauthorized moonlighting that caused damage to the employer. In the latter case the employee may lose his severance pay as well. The Israeli courts will have to rely on the implied duty of loyalty only in those rare cases where the dismissed employee had a fixed-term contract that did not prohibit moonlighting and the employee wanted to challenge the act of premature dismissal rather than the failure to serve notice or to grant severance pay. It is probably in this context, as well as when determining the severity of the offence under the Labor Code, that the court will have to determine whether or not the employer must prove actual damage as compared to potential damage to its business.

225

It would appear as though IB's work for K Company involved routine tasks and did not require the transfer of special know-how which IB had acquired while working for J Company, and as such the situation might be viewed as a minor offence. Cases in which the labor courts ruled that employees were not entitled to severance pay have arisen over either deeper involvement of employees with the competitor—becoming a partner or setting up a competing business—or the actual or potential transfer of know-how and trade secrets such as consumer lists.

Seriousness. From the above, one can infer that factors such as the use of skills developed in J Company, taking an outside job that requires the utilization of technological and business know-how not widely known outside J Company, and a share-ownership or high position in K Company would add severity to the offence. Apparently, the higher the position held by IB with J Company, the less actual damage would need to be proven. If IB is a lower level employee whose position requires no particular trust and provides no access to confidential know-how, the court will tend to require an actual, and not merely potential, conflict of interest in order to sustain summary dismissal and even a partial loss of severance pay.

Mitigation. Many years of seniority, a good performance record, and pressing domestic needs may be taken into account, even in the face of clear evidence of the likelihood of minor damage to the employer. The court may sustain the dismissal, yet order full severance pay as a deferred remuneration for good service.

Enforceability. The existence of a formal rule is more important in this scenario than in most of the nine others. This takes on more importance in cases when it is unclear whether someone in IB's position may cause damage to J Company by his moonlighting. The court may be much more permissive in scrutinizing such rules as compared to cases where the employer seeks to enforce a postemployment restrictive covenant. As in other disciplinary problems, the employee can present a good defence when he proves inconsistency in applying the rule to himself and others.

CONCLUSIONS

The private nonunionized enterprises in Israel and their unionized counterparts represent two extremely different models of industrial justice with regard to tenure and discipline. Practically speaking, the private nonunionized sector operates under the concept of employment at will. The employer is free to dismiss employees unless the dismissal is prohibited by a special statute (e.g., pregnant women) or violates the duty to act in good faith. Since the courts have not yet developed the criteria for good faith, this restriction has remained rather theoretical. As to discipline, the majority of these enterprises do not have a contractually binding disciplinary code that contains a list of offenses, punishments, and procedures for enforcement. Hence, they may legally utilize only the two polar extremes of punishment—warning and dismissal without either notice or severance pay.

In contrast, the unionized enterprises operate under an elaborate and well-entrenched model of tenure that severely encroaches upon the employer's freedom of dismissal, both substantively and procedurally. Almost all collective agreements stipulate in great detail employee obligations, grounds and procedures for dismissal, and a list of principal disciplinary violations along with their respective punishments. The common disciplinary code denies an employer the authority to act unilaterally. Any sanction beyond warning or, in extreme cases a forty-eight-hour inquiry suspension, must be decided upon by a joint labor–management conference. Cases of disagreement are referred to bipartite committees, which tend to be nonadjudicative and informal, and their decisions rarely include reasoning and are never made public.

Consequently, labor law has never developed a rich jurisprudence with regard to discipline. Practically speaking, there is no judicial review of the bipartite committees' decisions. Hence the jurisprudence regarding the annulment of severance pay is the only reliable source from which one can distill the courts' approach to industrial justice.

With the exception of the case regarding sobriety, all the scenarios could have been taken from the local industrial relations scene. The scenario involving collective action does not raise an issue in industrial justice since strikes and strikers are immune from discipline under Israeli law, and the immunity stretches to include illegal as well as legal strikes.

The common thread among the treatment of the scenarios has to do with aggravating and mitigating factors and enforceability. Thus, for example, repeated offenses are likely to be treated more seriously, provided that the employees were properly warned. The likely or actual damage to the employer and a lack of remorse may also contribute to the seriousness of the penalty. Among the mitigating factors that commonly are taken into consideration are long period of service, record of good performance, personal and family problems such as financial hardship or emotional stress. Equity considerations require that the employer act with patience and tolerance with an employee who has made an important contribution to the enterprise during a long period of high performance, or in cases where the misconduct was caused by circumstances that were beyond the employee's control. Israeli law does not call for more lenient treatment of union officials or managers. To the contrary, they are expected to be judged by higher standards of behavior.

Another basic tenet of Israeli industrial justice is the requirement that the disciplinary code be clear, precise, and well communicated to the workers and its norms be consistently enforced.

NOTES

1. Bagatz 257/73 *Zori Inc. v. National Labor Court,* 28 (I) PD 372, 384.

2. Women Employment Law 1954.

3. Discharged Soldier (Reemployment) Law 1949.

4. Labor Inspection (Organization) Law 1954.

5. Employment (Equal Protection) Law 1988.

6. Either with the same employer or at the same place of employment.

7. The Labor Court adopted the General Collective Agreement between the Manufacturers' Association and the Histadrut of 1962 as its guideline.

8. *Hatzofe v. Vilenzik,* 8 PDA 306; *Urbach v. Glezner* 14 PDA 92.

9. *Zori,* supra note 1; Bagatz 380/74 *Salman Salman v. The National Labor Court,* 30 (I) PD 495.

10. Note, however, that under King's Order in Council 1922 ministers retain a residual power to dismiss civil servants. Yet the scope of this power within the highly unionized and regulated public sector is controversial.

11. Dismissal of civil servants for disciplinary offences can be carried out only by the special disciplinary court.

12. *Shekem v. Dugin,* 19 PDA 141.

13. *Freed v. Beit Ya'akov,* 6 PDA 113.

14. *Shmuel v. The Construction Workers Insurance Fund,* 10 PDA 337.

15. Sick Pay Law 1976.

16. *Natasha Muhamad Nobil v. Yizrem,* 7 PDA 64.

17. *Haberman v. Portland,* 11 PDA 346.

18. Bagatz 239/83 *Milfelder v. National Labour Court,* 41 (II) PD 210.

19. State Comptroller Law 1958, s45A-F.

20. *Rozenzaig v. Tekes Katz,* 6 PDA 393.

21. Under Collective Agreements Law 1957 s5.19 participation in a strike is not deemed a breach of personal obligations under the employment contract. Section 24 of the law provides that an employees' organization shall not be liable for damages due to the infringement on its obligations under a collective agreement.

22. Settlement of Labor Dispute Law 1957 s37A-E.

23. *Ginstler v. State of Israel,* 8 PDA 3.

24. Bagatz 566/76 *Elko v. National Labor Court,* 31 (II) PD 197.

25. Asham 1/86 *Koka v. Broadcasting Authority,* 40(II) PD 406.

26. Civil Appeal 593/81 *Auto Plant Ashdod v. Histadrut,* 41 (III) PD 169.

7

ITALY

Francesco Liso and Elena Pisani

For a better understanding of Italian law relating to workplace justice, it is necessary to outline a brief history aimed at sketching the lines along which the most relevant aspects of the employment relationship have developed over the years. This paper will mainly focus on the managerial powers that are aimed at controlling the labor force; in particular we will consider the disciplinary power—the power exercised by the employer in reacting to an employee's behavior that violates an explicit or implicit rule of conduct.[1] This reaction has been expressed by two types of sanctions: expulsive sanctions, leading to the worker's dismissal from the workplace (adopted for the most serious violations), and conservative sanctions, those which presuppose the conservation of the employment relationship.

OVERVIEW OF THE SYSTEM

The development of employers' disciplinary power can be briefly divided into three periods that coincide with major historical watersheds in the history of Italy. The first period, from the unification of the nation (1861) to the beginning of the fascist period (1922); the second, the fascist era (1922–43); and the third, beginning when the new republican constitution was implemented (1948).

THE EARLY PERIOD

In the first period there was a very limited number of disciplinary rules relating to the employment relationship. The 1865 code, based on the Napoleonic code, had only a very brief section on the contract of employment, which was defined as a contract by which the subject committed himself to work under somebody else's orders (Art. 1627). In accordance with the antifeudalistic ideology, inspired by the need for full mobility of all the production factors, the civil code only stated that "nobody can commit himself to work under somebody else's orders except for a fixed term or for a specific work" (Art. 1628). There were no other rules that bound the contractual parties, and therefore the principle of full freedom of contract was guaranteed. Though the code provided nothing about contract termination, from this basic principle the practice was established that each party could terminate the contract at his or her will, provided notice was given (the same principle applied to renting a house).

Under the mask of the free contract of employment—that is, of the assumed parity between the two parties to a contract and, consequently, of their capacity to autonomously determine by agreement every condition of the contractual relationship—it was easy to legitimize all situations in which the capitalist could take advantage of economic power and set up business activity through the utilization of the weaker party's work. Therefore, the disciplinary power was not explicitly recognized in the law, but originated from the relationships established within the firm. Indeed, in the collective agreements themselves, when collective bargaining started to develop the existence of such power was taken for granted.

Such acknowledgment could also be found in the jurisprudence of the college of arbiters (*probiviri*).[2] At the beginning of the century, when labor law began to develop, the idea that disciplinary power was implicit in the employment relationship was also shared by the legal theory that legitimized disciplinary power on the basis of: (1) freedom of contract; (2) the necessity of discipline in the production process (Barassi: "Industrial organizations require order and discipline"); (3) the inefficacy of traditional judicial remedies (compensation for damages and cancellation of the contract) in employment relationships, these being inappropriate in counteracting violations of minor degree,

231

especially in an area where it was often difficult to quantify the damage. In the early period disciplinary rules had only two types of sanctions: fine and dismissal. Afterward the spectrum was expanded and included admonition and suspension.

Some of the principles that in the future would characterize the area of disciplinary sanctions were worked out and affirmed in the cases decided by the early arbitrators—for example, the principle of proportionality between disciplinary sanction and violation; the principle that dismissal as a disciplinary measure is justified only when the violation is so serious that it becomes incompatible with the employee's remaining in the workplace; the principle that fault must be the ground for sanctions.

While in the private sector the norms were rudimentary and the disciplinary power was legitimized by the framework of private autonomy, the situation was different in the public sector, where there was extensive legislation. The law explicitly granted public officials disciplinary power and established a full set of disciplinary sanctions. In this area, according to the prevailing opinions (which excluded the view that the relationship between the public authority and its employees was based on parity, as in the case of a contract), the disciplinary power was conceived as the consequence of the sovereign authority of the state.

The emergence of societal concern about workers' working and living conditions at the turn of the century (later than in other countries, due to delayed industrial development) generated legislation regulating some of the most intolerable aspects of the workers' conditions. In 1883 protective rules for work in the mining sector were passed; in 1898 compulsory insurance for work injuries was instituted; and in the following year rules for the prevention of work accidents were introduced. In 1902 women workers and—more extensively—child labor were given legislative protection, and in 1907 Sunday rest was regulated. The employment relationship, however, remained basically unregulated.

Indeed, immediately after the end of World War I basic laws relating to the employment relationship were enacted (1919), and in 1924 the same area was extensively regulated. However, the focus was concentrated on white collar workers, as these employees (at that time only a small number) were not organized, and therefore were not affected by the results of collective bargaining. In the legislation enacted in 1924 disciplinary power was not explicitly regulated, with the exception of the area of dismissal, where it was stated that the employee could be fired without notice if there was a just cause (when the fault was so serious that the employment relationship could not be continued, Art. 9). In this case the employee would lose the right to a specific indemnity that in the following years became known as dismissal indemnity, which went into effect when dismissal was given with due notice.

THE FASCIST PERIOD

In contrast to the first period, the fascist period was characterized by extensive legislation. In the employment relationship area, this was carried out mainly through collective bargaining, handled by unions, which under the totalitarian system had been absorbed into the state context.

Of special interest for our study, employers and union representatives were required to indicate "clear clauses regarding disciplinary rules" (Sec. 11 of the Labor Charter [*Carta del Lavoro*], 1927; in a 1928 law it was also stated that collective agreements could not be concluded if a regulation on disciplinary rules was not included). It is worth emphasizing here that in this period favorable conditions were created for a clear-cut definition of disciplinary power in private employment. In fact, the existing political and legal climate emphasized the supreme power of the employer within the firm organization. The ideology of freedom of contract was then hidden under a framework where a special emphasis was given to the employer's power, which was legitimized as a "function of national interest."

In the Labor Charter, in which the principles of the corporatist state were highlighted, a specific section was devoted to disciplinary power. This was Art. 19: "Disciplinary violations and employee's behavior that endanger the normal activity of the firm will be punished according to their gravity by fine, suspension from work and in the most serious cases by dismissal without notice and indemnity. The cases when the entrepreneur can inflict a fine, suspension or immediate dismissal without notice will be specified." This context explains why on the one hand disciplinary rules became widespread in all the firms; and, on the other hand, the contents of such rules became more articulated.

The 1942 civil code, enacted at almost the end of this period, included a more detailed regulation of the employment relationship that summed up the past experience and made explicit references to collective agreements as sources of law. This legislation had an important innovative feature: it applied not only to nonmanual employees, but also to manual workers and to the newly described position of manager/executive (*dirigente*).

In the new code, in tune with the corporatist ideology, the firm was perceived as an authoritarian and hierarchical structure where the employer was committed to follow "the principles of the corporatist state and the obligations deriving from them; as a consequence, he had to give account to the state of the decisions taken in the area of production and in the market" (Art. 2088). In other words, the firm was formally subordinated to the public interest, which reflected a centrally controlled economy, while, within the firm the employer, perceived as the "head," was granted a high degree of freedom (Art. 2086). This freedom of action was objectively emphasized by a system where industrial conflict was severely limited (strikes and lockouts were sanctioned penally) and, most important, ignored at the shop floor level (the suppression of the internal committee [*commissione interna*] was one of the first actions of the fascist regime). These principles were carried out in the name of solidarity between opposing interests of employers and employees and in the name of their subordination to the superior interests of the nation.

The civil code clearly stressed that the supremacy of the employer is the founding principle of the employment relationship ("The entrepreneur is the head of the firm and his collaborators are hierarchically subordinated to him," Art. 2086). The employee is "obliged to cooperate within the firm, where he works as a dependent and under the direction of the employer" (Art. 2086); the employee has to follow the dispositions regulating the execution of his work and the disciplinary work rules that are given by the employer and his staff, who are the employee's hierarchical superiors (Art. 2104).

The work organization (in particular as far as the exercise of powers in the employment relationship are concerned) was not subjected to specific rules, except for marginal areas. The firm, therefore, became the place where, for ideological reasons, the employer's power was emphasized.

In summary, the civil code emphasized the basic principles functional to the work organization that were applied within the firm (hierarchy, obedience, disciplinary power, unrestrained power of dismissal) and created an effective framework for the control of the labor force. And, though the legislative framework emphasized certain elements for ideological reasons, it reflected a faithful image of the typical employment relationship of the time.

In the area of disciplinary power the civil code stated that violators could be punished with disciplinary sanctions according to the seriousness of the violations and in compliance with the corporatist provisions (Art. 2106), that is, the provisions of the collective agreements. The code also confirmed what the law on private employees and collective agreements already stated: the possibility of immediate dismissal without notice for reasons that did not allow for the continuation of the employment relationship (Art. 2119).

FROM THE FOUNDATION OF THE REPUBLIC TO THE PRESENT

In the period that followed the fall of the corporatist regime, the regulation of discipline in the employment relationship operated in a legal system that was inspired by principles opposed to those that had characterized the previous period. These were solemnly proclaimed in the constitution enacted in 1948, where the need for equality among citizens was affirmed. It was stated that the aim of the republic was to remove the social and economic obstacles that restrict freedom and equality among citizens and prevent the fulfillment of the human being and the effective participation of all workers in the political, economic, and social life of the nation (Art. 3.2).

The workers' right to organize (Art. 39) and the right to strike (Art. 40) were recognized; on the other hand, employers were not given the right to lock out, in accordance with the principle of substantive equality. The constitution also stated that economic activity cannot be in conflict with social utility and cannot be performed in ways that endanger safety, freedom, and human dignity (Art. 41.2).

In other words, the new constitution rejects the rigid hierarchical conception of the employment relationship that was designed in the civil code. The opposing interests underlying labor–management relations within the firm are openly recognized, and therefore the conflictual nature of the relations within the enterprise is also recognized, while the settlement of the conflict is left to the free interaction of the parties. However, the

235

statement of certain values (even when so solemnly made) is not sufficient per se to provide for their effective implementation. In fact, in practice the conditions inside the factories did not change, even though workers had gained, through a national agreement signed in 1943, the reinstatement of the internal committees and therefore a limited bargaining power within the firm.

Indeed, the constitutional principles had little impact on how employment relationships were handled in day-to-day practices; the attitude of the jurists, who were not at all inclined to discuss the dogma of entrepreneurial prerogatives, contributed to the very limited impact of the constitution. The collaborative and paternalistic approach continued to characterize the ideology of the personnel offices within the firms. In practice, particularly in the 1950s, this attitude was expressed by the recurring practice of discrimination against union activists and dismissals; in brief, the employer had complete control over the labor force. The weakness of the trade union movement induced the leftists in Parliament to work out political proposals for the enactment of protective legislation and a worker's statute. Di Vittorio, the secretary of the major union, launched an appeal: "The constitution must go beyond the gates of the enterprise."

This goal began to be realized in 1966, in a period when the government was opened to an important force of the left (the Socialist Party) and the union movement acquired substantial weight. In 1966 law 604 met a long-standing union demand: the principle that dismissal cannot be at will, or *ad nutum* (literally, "with a sign of the head"). It must always be justified. This principle had been anticipated in a 1947 national collective agreement for the industrial sector and had been confirmed, with significant changes, in 1950 and 1965. The law, however, was deemed necessary for three main reasons: (1) the previous agreement covered only industrial workers; (2) it was binding only for those employers who were members of the association which had signed the agreement; and (3) its practical implementation resulted in a very disappointing experience.

The law established that there cannot be dismissal without just cause or justifiable reason. The concept of just cause, already stated in the civil code, Art. 2119, as "any cause which does not permit the relationship's continuation, not even temporarily," implies serious contractual violations or factors outside the employment relationship that eliminate trust between the

236

parties. Collective agreements enumerate several cases in which dismissal for just cause is allowed (see, below, the collective agreement in the metalworkers sector). Dismissal for just cause does not require notice.

Justifiable motive for dismissal can be subjective when related to a major contractual violation, or objective when caused by an economic or production-related reason. In both cases notice of dismissal is required. The burden of proof of just cause and justifiable motive is always on the employer's side. Objective justifiable reasons can be invoked only in cases where the employee cannot be utilized in other equivalent jobs within the firm.

The 1966 law also established that termination of the employment contract due to political, religious, or union activity is void, and therefore the employee has the right to be reinstated. In case of dismissal without just cause or justifiable motive, the employer can choose between reinstating the employee or paying a fine equal to a minimum of five and a maximum of twelve months' pay, based upon seniority of the employee and the size of the firm. The 1966 law also fixed procedures for dismissal. For instance, dismissal must be done in writing. The employee has the right to demand, within eight days, the reasons for dismissal, and the employer must give a written answer within five days. Within sixty days the employee may choose to challenge the dismissal.

At last an archaic principle of individualistic liberalism which the code itself had kept in force (despite its proclaimed ideology of social cooperation) was repealed. This principle was that, in case of termination of the employment contract, the two parties to the employment relationship were equal. Contrary to its apparent evenhandedness, this rule gave the employer a most effective tool for controlling the labor force.

The 1966 law showed greater understanding of the spirit of the constitution and reversed the approach established in the civil code insofar as it recognized the different positions of the parties to the employment contract. The purpose of the law was to balance the employer's interests in manpower flexibility with the employee's opposing interests in job security. In Italy, where labor market conditions have always been characterized by a mismatch between supply and demand, job security has been very important to the employee. According to the law, the employer's decision to dismiss can be challenged. The entrepreneur's power is not the source of its own legitimacy. This legiti-

237

macy now has to be based upon the need for efficient production, which has become not only the ground for exercise of the entrepreneur's power, but also the reference point for challenges to the employer's decisions.

The law, despite its importance in principle, had two limitations. First, an employer who has decided on a dismissal without just cause or justifiable motive was free to choose either to reinstate the employee or to pay an indemnity, once the judge has recognized the dismissal as unlawful. Thus, entrepreneurial power is not limited in its applicability, as its unlawful exercise is only loaded with an extra cost. Second, the new law had a rather restricted scope, as all employees in firms with less than thirty-six employees were excluded, and these small firms constitute the backbone of economic activity in Italy.

The real turning point occurred with the law passed in 1970 (law 300, the so-called Workers' Statute), during a period of strong political and social upheaval when the unions were gaining power inside workplaces. In brief, the law regulated in detail the disciplinary power (in its broader meaning) inside the workplace. The objective was to subject to some restraint managerial power, which until then had been practically unrestricted. This goal was pursued in two ways. The first way was to favor the formation of union structures within the firm by giving them certain rights designed to counter the employer's power. Among these rights was the right to set up union representatives in the workplace and the right to file suits in labor courts (for unfair labor practices). The second way was to limit those practices of the employer that experience had shown to be harmful to the dignity and freedom of the employee; these powers were all related to the direct or indirect control of the work force by the personnel department.

An example of the limits on employer power can be found in the controls established on the power of plant guards (Art. 3). For the same reasons, the manipulative control of cultural, recreational, and welfare activities unilaterally exercised by the firm was impeded (Art. 11). It was forbidden to carry out investigations into the employee's private life and personality that were not relevant for the evaluation of the employee's professional skills (Art. 8). New regulations were included regarding control over the employee's behavior. For instance, employees on sick leave could be checked on only by doctors of the National Health Services (Art. 5); searching at the exit gates of the firm was allowed only in limited cases and was to be performed in established ways (Art 6). It was forbidden to use audiovisual and other devices for the remote monitoring and control of employees (Art. 4). Employer discriminatory provisions were banned (Art. 15) and a specific procedure for the exercise of disciplinary power was provided for (Art. 7).

The law did not deny that the disciplinary function and the power to control were essential in the productive unit, but forbade certain paternalistic and authoritarian means of exercising them. In the new legislation the needs of the firm are not something that only the employer can determine, or something that is a priori lawful. These needs have to be based on real technical and functional requirements, which must in any event respect the dignity and freedom of the employee.

The impact of this law on personnel management has been considerable, especially if one considers that an important amendment was made to the law on individual dismissals. Unlawful dismissal is no longer punished only with an indemnity; reinstatement of the employee is required (Art. 18). The employer is therefore prevented from unlawfully terminating the employment relationship.

In conclusion, what we want to emphasize is that in previous historical periods entrepreneurial powers enjoyed an extensive range of action, first through the philosophy of freedom of contract and then through their full and formal legitimization, with no real limits from the law. With the law on individual dismissals and then with the Workers' Statute, the exercise of the entrepreneurial powers relevant to labor-force control has been subjected to regulatory provisions.

The new law affects the employment relationship by reducing the subjection of the employee and weakening the fiduciary and personal features that characterized the past experience. The courts, however, have not always endorsed this approach, and it is still possible to find decisions that are based on an old model of the employment relationship.

It should be emphasized that the Workers' Statute applies only to units with more than fifteen employees. To be more precise, fifteen is the threshold only for the application of union rights and for the employee's right to be reinstated, but clearly the absence of unions makes enforcement of the individual worker's legal rights more difficult.

The number of firms to which the Workers' Statute does not

apply is quite large. The small firms sector, which traditionally had always been very strong and extensive, was left out. In the 1981 census the percentage of workers employed in firms with less than sixteen employees was around 47 percent. The manufacturing system that operates in many Italian regions can also be an unintended consequence of the legal protection given to the employees of larger enterprises (Piore and Sabel, 1984). The law, because of its rigidities, certainly contributed to a remarkable phenomenon of firm decentralization—that is, splitting into smaller units, each employing less than sixteen employees.

Because the areas not covered by that legislation were so large and had expanded in recent years, the political demand for an extension of the Workers' Statute to smaller units increased. The demand has been in part accommodated by a new law (180/1990) that increases the coverage of legal restraints on individual dismissals, with the exception of domestic work and top management. But in smaller firms the law provides for indemnity, not reinstatement.

CURRENT LAW AND COLLECTIVE AGREEMENTS

At this point we should set out some conclusions regarding our discussion thus far. For this purpose, we will now sketch a synthetic picture of the rules concerning the exercise of the employer's disciplinary power. We must make a distinction between provisions of law and provisions of collective agreements. These are not alternative sources but reciprocally integrating sources.

Provisions of Law

The law provides that the employer can exercise its disciplinary power when the employee violates his or her obligations of diligence and loyalty (Art. 2106, civil code). The obligation of diligence concerns the performance of work with the diligence required by the nature of the work and by the interest of the enterprise, as well as the obligation to comply with the orders issued by the employer for the performance of the work and for the orderly functioning of the enterprise (Art. 2104). Loyalty includes the prohibition from engaging in business in competition with the employer and publicizing information concerning the organization and the methods of production, or using such information in a way that may damage the enterprise itself (Art.

2105). This is the set of norms that the law explicitly lays down regarding the employee's obligation of loyalty. However, both legal doctrine and case law expand its meaning and extend the prohibition to any behavior that may cause damage to the interests of the enterprise. In addition, Article 2106 lays down the principle of the proportionality of the sanction to the gravity of the violation; the implementation of this principle is left to collective agreements.

Substantial and meaningful rules that add to the civil code are contained in the Workers' Statute (law 300 of May 20, 1970). Article 7 of this law provides that:

1. The employer has to post disciplinary rules. Leading case law indicates that compliance with this provision constitutes an essential condition for the exercise of the disciplinary power (Cassation, S.U. n. 1208/1988). In other words, the violation of the publicity rule makes for the ineffectiveness of a sanction.

2. The posted rules must concern the procedures that must be followed, and above all they must list the violations and related disciplinary measures. In this way a fundamental principle of civilized jurisprudence is affirmed in the employment relationship, which is similar to the principle stated in criminal law.

3. The posted rules must be consistent with what is provided for in collective agreements, if they exist. The prevailing opinion is that this provision confirms that the disciplinary power is fully recognized. That is, it is not only power to react, but also power to indicate what behaviors are relevant.

4. With the exception of disciplinary dismissal, there cannot be disciplinary sanctions that result in the permanent transformation of the working relationship (for instance, demotion or pay reduction); moreover, a fine cannot exceed four hours' basic pay, nor can the suspension from work and from pay be longer than ten days.

5. The employer cannot impose any disciplinary sanction unless the employee is informed about the charges and can speak in his or her own defense. Notice of the alleged violation must be given in writing—with the exception, of course, of a verbal reprimand.

6. The employee can request assistance from his or her union.

With (5) and (6) another important principle of civilized jurisprudence is affirmed; the principle aimed at guaranteeing respect of the right to defense. In other words, it is not permitted to inflict a sanction on persons without allowing them to explain their reasons.

7. In any event, disciplinary sanctions (with the exception of oral reprimand) cannot be applied sooner than five days after written notice of a violation.

8. Disciplinary sanctions cannot be taken into consideration beyond two years after the violation. This provision plays an important role, especially in the cases of recidivism, which collective agreements consider as an aggravating factor.

9. The employee, if he or she does not choose to challenge a disciplinary sanction through the court, can have constituted, within twenty days from the notification of the sanction inflicted on him, and through the union if he chooses to do so, the establishment by the provincial labor branch of a conciliation and arbitration board. This board consists of a representative from each side and a third member chosen by the two parties, or, if there is no agreement as to the third member, one selected by the director of the labor branch. The disciplinary measure is suspended until a decision is reached by the board. The disciplinary sanction is also suspended when it is the employer who applies to the judge in order to confirm the legitimacy of the sanction.

As can be seen, the rules introduced in 1970 have promoted a major change in quality, in comparison to the previous situation. The "proceduralization" along the lines that we have just illustrated implies a noticeable structural modification of the employer's disciplinary power. The feature of an immediate the employer reaction which gave practical effectiveness to the employer's exercise of power, has disappeared.

As far as the optional procedures of conciliation and arbitration provided for by the law are concerned, we must stress that they have been rarely followed, though workers are given an incentive to use them by the suspension of the sanction when such procedures are initiated. Unfortunately, no empirical research has been carried out in this area and therefore information is very limited.

Generally, due to the traditionally adversarial philosophy of labor–management relations, arbitration in labor disputes has never had a significant role in Italy. The 1973 law on labor disputes proceedings acknowledged the reality of the scarce use of arbitration and preferred resort to courts. To our knowledge, resort to the arbitrators' board in the matter of disciplinary sanctions is invoked only when the employee and his or her lawyer believe that the case has a poor chance in court, and are trying to delay the sanction in the hope of solving the dispute through settlement on more favorable terms (reduction of sanction). The procedure for arbitration is therefore used more with conciliation in mind than for its own sake.

As already explained, the disciplinary power can be exercised not only through the imposition of "conservative" sanctions (i.e., those sanctions that do not imply employment contract termination), to which the provisions which we have discussed immediately above refer, but also through the imposition of sanctions terminating the employment contract.

We have already illustrated the oldest of the sanctions used by the employer in reaction to very serious violations: termination for just cause, without notice, as laid down in Article 2119 of the civil code. As in the past, the concept of just cause—even though with some mitigating factors, due to the subsequent evolution of the legislation—continues to refer not only to employee conduct that can be counted as a nonfulfillment of the obligations connected with the employment contract, but also to any conduct or fact that undermines the employer's trust in the employee.

Case law, in applying this concept, insists on the need to proceed to an evaluation of all the elements of the specific situation. The just cause concept cannot be invoked, cases affirm, in presence of an abstract evaluation only; it is necessary to evaluate the nature and the quality of the individual employment relationship, the parties' position, the employee's job content, and the loyalty implied by the job and by the type of enterprise. To justify dismissal the violation, in both its objective and subjective features, must be so serious that it does not permit the continuation of the employment relationship.

Moreover, the employer's disciplinary reaction amounts to discharging the employee for a justified motive (law 604/1966) when such employee has seriously failed to fulfill the obligations deriving from the employment contract. In this case a notice period is provided, insofar as the reasons causing the termination are less serious than those allowing the termination for just cause.

One of the main problems posed by the provisions of the Workers' Statute in matters of disciplinary power has been whether it could be used in the cases of dismissal for disciplinary reasons. The most restrictive interpretation, which the law

243

applies only to disciplinary measures with the exclusion of dismissal, has not prevailed. The controversy ended with a decision of the Constitutional Court (n. 338/1982) that stated that the first three paragraphs of the law (which guarantee the right of employees to be informed about disciplinary rules, to be informed about the charges, and to speak in their own defense and to be assisted by the union) must be applied to all dismissals having disciplinary character.

The solution of this controversy has generated another issue: whether this interpretation of the law should be applicable to small firms, to which regulations on dismissal were not applicable. This problem has been solved by the Constitutional Court with a recent decision (427/1989). The court decision attempted to fill the vacuum left by the exclusion of small firms from the legislation that regulated dismissal. The importance of this decision has now been overshadowed by a new law (law 108/1990) that has extended the protection against unjustified dismissals to all employees who were previously excluded (the only exceptions are domestic workers and managers/executives). As a consequence of this law, the protection of the employee does not now depend on the number of employees employed in the firm. Firm size is relevant only to the scale of remedies (indemnity or reinstatement). In the area where the law does not provide compulsory reinstatement, the employee, before going to court, is requested to try conciliation.

Discipline Established in Collective Agreements

Collective labor contracts regulate employers' disciplinary power, often by reproducing or integrating what the law already provides in the matter of procedural rules. Although there is not space here for a detailed comparative analysis of disciplinary provisions in specific labor contracts, we think it is worthwhile to give at least one example. This will be the provisions of the national contract of the private sector metalworkers—one of the most important contracts in the industrial sector, and therefore a good sample contract for our purposes. The use of one contract as an example is made more useful by the fact that it appears that there are no great differences in disciplinary rules among contracts (Fernex and Guglielmino 1983).

The metalworkers' contract, signed in December 1990, includes an article entitled "Relations in the Workplace," which sketches a sort of workers' code of behavior that also applies to relations between management and workers. The following is an informal translation:

In the employment relationship the worker is subordinated to his respective supervisors, as provided in the firm's organization. Relations among workers, at all levels of responsibilities in the firm organization, must be marked by reciprocal fairness and politeness.

In harmony with the worker's dignity, supervisors' relations with employees will be marked by collaboration and courtesy.

Everybody should abstain from inappropriate, offensive and insistent behaviors, particularly with reference to sex, which cause a situation of uneasiness on the part of the person to whom they are addressed, and which also are aimed at conditioning changes in working conditions on the acceptance or refusal of such behaviors. In order to prevent the above mentioned behaviors, the firms will adopt the initiatives proposed by the National Commission for Equal Opportunities.

The firm will not place a worker in the position of having misunderstandings concerning the persons (besides the worker's direct supervisor) with whose dispositions he is bound to comply. In addition, the firm must notify workers of the names and specific duties of persons in charge of surveillance of working activities.

The worker must respect the working time and fulfill all formalities prescribed by the firm to control attendance, with explicit prohibition against making changes or erasures on time cards or trying in any way to alter what the time clock indicates.

The worker who has not regularly punched in on the time clock will be considered late for work; when the worker cannot produce evidence of attendance at the workplace, he or she will be considered absent.

The worker must perform the job assigned with the prescribed diligence, comply with the dispositions of the contract and with those given by his superiors, take care of the premises and of anything with which he or she is entrusted (furniture, tools, machinery, etc.).

The worker is also responsible for the loss and for possible damage due to fault or negligence, as well as for arbitrary changes made by him or her in the above-mentioned objects. The evaluation of the damage must be objectively made and the worker must be notified of the amount of the damage in advance.

The amount of the losses and damages may be withheld from the worker's pay in installments, each one being not more than 10 percent of pay.

In case of termination of the employment relationship, the amount to be withheld will be taken from all the emoluments owed by the worker, with the exceptions laid down by law.

The worker must maintain absolute secrecy regarding the firm's interests; also, he or she will not take advantage, to the employer's damage, of what pertains to his or her job in the firm. The worker cannot perform any activity conflicting with the interests of the firm's production, nor use in any unfair competition, once the employment contract is terminated, information obtained during employment.

Agreements limiting the worker's professional activity after termination of the employment relationship are regulated by Art. 2125 of the civil code.

Violations of the above provisions will result in disciplinary actions, which may include dismissal for fault.

The metalworkers' contract provides for the following types of disciplinary measures: oral reprimand, written warning, fines (no more than the equivalent of three hours' pay, which includes basic wage plus cost of living adjustment), suspension from work and pay for up to three days, and dismissal. These measures must be the same as those laid down in the law.

The employee may incur written warning, fine, or suspension in the following situations, which are stated in the contract: (a) failure to show up for work or leaving the job without justifiable reasons, if the absence is not justified within a day, barring force majeure; (b) tardiness, suspension of work, or leaving early without a justifiable reason; (c) minor insubordination toward superiors; (d) deliberate slowness or negligence in the performance of work assigned; (e) damage to materials or property through carelessness or negligence; (f) evident drunkenness during work hours; (g) working outside the firm for somebody who is in the same business activity; (h) smoking where it is explicitly forbidden; (i) performing minor work after working hours using firm machinery; (j) in any other way violating the contract or committing any other action that adversely affects the discipline, morale, health, or safety of the firm.

Written warning is given for minor violations; fine and suspension for major ones. The fine paid is not considered reparation, and the money is paid into existing benefits and service funds within the firm or—in the absence of such funds—to the National Health Fund.

The national labor contract establishes when dismissal is to be invoked. There are two alternatives. One is dismissal with notice. The second is dismissal without notice. The first type of dismissal applies to: (a) insubordination; (b) serious but unpremeditated damage to firm materials and equipment; (c) carrying on minor work for others or oneself *without* the use of firm material; (d) brawling on the firm's premises, away from the worker's workplace; (e) leaving the workplace if the worker has been assigned specific surveillance, custody, and checking tasks; (f) unjustified absence for more than four consecutive days or absence three times in one year when the absences fall after a vacation day; (g) when the employee has been sentenced to a jail term for an action unrelated to work but for which oral reprimand, fine, or suspension are provided and which reflects negatively on the employee's morals; (h) recidivism in any of the violations when two suspensions have been given.

Dismissal without notice applies to employees who cause substantial moral or material loss to the firm or engage in any action within the context of the job that constitutes a crime under the law. For example, behaviors of the following nature would incur this penalty: (a) major insubordination to superiors; (b) theft within the firm; (c) abstraction of machinery or documents belonging to the firm; (d) deliberate damage to firm equipment and materials; (e) leaving the job or doing any other action when the safety of personnel or the plant could be thereby jeopardized; (f) smoking where it may jeopardize the safety of personnel or the plant; (g) carrying out major work for outside

247

parties or for oneself and/or using firm materials; (h) brawling in the workplace.

The agreement also establishes that in the case of dismissal without notice the firm, as a precautionary measure, can suspend the employee from work for a maximum of six days. The employer must inform the employee in writing about the relevant facts pertaining to the decision and examine the employee's response. If the dismissal is confirmed, it will be retroactive from the suspension.

THE PARTICULAR OBLIGATIONS OF EMPLOYMENT

In viewing the particular obligations of employment, several general principles should be kept in mind:

1. The employee's repeated violation of the same, or different, rules is undoubtedly an aggravating factor, even when such violation is not of the most serious type. Recidivism is explicitly cited in all national labor contracts as a factor justifying the most severe type of sanction. The law, however, provides that disciplinary measures cannot be taken into account after two years from their imposition.

2. The employee's good conduct in the past is a factor that favors a more benevolent evaluation of the violation, provided that the violation itself is not a very serious one. However, good conduct alone is not a sufficient ground to mitigate a very serious violation.

3. The employer's tolerance of similar violations in the past by the same employee or by others is irrelevant, as the principle of discretionality in the exercise of the disciplinary power applies. It may happen, in fact, that the employer decides to tolerate irregular violations by one single employee or by several employees in order not to interrupt production. However, the employer may decide at a certain point to react against one employee who has committed a particular violation or with a particular frequency. In one decision (Cass. 4382/1984) the judge repealed a disciplinary sanction imposed on an employee who had infringed a prohibition against smoking, not because this prohibition was not respected by anybody in the workplace, but because it was thought discriminatory insofar as it was aimed at damaging the employee, who was a union activist.

In other words, by virtue of this principle the employer's conduct is lawful even when the disciplinary sanction is not imposed on all employees who violated the rule but only on a restricted number of them, or even to only one employee (Cass. 4382/1984; Cass. 2433/1987). In the latter decision the fact that the employee's direct supervisor had committed the same violation and had not been punished was irrelevant. This interpretation was based on the criterion—quite widespread in case law—according to which the principle of parity of treatment does not exist in our system. But it must be pointed out that in the last year some case law—not concerned with industrial justice—has begun to apply this principle, stating that a disparity of treatment is lawful only if justified.

4. In general, while the presence of economic damage to the enterprise may be an aggravating factor, the absence of such damage is not per se a mitigating circumstance, if the action were potentially apt to cause economic damage (Cass. 2846/1987; Cass. 8723/1989). In the evaluation of a cause justifying dismissal, and therefore of its lawfulness, the weight given to the eventual damage borne by the employer is very limited (Cass. 4728/1989). Instead, according to case law, the only relevant factor is the destruction of the employer's trust in the employee (Cass. 659/1990).

In summary, damage borne by the employer is not a precondition for a disciplinary action. Should damage occur as a consequence of a violation within the enterprise, then the employee is responsible to compensate the employer for the damage.

SUBORDINATION

Case Scenario

JD, a janitor at A Manufacturing Company, is assigned the task of waxing office hallways. He completes one hallway. His supervisor, FF, inspects the hallway and says to JD, "Do this floor again." JD replies "No," and walks away.

Analysis

The employee's disobedience of an order given by his supervisor is undoubtedly grounds for a disciplinary sanction. It is indeed one of the most serious cases of unlawful conduct, insofar as it opposes the most substantial element of the subordinate employment relationship, which is characterized by the employee's obligation of obedience to the employer's guidelines concerning either work performance or discipline.

Unlawful conduct implies also that the order given is lawful. It would not be such if the order means that the employee's health is jeopardized, or that the employee is asked to perform work that is not included in his or her duties (Cass. 2231/1984).

Seriousness. If the employee's disobedience is aimed at explicitly contesting the employer's power of managing employees, we have a case of insubordination. The concept of insubordination, in fact, includes not only the employee's refusal to comply with the supervisor's directives, but also any behavior that seriously contests and offends the supervisor in his or her capacity of giving legitimate orders (Cass. 5804/1987; Cass. 6945/1986). The latter decision concerned an offensive letter sent by an employee to his employer. The court decided that the letter could not be considered just a private action between the two.

In other words, in the concept of insubordination an attack on the employer's managerial function is considered a more serious element than the nonperformance of the work itself. A series of acts of disobedience, even of minor importance, can be grounds for dismissal, as they are evidence that the employee's personality does not tolerate discipline.

Many national labor contracts explicitly include insubordination in the causes for dismissal. In some of them there is a scale of seriousness. For instance, in the metalworkers' contract there are three levels of insubordination: slight insubordination, for which the employee is given a disciplinary sanction but maintains his or her job; insubordination, which is grounds for dismissal with notice; and serious insubordination, which is grounds for dismissal without notice.

The most serious sanction can be inflicted when the supervisor is offended or threatened, or when there is an act of violence. Previous cases of the employee's refusal to obey orders can be considered an aggravating factor, even if the last refusal is not really serious. The presence of other workers is undoubtedly considered an aggravating factor.

Mitigation. Provocation is a mitigating factor as to the seriousness of the employee's disobedience. The use of offensive expressions on the part of the employer, or the imposition of a useless act of work requested only with the aim of vexing or provoking the employee, is a provocation. In Cass. 5804/1987 and

Cass. 3199/1987 the judge stated that it is necessary to find out whether the employee's behavior was determined by his supervisor's behavior.

One major question concerns whether provocation can preclude unlawfulness of the refusal to obey. Our opinion is that when provocation affects the employee's dignity, he or she has a legitimate right to disobey, provided the refusal can be seen as reasonable and consistent conduct and therefore in good faith. In fact, according to a general principle of civil law, one of the two parties to a contract can refuse to fulfill his or her obligation if the other party does not fulfill his or her obligation. However, the obligation must be fulfilled if a refusal would not be in good faith (Art. 1640, civil code).

Despite what has just been said, the Court of Cassation (Italy's highest court, except for constitutional questions) seemed to have held the opposite opinion when it stated (Cass. 3204/1985) that the employer's impolite expression cannot be grounds for exempting the employee from complying with an order. It is worth noting, however, that the case was a peculiar one: the employee was using the office telephone to make a private call. With the exception of the above mentioned cases, the employee's opinion whether the work performance requested is appropriate has no relevance. In fact, the courts follow the principle according to which neither the judge nor the employee can criticize the directions given by the employer to the employee on how he or she should perform the work. The only exceptions are either when such directions are clearly impossible to follow or when they are unlawful (Cass. 7381/1983; Cass. 6213/1981).

A mitigating circumstance could be the employee's justification that the requested work is noxious to his or her health. Another mitigating circumstance is the irrelevance of the requested work to the overall economic activity, provided the refusal does not imply a real case of insubordination (Cass. 1355/1984). In the latter case, as already noted, the damage received by the employer as a consequence of the employee's conduct is irrelevant.

In evaluating the seriousness of a refusal to perform work, it does not make any difference whether the employee is a union representative or not. In fact the employer maintains all of its powers toward employees who are union representatives, with the exception of cases when they are lawfully exercising their union rights (for instance, the right to have time off). In other words, union representatives in the workplace are always bound to comply with the obligations of their employment contracts (Cass. 2314/1980). Nor can they invoke the principle of trade union freedom (Art. 14 of the Workers' Statute), since this article does not imply that the individual employee, even though he or she is a union representative, is indiscriminately authorized to interrupt work activity in order to discuss union matters (Cass. 1066/1978; 5711/1984; 3508/1986).

As far as national labor contracts are concerned, the metalworkers' contract, already mentioned, has a scale of seriousness. The textile workers' contract excludes insubordination as a ground for dismissal in cases where there are mitigating reasons, or when the insubordination is so minor that it did not cause any damage to discipline in the workplace.

SOBRIETY

Case Scenario

RR, a laborer on the loading dock of B Trucking Company, is observed by his supervisor, JB, reaching into the pocket of a coat that is hanging near his workplace. JB observes RR bring something to his mouth, appear to swallow, and then replace it in the coat. JB approaches RR and asks, "What are you drinking?" RR reaches into the pocket of the coat and hands JB a bottle that contains an alcoholic beverage. JB forms the opinion that RR's breath smells strongly of alcoholic spirits and that his eyes are unfocused.

Analysis

The employee who is found drunk in the workplace is certainly liable to be punished. In fact, this condition negatively affects the work performance. The employer's disciplinary sanction given on the ground of moral criticism is not legitimate.

Since case law on this subject is very rare, we are inclined to think that this violation is not very frequent. However, it is often referred to in national labor contracts, which provide for minor sanctions (fines or suspension), provided there is no recidivism.

Seriousness. It is clear that the drunker the employee is, the more serious will be the violation, as that will affect the work performance severely. Whether the lack of sobriety is caused by alcohol or drugs should not make any difference. However, in the case of drug addiction another major aspect becomes prominent: the employee's unreliability and, therefore, loss of trust on the part of the employer. For instance, the lower court of Bari stated that a bank employee's dismissal was lawful because the employee was not only a drug addict but a drug dealer. There are also decisions upholding the lawfulness of dismissals of bank employees who had been convicted of drug-related offenses. One of these decisions emphasized the damage sustained by the bank from rumors and bad publicity (Cass. 5321/1988). It is worth noting that a new law on drug addiction has been enacted (law 162 of June 26, 1990) which provides for job conservation without pay for a maximum of three years for those workers who intend to detoxicate in appropriate treatment centers.

Lack of sobriety in the workplace may constitute a particularly serious violation when, due to the employee's duties, damage may be caused to other workers or to the employer's assets. The new law on drug addiction also provides that, in the case when an employee is caught under the influence of drugs, the employer is obliged to suspend the employee from his or her duties if such duties imply risks to the health or safety of third parties.

SECURITY OF EMPLOYER'S PROPERTY

Case Scenario

PR, a clerk employed by C Gourmet Foods Company, is observed by two supervisors taking company products out of a packing box, concealing them on his person, and walking out the door with them. He is apprehended after he exits the store, and admits taking the products.

Analysis

Subtraction from the employer's assets—which is the crime of theft—constitutes a very serious disciplinary violation. It is grounds for dismissal without notice and is often laid down in the national labor contracts as being among the most serious violations.

Seriousness. The value of the assets taken is irrelevant to an evaluation of the seriousness of the violation (Cass. 4728/1989). It is also irrelevant if such assets were leftovers (Cass. 1461/1988: the court decided that the dismissal of a hotel servant was lawful despite the fact that she had taken food that clients had left untouched). However, there are some exceptional cases where judges have decided that there was no just cause for dismissal for two reasons: the value of the assets and the employee having had no previous discipline.

Mitigation. In the case of a theft that was motivated by the employee's urgent need to, say, supply medical treatment for a relative, this might affect the scale of the penal sanctions (Art. 626, criminal code procedure) but is not relevant to discipline. However, a case might occur where the magistrate would decide that the employer's trust in the employee was not compromised because of the circumstances.

PEACEFUL WORKPLACE

Case Scenario

MM is a clerk for D Department Store. NN is another clerk in the same department store; he is physically larger than MM. While MM is moving some heavy equipment from one area to another, NN says, "I'm surprised that you did not ask a real man like me to handle this job." MM, angered, strikes NN on the jaw, knocking him down. NN gets up and walks away.

Analysis

The maintenance of peaceful relations in the workplace constitutes one of the basic principles of any organization. This is the reason why major national labor contracts include a general provision stating that workers must maintain reciprocal correct and fair relations. Violence in the workplace is also very frequently listed as a cause for dismissal.

Seriousness. Aggravating factors are: when the violence caused physical injury; when other employees or the employer's assets were jeopardized; when the event occurred in other employees' or clients' presence; when the violence affected the outcome of the productive activity. It is worth noting that the metalworkers' contract considers it a more serious violation if a fight among workers occurs within the workplace than if it takes place outside. The former is punished with dismissal without notice, the latter with dismissal with notice.

Mitigation. Provocation does not necessarily constitute a mitigating factor, except in the case when it may be considered to give rise to a legitimate act of self-defense. The presence of factors such as seniority and the absence of a previous personal history of violence seems to be irrelevant vis-à-vis a serious event such as a fight among workers.

OFF-DUTY CONDUCT

Case Scenario

TT, head salesclerk for E Toy Store, participates in a white supremacist demonstration. He is arrested for disorderly behavior and a photograph of him handcuffed to a post and snarling at police is printed in the local newspaper, along with his name and the name of his employer.

Analysis

Over the years the case law has progressively come to acknowledge the principle that, as a rule, facts pertaining to the employee's private life are not grounds for termination. While changes in morals and life-style contributed to the development of this tendency, an important role was played by the Workers' Statute, which sets forth in Art. 8: "Employers shall not, for recruitment purposes, as well as during the employment relation, carry out investigations, including the use of third parties, concerning workers' political, religious, or union views, or concerning matters not pertaining to the evaluation of the worker's skill." Following this principle, the Cassation Court held unlawful a clause in a national labor contract that provided for the possibility of termination for an employee in case he or she were penally sentenced for an action which—though not connected with the employment relation—had damaged the employee's reputation. However, the court, on the basis of Article 8, also held that the employee's conduct can be grounds for a just cause dismissal when, because of the seriousness and nature of the action, the employee may be ascertained to be professionally unfit for the continuation of the employment relation.

Seriousness. The principle is that private life is irrelevant, but may become relevant if it has repercussions in the employee's work performance. Although professional unfitness would seem to require relevance to employment of behavior, this requirement has been rather narrowly interpreted. Case law has always followed the criterion that the relationship is based

255

on the trust that the employer must place in the employee, which must not be harmed in any way by the employee. Therefore, the employee's off-duty conduct becomes relevant not only as it relates to the particular type of work performed, but also as it pertains to the characteristics of the business organization within which the employee's work performance takes place.

In compliance with these principles, the Cassation held, for instance, that a sentence for acts against sexual morality is irrelevant in the case of an employee whose job was moving goods in an airport (6317/1985). Vice versa, it was stated that drug addiction of a bank employee, and the fact that he also sold the drug, constituted grounds for dismissal (Cass. 5321/1988). The court ruled similarly in the case of a bank employee who had issued bad checks. In other words, case law holds that the employee is professionally unfit when his work performance requires trust in a broad area, including reliability and honesty in private life (Cass. 5428/1987). It is worth noting that most of the decisions of this type refer to bank employees.

On the basis of these guidelines, we shall now try to evaluate the scenario. First, what reasons could justify TT's termination from a general point of view? In our view, only two elements could be used to justify it: the negative impact (potential or real) on the business of the firm, and the negative impact on relations within the firm.

However, the dismissal might be held lawful only in case TT's conduct constituted a crime. If, instead, TT's conduct was deemed to be a mere exercise of his freedom to express his own beliefs, it may be more difficult to justify his termination. One could even go further and say that TT's termination might be held unlawful if his conduct is of the kind that makes the employer's decision susceptible to being held to be discriminatory. It is worth remembering that—as stated in Article 15 of the Workers' Statute—an employer's disciplinary sanction taken on the grounds of the employee's union or political activity or on the grounds of sex, religion, or citizenship is null.

ATTENDANCE

Case Scenario

JJ is a nurse's aide at F Nursing Home. Because of an illness, her attendance at work has been erratic for two years. During that period she has missed 30 percent of her scheduled working days. During the last month she has missed 20 percent of her scheduled working days. All of these absences were excused. She then misses three days of work, without notifying her employer, because she decides to extend her holiday.

Analysis

Two aspects must be separated: the first is absenteeism caused by health problems; the second is unjustified absence. The first aspect poses the following problem: To what extent is the employer obliged to tolerate the too frequent illnesses of an employee?

From this perspective the problem has no relation to the disciplinary power. Case law has applied the principle—set forth in Article 2110 of the civil code—that the employer is forbidden to terminate a sick employee unless the illness is prolonged beyond a given time. National labor contracts specify the length of such period. Usually it is six, nine, or twelve months for employees whose seniority is respectively three, six, or more than six years. This principle—which implies that the negative repercussions of the employee's absence for illness are irrelevant to the work organization—has been applied in cases involving erratic attendance due to illness (Cass. 2072/1980).

When national labor contracts do not indicate the overall duration of sick leave (as in cases of erratic illness), the judge may do it on the basis of equity. Judges have been inclined to relate the length of the sick leave permitted to the duration of the national labor contracts, which is three years. If we take the metalworkers' contract as an example, an employee having seniority longer than six years, who in the previous three years had been sick for no longer than twelve months, could not be fired.

The second aspect directly concerns the disciplinary power and focuses on one of the major issues in the employment relationship: the fulfillment of the obligation of the agreed performance. All national labor contracts provide very detailed provisions on this issue, among which are:

1. The obligation to justify the absence by the following day, unless there is a justified impediment to doing so. Violation of this obligation may be punished by a fine. It is worth noting that the national labor contract for the commerce sector requires the

immediate communication of an absence and for written justification within forty-eight hours.

2. An occasion of continuous unjustified absence for more than a given number of days (three in the construction workers' contract, four in the metalworkers' contract, five in the chemical worker's) is considered a serious violation that may lead to dismissal. The purpose of such severe punishment is to deal with the problem of absenteeism.

PERFORMANCE

Case Scenario

HH is a warehouseman for G Distributing Company. G has instituted a program that determines levels of productivity for warehousemen. This program meets accepted professional standards for such programs. Over a period of two months HH fails to produce at the prescribed levels, consistently falling 10 percent below the standard. He is warned that he will be terminated if he fails to improve his productivity within two weeks. HH claims that the standards of the new system are impossible to meet. He proves that prior to the institution of the new system he was given above average evaluations by his supervisor for producing at his current level, covering a period of ten years.

Analysis

The employer has the right to fix minimum standards for the employee's performance and the employee is obliged to meet them. The only condition is that the strain of performance required to meet the minimum standards must not exceed the average standards for that specific work. This statement is consistent with Article 2104 of the civil code, which states that "the employee must use the diligence required by the nature of the performance." However, it must be noted that such standards are not meant to be used as a way to transfer the risk concerning the profitability of the employee's work to the employee, as such risk, by definition, belongs to the employer. In fact, it is a specific feature of the employment contract that the employee does not commit himself or herself to reach a certain result but to perform a predetermined activity by following the guidelines given by the employer.

Seriousness. The employee who is unable to meet the

required standards can be considered in default. The diligence which he or she is obliged to use is not measured by the employee's personal capacity but is objective, having reference to the skills described in the employment contract. In brief, reference must be made to the average performance requested of an average employee covering the same position in a similar technical context.

The fact that the employee is unable to meet the minimum standards does not mean that the employee is liable to be dismissed on the grounds of serious default. Some interesting decisions on this matter concern the work performance of insurance companies' agents, who are bound to meet a given productivity standard. These decisions state that unmet standards are not direct grounds for dismissal even though such a serious consequence is laid down in the employment contract, either collective or individual. The judge must verify the existence in fact of a just cause for dismissal. In brief, the judge must verify (1) that the agreed standards can be met by an average employee working in the same activity and in the same area; (2) that the agent's lack of efficiency—as compared to the agreed minimum standards—is so much below the standards that it can be considered a serious default of the work performance; (3) whether the lack of efficiency derives from the employee's negligence (Cass. 3062/ 1987); Cass. 6616/1987 repealed a decision that had ascribed nonfulfillment of the work performance requirements to the employee without taking into consideration that the employee worked in an area where there were no former clients.

Mitigation. A mitigating factor may be the rather unlikely event that the employee's below standard performance has no impact on the employer's costs and no negative influence on other employees' conduct. If the employee does not have the capacity to perform the work assigned, he or she can be dismissed. Such capacity, however, must be implicit in the type of job for which the employee was hired. Also, the employee cannot be fired if the employer who hired the employee was fully aware of the incapacity. If the employee's incapacity is attributable to difficulty in adjusting to the technical characteristics of new machinery introduced in the enterprise, the employee's dismissal can be justified only if he or she cannot be moved to another job. In this case, however, the dismissal should not be for disciplinary reasons but for reasons attributable to the work organization.

LOYALTY

Case Scenario

JS, a teller for H Bank, during an appearance on a television consumer information program states that her employer regularly fails to advise customers when they make mistakes in favor of the bank, but promptly corrects mistakes made in favor of the customers.

Analysis

This employee is publicizing information concerning the business activity of the firm where she works. This case falls under Article 2105 of the civil code entitled "Loyalty Obligation," which states that the employee "must not publicize any information concerning organization and production methods of the firm or make use of it in such a way as to cause damage to the firm itself." Even more clearly, the case could be placed in the framework of the more general principle—though such principle is not explicitly stated in the law but only inferred through a not unanimous interpretation of the jurists—according to which an employee ought to abstain from any behavior likely to cause damage to the firm or to the firm's image. However, a question that arose—especially after (and as a consequence of) the enactment of the Workers' Statute—was whether this principle should be mitigated by virtue of the right that citizens enjoy to freely express their thinking.

Seriousness. The balance between opposing interests—the right to criticize on one hand, the interest of the firm on the other hand—is a very delicate one. Indeed, there is a tendency to permit the exercise of the right to criticize rather extensively when it is used during union activities, insofar as such a right could be used as a tool to promote collective self-protection. A case can be cited of workers who—in order to safeguard their interest in work without risking their lives, and in search of solidarity from the community—informed the press that their employer did not comply with regulations aimed at preventing work accidents. On the other hand, the evaluation of the right to criticize—when it is exercised in a different perspective—may be a really difficult one.

On this subject guidelines have been provided by a Constitutional Court decision concerning the case of two employees of a hospital who during a TV interview discredited their employer and then sent a statement of the facts to the general attorney. The decision (Cass. 1173/1986) fixed the following principles, which must be observed by the judge in making decisions: (a) evaluate whether the behavior as a whole turns out objectively to damage the employer's reputation; (b) evaluate whether the charges if defamatory were expressed on behalf of interests deemed by the legal system as being at least as important as the interests injured by the defamation itself; (c) evaluate whether the modes in which the judgments were expressed and circulated were reasonably adequate to the need to protect these interests, and whether the actions denounced by the employee were true entirely or in part and had been carefully verified by the employee.

RESTRICT COLLECTIVE ACTION

Case Scenario

JJ, a machinist at I Manufacturing Company, becomes angry because he believes that his supervisor is treating him and other employees in a disrespectful manner. In protest, he persuades the other employees in his work group to leave work together in the middle of their scheduled work shift and not return until the next day.

Analysis

The action described in the scenario seems to have all the qualifications to fall under the exercise of the right to strike. JJ's defending counsel would certainly argue in support of this thesis and the judge might well accept it, because all the elements required for a strike are there: collective abstention from work for purposes of self-protection. In the Italian system the right to strike is not specifically regulated (with the exception of the public essential services sectors, for which a law was enacted in 1990), and it is also a right held directly by each individual worker—who, however, must exercise it collectively—but is not held by unions.

Seriousness. The facts that the strike action was spontaneous and that its purpose was simply to protest against the supervisor's disrespectful behavior are not sufficient reasons to negate its lawfulness. However, the question whether this was really a strike could be debated if the abstention was not justified by the purpose of protecting the workers' professional interests (for instance, if

261

the reason of the abstention was to watch a soccer match). Provided that such abstention can be qualified as exercise of the right to strike, the duration of the abstention is irrelevant. The same can be said with regard to the effects of the abstention on production. Certain anomalous strike modes: "hiccup" strike, "chessboard" strike, etc., may be unlawful on the grounds of being in bad faith.

Putting a strike into effect is not a legitimate reason for actions that in a normal situation would be considered unlawful from the disciplinary point of view. Therefore, threatening a supervisor is not permitted (though provocation by the supervisor can be considered a mitigating factor), nor is violence or the destruction of property.

The number of workers involved in the action is irrelevant, provided that the action can be defined as a union action and not the sum of individual abstentions from work, the lawfulness of which would be evaluated under the general provision that states that one party's performance is not due when the other party does not fulfill its own (*eccezione di inadempimento*). It is, however, clear that the more numerous are the workers abstaining from work, the greater the chances for the action to be considered a strike. In the case that only a few workers abstain from work, the chances that such action will be recognized as a strike are greater if a union is involved. Whether JJ was or was not the leader would be relevant only in the case that such action was not recognized as being the exercise of the right to strike and therefore was unlawful from the disciplinary point of view (with the exception of what we already said in the matter of *eccezione di inadempimento*).

AVOID CONFLICT OF INTEREST

Case Scenario

IB, a systems analyst for J Company, has access to private computer systems of his employer. IB accepts a string of freelance, relatively routine programming jobs for K Company, a competitor of his employer, performing the work at his home.

Analysis

Very likely IB's behavior would be considered a violation of the provision set forth in Article 2105 of the civil code, according to which "the employee must not engage in business in his own name or on behalf of somebody else that may result in a competition with the employer." This provision is given a very extensive interpretation, being applied even beyond the case illustrated in the scenario. It has been used in all cases in which a conflict of interest—either potentially or in reality—is involved. For instance, in Cass. 1711/1987 the judge decided that the dismissal of a bank employee who had set up a financial company in competition with the bank was lawful. The fact that the employee's financial activity covered a very limited geographical area and involved a limited liability company (i.e., with legal status) was irrelevant to the judge.

Again, the case of a company manager who had his wife become a shareholder of a company competing with his own was considered by Cass. 3719/1988 to have a conflict of interest. The same provision, set forth in Article 2105 of the civil code, was applied to the case of a company manager who aimed at having a competing company hire one or several employees of his own company (Cass. 6342/1987).

Seriousness. It is clear that there can be a disciplinary violation on the grounds of conflict of interest even though there are no specific company rules prohibiting such conduct. As far as a connection between the jobs performed in both places is concerned, it is worth noting that if the employee's contribution to the competing company is of a creative kind, there is a conflict of interest, especially if in the second activity the employee makes use of training and skills acquired in his work with the first employer.

Experience shows that it is the most highly qualified employees, with a high degree of responsibility, that are involved in this kind of violation. In fact, the principle that the loyalty obligation increases and becomes more and more pervasive according to the employee's position in the hierarchical grade scale is frequently affirmed (Cass. 2372/1986). On the contrary, it is difficult to prove that there is a conflict of interest when the work performed in a competing company is merely clerical.

Disclosure of a company's private information is a disciplinary violation that is regulated separately. Article 2105 of the civil code states a prohibition against disclosing information concerning work organization or production methods.

CONCLUSIONS

The Italian system of industrial justice, as it has developed over its history, regulates the employer's disciplinary powers rather extensively, through both law and collective agreements. It maintains the right of the employer to impose discipline, but significantly constrains it so that it is no longer possible to dismiss "with a sign of the head" at the employer's sole discretion. A main principle of the system is the requirement that the employee be worthy of the employer's trust. Loss of trust is treated as an extremely serious matter. With respect to remedies for unlawful termination, Italy is one of those rare countries where reinstatement is rather broadly available.

As to the particular obligations of employment, Italian law treats insubordination severely, as destroying a fundamental requirement of the employment relationship. Violations of the sobriety obligation appear to be rare. Security of the employer's property and the obligation to be peaceable at the workplace are enforced rather strictly. Off-duty conduct is judged depending on its impact on the firm's business or relations within it. As to attendance, a failure to attend work because of illness is not a disciplinary matter, but can lead to dismissal if it is too extensive. Intentional absenteeism is a disciplinary offense that is regulated in some detail in the law and in collective agreements. Performance is judged by objective standards based upon what it is reasonable to expect of the average employee. Loyalty is a clear obligation, but is balanced with the employee's interest in free action. There is no meaningful legal obligation to avoid collective action, as employees maintain a right to strike. The obligation to avoid a conflict of interest, on the other hand, is quite broad and derives directly from provisions in the civil code.

All in all, the Italian system is a mature one that has been rather carefully crafted over a long period. It focuses on maintaining the essential obligations of employment so that the enterprise can operate efficiently, while at the same time attempting to guarantee basic rights and dignity to employees.

NOTES

1. The authors would like to acknowledge the contributions to the research for this chapter by Dr. Claudio Pelligrini of the University of Rome.

2. Disciplinary power was considered by the arbitrators as constituting a structural element of the employment relationship. The college of arbiters was established by law in 1893, following the French experience, with the purpose of settling—on the basis of

equity—disputes that arise in the workplace. The arbitrators were part of a special jurisdiction. The president of the panel was appointed by the public administration and the other members were elected by employers' and employees' representatives. These colleges were abolished during the fascist period, when ordinary courts were given exclusive jurisdiction over dispute settlements. As these colleges were required to issue decisions based on equity in a context where there were no laws regarding the employment relationship, they had to take into account both usage and customs.

REFERENCES

AA. VV., *Il patere disciplinare, Quaderni di diritto del lavoro e delle relagioni industriali,* n. 9 (Turin: UTET 1991).

AA. VV., *Le sanzioni disciplinari nella contrattazione collettiva.* Milan: Giuffrè ed., 1966.

Assanti, Cecilia. *Le sanzioni disciplinari nel rapporto di lavoro.* Milan: Giuffrè ed., 1963.

Bortone, Roberta. "Commento all' art. 7," *Lo Statuto dei lavoratori,* Commentario diretto da Gino Giugni. Milan: Giuffrè ed., 1979.

Fernex, Bruno, and Emilio Guglielmino. *I Contratti Nazionali dell'industria.* Rome: Ediesse: 1983.

Ghera, Edoardo. *Diritto del lavoro, Il rapporto di lavoro.* Bari: Cacucci ed., 1989.

Ghezzi, Giorgio, and Umberto Romagnoli. *Il rapporto di lavoro.* Bologna: Zanichelli, 1987.

Liso, Francesco. *La mobilità del lavoratore in azienda.* Milan: Angeli ed., 1982.

Montuschi, Luigi. "Commento all' art. 7." Ghezzi, Mancini, Montuschi and Romagnoli, *Statuto dei diritti dei lavoratori.* Bologna: Zanichelli, 1979.

———. *Potere disciplinare e rapporto di lavoro.* Milan: Giuffrè ed., 1973.

Pera, Giuseppe. *Diritto del lavoro.* Padua: Cedam, 1991.

Piore, Michael, and Charles Sabel. *The Second Industrial Divide: Possibilities for Prosperity.* New York: Basic Books, 1984.

Veneto, Gaetano. *Contrattazione e prassi nei rapporti di lavoro.* Bologna: Il Mulino, 1974.

Vigorita, Luciano Spagnuolo, and Giuseppe Ferraro. "Sanzioni disciplinari," *Commentario dello Statuto dei lavoratori,* diretto da Ubaldo Prosperetti. Milan: Giuffrè ed., 1975.

8

SPAIN

Antonio Ojeda-Aviles

OVERVIEW OF THE SYSTEM

In Spain, as in the other countries under study, there exist several ways to terminate a labor contract. These can be placed in three categories: (1) by mutual agreement, (2) for causes that can be attributed to the employee, and (3) for causes attributable to the employer.

Types of Termination of Contract

Source of Termination	Voluntary	Involuntary
Mutual Agreement		
Employer	Disciplinary or economic reasons	
Employee	Resignation or quitting	Disability, old age, or death

At times the *cause* and the *initiative* for termination of a contract do not coincide in the same party. This is what occurs when there are infractions or faults on the part of the employee, as where the employee's attitude leads to the dismissal but the initiative is taken by the employer. In other cases they do coincide, as where a worker quits of his own free will.

When a contract is terminated for a reason attributable to the employer, that reason may be the impossibility of compliance (death of the employer), nonliability (disability or retirement), or the desire of the employer arising either from faults or nonfulfillment of duties on the worker's part or from economic difficulties in the company. The matter that will be the center of our attention here is the termination of a contract by the desire of an employer as a result of faults committed by the employee, which we will call *disciplinary firing.* Spain's law on this subject is characterized by the following:

1. Legalism. The loss of a job in Spain, although not only in Spain, is a personal tragedy, since it will be very difficult, if not impossible, for a large proportion of the unemployed to find a new job; in this country the unemployment rate is 15 percent of the registered active population (those persons between the ages of sixteen and sixty-five registered in job placement offices), and mechanisms for promoting employment and retraining workers are deficient. Thus the Parliament has intervened in this matter in order to regulate, in detail, the major aspects of this issue. These regulations are contained in Law 8/1980, the Workers' Statute.

2. Cause. "Employment at will" does not exist in Spain. In fact, the opposite principle holds; an employee cannot be fired without justification. Firing can only take place as a result of the causes established in Article 54 of Law 8/1980, and these causes, seven in total, are enumerated in detail. These causes practically coincide with those which are being examined in this book:

a) absenteeism and lack of punctuality;
b) insubordination and disobedience;
c) verbal or physical abuse;
d) bad faith or abuse of confidence;
e) lack of productivity;
f) drunkenness or drug addiction;
g) illegal striking or illegal behavior during a strike.

3. Formalization of the act of dismissal. The employer must observe certain formal requirements when firing a worker. These are likewise established by Law 8/1980, and if not followed lead to the dismissal being declared a nullity on a question of form. They consist of written communication of the termination of the

contract to the employee as well as notification of the date or moment the termination will be effective.

4. A lack of symmetry regarding prerogatives in terminating a contract. According to Spanish legislation an employee may quit his or her job without having to allege a cause, as it is understood that the reasons must be important to give up a job in a country where jobs do not abound. As a rule he or she is only required to give advance notice of between fifteen days and three months.

The effect of a dismissal, carried out with just cause and following the established procedures, is the termination of the contract. To the contrary, if it were carried out abusively, which means without justification, the employer must choose between readmitting the worker or paying compensation of forty-five days' salary for each year the worker has been employed. If there has been a defect of form in the dismissal, it will be declared null and the employer will be required to reinstate the employee, paying him the back salary due, and then dismiss him again.

Nevertheless, special rules apply when the employer's motives are unconstitutional (discrimination) or the employee is an employee or union representative: the dismissal is considered nonexistent ("null and void") and the employer must reinstate the employee. A settlement providing only compensation is not permitted.

A REVIEW OF DISMISSALS IN SPAIN

Unlike in other countries, where it is necessary to distinguish between procedures regulated by collective bargaining agreements (arbitration) and procedures regulated by law (judicial rulings), in Spain there exists a complete uniformity in the procedure governing the review of dismissals which are presumed invalid, and it is found in the Law of Labor Procedure of 1990 (it was formerly regulated by the law of 1980). Legislators still believe that the matter is too important to be left in the hands of private citizens, and unions and employers accept the state legislation to avoid broader conflicts. Undoubtedly they could turn to private arbitration, but specific technical problems exist which, along with a generally accepted reliance on the courts, in effect block this solution.

There are two types of labor courts with jurisdiction in the area of disciplinary firings: at a basic level *(a quo)* are those located in each provincial capital and in large cities; at a higher level *(ad quem)* we encounter the Superior Court in each region. In the special case of firings for union-related reasons (or discrimination in general) there is a third recourse in the country, the Constitutional Court, and additionally there is a fourth and final level of recourse available to an individual worker for the review of his dismissal: the European Court of Human Rights in Strasbourg. The initial procedure is relatively quick because it is exempt from formalities: there is a trial in one sitting, which normally lasts one hour and which has been preceded by an attempt at reconciliation, and a verdict is reached by the judge approximately one month later. If a decision is made to appeal to the regional Superior Court, its verdict will be handed down three months after the appeal was made. Delays in reaching verdicts are mainly due to the large number of cases that are taken to court, since no one uses private arbitration to solve their disputes. The history of the frequency of disciplinary firings in recent years is set out in figure 1.

Figure 1

Dismissals Between 1978 and 1988

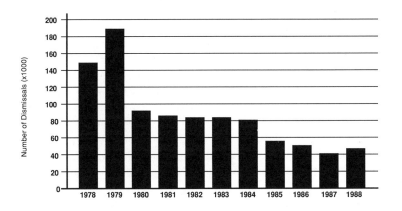

In conclusion, there are two additional points:

1. Collective contract agreements make provision for oversight committees designated from among the signing parties;

269

their purpose is to interpret and apply the agreement, but they have no jurisdiction in the area of disciplinary firings.

2. In some cases there exists union control over these dismissals; specifically, when the worker fired is a union member, the union must be informed by the employer and may take action against the dismissal even though the affected member does not wish to do so, as long as the employee does not explicitly oppose the union's initiative.

HISTORICAL EVOLUTION OF DISCIPLINARY FIRINGS

As with the American law of master and servant, the need for just cause for dismissal appears at the end of the nineteenth century for those labor contracts which specify a determined length of time for the contractual relationship. We find in Article 1584 of the Civil Code of 1889 that the employer cannot fire the employee before the time agreed to in the contract, and if he does so, he must compensate the worker with fifteen days' salary. Likewise, Article 300 of the Commerce Code of 1885 determined for mercantile employees what the just causes were that would permit a merchant to fire them *ante tempus,* and those causes are related to some of the ones that presently exist: fraud or abuse of confidence, carrying out commerce in one's own interest, and serious disrespect. On the other hand, for labor contracts of undefined term, just cause was not necessary to rescind them. This could be done at will by either of the parties, but the Commerce Code nevertheless required advance notice of one month or its equivalent in money (Art. 302).

In 1928 the courts established an accelerated procedure for reviewing the legitimacy of firings with respect to contracts for specified terms of duration: if the dismissal were considered unjustified, the employer was forced to reinstate the worker; if this was not acceptable to the employer, he was condemned to pay compensation based on the damages incurred during the time it took for the worker to find a new job.[1]

In 1931 we encounter the current regulation in the Labor Contract Law of that same year,[2] which increased the number of just causes for firings and extended to all types of contracts, whether temporary or permanent, the need to demonstrate just cause. The causal system in Spain dates from that time, and has endured changes in political regimes and laws since then, including a republic, a dictatorship, and a monarchy, which respectively promulgated the laws of 1931, 1944, and 1980 in this area.

As can be seen, collective bargaining plays no role in the evolution and consolidation of the Spanish system of justified cause for firings, and neither does arbitration nor even jurisprudence, to which, however, is owed the creation of the concept of "null and void" dismissal when the cause is unconstitutional. It has been the legislators who, of their own accord, have promoted almost all the changes, and there is no apparent trace of influence by the judiciary, arbitration, or negotiation. Some collective contract agreements have expanded the guarantees established in the law that favor workers, and this has been upheld by the courts, but always on a secondary level. The causes that we will examine below are therefore found in the 1980 law, and their interpretation will be seen through rulings produced in the courts of law.

THE PARTICULAR OBLIGATIONS OF EMPLOYMENT

Before embarking on an analysis of each of the just causes for dismissal in Spain, we must remember that in Spain the review of firings takes place after these occur and in the courts. It seems useful to visualize the percentage of cases reviewed by the courts in the last few years, as this will give an idea of which causes are of most importance. As no statistics are available regarding this subject, I have used the procedure of counting one by one the judicial decisions handed down between 1984 and June 1990. These are shown in Figure 2.

SUBORDINATION

Case Scenario

JD, a janitor at the A Manufacturing Company, is assigned the task of waxing office hallways. He completes one hallway. His supervisor, FF, inspects the hallway and says to JD, "Do this floor again." JD replies "No," and walks away.

Analysis

This scenario would come under the cause specified in Article 54.b of the law of 1980, "insubordination and disobedience on the job," owing to the generally accepted principle in labor relations *solve et repete*—comply and then complain. However,

271

Figure 2

Percentage of Judicial Decisions *

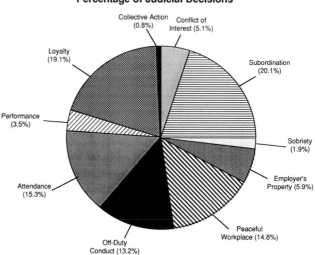

* Failure of percentages to total 100 is caused by rounding

the disobedience must be definite and unjustified, according to jurisprudence,[3] and it is this last requisite which may possibly be used as the basis for the judge to declare the dismissal null. Indeed, jurisprudence provides the worker with a *ius resistentiae* in extreme cases of orders that put his life or physical safety at risk, those that are degrading, or those that are clearly illegal. And since in Spain janitors ordinarily are not given cleaning tasks—these being considered humiliating and so to be performed by women of humble social origins—but rather duties with authority—control of access at the entrances to the building—they would probably have the right to refuse to carry out this kind of task. In recent years, perhaps due to the greater number of firings as a result of the economic recession, the courts have restricted the rights of employers in cases of disobedience, supporting refusal to carry out illegal orders, even though these were not "manifestly" so.[4] Only when the employer has an objective reason to ask the janitor to carry out a cleaning task on a specific occasion (for example, due to leakage of sewage when the cleaning worker is not on duty) would it be legitimate for the employer to require services other than those contracted, invok-

272

ing what is called managerial *ius variandi* (Art. 23, law of 1980). As stated in the decision of February 6, 1990, handed down by the Superior Court of Vasconia, "Jurisprudence requires that the disobedience be open, clear and without basis, being a necessary requirement on the part of the employer legitimacy in giving the order, unequivocal refusal by the worker to carry it out and serious and transcendent consequences of noncompliance."[5]

Seriousness. Of course, if cleaning were included in the collective agreement as a duty of the janitor, the disobedience of the janitor would be serious, although in this case it would not in itself justify dismissal but only a warning or a lesser suspension of employment and salary. Only when the disobedience is of extreme gravity can one incident be sufficient cause for dismissal, according to jurisprudence,[6] meaning in this case that the repetition of disobedience is necessary and that this refusal be the last in a chain for the dismissal to be legal. Another complicating factor is the necessity or importance of the order: waxing the main hallway on the day of a visit to the company by a high public officeholder is one thing and waxing a side hallway on an ordinary day is another. Similarly, "habitual" orders are considered less important than "exceptional" orders, such as one to change one's place of work.[7] Lastly, great importance is given to the way the order affects the collective, that is, the effect the order may have on the rest of the personnel, either because other workers are present or because the company finds itself immersed in a situation of collective labor conflicts. The law of 1980 speaks of "lack of discipline and disobedience" to mark the importance given to this aspect.

Mitigation. An illegal order or one of degrading nature does not have to be obeyed. When the order does not reach these limits but contains a certain degree of frivolousness or is otherwise out of place, disobedience constitutes a fault and can be sanctioned but not with the maximum penalty of dismissal. Dismissal is also inappropriate in cases where another procedure is habitually used, being more adequate,[8] or when the disobedience is based on a right which probably excuses the infractor.[9]

Enforceability. Since the nonfulfillment of orders must be "conscious, radical and unjustified," the case of an order that lacks sufficient unambiguous clarity—for example, giving an order for a worker to wax a hallway when he has time—cannot be a cause for dismissal.[10] In the scenario being considered (the disobeying of the second order, not the first), if the purpose of the second order was a reprisal or was not justified because of the condition of the floor tiling, the requirement of good faith on the part of the employer is probably violated, since the employee must "comply with the specific obligations related to his position according to the rules of good faith and diligence" (Art. 5.a, law of 1980).[11]

SOBRIETY

Case Scenario

RR, a laborer on the loading dock of B Trucking Company, is observed by his supervisor, JB, reaching into the pocket of a coat that is hanging near his workplace. JB observes RR bring something to his mouth, appear to swallow, and then replace it in the coat. JB approaches RR and asks, "What are you drinking?" RR reaches into the pocket of the coat and hands JB a bottle that contains an alcoholic beverage. JB forms the opinion that RR's breath smells strongly of alcoholic spirits and that his eyes are unfocused.

Analysis

Seemingly RR has been caught drinking alcohol in large quantities on the job, which in itself is not generally considered to be a serious fault in Spain. Thus the collective contract agreements must be consulted to determine whether it is listed as a fault for certain occupations. In the cases of drivers of road vehicles or pilots of aircraft or ships, mere consumption can lead to dismissal, but in general being caught drinking on the job constitutes a fault of slight or moderate importance, not a very serious one. Therefore the law of 1980 only considers habitual drunkenness or drug addiction if it has a negative effect on job performance (Art. 54.f) as cause for dismissal. Consequently there are activities (artistic ones, for example) where chronic drunkenness or drug addiction does not permit an employer to fire a worker so long as his performance is outstanding while under the influence of these stimulants. Spain, with its culture of beverages with moderate alcohol content (wine), does not suffer the same alcohol-related problems as countries with a culture of strong spirits (vodka in Sweden and other countries of northern Europe). From a statistical point of view, in the last few years almost as many cases related to drug addiction as to drunkenness have reached the courts.

In areas where drinking does not constitute a serious fault, it can become one when the employer orders the worker who has been caught drinking not to do so again. If the fault reoccurs it will then be considered a case of disobedience, and can be sanctioned as such. Another way of firing a worker indirectly is because of poor performance, which is also listed as a just cause in the law of 1980. Thus, jurisprudence has established that on certain occasions this cause for dismissal can be absorbed in others included in the law of 1980 and, therefore, it should be voided.[12] In any case the courts are stricter than the law itself when they deal with these cases, reflecting the trend of the society toward rejection of drunkenness, and have ruled on several occasions that to repeatedly arrive at work in a drunken state constitutes cause for dismissal.[13]

Seriousness. Without doubt the seriousness of this behavior reaches its height when the safety of work mates or clients or company property is put in danger. Thus, the driver of a bus carrying passengers who is caught by the highway police with a blood content of alcohol only slightly above that permitted can be fired because "extreme diligence in driving the vehicle can be demanded of him, due to the risk that driving in that [drunken] states constitutes, not only for the passengers, but also for other drivers on the road, it being thus unnecessary to show that this behavior is habitual, and of no importance whether an accident actually occurred or not," states the decision of the Central Labor Court of February 11, 1986. This decision concludes with the following Latin dictum: *ebrius punitur non propter delictum, sed propter ebrietatem* (the drunk should be punished, not because of the misdeed, but for his drunkenness). In other cases drinking is considered incompatible with the duties of the position, and a single occurrence is sufficient for the court to consider dismissal justified, as occurs with employees who deal directly with the public.[14] Thus, a ladies' hairdresser may be fired because the drunkenness affects "that complex and personal employee-client relationship which implies or may imply anything from an evident risk of physical danger to a certain result which negatively affects an aesthetic goal."[15]

Mitigation. Alcoholism was judged to be beyond the individual's control in some sentences handed down a few years ago, as it was an illness that had to be distinguished from drunkenness, until the Supreme Court rejected this doctrine for good.[16] Presently only repetition and a negative effect on performance are taken into account, independent of whether the worker is ill

275

or is undergoing treatment. The fact that a worker is going through a temporary state of psychic stress can be invoked as an extenuating circumstance in these cases, if the worker's prior behavior on the job is irreproachable.

Enforceability. Sporadic drinking, which is consented to in virtually all sectors, is not the behavior being discussed here. Numerous public institutions (for instance, universities) have bars, cafeterias, and restaurants on the premises where employees drink alcoholic beverages even during work hours. Only repeated drunkenness that negatively affects performance is cause for firing. This is why these particular aspects (repetition and negative impact on performance) must be proved in the subsequent trial: "If the employer has no record of the number of times an employee has arrived at work drunk, nor of the degree of drunkenness, and cannot show the negative impact on the worker's job performance," other sanctions may be imposed but not dismissal, states the decision of the Supreme Court of May 29, 1986. It is important to note that prior tolerance of this behavior does not impede the firing of the employee when the employer decides to do so, precisely because a repeated occurrence of this behavior is a requirement for dismissal. Neither cooperation on the part of the worker, in our scenario the worker showing the bottle, nor signs of repentance on his part impede his being dismissed.

SECURITY OF EMPLOYER'S PROPERTY

Case Scenario

PR, a clerk employed by C Gourmet Foods Company, is observed by two supervisors taking company products out of a packing box, concealing them on his person, and walking out the door with them. He is apprehended after he exits the store and admits taking the products.

Analysis

Theft is not an independent just cause for firing in the law of 1980, but is encompassed in Article 54.d, "transgression of contractual good faith, and likewise abuse of trust in the discharge of one's work". As a breach of the duties implied by contractual good faith, repetition is not required for the maximum penalty to be applied,[17] regardless of the damages caused or the regret or cooperation shown, as we see in the case under consideration where the employee admits having stolen the products. Nevertheless, in cases of minor thefts of small value the courts may decide that lesser penalties are in order. It must be noted that in numerous cases employees have retained sums of money or goods belonging to their company in an attempt to receive compensation for money owed by the company.[18] The courts condemn this action and judge it to be just cause for dismissal. On other occasions the theft is only presumed, not having been proved legally, in spite of which it constitutes sufficient cause for dismissal.[19] As is logical, not only the thief but also those who aid and abet the robbery are punished.[20] Crimes in which the company is involuntarily involved as a party also lead to the same consequences.[21] Lastly, at times there exists a certain liberality on the part of the employee with regard to company property; the employee "borrows" money[22] or makes private use of company installations.[23] A great majority of acts against company property fall into this heterogeneous category, with cases of out-and-out robbery being rare.

The labor courts have repeatedly decreed that dismissal for theft is legitimate even when there has been no criminal conviction, as this comes under the heading of bad faith or abuse of trust in the law of 1980, which is much broader in content than criminal statutes. There is even the possibility that in the same case a presumed thief may be found innocent in a criminal court, for lack of evidence, and nevertheless be considered guilty by a labor court.

Seriousness. The courts generally place emphasis on the fact that the appropriation took place without the company's consent, that the acts against the company's property were unauthorized. On one occasion the transaction (in banking) was carried out under totally normal circumstances and even, supposedly, for the company's benefit, but owing to the lack of consent and because of having placed the company's assets at risk, the act constituted cause for dismissal.

Mitigation. In many companies there is a certain tolerance of the use of some company products or materials by employees for their personal use, such as coal at a coal mine, office supplies in offices, etc., as long as the value of these items is insignificant. In some cases the courts do not take into account the custom of each company, which is difficult to prove, but the policy which would logically apply to the sector. For example, less importance is given to a product in the sector where it is manufactured than in the sector where it is marketed.

We have already seen that the taking of sums of money in "direct payment" of inadequate salaries does not prevent an employee from being fired, since no one can take justice into their own hands. Neither does regret after the fact nor even the return of the sum stolen; this "may have transcendence under the penal code but not in the jurisdiction of labor law, which punishes the breach of good faith as the cause of disciplinary firing," states the decision of the Superior Court of Madrid of March 14, 1990.

Committing irregularities with the authorization of a superior does not free an employee from responsibility either, as long as we are clearly dealing with a case of illegality and not merely a risky operation or one that falls into a "grey" area.[24]

Enforceability. As most of the cases reviewed are not straightforward robberies, but self-interestly abusing or "taking liberties" with company property, the degree to which this kind of behavior has been tolerated on previous occasions is a determining factor in whether it is considered to be a serious fault. The same can be said of actual thefts. In the scenario being studied if the products were food for that night's dinner, or a few light bulbs to replace a few burned-out ones in the employee's home, it would be difficult to fire him—although this behavior could not be repeated. On occasions such a situation leads to a reciprocal attitude between employer and employee to the effect that "neither of them can jump from permissiveness to the maximum penalty without prior warning," as is stated in the decision of the Supreme Court of September 12, 1986. The same court likewise pointed out in a decision taken on January 8, 1984, that "the company created an atmosphere of tolerance toward certain practices, and not having given due warning to company personnel, cannot use these practices as a cause for dismissal since this would be a breach of the good faith and loyalty that employees and employers owe each other."

PEACEFUL WORKPLACE

Case Scenario

MM is a clerk in a department store. NN is another clerk in the same department store; he is physically larger than MM.

While MM is moving some heavy equipment from one area to another NN says, "I'm surprised that you did not ask a real man like me to handle this job." MM, angered, strikes NN on the jaw, knocking him down. NN gets up and walks away.

Analysis

The law of 1980 is quite strict in the area of orderly behavior in the workplace and prohibits any disorderly conduct with a broad range of provisions. According to Article 54.c, "Verbal or physical offenses toward the owner of the company or company personnel or members of their families who live with them" are considered cause for dismissal. Verbal as well as physical violence is punishable whether directed at the owner, co-workers, or their families. The courts have broadened the groups of people offended, once condemning a football player for making disrespectful gestures toward "the spectators, provoking their anger and inciting them to public disorder."[25] Offenses to a company's customers are also included.[26] With regard to where these offenses take place, a violent attitude away from the workplace is punishable if it is job related. Concerning the act itself, the concept of physical or verbal violence is very broadly interpreted by the courts, even encompassing sexual abuses or propositions,[28] threats,[29] or even lack of consideration or respect in certain special circumstances.[30]

In any case the courts have an ample degree of freedom to judge the circumstances leading to the violence, especially verbal violence. Simple blasphemy, if reiterated, is cause for dismissal if it occurs on a public means of transportation,[31] while an insult uttered during an argument "in a moment of nervousness, taken together with the hurt feelings of an employee who has been the object of a sanction which the courts later decide was inappropriate, along with the harsh nature of the job [mine work]," may be subject to a reduced sanction.[32]

Seriousness. The transcendence of the offense, its notoriety for having taken place in front of other people or because it later is reported in the mass media, can lead to a more severe sanction due to the greater harm done to the prestige or the good name of the affected party.[33] Thus, for example, the same insult is considered differently if it is spoken or written in a letter, with the latter being judged more serious.[34] An offender's good cultural background or the fact that he occupies a position of responsibil-

279

ity or command make the penalty more severe.[35] On the other hand, physical violence, even if only threatened, is always serious even though it is an isolated case, whereas a verbal offense is not always sufficient cause for dismissal.

Mitigation. The courts always take very much into account the labor environment, that is, the type of activity being carried on where the violence or offense takes place. This is because certain language commonly used in some sectors will be judged totally improper in others. With regard to provocation by the person who is then verbally or physically attacked, there is a long list of decisions that treat provocation as an extenuating circumstance and even an exemption from any sanction. For dismissal to be justified there must be an "aggressive priority of the sanctioned worker," this being defined as a clearly unjust and unilateral action.[36] Firing is not permitted when, for example, a worker assaulted another who had called her "a whore,"[37] nor in the case of the worker who used defiant and offensive language in addressing a co-worker belonging to a rival group who had insulted him when he returned to his post following an absence.[38] The behavior of the offended party can have an influence in ways other than provocation on the degrading nature of the fault committed. Thus there was no insult to the honor of a businesswoman since on the one hand "she consented to be photographed nude and later showed a passive attitude to the exhibition of the photographs, giving no sign that she felt her intimacy had been violated, and on the other, there is a limited degree of repercussion in the workplace where the events took place."[39] Likewise, it is considered an extenuating circumstance if an insult is spoken during a heated argument, as the intent to do harm is diminished.[40] An insulted superior's attitude that is contrary to employees' rights is also considered an extenuating circumstance, impeding dismissal but not a lesser sanction.[41]

On occasion it is not a question of extenuating circumstances, but the fact that the behavior punished by firing is not sufficiently serious for this maximum penalty to be applied—for example, telling a superior to "go to hell" when he reprimands the subordinate.[42] Conversely, the seriousness of the act is not lessened by circumstances that affect the will of the offender, such as when under the influence of alcohol he or she threatens co-workers with a knife or when a worker insults and harasses co-workers for a period of two weeks due to a crisis of neurotic anxiety.[43]

Enforceability. A single action need only be sufficiently serious to constitute a cause for dismissal, there being no requirement for repetition.[44] This is the case in all acts of physical offenses, and it can also suffice in the case of verbal ones. A physical aggression need not actually be carried out, but only attempted, for it to be sanctioned with dismissal. It is even irrelevant whether the employee commits the fault directly himself. He need only be the instigator—for example, by inciting his wife to insult his boss as he leaves the factory.[45]

OFF-DUTY CONDUCT

Case Scenario

TT, head salesclerk for E Toy Store, participates in a white supremacist demonstration. He is arrested for disorderly behavior, and a photograph of him handcuffed to a post and snarling at police is printed in the local newspaper, along with his name and the name of his employer.

Analysis

In principle, Spanish legislation holds that a worker is free to act as he sees fit off the job and that only nonperformance of his duties at work can lead to sanctions by the company. Because of this the law of 1980 makes no mention of faults related to off-duty conduct. The company can in no way determine what a worker must or must not do in his free time. Nevertheless it must be taken into account that some of the faults punishable by firing which appear in Article 54 of the law of 1980 have aspects that may occur outside the labor contract. We have seen how a worker can be sanctioned for *arriving* at work drunk, or for verbal or physical offenses against co-workers due to work-related matters, even though these take place off-duty. Later we will study the case of the employee who works for a competing firm in his free time, creating a conflict of interest. But where there are more cases involving respect for the worker's private life is in the area of loyalty and good faith. These can be, and in fact are, breached in a variety of situations outside the labor relationship, such as when statements are made to the press that are harmful to the interests of the company. This topic is directly related to, for example, whistleblowers, toward whom Spanish courts have traditionally shown repulsion based on an antiquated concept of company loyalty. The Constitutional Court has not followed this concept in two sentences, 89/1985 and 6/1988, by which it annulled the dismissals caused, respectively, when a psychiatrist criticized his hospital in a television interview and when a public functionary criticized his ministry in the press for favoring a certain newspaper in the publication of announcements.

Of all the cases in which a worker's off-duty behavior is cause for dismissal, there is one which has led to a multitude of judicial decisions in the last few years: When a worker falls ill and is ordered by his doctor not to work for a certain period of time, the fact that he is then discovered performing some kind of strenuous activity (going out twice on the same night,[46] going on a hunting trip,[47] helping to organize an activity for charity, helping out in a small family business a few hours a day[48]) or, of course, is discovered working,[49] is considered a serious breach of good faith and cause for automatic dismissal.

Seriousness. The prestige of the company and its products is of special relevance in measuring the importance of the conduct being judged. The same behavior might well deserve different sanctions according to whether it occurs in a large city or a small town, whether it receives exposure in the mass media or is known to only a small group of people. In the case we are studying, the courts would probably reject the firing of the racist employee because after the weighing of the two conflicting interests, it would be decided that the job of the employee is of greater value than the possible economic losses for the company, however scandalous TT's political and social behavior might seem to us.

Mitigation. Protection of employment and the privacy of a worker in Spain covers even those cases where a worker is arrested and accused of having committed a crime—for example, murder or a robbery with violence. Only after the trial has been held and the worker found guilty and sentenced can the employer fire him for faults of attendance at work (for the time he is in prison), since otherwise he would have the right to be reinstated in his job (Art. 45.g, law of 1980).

Enforceability. Of course, prior tolerance of similar behavior by the employee himself or his co-workers plays an important role here in carrying out a dismissal, but there is also something we could call the standardization of the behavior. For example, if an employee who is not working due to illness happens to drive an automobile, it is not sufficiently damning or important enough to be used against him in a case for dismissal.[50] Likewise, making a strenuous effort or doing hard work during time off due to illness will be allowed if it has a beneficial effect on the patient, as is the case with stress-related or psychic illnesses.

In general it can be said that the presence of a fundamental right favoring a worker neutralizes the reaction of the businessman who has been harmed: the freedom of expression, opinion, and information play a decisive role in this area.

ATTENDANCE

Case Scenario

JJ is a nurse's aide at F Nursing Home. Because of an illness her attendance at work has been erratic for two years. During that period she has missed 30 percent of her scheduled working days. During the last month she has missed 20 percent of her scheduled working days. All of these absences were excused. She then misses three days of work, without notifying her employer, because she decides to extend her holiday.

Analysis

The scenario combines aspects of two different situations, justified and unjustified absence from work. While the former can never give rise to sanctions or dismissal, except when the situation reaches such proportions as to make the post unproductive, the latter does call for penalties in proportion to the length of the unexcused absence. This point is regulated in the collective labor agreements. The general rule is that three successive days' absence without permission is cause for dismissal. A higher number of nonconsecutive days of unexcused absence from work during a month—for example, six days—is also a basis for the worker being fired. Below these figures the worker can be sanctioned with suspension from work and salary, transfer, or demotion as the maximum penalty. Lack of punctuality on arriving at and leaving work is computed along with actual absence from work. Article 54.b of the law of 1980 classifies as a cause for dismissal "repeated and unexcused absence or lack of punctuality at work."

With reference to excused absences, only when they are so numerous as to make that worker's post unproductive is dismissal permitted through what the law of 1980 calls "objective dismissals," that is, those in which the worker is not to blame, and therefore in which advance notice must be given and compensation provided. This compensation is set at twenty days' salary for each year the worker has been with the company up to a maximum of twelve months' pay. Article 52 of the law of 1980 states that the contract may be terminated by the company when absences, even justified ones, reach 20 percent of the scheduled working days in two consecutive months or 25 percent in four nonconsecutive months during a one-year period, provided that the general rate of absenteeism in the work center is higher than 5 percent during the same period of time. Days missed because of legal strikes cannot be counted, nor can sick leaves of twenty days or more. Thus these rules are aimed at short and frequent absences of all types, especially those due to minor illnesses. The difference in compensation between objective dismissal and dismissal without just cause is that in the latter, compensation must be more than twice as much, forty-five days' wages for each year worked; on occasion the worker must be reinstated with the alternative possibility of compensation being nonexistent.

The difficulties in applying objective dismissal are a result of it being based upon excessive propensity to illness which is almost unworkable and thus little used. On the other hand, the reason of unjustified absence constitutes one of the most important chapters in the area of termination of labor contracts in Spain.

Seriousness. Not giving due justification for the missed workdays can lead to sanctions and, if the absence is for more than three days, dismissal. In the case study JJ can be fired automatically for missing three days without permission, although this step could also be taken because she has missed 20 percent of her scheduled workdays in the previous two months, a case foreseen in the law of 1980. The difference is that in the first case she is not entitled to compensation, while in the second case she is. Under especially serious circumstances it is not necessary for the unauthorized absence to be of three days' duration; depending on the harm done to the company or the importance of the work being carried out by the employee, a shorter absence may be considered sufficiently serious to merit dismissal if it were unjustified.

Mitigation. The courts weigh the justification given by the employee to determine whether or not the dismissal is valid. Seniority is not in itself an extenuating circumstance, but will be taken into account when another excuse is also offered. For example, if JJ has been with the company for a long time, almost any justification, weak though it may be, will protect her from being fired; if the reason for prolonging her vacation was to visit her sick mother, the court might combine this with her seniority and rule in her favor.

Enforceability. The law of 1980 requires prior notification and justification for an absence to be protected from sanctions. The courts interpret this to mean that notification of the absence must be given in advance, and the justification as soon as possible, although not necessarily at the same time as the notification. However, it is clear that if the worker puts off providing justification until he is fired[51] or until the trial itself,[52] he is violating contractual good faith, which is a cause for dismissal that will be examined below.

Some courts have ruled that not having given advance notice is sufficient cause for dismissal, even though reasonable justification exists and later notification is given.[53] But these are extreme cases, and the courts pay more attention to the fact that a worker has given notification as soon as he was able to and to the actual reasons for the absence.

PERFORMANCE

Case Scenario

HH is a warehouseman for G Distributing Company. G has instituted a program that determines levels of productivity for warehousemen. This program meets accepted professional standards for such programs. Over a period of two months HH fails to produce at the prescribed levels, consistently falling 10 percent below the standard. He is warned that he will be terminated if he fails to improve his productivity within two weeks. He fails to do so. HH claims that the standards of the new system are impossible to meet. He proves that prior to the institution of the new system he was given above-average evaluations by his supervisors for producing at his present level, covering a period of ten years.

Analysis

Two preliminary observations must be made here. First, productivity 10 percent below the productivity standard or *aver-*

age may not fall below the *minimum* productivity that the most frequently used systems (in Spain these are the Bedaux and the Centesimal) establish, in which case the worker cannot be sanctioned.[54] The consequence of low production is that the employee earns less than fellow workers. The other observation is that in the case under study the company passes from a situation where productivity has not been measured to one where it is. This in Spain is categorized as a substantial change in the contractual agreement and as such requires the consent of the workers' representatives or, if this is not possible, the authorization of the Labor Administration. Generally speaking, the new situation is regulated through the collective labor agreement, to avoid employee resistance.

The law of 1980 makes provision for dismissal due to both voluntary and involuntary low productivity. Thus, Article 54.e sanctions the continuous and voluntary decrease in normal or agreed-upon productivity. Article 52 of the same law sanctions an employee's ineptitude learned of or developed after his being hired by the company. This constitutes a kind of objective dismissal with half compensation being mandated, as neither party is at fault. Article 52 also allows objective dismissals when an employee is unable to adapt to technical innovations in his post, provided that the company offers adequate training courses for the innovations or new equipment. In the case under study we are not dealing with technical changes, but with the measurement of productivity.

Seriousness. In the scenario HH's normal productivity has not dropped nor is he more inept than before. The only difference is that the company seems to have raised its demands. There is nothing he can be criticized for, even if his 10 percent shortfall is below the minimum established, because the company has knowledge of his level of performance and has accepted it for years. It is the company that has modified its contractual offer and, according to Spanish legislation, should have obtained authorization. For his part the worker could leave with compensation of twenty days' pay per year of service, with a maximum of nine months' pay.

Quite a different case is when the modifications of work conditions come about at the request of the worker. If he then does not meet the minimum productivity standards of the new situation, he may be fired.[55] Or if a low initial performance is observed and it is voluntary on the part of the employee, the

286

maximum penalty may be applied, even though the decrease in productivity mentioned in the law does not exist.[56]

Mitigation. The comparison between prior and present productivity must be made under normal conditions, for if the decrease in productivity were the result of a period of illness it would be justified.[57] With regard go this, it would be well to mention an important point of Spanish law: even if an employee becomes partially incapacitated as a result of illness or an accident, he must be reinstated by the company (Art. 45.5, law of 1980), although with his salary lowered proportionally to his loss of productivity.[58]

Enforceability. In order to fire a worker the courts require that the drop in productivity be continuous and voluntary, as the law sets forth. A sporadic reduction in productivity will not lead to dismissal although, as we will see below, perhaps this would become a case of bad faith, depending on the seriousness of the circumstances. The same may be said of the voluntary nature of the behavior; if it is involuntary but can still be attributed to the employee, it could be considered a case of ineptitude. If, on the other hand, the employer is responsible (equipment breakdown, lack of raw materials, a change in contracted working conditions), the worker will lose his wages during the period of inactivity or may be required to recover the time lost, but he or she may not be fired. What happens is that willfulness on the part of the employee is assumed when his productivity decreases, unless a legitimate motive is demonstrated, or when other circumstances indicate willfulness. Thus, in the decision of the Supreme Court of March 28, 1985, employees were fired after having been found on several occasions sleeping in the lavatory, it being known to the company that they sometimes left work and went to help a relative with some construction work: "They arrived at work not sufficiently rested—leading to low productivity—because of a freely taken decision to involve themselves in construction work in their free time."

A question that the courts must often ponder is how to evaluate low productivity. They commonly compare the employee's present performance with his past productivity, since the law requires that there be a decrease. When this is not possible, a comparison is made between the employee and his co-workers. In any case the decrease must be clear; there must be an "enormous drop,"[59] "a decrease of two-thirds,"[60] if the courts are to accept the dismissal in cases where there are no scientific standards of measurement. Further, the established minimums must be reasonable, which may not be the case in such activities as door-to-door selling or sales work. For example, according to a Supreme Court decision of October 20, 1986, a productivity clause in a labor contract is only valid provided it is not abusive.[61]

LOYALTY

Case Scenario

JS, a teller for H Bank, during an appearance on a television consumer information program states that her employer regularly fails to advise customers when they make mistakes in favor of the bank, but promptly corrects mistakes made in favor of the customers.

Analysis

Cases of disloyalty are frequent in Spain, perhaps because it serves as an escape valve for the pressure that exists due to the fact that dismissal at will does not exist. Article 54.d of the law of 1980 includes disloyalty as a just cause for dismissal, defining it as a breach of contractual good faith. The law is very broadly worded, which permits its frequent application. A great deal of what we have said when discussing theft and verbal or physical offenses can be repeated here. One single incident of bad faith can justify dismissal, regardless of the amount of economic loss incurred by the company. Only a loss of confidence in the person capable of perpetrating such an act need be present, and "when dealing with a loss of trust, degree cannot be established."[62] A wide range of cases exists: a security guard who goes to sleep on duty,[63] cases of sexual abuse committed while working,[64] clocking in for a work mate so that his or her absence will not be noticed,[65] a lack of attention on the part of a ship's captain leading to the grounding of the vessel,[66] and finally classic cases of theft or accounting irregularities. All in all, any deviation from what is understood to be honest and loyal behavior, regardless of its material consequences, is cause for dismissal. As we have said, some cases which in other countries are held to be independent causes for dismissal, theft and off-duty conduct, fall under this heading in Spain. In addition, in the last few years other cases typical of the society in which we live have been added in this area:[67] the introduction, sale, or consumption of drugs in the workplace—which, if leading to addiction with a negative influence on performance, could be included in another cause for dismissal, as we have already seen—and tampering with computer programs.[68]

We have also already seen how the scenario being analyzed is related to the area of off-duty conduct, linked with the problem of whistleblowers. When discussing that point reference was made to two decisions of the Constitutional Court which decided in favor of the employees. Both cases dealt with government employees and the right of the public to information. But when it is a matter of private enterprise and the employee makes serious accusations about the safety of a product, which later cannot be proved, the result is justified dismissal.[69]

Seriousness. Holding a post of responsibility in the company is usually considered greater reason for dismissal, since the law holds that the worker is in a more favorable situation to misuse confidential information or other company property.

Mitigation. Regret on the part of the employee does not lessen the seriousness of the action, since the result is that "the trust deposited in him" has vanished, independently of whether his subsequent reinstatement would harm the company.[70] Neither is the extent of economic losses caused to the company, no matter how small, a factor in blocking dismissal. According to the decision of the Supreme Court of December 9, 1987, "The causing of damages is not the essence of the infraction, but rather the breach of loyalty, of good faith." This aspect of the doctrine has been so often repeated by the court that it is universally known, both in cases of theft and of damage to or breakage of company property.

In these cases the fault on the part of the employee need not be intentional, simple negligence being sufficient, or "the grave and undeniable negligence attributable to a person who, because of the position of trust assigned to him, was obligated to show special dedication and diligence in carrying out his duties, but due to what can at least be described as a lack of interest and neglect shown by the said worker in the case being judged, caused serious damage."[71] Likewise when the director of a television program allows some of the participants to mention brand names of products on the air, breaking the rules, "there is undoubtedly a subjective element of blame or inexcusable negligence on his part."[72]

Enforceability. Almost any abuse of trust is punishable with the maximum sanction according to Spanish legislation. But there exists a protected area where dismissal is not allowed even when certain types of irregular conduct on the part of the company are made public. This is when it is done by the worker in defense of his own interests in court. An employee cannot be fired for complaining about salary or asking for the adoption of safety measures that affect him or her. The same is true for shop stewards who complain on behalf of their work mates, or who denounce illegal actions carried out by the company.[73]

On some occasions the circumstances are unclear and the courts may adopt contradictory decisions based on these particular circumstances. We saw in the case of off-duty conduct that a worker who is recovering from an illness can sometimes do strenuous exercise if it helps cure him, in spite of it appearing unreasonable. The same occurs when the director of a bank causes accounting irregularities and hides money in different parts of the bank because of fear that the branch office is going to be robbed.[74]

RESTRICT COLLECTIVE ACTION

Case Scenario

JJ, a machinist at I Manufacturing Company, becomes angry because he believes that his supervisor is treating him and other employees in a disrespectful manner. In protest, he persuades the other workers in his work group to leave work in the middle of their scheduled work shift and not return until the next day.

Analysis

In Spain, Italy, and France, unlike Germany, Sweden, Great Britain, and the United States, the right to strike is an individual right which can be exercised by a group of workers without union support. It is enough to call an assembly and for the majority of those present to vote to go on strike. A decree law of 1977 regulates the requirements that the strike must comply with for it to be considered a right. Those requirements make it difficult to organize strikes without union support, although it is theoretically possible. Apart from calling an assembly and having a majority of those present vote in favor, advance notification must be given to the company and the labor authorities, and a strike committee must be set up to carry out negotiations.

Seriousness. In the case under study, the employees decided to leave work without having held an assembly to see if a majority favored this action. Neither was five days' advance notice, required by Spanish law in the private sector (ten days' in the public sector), given, and the workers failed to name a strike committee to hold talks with the company. Thus, it is an illegal strike, and JJ and the *active* participants may be fired, but not the ordinary participants.[75] Active participation is, as defined in the decision of the Central Labor Court of July 7, 1977, "a personal and individualized activity which makes the fired worker stand out from the group." The criteria are, of course, not uniform. It is judged legal to fire the worker who instigated the illegal strike[76] or incited others to strike illegally, or one who "took a leading role in the group which marched through several departments of the factory,"[77] but not those who only gave out information[78] or attended a meeting of delegates.[79] In the scenario, it seems that JJ is the only active participant, while the other employees are only ordinary participants. However, employees who commit acts during a strike that are grounds for dismissal can be fired, even when they are not active participants and even if the strike is legal. The contractual relationship is only suspended, and therefore the strikers maintain their obligation of good faith with the company; noncompliance is covered by the same parameters as if the contract were still in full effect. Offenses, conflicts of interest, press releases, and so on can be cause for dismissal for the ordinary strikers.[80]

Mitigation. When the just causes for dismissal are determined by law, as is the case in Spain, there are very few mitigating circumstances once the employee's conduct has been clearly identified with the cases set forth in the law. Since the basic requirements for the strike to be considered legal are missing, the active participants can be fired. The judge must determine the degree of "activism" of the specific employee. Thus, decision 13/1986 of the Constitutional Court considers inappropriate the dismissal of a worker who joined a general strike whose organizers had failed to give advance notice to the company.

Enforceability. On numerous occasions an agreement is reached at the end of a strike to the effect that no sanctions will be imposed, or that those imposed will be rescinded.[81] On other occasions there has been an announcement by the company

291

prior to the strike that no sanctions will be imposed, and jurisprudence has considered this to be valid at times, although there has been a trend toward considering this invalid.

Once again the seriousness of the infraction is evaluated without regard to the economic loss suffered by the company, or even to the length of the strike. What is important is that the stoppage is illegal, so no matter how long it lasts, the active participants are subject to dismissal. Even a warning strike lasting one minute, for example, may be cause for dismissal if it has not been legally called. In practice, however, it is difficult to find a case where this has happened.

AVOID CONFLICT OF INTEREST

Case Scenario

IB, a systems analyst for J Company, has access to private computer systems of his employer. IB accepts a string of freelance, relatively routine programming jobs for K Company, a competitor of his employer, performing the work at his home.

Analysis

The law of 1980 constrains an employee from *disloyal* competition with the business of his employer in its Article 21.1, which states: "A worker may not be employed by more than one company when disloyal competition is deemed to exist." The courts, however, continue to apply the previous rule, which was supposed to be superseded by the present legislation. Previously, any work in a business similar to that of one's employer was considered to be illegal, whether it was disloyal or not. In any case the law includes dismissals for this cause in Article 54.d, for reasons of bad faith and abuse of trust.

Under Spanish law it does not matter whether the competitive activity was carried out by the employee autonomously or for another employer, nor is the economic loss to the employer, if any, of consequence. This characteristic is common to all infractions that fall under the heading of bad faith or disloyalty. The typical case, as expressed in the decision of the Supreme Court of November 16, 1988, is when "the employee is employed by the suing company and is at the same time an officer in a company dedicated to the same ends, offering the services of the latter to customers of the former, which clearly proves market competition. This leads to a conflict of interest, which places the employee in the situation of breach of contractual good faith stipulated as a cause for dismissal".

Seriousness. Although the typical scenario is that of an employee who uses his knowledge of the company's clientele or the company's procedures to improve the competitor's business or his own business, the courts only require that his external activity be detrimental to his employer.[82] Therefore, it is taken very much into account whether the employee's activities take place in a small town or in a large city, if there is a large clientele or a small one, or if the product is easily marketable or not. Seriousness increases when the employee occupies a managerial post in the competing company, is a founder of it or a shareholder in it. This occurred when three electronics experts working for a company "founded a P.L.C. where one was president, another a member and the third the secretary of the board of directors," claiming that the aim of the company was to make up for production deficiencies of the company that employed them.[83] This circumstance calls for dismissal even when the activity of the competing firm is not identical but only similar.[84] "High-level participation" in the competing company may be known to and even promoted by the employing firm, which uses the connection as a form of control; this may be frustrated by the attitude of the employee, and it is then possible to fire him.[85] Of course, the same situation may arise when the worker carries out important duties in the original company, since it is assumed that he has access to important confidential information which he uses to benefit the competing firm.[86]

On some occasions it has been presumed that working for another company in the same field was disloyal because the employee's wife formed part of the management of that company.[87] And dismissal has been applied to cases where employees were temporarily not employed by their companies, when the work for the competing firms was detrimental to their original companies.[88]

Mitigation. Since this situation is included in the area of dismissal for bad faith and disloyalty, it is difficult to find extenuating circumstances when the employee has gone to work for a competing firm. Nevertheless, the complicating factor of damage done to the original company may not exist if the employee does not have significant responsibilities in either company. The dividing line between what is and is not significant is drawn by the courts. It must not be forgotten that the courts have approved dismissals of workers who were simple employees of both firms but were in possession of key knowledge; thus, salesmen (they know the original company's clientele)[89] or designers of electrical installations[90] have been fired for conflict of interest.

Seniority in the original company is not considered to be an extenuating circumstance but, in fact, just the opposite. In Spain the seniority system is little used, and the courts would probably consider that a worker with long years of service in a company possesses more information about it and owes it more loyalty than a recently hired employee.

Enforceability. This cause of dismissal is not applicable when the geographical area of operation of the two firms is different, or when the activities of the two firms are not identical or similar. Above all, the courts stipulate that if the original company authorized the employment of the employee in the competing company, they cannot then fire him or her for that reason.[91]

CONCLUSIONS

In Spain, disciplinary dismissals face strong legal controls. These controls originate with having a statutory requirement of justified cause for dismissal. The requirements are specifically written into the dismissal act. There is also judicial control of the entire process when a worker claims that an employer has imposed an excessive or unjustified sanction. In the process of judicial review, however, there is a certain degree of weakness in these controls, which arises from loose interpretation of such justifiable causes for dismissal as "abuse of confidence." The reality of disciplinary dismissal law therefore differs from its apparent clarity of design. However, in the last three years there have been notable decreases in the number of both dismissals and court reviews of dismissals, probably due to new work contracts, approximately 90 percent of which comply with the government's temporary guidelines on dismissals.

NOTES

1. Rodríguez-Piñero/Fernández/Cruz, *Derecho del Trabajo,* vol. 2 (Seville, 1990), p. 260. Economically times were bad, as almost always in Spain, and politically there was a paternalistic dictatorship that was trying to imitate some aspects of national socialism already in place in Italy and Portugal.

2. That same year the Republic had been established, radicalized to the left with the world economic crisis and governed by the Socialist Party.

3. Supreme Court ruling, 12 Feb. 1965.

4. Supreme Court ruling, 9 June 1987.

5. In the same vein, the Supreme Court ruling of 17 Nov. 1987. The rulings of this same court of 4 Feb. 1989 and 4 Apr. 1990 require that the disobedience be "serious, worthy of blame, of far-reaching consequences or notoriously insubordinate and unjustified."

6. Rulings of the Central Labor Court (replaced in the current system by the regional superior courts), 11 and 25 Jan. 1983.

7. Rulings of the Supreme Court, 3 Jan. 1990, and the Superior Court of Madrid, 5 Dec. 1989.

8. Ruling of the Supreme Court, 4 Apr. 1990: a sick collections agent who is fired for not delivering collected funds to the company when habitually the company, under such circumstances, sends another employee to get them.

9. Ruling of the Supreme Court, 29 Mar. 1989: in spite of an order to be present at work the last day of the year, dismissed workers did not report because their contract afforded them one unexcused absence per year, and this was the last day to take advantage of it.

10. Rulings of the Supreme Court, 14 Feb. 1989, and the Superior Court of Vasconia, 30 Mar. 1990.

11. Ruling of the Supreme Court, 14 Feb. 1989, among others.

12. Ruling of the Central Labor Court, 14 Dec. 1982.

13. Rulings of the Central Labor Court, 14 May and 13 June 1986.

14. Rulings of the Central Labor Court, 3 and 8 Mar. 1983.

15. Ruling of the Central Labor Court, 2 Feb. 1988.

16. Ruling of the Supreme Court, 3 June 1963.

17. Thus, the ruling of the Supreme Court, 29 Oct. 1988: the taking of two undershirts. Ruling of the same court, 9 Dec. 1986: prohibited banking operations, even though no economic damage caused to the company. Ruling of Central Labor Court, 21 Sept. 1988: overturning the judgment of the lower court, which had considered unlawful the dismissal of a cleaning woman who had taken several kitchen utensils, on the grounds that the theft was not sufficiently serious. Ruling of the Superior Court of

Madrid, 7 Nov. 1989: appropriation of two packets of correspondence entrusted for transport.

18. Ruling of the Supreme Court, 15 Dec. 1986: a worker was declared permanently disabled and the company paid him $11,205 but later obtained a reclassification stating that he was temporarily disabled; the worker refused to return the money. Ruling of 26 Apr. 1988: a worker took company documents and refused to return them when the president of the company ordered that he do so. Ruling of the Supreme Court, 5 Mar. 1990: a worker appropriated significant sums of money collected from company clients, claiming that the company owed them to him for wages not paid.

19. Ruling of the Supreme Court, 16 Mar. 1987: to secure a bag a watchman offered a padlock that was his personal property; the bag was later found open with $1,000 missing from it. Ruling of the Supreme Court, 25 July 1988: while serving as comptroller the manager of a branch bank executed important transactions that he did not communicate to the company.

20. Ruling of the Supreme Court, 18 Nov. 1988: furnishing a blank check from the institution to a woman who later cashed it for $150,000; ruling of the same court, 18 Nov. 86: transporting a co-worker by car so that he could sell several boxes of paper stolen from the company.

21. Flight attendant for an airline who tried to smuggle gold coins in the handle of a tennis racket.

22. Ruling of the Supreme Court, 11 Mar. 1987. In a case decided by the Central Labor Court, 31 Jan. 1989, a worker took money from his supervisor without permission, leaving a note in which he informed the supervisor of his action. Ruling of the Supreme Court, 27 Sept. 1988: a manager put company funds into his own accounts for a certain period of time in order to collect the interest.

23. In the Supreme Court ruling of 20 July 1987, a female hotel employee took a room key and spent the night in that room with an unidentified person: theft of use.

24. Ruling of the Supreme Court, 24 June 1986: over a period of months a bank employee was responsible for certain financial irregularities; his activities had been authorized by the branch manager, who was engaged in the same irregular transactions.

25. Ruling of the Supreme Court, 19 May 1986.

26. Ruling of the Central Labor Court, 1 Mar. 1983.

27. Ruling of the Central Labor Court, 23 May 1983.

28. Ruling of the Central Labor Court, 22 Mar. 1983.

29. Ruling of the Central Labor Court, 24 May 1983.

30. Alleging that the boss had slept with a female reception-ist, threatening her that if she told the truth he would "beat her brains out"; ruling of the Supreme Court, 3 July 1984. Also, rul-ing of the Central Labor Court 15 Feb. 1983.

31. Ruling of the Supreme Court, 2 July 1986.

32. Ruling of the Supreme Court, 9 Apr. 1990; in the same vein, ruling of the Supreme Court, 12 Apr. 1984.

33. Ruling of the Central Labor Court, 15 Feb. 1983.

34. Rulings of the Supreme Court, 24 Nov. 1987 and 3 Oct. 1985.

35. Ruling of the Central Labor Court, 22 Mar. 1983.

36. Rulings of the Supreme Court, 24 Jan. 1967; 31 May and 3 Oct. 1968; 26 June 1978; 10 Sept. 1982; and of the Central Labor Court, 22 June 1981; 6 and 28 Feb. 1979; 11 Oct. 1978.

37. Ruling of the Central Labor Court, 7 Feb. 1984.

38. Ruling of the Supreme Court, 16 Feb. 1990.

39. Ruling of the Supreme Court, 13 Apr. 1987.

40. Ruling of the Supreme Court, 17 Dec. 1985.

41. Rulings of the Supreme Court, 3 Mar. 1986 and 26 Dec. 1988.

42. Ruling of the Supreme Court, 22 May 1987. In the same vein is the ruling of the same court 13 Nov. 1986.

43. Ruling of the Supreme Court, 27 Oct. 1987.

44. Ruling of the Supreme Court, 23 Feb. 1960.

45. Ruling of the Central Law Court, 23 June 1982.

46. Ruling of the Supreme Court, 1 Dec. 1986. For attend-ing a festival, see ruling of the Supreme Court, 7 May 1987.

47. Ruling of the Supreme Court, 7 Dec. 1984.

48. Ruling of the Superior Court of Madrid, 2 Oct. 1989.

49. Ruling of the Superior Court of Madrid, 8 Mar. 1990. Rulings of the Supreme Court, 25 Feb. 1990; 3 Apr. 1987; 29 Jan., 31 May, 15 July, 8 and 30 Oct., and 22 Dec. 1986; 2, 7, and 12 Mar., 2 and 31 Oct., 30 Sept., 3 Dec., and 26 July 1985; 9 May 1984, among many others.

50. Ruling of the Supreme Court, 22 Dec. 1986. In contrast, repeatedly driving a small motorcycle is so considered: ruling of the same court, 13 Mar. 1984.

51. Ruling of the Central Labor Court, 6 Oct. 1987.

52. Ruling of the Central Labor Court, 4 Apr. 1989. Cf.

Albiol, *El despido disciplinario y otras sanciones en la empresa* (Bilbao, 1990), p. 42.

53. Ruling of the Supreme Court, 8 Oct. 1980.

54. In the case of the ruling of the Supreme Court of 23 Feb. 1990, however, standard productivity was 50 percent and minimum 40 percent.

55. Ruling of the Supreme Court, 2 Oct. 1985: change from section head to salesman.

56. Ruling of the Supreme Court, 28 Mar. 1985: during a two-month period several workers reported for work but did not perform their jobs because their employer was not paying them the salaries they demanded.

57. Ruling of the Supreme Court, 15 July 1987.

58. Ruling of the Central Labor Court, 10 Jan. 1989: an office worker who cannot type normally with his left hand.

59. Ruling of the Central Labor Court, 24 May 1988.

60. Ruling of the Supreme Court, 20 July 1989.

61. In the same vein, rulings of the same court 13 Nov. 1986 and 23 Feb. 1990.

62. Ruling of the Central Labor Court, 14 Oct. 1982.

63. Ruling of the Supreme Court, 10 Dec. 1984.

64. Ruling of the Supreme Court, 26 Feb. 1986: male hospital employee with female patient; ruling of the Supreme Court, 20 Nov. 1987: watchman with two girls whom he apprehended stealing from department stores.

65. Ruling of the Central Labor Court, 13 July 1982.

66. Rulings of the Supreme Court, 30 Apr. 1986 and 8 Oct. 1988.

67. Ruling of the Supreme Court, 18 Mar. 1987: croupier in a casino; ruling of the Central Labor Court, 19 Nov. 1987: an employee who introduced drugs into a prison.

68. Ruling of the Superior Court of Murcia, 19 Dec. 1989.

69. Ruling of the Supreme Court, 27 May 1987: making serious accusations during a press conference, in the middle of a company's summertime advertising campaign promoting consumption of beer. Ruling of the Constitutional Court 120/1983: note in press on the scant preparation of teachers hired by an academy to administer exams during a strike.

70. Ruling of the Supreme Court, 2 Feb. 1984.

71. Ruling of the Supreme Court, 6 Apr. 1984.

72. Ruling of the Supreme Court, 13 Nov. 1989.

73. Ruling of the Supreme Court, 28 Oct. 1987: a represen-

tative who claimed to have received false votes from the personnel director in connection with a workers' assembly.

74. Ruling of the Supreme Court, 9 Dec. 1986.

75. Currently there is debate over whether this requirement of active participation applies or whether it suffices to determine if the noncompliance was serious and blameworthy in order to assume that there has been a breach of good faith and with it grounds for dismissal as specified in Art. 54.d. See Martínez Emperador, *La participación en huelga como causa de despido disciplinario: marco regulador,* apud VVAA, *Estudios sobre el despido disciplinario* (Madrid, 1989), pp. 4077ff.

76. Ruling of the Central Labor Court, 25 Apr. 1977.

77. Ruling of the Supreme Court, 1 Oct. 1979.

78. Ruling of the Supreme Court, 9 June 1979.

79. Ruling of the Supreme Court, 1 Oct. 1979; distinct from the ruling cited in note 77.

80. For example, enforcements: ruling of Constitutional Court 254/1988.

81. Ruling of the Central Labor Court, 19 Oct. 1977.

82. Ruling of the Supreme Court, 18 July 1989.

83. Ruling of the Supreme Court, 27 Sept. 1989. Also, ruling of the Supreme Court, 26 July 1988: stockholder in a competing company; and ruling of the Supreme Court, 22 Feb. 1990: founding partner.

84. Ruling of the Supreme Court, 12 July 1988: founding partner in a competing company.

85. Ruling of the Supreme Court, 25 Apr. 1988: the employee was a member of the board of directors of a competing company and went on to become its president, with the opposition of the company for which he worked.

86. Ruling of the Supreme Court, 26 July 1989.

87. Rulings of the Supreme Court, 21 May 1986, 3 Nov. 1988, and 16 Mar. 1990.

88. Ruling of the Supreme Court, 18 July 1988: radio station employee who took a year's leave and produced the same show for a competing company.

89. Ruling of the Supreme Court, 17 Dec. 1987.

90. Ruling of the Supreme Court, 13 Mar. 1986.

91. Rulings of the Supreme Court, 26 Jan. 1988 and 7 Mar. 1990.

9

THE UNITED KINGDOM

Karl J. Mackie

OVERVIEW OF THE SYSTEM

For most employees in the United Kingdom[1] the principal legal rules setting out their rights in a case of termination of employment are the modern (post–1971) statutory rules concerning unfair dismissal.[2] Discipline and dismissal practices have traditionally also been considerably affected both by personnel management approaches in different industries and companies and by the influence of trade union collective bargaining. However, the legislation on unfair dismissal appears to have had the effect (as intended) of providing for more standardization of employer practice and employer–union agreements across industries. Personnel and industrial relations practices nevertheless remain important in terms of the practical rights of employees prior to termination, as only in exceptional instances (usually involving special contractual conditions or in relation to holders of a public office of some kind) do the courts intervene to *prevent* a termination of employment or correct a disciplinary injustice by an employer rather than adjudicate on the legality of a dismissal once it has taken place. However, these background factors are taken into account in legal decisions on the fairness of a dismissal, and so will be considered in relation to the discussion on unfair dismissal in this chapter.

The legislation on unfair dismissal is discussed in more detail below and is applied to the various scenarios considered in this book. Traditional common law rules continue to apply to termination of employment situations and to interact with the law of unfair dismissal in some respects. (An interaction which will grow in the future in the light of a likely grant of jurisdiction over certain contractual matters to industrial tribunals, s131 Employment Protection Act 1978.) The approach at common law to termination of employment will therefore be considered first.

SUBSTANTIVE AND PROCEDURAL RULES OF THE EMPLOYMENT OBLIGATION

THE COMMON LAW FRAMEWORK

Essentially the common law (judge-made) rules on employment evolved in the eighteenth and nineteenth centuries out of "master and servant" law to regard the relationship between an employee and employer as regulated by the "contract of employment." The terminology of "master and servant" persisted, however, well into the twentieth century. Its presence is still echoed in the distinction employment lawyers would draw (important for statutory rights as well as common law ones) between a contract *of service* (employee) and contract *for services* (an independent contractor or self-employed worker).

No special code of law was devised by the courts for contracts of employment, the same general legal principles applicable to commercial and other contracts being in theory applied to an individual's dispute with an employer which might come before the court. The rights as between an employer and employee were held to derive from an assumed bargain made (on equal terms) between the individual employee and the employer once an employee had begun, or contracted to begin, to work for the employer. This view was sustained as the basis of legal interpretation of disputes over employment terms despite the reality that many employment relationships were begun and sustained on the basis of a minimal oral agreement. (A requirement to reduce into writing some of the main terms or conditions of the employment relationship was only introduced by statute in 1963; see now Employment Protection [Consolidation] Act 1978 s1, as amended.)

Where the parties had not explicitly discussed an aspect of

the relationship that became a source of dispute (e.g., a right to pay during a sickness absence or the right to earn commission or to stay in one place of employment), the courts might still imply a term if they could find it was incorporated into the contract under general contractual principles—for example, that the parties' acts clearly indicated that an agreement had been reached, or if it was a term that would have been obviously needed to give business effect to the arrangement in the first place. Some terms—for example, duty to provide faithful service and to obey an employer's reasonable and lawful orders; duty to pay wages and to take care of employees' safety—were regarded as standard implied terms under the common law conception of the employment relationship.

Such an approach, of applying an abstract legal concept to a diverse and complex human transaction, gives rise to difficulties, and made it often unpredictable how the courts might interpret a contract in a particular case. In particular, a curiosity of the law was its abstention from legal recognition and enforcement of collective agreements between employers and trade unions. The exception to this was where the court found that a term of a collective agreement had been incorporated into the individual's contract and hence was enforceable at law (in the name of the individual, not the union). This could arise by means of an explicit agreement between the employee and the employer, or where the courts found it was an implied term in the contract and the term was an appropriate one for incorporation into an individual contract. Individual legal rights under the many collective agreements that provide for disciplinary and termination procedures (including independent arbitration) are therefore often complex in terms of their common law position, not assisted by the fact that it is in turn uncommon for employees in such situations to take legal action at common law. (One should note the readiness of the courts to find that procedures in some contexts do impose more substantial requirements on the employer in terms of adherence to procedure or to the rules of natural justice—where there is a statutory or public office status attaching to the particular employment or a clear contractual right to special procedural provisions.)[3]

In relation to termination of employment, the common law rule was that an employer could dismiss an employee for any reason or no reason; employment was terminable by either side at will, subject to any conditions imposed under the contract of employment. Only in circumstances therefore where there was breach of a term of the contract could termination give rise to a claim for damages. Only in very unusual situations would the courts award continued employment or reinstatement. This breach of contract action was referred to as wrongful dismissal (as opposed to the modern statutory right to claim unfair dismissal).

The most common term implied or explicit in relation to dismissal was a requirement to give contractual—or in the absence of an explicit term, reasonable—notice. (No statutory requirement for minimum notice was imposed until 1963.) However, the employer still had an implied right at common law to dismiss without notice (summary dismissal) where the employee was guilty of a fundamental breach of contract. The employer could accept this repudiation of the contract and dismiss and/or sue for damages, a less common approach. (Employees faced with a repudiation are in a similar position in terms of a right to resign without notice and/or claim damages.) The most common case law arising from wrongful dismissal actions therefore concerned situations where an employee had been dismissed without notice, usually for "gross misconduct" of some kind, who claimed to be entitled to proper notice and therefore pay during, or in lieu of, notice. The courts would be asked to determine whether there had been a wrongful dismissal in that either proper notice had not been given or because the misconduct did not amount to conduct serious enough to justify the employer acting as if the contract could be terminated summarily.[4]

Wrongful dismissal still exists as a legal right at common law, requiring a claim to be made through the ordinary civil courts. It is not, and was not, a frequent legal action because the majority of employees did not seek redress for dismissals through the courts, in part linked to the fact that damages for loss of a period of notice would not amount to a great deal for the majority of employees. However, the action is still useful for employees who do not qualify for a claim of unfair dismissal or who are dismissed with a significant period of employment still to run (as in the case of the fixed-term contracts of many senior managers) or for whom damages for lost earnings or other contractual entitlements might exceed the statutory maximum compensation available in an unfair dismissal action.

Finally, one should note an important irony of current English law in relation to the law of contracts of employment. Not only do the common law rules on wrongful dismissal continue to exist, but the interpretation by the courts of the modern statutory law of unfair dismissal has led to considerably more attention being given to contractual issues even in these cases, in order to decide details of entitlement and questions of fairness. This has led to what some consider to be a more elastic concept of contract than can be found in traditional rulings or in commercial contract interpretation despite the apparent formal equivalence.

STATUTORY PROTECTION AGAINST UNFAIR DISMISSAL

For the majority of employees the statutory right to claim unfair dismissal is the most important legal route to seeking redress over an unjust termination of employment. The right was enacted first in 1971 in an attempt to defuse one important area of industrial conflict and bring more order to employer discipline and dismissal practices.[5] It has survived substantially intact, although it has been amended in detail over the years. The main text of the legal rules is set out now in the Employment Protection (Consolidation) Act 1978, as amended by a number of acts during the 1980s. One of the most significant amendments during the period of office of Conservative governments since 1979 has been to lengthen the period of employment required by an employee in order to claim unfair dismissal. It had been reduced by 1979 to six months' employment, then was raised again during the 1980s to its present level of two years' service.[6]

The statutory right requires an employer, where there has been a dismissal, to prove to an industrial tribunal that he had a valid reason for dismissal (thus ending the common law position that a dismissal could be at will), and then requires the industrial tribunal to decide whether in all the circumstances the employer acted reasonably in dismissing the employee for that reason. There are five aspects of unfair dismissal law to consider: (a) grounds for eligibility for claiming unfair dismissal; (b) the statutory definition of a valid reason for dismissal; (c) the criteria for reasonableness in judging a dismissal fair or unfair; (d) the remedies available from the tribunal; and (e) the nature of, and procedure before, the industrial tribunals.

Eligibility

One of the main qualifications for an employee to claim unfair dismissal is to have served an appropriate length of time with the employer. An employee requires two years' service with an employer, working (or contracted to work) a minimum of sixteen hours a week, before he or she has a right to claim unfair dismissal. Employees who work between eight and sixteen hours become eligible after five years. Only employees below normal retiring age in the organization or the age of 65 can claim. (The service requirements are not applicable if dismissal is on the grounds of trade union membership or activities or because of nonunion membership.) Finally, and another vital element of entitlement, an employee must bring a claim for unfair dismissal within three months of the effective date of dismissal or the claim is barred. Tribunals have the power to waive this time limit, but only in exceptional circumstances preventing an earlier claim.

The legal rules apply to most employment situations, including government employment (strictly speaking, "Crown" employees in British constitutional law), although a few employment areas are specifically excluded—for examples, employees who normally are employed outside Great Britain, employees excluded on grounds of national security, and employees on contracts for a fixed term of a year or more where they agree in writing to waive their legal right to claim unfair dismissal at the end of the contract term.

The employee must prove that there was a "dismissal" and within the statutory definitions (s55.2.). In the majority of cases this is not an issue, but there are occasions where employers may claim an employee resigned or the contract came to an end in other ways. Apart from termination of the employment contract by the employer and nonrenewal of a fixed-term contract, the statute classifies as a dismissal cases where an employee resigns because the employee's conduct entitled the employee to treat his employment as at an end—that is, where the employer is guilty of a breach of contract of a fundamental term or a breach going to the root of the contract.[7] This last type is commonly called constructive dismissal.

Finally, industrial tribunals do not have jurisdiction over dismissals of those taking part in industrial action (or involved in an employer lockout) unless a dismissed employee can show discrimination in terms of selective dismissals amongst those taking part or selective reemployment offers within a three-month period after his dismissal (s62). Selective dismissals of those involved in "unofficial" action will also be excluded from

305

tribunal jurisdiction once the provisions of the Employment Act 1990 come into force.

Reason for Dismissal

The employer must prove that it had a valid reason (or if more than one reason, a valid principal reason) for dismissal. The 1978 Act (s57.1 and 2) lists five categories of legally acceptable reasons, relating to capability or qualifications to perform the work; conduct; redundancy (no longer required for the employer's business); illegality (continued employment would lead to breach of a statutory duty or restriction); "some other substantial reason" to justify dismissal of an employee in that position.

Dismissal is automatically unfair, therefore, if the employer cannot show a reason for a dismissal and that the reason falls within one of the statutory headings. Dismissal for union membership or activities or for nonunion membership or because an employee is pregnant are explicitly classified in the statute as automatically unfair reasons.

Reasonableness

In most cases there is little difficulty for employers to prove a reason for dismissal. Therefore the majority of unfair dismissal cases turn on the evidence relating to the detailed circumstances of the dismissal. To determine whether the dismissal was fair or unfair, given the employer's principal reason, the tribunal has to find "in the circumstances (including the size and administrative resources of the employer's undertaking) the employer acted reasonably or unreasonably in treating it as a sufficient reason for dismissing the employee; and that question shall be determined in accordance with equity and the substantial merits of the case" (s57.3 as amended by the Employment Act 1980).

The statute therefore allows tribunals to exercise flexibility in their judgments according to the particular facts of the case. Reasonableness is not precisely defined. However, three elements are worth noting in relation to the later commentary in this chapter on the scenario variations: the nature of a "reasonable employer," procedural matters, and the question of consistency in employer actions.

The Reasonable Employer. Appeal court judgments have

306

laid stress (not always with the same emphasis) on the point that the tribunals are the judges of fact under the legislation, including questions of reasonableness. Thus it is possible to have inconsistent judgments by tribunals of apparently similar circumstances without raising a point of law. However, the test is not what the tribunal itself would have done in the circumstances but what it judges a reasonable employer might have done. That is, there is a "band of reasonableness" within which one reasonable employer might have dismissed while another would merely have warned an employee about the conduct.[8]

The norm underlying the approach of tribunals is to be guided by what they perceive as good industrial relations practice (which usually represents the personnel practice of well-developed companies), sometimes referred to more obliquely as an ability to apply "industrial common sense." Allowance is made for differences in the size of the employer involved, although this usually has most explicit impact in relation to questions such as the formality of procedures and number of appeal stages. This norm is reinforced in a Code of Practice relating to dismissal and discipline[9] issued under powers given to the Advisory Conciliation and Arbitration Service, an independent statutory agency concerned with the improvement of industrial relations (Employment Protection Act 1975, ss1–6). The code is admissible in evidence before a tribunal and must be taken into account where relevant. It sets out what is seen as standard good practice in employer handling of disciplinary rules and procedures, including a recommendation of the need for involvement of employees in drawing these up. This would include such matters as rules being communicated effectively to employees, rights to a warning or series of warnings relating to possible dismissal (except in cases of gross misconduct justifying dismissal without notice), rights to hearing details of the case against them, rights to be consulted on a management decision or to reply to a charge against them, rights to be accompanied by a union official in a disciplinary hearing, rights to an appeal to a higher level of management, and so forth.

Procedure and Substance. Employers are entitled to rely on generally accepted standards of conduct in employment, including the common law rule that summary dismissal is still an accepted option in the case of gross misconduct.[10] Where an employer seeks to create rules specific to a business—for example, unacceptable standards of dress or work methods—there would normally be an expectation that such rules would be clearly communicated to employees, although tribunals are ultimately bound by the statutory test of reasonableness, not by the employment rules or contract.[11]

A failure to follow good procedures can also make a dismissal unfair—for example, because the employer failed to find out the full circumstances of the employee's case or to explore a suggestion of alternative employment that might be suitable in a case of incapability. An important decision in the House of Lords in 1987 reaffirmed the importance of procedural requirements.[12] Tribunals are bound to consider the fairness of an employer decision in terms of what was known to it at the time of dismissal, not on the basis that the decision would have been the same if a proper procedure had been followed. Only where it would have been clearly futile to follow procedures can an employer claim to sidestep such requirements.

Consistency. The question of consistency of treatment of employees in similar situations is a relevant consideration; the statutory test talks of "equity" considerations.[13] However, this must be tempered with flexibility in the light of the individual circumstances of each case. Lack of consistency may indicate to employees that certain categories of conduct are not dealt with by dismissal or may indicate that the employer's real reason for dismissal is not the purported one.[14]

Remedies

The 1978 Act sets out three categories of remedy if the tribunal finds a dismissal unfair—reinstatement, reengagement, or monetary compensation. The difference between the two reemployment orders is that in reinstatement, the tribunal order treats the applicant in all respects as if he had not been dismissed; in reengagement the tribunal may order reemployment on somewhat different terms from that originally held (e.g., different place or hours of work), although the act makes clear that reengagement should be, as far as reasonably practicable, as favorable as reinstatement. It is in the tribunal's discretion which of the three orders to make. In exercising its discretion on reemployment, the tribunal has to take into account the wishes of the complainant, whether it is practicable for the employer to comply with a reemployment order, and whether it would be just to make the order where the complainant caused or contributed to his dismissal in some way.

Compensation is made up of two elements: a basic award and a compensatory award. The basic award is calculated as a length of service payment and is broadly equivalent to the payments required by statute to workers made redundant—a calculation based on a number of weeks' pay according to length of service and age. The current (1990–91) maximum payment under this scheme is £5,520. The compensatory award is "such amount as the Tribunal considers just and equitable in all the circumstances having regard to the loss sustained by the complainant in consequence of the dismissal in so far as that loss is attributable to action taken by the employer" (s74). Typical areas of loss calculation are lost earnings from the date of the dismissal, loss of future earnings where the complainant is still unemployed or in a new job with lower earnings, loss of pension benefits or medical insurance, expenses in seeking work, etc. There are some deductions that can be made by the tribunal in calculating total loss, in particular if the complainant contributed to his own dismissal (e.g., by the degree of misconduct) or failed to mitigate his losses (e.g., by not taking up an offer or opportunity to find employment after dismissal). The level of deduction is normally in the region of 25–75 percent but can be 100 percent. The tribunal cannot award more than £8,925 as a compensatory award. (Like the basic award, this limit is reviewed annually by the Secretary of State for Employment to take account of changes such as in earnings and inflation, but has not always been increased on an annual basis or in line with these changes.)

The terms of the statute make clear that reemployment orders were intended to be the primary remedy, but in practice such orders are rare, made in less than 3 percent of successful claims. (There is scope for debate about the true causes of this, but it is evident that few employees wish to go back to their employer by the time an unfair dismissal decision is handed down.) Where an employer fails to comply with a reemployment order, the sole remedy is an extra compensation payment, generally thirteen to twenty-six weeks' pay in addition to the compensation award. Higher compensation for failure to reemploy is ordered if the dismissal is by reason of sex or race discrimination, or because of union or nonunion membership. Average tribunal awards, however, are low (less than £2,000).

Industrial Tribunal Practice

The industrial tribunals are effectively specialist labor courts dealing primarily with individual statutory employment rights, not only dismissal but various other claims such as sex or race discrimination in employment. Over 80 percent of their case load, however, concerns unfair dismissal claims. Their designation as tribunals indicates the intent that they should be less formal and speedier than the ordinary courts, as well as exercising specialist expertise. While it is true that industrial tribunals are less formal than courts—for example, trade union officials or citizen rights' or other lay organizations can act as advocates for the parties—and that they do hear cases more quickly, there have been criticisms of their formality and tendency to legalism.[15] It is common practice for lawyers to be engaged to act for parties (more so on the employer's side; there is no eligibility for state legal aid for representation before industrial tribunals). Criticisms of legalism are perhaps unfair given the fact that tribunals are required to act in accordance with statutory rules and that their decisions are subject to appeal on points of law. Appeals from industrial tribunals can be taken to an employment appeal tribunal, and from there into the higher courts, the Court of Appeals and the House of Lords. (Legal aid is available on appeals.) Criticisms of formality may have more substance; tribunals follow standard adversarial court procedures of examination and crossexamination of witnesses giving evidence under oath.

The tribunal is composed of a legal chairman who directs the proceedings and two lay members, one of whom is drawn from lists submitted by trade union organizations, the other from employers' organizations. In the employment appeal tribunal the chairman is a high court judge. Decisions are made on a majority basis, although most judgments are unanimous. The procedure of bringing an industrial tribunal claim is initiated by an applicant making a simple complaint in writing within three months after dismissal, which leads the tribunal to issue a form to the employer seeking a reply on the complaint and making arrangements for a hearing or preliminary hearing date. Where an individual makes a complaint of dismissal (or would be entitled to do so and initiates this), a conciliation officer will attempt to help the parties reach a settlement before the stage of a tribunal hearing. The conciliation is provided by a separate independent statutory agency, ACAS, which also acts in collective disputes. ACAS conciliation, mediation, or arbitration of dismissal claims may also take place independently of any industrial tribunal claim, usually under a collective agreement or on a trade union–employer request. This is not a legal rule-based system, however, except in the sense that it is part of ACAS's general statutory duties to assist settlement of industrial relations disputes.

Some thirty to forty thousand claims a year are made to the industrial tribunals. The majority of these are withdrawn or settled (in roughly equal proportions) before a hearing date is reached. Only around a third of cases reach a full tribunal hearing annually, applicants commonly being successful in less than a third of the cases heard.

THE PARTICULAR OBLIGATIONS OF EMPLOYMENT

The discussion on the various scenarios draws primarily on the law of unfair dismissal as outlined. As should be clear from the outline, tribunal judgments on the fairness of a dismissal are inherently influenced by the factual circumstances and variations present in individual cases, making predictions of outcome often uncertain. Judgments of reasonableness often tend to reflect a complex of circumstances rather than a single factor. It should also be stated here that of course the outcome of many of these scenarios in the real world may not be a tribunal action at all; a trade union may successfully negotiate a lesser penalty for the employee, or the employee may accept the dismissal rather than face the anxiety or cost of legal action over a dismissal.

SUBORDINATION

Case Scenario

JD, a janitor at the A Manufacturing Company, is assigned the task of waxing office hallways. He completes one hallway. His supervisor, FF, inspects the hallway and says to JD, "Do this floor again." JD replies "No," and walks away.

Analysis

The duty to obey lawful and reasonable orders is inherent in the common law conception of the employment relationship, one of the fundamental implied terms in any contract of employment. Insubordination will always therefore be treated by tribunals as a reason for dismissal within the 1978 Act under the heading of conduct. However, the fairness of dismissal for this cause will depend on the wider issues of reasonableness—the nature of the order and of the refusal, the circumstances surrounding it, and the reason for refusing to carry it out.[16] Such circumstances often have to be cumulative in effect, rather than relating to a single incident of disobedience, before a tribunal will find unfair dismissal. If an order is unlawful or unreasonable in terms of common industrial relations practice or outside the terms of the contract or job description, dismissal is likely to be unfair.[17]

Seriousness. Factors that emphasize the aspect of insubordination—accompanying abuse from the employee or threats, particularly of clearly accompanied by an assault—would tend to influence a tribunal toward a finding of reasonableness. The most important factor in determining reasonableness of dismissal, however, would be repetition of this insubordination. But, even in such a case it would be unusual for a tribunal to find a dismissal fair unless there had been a proper series of warnings before the employee was dismissed—for example, disciplinary interview and written warning or suspension. Tribunals might be willing in practice to ignore formal disciplinary action if the evidence indicated that the employee had a number of previous informal warnings and was well aware of the likely consequences of his actions.

Observation by other employees might be a factor, but not usually of importance. Rarely mentioned in tribunal decisions, its importance lies more in its evidential significance: there would be confirmation of the supervisor's evidence should the employee deny the incident took place, by calling the other employees as witnesses.

Procedural protection for the employee by means of the series of disciplinary interviews is seen as an accepted part of good industrial relations practice. A single incident of insubordination is infrequently a justification for dismissal as compared to a lesser disciplinary penalty. It is also seen as appropriate because there might be circumstances in the employee's situation that would diminish the seriousness of the insubordination. This would be true, for example, if the employee genuinely believed that his health was at risk, that the order was contrary to

312

rules or law, was countermanded by another managerial order, was outside the terms of his contract or his job description, or was unreasonable. In all these cases the tribunals would expect the employer's reasonable investigation of the case to have unearthed this belief, and there would be an onus on the employer first to consider or investigate its validity. If the employee view was invalid, the employer could then properly warn the employee, if appropriate consultation had failed to change his view, that continued disobedience could lead to either further disciplinary action or dismissal.

Tribunals would be less ready to accept as a valid reason for refusal the employee's personal appraisal that the work was unnecessary, as it is an accepted managerial function to issue work instructions. However, they would expect an employer to have some justification for the instruction, and again there should have been a clear series of warnings or lesser disciplinary penalties prior to dismissal.

Mitigation. Dismissal would be particularly inappropriate as a disciplinary response to a single act of insubordination where the employee had been provoked by the supervisor, had a good work record, or was a long-serving employee. It would be legally irrelevant whether the employee was or was not an employee representative[18] unless his refusal related to his concerns as a representative as such—for example, a need to challenge a particular order as outside a job contract requirement. In practice, however, both employers and tribunals would treat such a case a little more carefully as a possible instance of victimization for union activities. The Code of Practice recommends that a case against a union representative be discussed with a full-time union officer.

Enforceability. Consistency in the employer's conduct is seen as an important element in tribunal considerations of reasonableness. Failure to warn about previous incidents or to take similar action against employees who had committed similar misconduct would detract from a claim of reasonableness. The employer can avoid the difficulty of having been lax in the past over a practice by making clear to employees that a particular type of conduct is in the future to be treated more severely despite any earlier practice—for example, by a works notice or circular. In relation to a single employee's misconduct, employers often argue before tribunals, and tribunals often accept, that inconsistency in treatment of misconduct by one employee over time is only evidence of the

313

employer's goodwill and tolerance, which had justifiably now worn thin. Nevertheless, in the latter case the tribunal would usually still expect some intimation to the employee that dismissal was a likely option for any further misconduct.

SOBRIETY

Case Scenario

RR, a laborer on the loading dock of B Trucking Company, is observed by his supervisor, JB, reaching into the pocket of a coat that is hanging near his workplace. JB observes RR bring something to his mouth, appear to swallow, and then replace it in the coat. JB approaches RR and asks, "What are you drinking?" RR reaches into the pocket of his coat and hands JB a bottle that contains an alcoholic beverage. JB forms the opinion that RR's breath smells strongly of alcoholic spirits and that his eyes are unfocused.

Analysis

Traditionally an employee who was under the influence of alcohol at work would be regarded as being in breach of the contract of employment in a willful manner, therefore subject to disciplinary penalties. This is still an accepted approach in many employment situations. However, with the recognition of alcoholism as a medical disease, there may also be a shift toward treating employees with symptoms of alcoholism along similar lines to those with other forms of health problems. An employer would therefore be expected to investigate a case and, if the investigation revealed a possibility of alcoholism, to counsel the employee to accept treatment and to go on sickness absence or other monitored regime. If, however, after reasonable effort the employer were unsuccessful or the employee failed to recover, the employer would be entitled to dismiss the employee for lack of competence to perform the work for which he or she was employed.

The tribunals would adopt the same emphasis on proper procedures being conducted as described under the first scenario, that is, warnings about the consequences of repeated action and a series of lesser disciplinary penalties in an attempt to correct the behavior before dismissal.

Seriousness. If the employee is drunk, as opposed to merely in the act of drinking, this is more likely to lead to a fair dismissal as an act of gross misconduct. This is even more the case where there could be potential damage to valuable property, to other employees' safety, or to the employer's reputation, and almost certainly so in the case of actual damage. Where an unlawful intoxicant (such as certain drugs) had been or was being used during working hours, this would give the employer a stronger right in all circumstances to dismiss the employee.

Mitigation. A claim by the employee that he is an alcoholic (or evidence that the employer should have known of this) and seeking treatment might lead a tribunal to suggest that the employer acted unreasonably if it failed to treat the case as one comparable to a case of a disability or sickness—that is, give the employee the opportunity to show he or she can recover. Where the employee merely asserted this without evidence, however, this would normally be insufficient to persuade a tribunal. If the employee had already caused damage but had failed to warn the employer of his problem, this might also be ground for the tribunal to find that the employer had acted fairly in dismissing.

If there were evidence of a well-known works practice to imbibe beer or other alcoholic beverage, the employer could not claim the misconduct to be gross misconduct without taking action to bring its seriousness to the attention of all employees and to root out the practice. This, however, relates to consistency rather than the nature of the industry, since it may be the case that some industries that produce a beverage may take an even more serious view of employees consuming it during working hours than would an outside industry. The fact that the offence is not spelled out in works rules is not in itself conclusive, although a finding of reasonableness is more likely where offences leading to dismissal are clearly indicated.[19]

Enforceability. The approach to consistency of treatment has already been described. This also in theory applies to consumption by supervisor and managerial grades, although in these cases there might be different arguments regarding potential damage to property or other employees' safety.

SECURITY OF EMPLOYER'S PROPERTY

Case Scenario

PR, a clerk employed by C Gourmet Foods Company, is observed by two supervisors taking company products out of a

315

packing box, concealing them on his person, and walking out the door with them. He is apprehended after he exits the store, and admits taking the products.

Analysis

The offence of dishonest taking of employer property is treated as one of the most serious cases of misconduct, a breach of the fundamental term of loyalty in a contract of employment.[20] It will often lead to a summary dismissal and a finding of fair dismissal. Most tribunal cases in this area concern situations where employees have denied the offence, and the tribunal's role is to establish from the evidence whether the employer acted reasonably in dismissing for a suspected offence. An employer in a case of suspected theft would be expected to show that it genuinely believes the employee is guilty of misconduct, that it has conducted an investigation that is reasonable in the circumstances, and that it has then reasonable grounds for belief that the employee is guilty.[21] The important point stressed in the tribunal decisions is that the employer does not have to satisfy itself of the employee's guilt to the extent that would be required in a criminal court, where the standard of proof is beyond reasonable doubt.[22] The employer's decision is on the separate issue of reasonableness and is in relation to the effect on its trust of the employee; an employee may therefore validly be dismissed for theft even if acquitted of the same offence in a criminal court.

Seriousness. The value of goods stolen is not an especially determinant factor at law, although one can guess that in practice industrial tribunals would expect that for certain trivial amounts in terms of property value there would be a warning rather than dismissal in the first instance. This would probably be more true of certain types of property (e.g., waste) than cash. There are circumstances where even trivial thefts could be seen as serious, such as where an employer has had a series of thefts, or an industry is prone to theft problems (e.g., department stores). At the end of the day it is not for the tribunal to substitute its own view of seriousness.[23]

Knowledge of the act by other employees is not relevant given that the issue is trust between the employee and employer. The fact that goods were abandoned is not in itself sufficient to excuse an employee, but it would be a factor in a tribunal looking for evidence that the employer made it clear to employees that such practices were not condoned.

Mitigation. The needs of the employee could be taken into account by the tribunal in that the employer would be expected to follow a disciplinary procedure that allowed the employee to reveal his situation—that is, an interview putting the charge to the employee, even in cases that might seem clear.[24] If the employer had followed such a procedure, the employee's circumstance—whether family needs or the problems of job stress—would be relevant, but not necessarily where there was a serious theft as against one involving a product of minor value. A previous record of dishonesty in relation to that employment would count against the employee, but criminal offences as such are not usually relevant and in some cases are required by statute to be ignored (Rehabilitation of Offenders Act 1974). Length of service is relevant,[25] particularly where there might be doubt as to the fact of an offence or its seriousness; in itself it may only lead the employer to suspect that the employee may have been guilty of offences for some time.

The existence of a works custom of allowing employees to take home small amounts of goods would be of considerable importance to an employee's case, unless the evidence clearly indicated that the employee was not following normal procedure in relation to such goods and was well aware of the normal practice.

Enforceability. Again consistency is vital in an employee knowing what to expect; therefore, ignoring past employee thefts could be fatal to a claim of reasonableness unless it was shown that the employer's change of heart had been clearly communicated (although a claim of employer inconsistency is probably less effective in this context unless the employee has very clear evidence).

PEACEFUL WORKPLACE

Case Scenario

MM is a clerk in D Department Store. NN is another clerk in the same department store; he is physically larger than MM. While MM is moving some heavy equipment from one area to another NN says, "I'm surprised that you did not ask a real man like me to handle this job." MM, angered, strikes NN on the jaw, knocking him down. NN gets up and walks away.

Analysis

Fighting or an assault in the workplace is another category of offence that is well established as an instance of gross misconduct, often set out in works rules as a category of offence justifying summary dismissal in the absence of appropriate mitigating circumstances. Tribunals treat it along similar lines and might expect employees to be aware of its seriousness even in the absence of an explicit works rule.[26]

Seriousness. Evidence that another employee provoked a response would alter any estimate of whether it was reasonable to dismiss. Sufficient provocation would lead to a requirement that a lesser penalty should be imposed, unless the response was exaggerated in relation to the provocation. In particular, a tribunal might wish to be assured that there was not unfair discrimination in the treatment of the two employees; if both were at fault or involved in fighting, both might be dismissed. A definite injury to the other employee or use of a weapon would be clear evidence of a serious breach of employment rules (or terms of contract), whereas a brief tussle would raise problems for management of whether the incident merited dismissal as the disciplinary reaction rather than a lesser penalty. Similarly, incidental damage to property, or a vicinity where there might occur such damage or other dangers to health and safety or interference with production, would tend to increase the evident seriousness of the offence albeit not strictly part of the employee intention.

The presence of other employees would not alter the seriousness of the offence (it would alter management's ability to obtain evidence in the event of dispute over what exactly occurred), but the presence of a customer would be likely to contribute to the perceived seriousness of the incident whether or not it affected the customer's business orders. The employees' respective job duties would only affect a decision if this could have led the actions of one to amount to a substantial provocation.

Mitigation. A record of fighting would ensure a finding of fair dismissal, but even in the absence of this a clear outburst of violence could also be grounds for fair dismissal in the absence of provocation or other mitigating factors. However, seniority and a good record or good previous relationship could make it likely that a tribunal would expect a warning rather than dismissal as the appropriate reasonable employer response.[27]

Enforceability. The question of consistency of treatment is similar to that described in relation to earlier scenarios.[28]

OFF-DUTY CONDUCT

Case Scenario

TT, head salesclerk for E Toy Store, participates in a white supremacist demonstration. He is arrested for disorderly behavior, and a photograph of him handcuffed to a post and snarling at police is printed in the local newspaper, along with his name and the name of his employer.

Analysis

The general approach taken by tribunals to off-duty conduct, in particular criminal offences, is that the employee's private life is his own affair unless it reflects adversely on the employer's business in some way. In the latter case the employer may be entitled to regard the employee as no longer suitable for its employment. This is particularly apt where employees are in positions of trust or control of equipment or money and are convicted of an outside offence that indicates that trust cannot be placed in them. It also applies where the offence might lead to damage to the employer's reputation with customers or the public[29] or where the offence might cause difficulties with other employees at work. In this case TT has brought unwelcome publicity to his employer, and may cause damage to relations at work if there is an employment force of mixed racial origins.

Seriousness. The question of a criminal conviction in this case is not crucial, given the publicity. The key question is whether the employer can act reasonably in dismissing for this conduct. A more serious offence might have a bearing on this reasonableness, but again only if it affects the employment position—for example, because of publicity or a long prison sentence. (In the latter case employers should generally treat the case as they might a long-term sickness absence unless there were other aspects of the offence affecting the employment relationship, as here.) An absence of publicity would therefore be relevant to the reasonableness of dismissal; employers have no inherent right to take a moral stance on the off-duty conduct of

319

employees. Evidence of an impact on sales or relationships at work would, however, enable the employer to advance an argument as to the relevance of the conduct to the employment relationship.

Mitigation. Seniority in terms of a previous good employment record would have a bearing on reasonableness, as would any claim by the employee that he was not at fault but was provoked. In the latter case particularly the employer would be expected to have conducted a reasonable investigation of the background before coming to a conclusion.

Enforceability. If TT had been previously arrested for a similar offence, the employer could clearly act to dismiss if there had been a warning about a future occurrence leading to dismissal. However, in a case of this nature, the tribunal would be likely to view the incident as serious enough to merit a dismissal for a first offence or for a repeated offence even if no action was taken against an earlier one. Inconsistency of treatment of other employees would, however, make it likely that the dismissal could not be upheld. If the inconsistency related to more favorable treatment of a black employee, TT could claim racial discrimination as well as unfair dismissal.

ATTENDANCE

Case Scenario

JJ is a nurse's aide at F Nursing Home. Because of an illness her attendance at work has been erratic for two years. During that period she has missed 30 percent of her scheduled working days. During the last month she has missed 20 percent of her scheduled working days. All of these absences were excused. She then misses three days of work, without notifying her employer, because she decides to extend her holiday.

Analysis

Attendance for work is at the root of the contract of employment in most cases, therefore a serious matter for the employer where it is outside the band of reasonable sickness absence, even if these are excused (medically certified) absences. It allows an employer to dismiss for reasons of incapability. It is within the employer's rights to define what is expected by way of attendance, although an extreme view of this by an employer would no doubt be rejected by an industrial tribunal as unreasonable. A clue to a reasonable period in any employment might be obtained from the length of entitlement to sickness pay, but this is not conclusive, as other factors such as the needs of the employer to get the work done have to be considered. However, unlike some of the areas of misconduct, there is a greater onus in practice on the employer to make it clear to employees in general or any particular employee how much absence will be tolerated. An employee should be consulted about the absences and employer options for action, particularly if there is an underlying medical problem,[30] and if necessary warned about the possible consequences of further absences.

Alternative employment should be considered in the case of a likely incapacity problem. In this case, however, the issue is one of absences and erratic attendance as such rather than a long-term incapacity requiring detailed medical consideration. JJ could only be dismissed fairly if the employer had clearly warned her about the consequences of further instances of absenteeism after earlier consultation with her on the reasons for nonattendance.

Seriousness. The employer is entitled to define what is expected by way of attendance, although in theory a tribunal has the power to say that a particular level is unreasonable in terms of a dismissal. Dismissal for missing a day after a holiday would be likely to fall into the unreasonable category unless there had been clear warning of the likely consequence after a history of absence. The employer can dismiss fairly even if there has been a clear medical reason for absence[31] provided there has been sufficient consultation with the employee, exploration of the possible alternative jobs with the employer that might be suitable if the employee's absence was partly job-related, and failure to find a suitable alternative. Where there is a less clear reason for absences, and especially in the absence of any medical certificates, a warning procedure is generally accepted as more appropriate. If the employee can point to a downward trend either in terms of less absences in the recent period or in terms of a doctor's note that she will fully recover soon, an employer would be expected to treat the case more leniently. However, if the employee had been warned about absences being unacceptable and merely shown a statistical improvement, the employer could continue to carry out the action specified in the original warning.

Mitigation. Seniority, evidence of being a good employee,

321

knowledge by the employer that the employee has pressing domestic problems—all these make it more likely that a tribunal will find a dismissal unfair in the absence of a reasonable length of time in which the employer has attempted to manage the problem other than by dismissal.

Enforceability. Tribunals would be especially concerned that employers followed the Code of Practice and good industrial relations practice in this type of area. They would expect clear rules known by employees and interpreted and enforced consistently. In the case of a definite illness incapacitating the employee, they would expect appropriate consultation and consideration of other work arrangements to assist the employee. Consistency of treatment of all employees would be important. Absence of rules or a written policy on the subject would likely be held against employers with sufficient size and administrative resources but would not prevent a small employer winning a case so long as in practice it had taken similar steps of clear warning or consultation, etc., as might be required under the larger organization's more formal policies.

PERFORMANCE

Case Scenario

HH is a warehouseman for G Distributing Company. G has instituted a program that determines levels of productivity for warehousemen. This program meets accepted professional standards for such programs. Over a period of two months HH fails to produce at the prescribed levels, consistently falling 10 percent below the standard. He is warned that he will be terminated if he fails to improve his productivity within two weeks. HH claims that the standards of the new system are impossible to meet. He proves that prior to the institution of the new system he was given above-average evaluations by his supervisor for producing at this current level, covering a period of ten years.

Analysis

A duty to use care and skill to perform one's work competently is a fundamental implied term of the employment contract and recognized in the statutory reason for dismissal on grounds relating to capability. However, the employer will be expected to provide the conditions to make adequate performance possible by way of proper equipment, training, working

322

environment, investigation and consultation over difficulties, consideration of alternative employment, and—except in the case of a serious incident[32]—warnings about a need for improvement, before dismissal.[33] Warnings are a difficult aspect of this area of dismissal as, like some types of sickness absence, they may be quite inappropriate to the employee's incapability problem. They are most appropriate for situations where there is a suspected element of willful incapacity in the employee's performance. In other words, would a warning do any good?[34] Nevertheless, the employee in any case should be clearly forewarned of the likely result if there is a failure to improve. In instances where there has been a change of technical system or technology, there is particularly a need for the employer to consult and provide proper training. At the end of the day, however, the employer has a right to change working methods and technology used[35] and can dismiss provided it has followed appropriate procedures and considered alternative employment opportunities.

Seriousness. Perhaps the most important factor in such a case is whether the failure of performance actually affects the employer's business in some way, although ultimately this is a question of reasonable belief rather than proof of incompetence, and in some job roles measures of competence are not clear-cut. In this scenario there is some suggestion that the new program is to a degree an artificial monitoring system rather than one that produces evidence of damage to production, increased costs, or lost profits. To the extent that these can be evidenced, HH can be dismissed with fair dismissal as the likely outcome, subject to the considerations described above. The extent to which his performance falls below the average may also be relevant. If he has shown signs of improvement, this is an argument for the employer to persist in waiting for improvement. If the new system is proving too difficult for the aptitudes of this employee, he should be consulted on whether there is some need for retraining or alternative work he could do for the employer.

Mitigation. Again seniority or a good employment record would count toward the employer making more effort to correct the problem.

Enforceability. If there were evidence that other employees were failing to meet the standard, this would certainly prevent a fair dismissal of HH. This would also be likely if there had been evidence of adverse health effects of the new system, or failures to warn or consult on improved performance.

LOYALTY

Case Scenario

JS, a teller for H Bank, during an appearance on a television consumer information program states that her employer regularly fails to advise customers when they make mistakes in favor of the bank, but promptly corrects mistakes made in favor of the customers.

Analysis

Employers can expect that employees do not act in a manner that might damage their business under the implied obligations of loyalty and fidelity at common law.[36] This would fall under the heading of conduct or "some other substantial reason" in terms of the statutory tests. The difficulty raised in this scenario is the extent to which there is a degree of public interest involved, which suggests a need to balance public considerations with the employee duty. Even assuming that the employee could justify her statements before a tribunal, the employer is likely to argue that JS could have raised the matter through internal procedures or drawn the issue to the attention of outsiders without active participation in the program.

Seriousness. Factors that add to the seriousness of the damage to the employer, such as a peak-hour program appearance or evidence of a public response, would make the employer's dismissal more justifiable. If there were evidence that the employee was motivated merely by a desire to annoy the employer, or spoke out on the basis of flimsy evidence, or knew that what she was saying was untrue, these are all factors that would make the employer's decision more reasonable. If JD had been drawing attention to an unlawful practice of the employer, however, a claim of reasonableness would be difficult to sustain. Finally, tribunals would be likely to take account of the industry, but more in terms of the likely damage to the employer from an employee allegation; a leading bank would be assumed to suffer greater damage than a little-known business.

Mitigation. Other factors in JS's situation, such as mistreatment of her by the employer, would be taken into account in assessing how reasonable a decision to dismiss would be. Similarly, if JS held a position of employee representative, the employer would need to show more care in handling the situation because of possible allegations of victimization. However, the fact of being an employee representative does not as such permit acts of disloyalty; information obtained by a position on the board of the company would merely emphasize a further fiduciary duty of confidentiality.

Enforceability. The existence of a clear rule preventing employees making public statements on the bank's affairs would add to the reasonableness of the employer's decision, although a tribunal might ignore a clause that attempts to prohibit disclosure of unlawful acts by the bank. The duty of loyalty would probably be regarded as sufficient, however, to justify a dismissal even in the absence of a formal rule or a claim from the employee that the rule was not communicated to her, unless there was a sufficient public interest element.

RESTRICT COLLECTIVE ACTION

Case Scenario

JJ, a machinist at I Manufacturing Company, becomes angry because he believes that his supervisor is treating him and other employees in a disrespectful manner. In protest, he persuades the other employees in his work group to leave work together in the middle of their scheduled work shift and not return until the next day.

Analysis

At common law, collective industrial action is generally regarded as a clear breach of contract justifying the employer in terminating the contract. Statutory reforms in English law have led to a number of immunities for organizers of industrial action in terms of protection against injunctions and claims for damages for inducing breach of contract.[37] However, the statutory immunities do not extend to protection against dismissal for breach of contract. Indeed, the 1978 Act specifically prevents a tribunal determining whether a dismissal was fair or unfair where the employee was dismissed while taking part in industrial action, unless there have been selective dismissals amongst those taking part or unless there have been selective reengagement offers made within three months after dismissals have taken place within the same establishment (s62 as amended). JJ in this case could, however, bring a claim because the dismissal apparently did not take place until he returned to work. Even if it took place before that, he could claim if the others have not been dismissed.[38] However, his protection may be less once the provisions of the Employment Act 1990 come into force; selective dismissals outside tribunal jurisdiction will be possible where the action is unofficial as defined in the act—that is, if it involves union members whose union has not authorized or endorsed the action. Where selectivity is proved or where there has been no dismissal during the action to trigger the effect of s62, dismissal is assessed according to the normal statutory tests of asking for the employer to prove a reason and then assessing reasonableness. As no specific guidance is given to tribunals in this area, it can be a difficult task to assess reasonableness. Where there had been selectivity, the test would revolve around the question of the criteria for the employer's selection. The presence of a "genuine" grievance would assist the tribunal to find a dismissal unfair—for example, if management had failed to act on complaints or on bad working conditions.[39]

Seriousness. The length of the walkout or damage to production would be factors in the tribunal's consideration of reasonableness. JJ's position as leader would probably not justify dismissal on its own without further evidence of misconduct. Gross misconduct other than the walkout would, however, be taken into account in assessing fairness—for example, evidence of JJ's participation in abuse of the supervisor, violence, or damage to property. The employer would still be expected to meet normal procedural requirements in cases of misconduct of holding an investigation and giving JJ an opportunity to put his side of the story.[40]

Mitigation. JJ's service would be taken into account in assessing the reasonableness of any decision by the employer to dismiss. Evidence that the action was in response to unreasonable supervisor requests would support a finding of unfair dismissal, while if the supervisor was merely trying to apply proper rules, industrial action would more clearly be seen as serious misconduct.

Enforceability. An absence of rules against strikes would not oust the common law view of strikes as fundamental breach of contract. A collective bargaining agreement prohibiting strikes, assuming it met the legal requirements for valid incorporation into the individual contract (Trade Union and Labour Relations Act 1974 s18), would merely confirm this common law rule, although a tribunal might in practice take some account of the fact that the parties had gone to the trouble of formalizing the position.

AVOID CONFLICT OF INTEREST

Case Scenario

IB, a systems analyst for J Company, has access to private computer systems of his employer. IB accepts a string of free-lance, relatively routine programming jobs for K Company, a competitor of his employer, performing the work at his home.

Analysis

Tribunals would again have regard to the common law background to this scenario: the implied duties on the employee of loyalty and good faith.[41] However, they would expect there to be evidence that the activity was capable of doing damage[42] and that the attention of the employee was drawn to this, assuming that it was not obvious.

Seriousness. The presence of a formal rule is important but not conclusive in allowing a tribunal to reach a decision that an employee was guilty of a disciplinary offence in this situation. A crucial factor in terms of whether it merited dismissal or a lesser penalty would be the question of whether IB was undermining his employer's business rather than whether the work was identical or whether IB was using skills developed in J Company. Damage could be demonstrated if there was evidence of a transfer of technology or trade secrets or confidential customer lists, or if the employer could claim a reasonable suspicion that such transfer was taking place or likely to take place. Share ownership in K would be a factor justifying such suspicion, or the fact that J had access to such information and was working for a competitor. Such circumstances have led to employees being dismissed fairly even on the ground that their *spouses* have been working for the competitor or setting up a business in competition.[43]

Mitigation. Seniority or pressing domestic financial circumstances could be argued in IB's favor but are unlikely to outweigh clear evidence or likelihood of damage to the employer.

Enforceability. The more obvious the damage that might be done by someone in IB's position, the less relevant the need for a formal rule or for clarity of rule. (The position is quite different where employers seek to enforce covenants preventing work for competitors after an employee leaves.) An employee in a senior position especially would be taken to know he should not work for a competitor in a way that might undermine his employer. In appropriate cases, the employee can again rely on inconsistency of employer application of the rule (to himself or others) in arguing that a dismissal is unreasonable.[44]

CONCLUSIONS

In terms of legal rules, it would be possible to argue that unfair dismissal legislation in the United Kingdom has revolutionized the employment relationship. The shift from the legal capacity to dismiss for any or no reason with appropriate contractual notice, to a position where a dismissal may have to be justified before a public body as reasonable, represents a radical reform. Some indication of its impact can be gauged from the campaign of protests conducted by employers against the legislation from its inception. It is still possible to find remnants of an employer folklore of the 1970s (small employers in particular) that it is impossible to dismiss people now. Legal reforms by Conservative governments since 1979 have reflected the desire to free employers of this "burden", although the substance of the legal framework has remained.[45] The majority of employers now accept and live happily with the legislation. Many would praise it for the way it has forced employers to pay attention to their personnel standards and practices, and brought a greater consistency and orderliness into employment practices.

This "revolution," however, can also be seen by critics as a mythical one other than in terms of its effect on personnel practice.[46] There is disappointment for those who saw the unfair dismissal rules as ushering in a new era of a job as a form of property right, where industrial justice would shift toward employee interests. In a number of respects the legislation has failed to achieve this. First, in assessing fairness tribunals have resorted to notions of "industrial common sense" and the "reasonable employer." These have therefore tended to follow existing (common law) values in terms of attitudes to insubordination, industrial action, and so on, although collective bargaining and employer practices pre–1971 had in many ways provided a floor of protection, in practice if not in legal theory, to such standards. The continuing application in the tribunals of these common law values means that the success rates for employees before the tribunals are low. There-fore, the claim that it is now impossible to dismiss someone fairly is indeed folklore rather than practice. Second, the reemployment orders that were intended to be the primary remedy are used on few occasions in practice. Third, the nature of the tribunals as a legal institution has proved inhibiting for applicants, both in terms of the weight of legal references, case law, and formal procedures which the tribunals seem to follow, and in terms of the costs of employing legal assistance for representation. Finally, the rewards for a successful applicant in terms of compensation are usually low, no real obstacle to an employer who wished to rid itself of someone.[47]

What is the reasonable judgment as to employer or union "folklore" on tribunals? The use of the criterion of reasonable-ness in the legislation, rather than of any more explicit criteria, has almost inevitably ensured an adherence to the dominant value system of British society in relation to employment prac-tices. It could hardly have been expected to be otherwise. A fail-ure in this respect is really more a failure of politicolegal reform than of the tribunals' judgments. Nevertheless, as the details of the scenarios indicate, there is scope for tribunals to shift stan-dards generally at least, toward those of more "enlightened" employers. The range of reasonable employer actions test could have been enormously restrictive, but the tribunals in practice seem to follow their own judgments of what is reasonable rather than strictly adhering to the test. What inchoate notion of employer they may be following in those judgments can be diffi-cult to define, although the personal experience of tribunal mem-bers must be significant.

The loose criterion of fairness also gives considerable scope for tribunals to respond to the emergence of new social values in employment relations, as for example in relation to alcoholism. Reasonableness is a moving social target, but of course it may move either toward or away from employer prerogative, depend-ing on the dominant interest groups and values in a particular period. Many would say that tribunal decisions have clearly moved toward employers' prerogatives in the 1980s, but the pen-dulum may shift again. However, it is also worth stressing, par-ticularly in the light of recent case law on procedural aspects of fairness, that procedural justice legal standards are now higher than they have ever been in the employment relationship in the United Kingdom.

In the near future reformers' attention is more likely to turn to the other criticisms mentioned of the system. Even where dismissals are judged unfair under current values, there is minimal job reinstatement and compensation levels that are arguably derisory set against the seriousness of dismissal as a personal experience. Lack of legal aid and the presence of formalism in tribunal practice compound the problem for applicants seeking justice. Restrictions on claims from new employees and part-timers mean large numbers of employees are still without any effective legal remedy when they are dismissed. On the other hand, government spokesmen argue that the legislative burden on employers needs to be restrained in order not to inhibit employers from taking on employees. We are back to a discussion on the question of what is reasonable.

NOTES

1. It is important to note that the United Kingdom has separate legal systems for Scotland, Northern Ireland, and England and Wales, the Scottish system in particular drawing on a different legal tradition. While the law of unfair dismissal applies to all three, minor differences may be found, e.g., in terminology or court structure. References to the common law position in this chapter and to the legal rules on contracts of employment are based on the law of England and Wales.

2. Other legal rules may be relevant to some instances of cases of discipline and dismissal, principally rules arising from the contract of employment, from the sex and racial discrimination legislation, and from the statutory rules which provide for compensation for length of service for workers dismissed on the grounds of redundancy. An employee dismissed and compensated for redundancy may still claim unfair dismissal as described in this chapter—e.g., because he was unfairly selected for redundancy. See, e.g., *Williams v. Compair Maxam* [1982] IRLR 83. For a general introduction to the law of employment see Lord Wedderburn, *The Worker and the Law,* 3rd ed. (London: Penguin, 1986); N. M. Selwyn, *Selwyn's Law of Employment,* 6th ed. (London: Butterworths, 1988); J. Bowers, *Employment Law* (London: Blackstone Press, 1990).

3. See, e.g., *McClelland v. Northern Ireland General Health Services Board* [1957] 2 All ER 129, HL; *Ridge v. Baldwin* [1964] AC 40, HL; *Malloch v. Aberdeen Corporation* [1971] 1 WLR 1578.

4. The courts acknowledged that considerations of what constituted gross misconduct might change with changing social conditions; see *Wilson v. Racher* [1974] ICR 428 CA.

5. The idea was first mooted in a major Royal Commission review of industrial relations; Donovan, *Royal Commission on Trade Unions and Employers' Associations 1965–1968* (London: HMSO, Command 3623, 1968).

6. This and other reforms of employment law have been justified by government spokesmen on the grounds of free market approaches to industrial relations. For a commentary on the reforms, see K. J. Mackie, "Reform: An Overview," *A Handbook of Industrial Relations Practice,* rev. ed., ed. B. Towers (London: Kogan Page, 1989).

7. For the leading case which led to this contractual interpretation of entitlement in the statute, see *Western Excavating (ECC) Ltd v. Sharp* [1978] QB 161.

8. *British Leyland (UK) Ltd v. Swift* [1981] IRLR 91, CA.

9. *ACAS Code of Practice 1: Disciplinary Practice and Procedures in Employment* (London: Advisory Conciliation and Arbitration Service, 1977). ACAS has recently issued an advisory handbook with fuller guidance on dismissal and disciplinary practice, but it does not have the legal status of a code: *Discipline at Work: ACAS Advisory Handbook,* 1987.

10. *Retarded Children's Aid Society v. Day* [1978] ICR 437, CA.

11. *Ladbroker Racing Ltd v. Arnott and Others* [1983] IRLR 154, Ct of Sess.

12. *Polkey v. A. E. Dayton Services Ltd* [1987] 3 All ER 974, HL.

13. *Post Office v. Fennell* [1981] IRLR 221, CA.

14. *Hadjiannou v. Coral Casinos Ltd* [1981] IRLR 352, EAT.

15. See, e.g., L. Dickens, M. Jones, B. Weekes, and M. Hart. *Dismissed: A Study of Unfair Dismissal and the Industrial Tribunal System* (Oxford: Blackwell, 1985); Karl J. Mackie, "Industrial Tribunals—What Next?" *Industrial Relations Journal* 19, no. 2: 89–92; Justice, *Industrial Tribunals,* A Report by Justice (London: 1987).

16. *UCATT v. Brain* [1980] ICR 779, EAT.

17. See *Morrish v. Henly's (Folkestone) Ltd* [1973] 2 All ER 137, NIRC; *Payne v. Spook Erection Ltd* [1984] IRLR 219; *Wilson v. IDR Construction* [1975] IRLR 260. Compare the common law case *Laws v. London Chronicle (Indicator Newspapers Ltd* [1959] 1 WLR 698, CA.

18. *Fowler v. Cammell Laird (Shipbuilders) Ltd* [1973] IRLR 72.

19. *Distillers Company (Bottling Services) Ltd v. Gardner* [1982] IRLR 47, EAT.

20. See, e.g., *Sinclair v. Neighbour* [1967] 2 QB 279, CA.

21. *British Home Stores v. Burchell* [1980] IRLR 379, EAT.

22. *Ferodo Ltd v. Barnes* [1976] ICR 439, EAT.

23. *Trusthouse Forte Hotels Ltd v. Murphy* [1977] IRLR 186, EAT.

24. *Tesco (Holdings) Ltd v. Hill* [1977] IRLR 63.

25. *Johnson Mathey Metals Ltd v. Harding* [1978] IRLR 248, EAT.

26. *Parsons & Co Ltd v. McLoughlin* [1978] IRLR 65, EAT.

27. *Taylor v. Parsons Peebles NEI Bruce Peebles Ltd* [1981] IRLR 119.

28. *Post Office v. Fennell* [1981] IRLR 221, CA.

29. *Richardson v. Bradford City M. C.* [1975] IRLR 296.

30. *East Lindsey District Council v. Daubney* [1977] ICR 566, EAT.

31. *International Sports Co Ltd v. Thomson* [1980] IRLR 340, EAT.

32. *Taylor v. Alidair* [1978] IRLR 82.

33. *James v. Waltham Holy Cross UDC* [1973] IRLR 202, NIRC.

34. *Littlewoods Organization Ltd v. Egenti* [1976] ICR 516, EAT; *Winterhalter Gastronom Ltd v. Webb* [1973] ICR 245, NIRC.

35. *Cresswell v. Board of Inland Revenue* [1984] 2 All ER 713.

36. For an interesting discussion of this in the context of industrial action, see *Secretary of State for Employment v. ASLEF (No 2)* [1972] 2 QB 455, CA.

37. These immunities have been substantially reduced since 1979; see Mackie, "Reform: An Overview."

38. A third (unlikely) route by which JJ could claim unfair dismissal in circumstances similar to those described in the scenario is a claim of what is termed constructive dismissal. The 1978 Act allows an employee to claim dismissal where he resigns by reason of the employer's conduct. The test laid down by statute and case law for establishing such a resignation as a dismissal is that the employer must have been guilty of breach of a fundamental term of the contract and that the employee resigned in consequence. Constructive dismissal decisions in the tribunals

appear to have established as a term a need for mutual trust and respect. However, JJ would have to prove serious incidents of disrespectful behavior by the supervisor, and probably that other managers took no action despite being alerted to the problem. JJ would be unable to take this route because the statute requires a deliberate termination by the employee. Here there has merely been a walkout followed by a return to work.

39. *Burns & Davies v. Ideal Timber Products Ltd* [1975] IRLR 19.

40. *Mclaren v. National Coal Board* [1988] ICR 370, CA.

41. *Hivac Ltd v. Park Royal Scientific Instruments Ltd* [1946] Ch 169, CA; *Smith v. Du Pont (UK) Ltd* [1976] IRLR 107. See also *Faccenda Chicken Ltd v. Fowler* [1987] Ch 117, CA.

42. *Nova Plastics Ltd v. Froggatt* [1982] IRLR 146, EAT.

43. *Foot v. Eastern Counties Timber Ltd* [1972] IRLR 83.

44. *Frame v. McKean & Graham Ltd* [1974] IRLR 179.

45. Mackie, "Reform: An Overview."

46. See the references in note 15.

47. A judgment which a recent government reform implicitly acknowledged by providing a special award system for those dismissed for nonunion membership, also applicable in cases of dismissal for union membership or union activities.

10

THE UNITED STATES

Hoyt N. Wheeler and Dennis R. Nolan

Understanding the substantive rules of industrial justice in the United States is both troublesome and worth the trouble. It is worth the trouble because, in addition to being of interest in their own right, these rules go to the very heart of the American employment relationship. Since employment is one of the crucial human relationships in any modern society, comprehension of it illuminates an important aspect of the overall society. However, it is troublesome. This is partly because, like other elements of the American industrial relations system, the industrial justice subsystem is divided between a nonunion sector and a smaller union sector.[1] In the nonunion sector, comprising 84 percent of the labor force, employees are protected by several narrow statutes and by judicial decisions interpreting express or implied employment contracts. Employees in the union sector have the additional protection of a body of private law developed by labor arbitrators.

To describe this complex system, we will begin with the legislative and judicial rules applicable to all employees. This section includes a treatment of the historic common (i.e., judge-made) law of "master and servant," which contains the oldest body of formal American law on termination of employment. We will then set out the general rules and procedures governing the unionized sector. Finally, we will provide a detailed analysis of the substantive law of industrial justice as applied to specific scenarios set in the unionized sector.

OVERVIEW OF THE SYSTEM

The American common law holds that the employment relationship is terminable at will. That is, in the absence of an express agreement to the contrary, either the employer or the employee can end the relationship at any time, without notice or compensation. In its purest form this means that the employer can define the obligations of employment and punish perceived breaches of these obligations, so long as this violates no specific legal stricture. In an early but accurate formulation one judge stated that a party could end the relationship "for good cause, bad cause, or no cause at all." The employee is assumed to consent to this rule when accepting a job and can leave and find another job if the employer's actions are unsatisfactory.

To the extent that employment at will remains the law, one could say that there is no general American law defining the obligations of employment or limiting discipline and termination. However, legislatures and courts have created special exceptions to this rule. In addition, some employees have express contracts of employment that will be enforced by the courts according to their terms under the still extant law of master and servant.

The earliest legislation limiting employer discretion to discipline or terminate was contained in statutes protecting the right of employees to form and join trade unions. In the 1890s, both state laws and the Federal Erdman Act, which applied to railroads, prohibited termination of employees for union activity. These statutes were, however, declared unconstitutional by the United States Supreme Court because they interfered with liberty of contract. Later attempts to prevent antiunion discrimination on the railroads succeeded, both in a Federal administrative order issued during World War I and in the 1926 Railway Labor Act. In 1935 Congress passed the National Labor Relations Act (Wagner Act), which covers most private employment and guarantees employee rights to form unions and bargain collectively. It also prohibits employers from discriminatory actions against employees who exercise their rights under the act.

Starting with state statutes on workers' compensation, the first of which was enacted in 1911, state legislatures incorporated nonretaliation provisions in laws regulating employment conditions. Workers' compensation laws typically provide that an employee cannot be terminated for filing a claim for benefits under the law. The Federal law regulating minimum wages and overtime pay, passed in 1934, similarly prohibits employers from discharging or otherwise discriminating against employees for exercising their rights under that act. A comparable provision is found in Federal occupational safety and health legislation adopted in 1970.

The broadest limitations on the employer's power to discipline or terminate come from equal employment opportunity legislation. Title VII of the Civil Rights Act of 1964 prohibits discrimination because of an employee's race, color, religion, sex, or national origin. In 1967 the Age Discrimination in Employment Act instituted protections against discrimination or termination on the basis of age. In 1973 and 1974, respectively, Federal laws were passed protecting handicapped workers and Vietnam veterans. In 1992, a new Federal law protecting disabled workers took effect.

Recent legislative protections of employees have come in the form of Federal legislation on plant closing and polygraphs (lie detectors), both passed in 1988. The plant closing bill obliges employers in some circumstances to provide advance notice of employment termination. The polygraph bill restricts the types of cases in which employers can require employees to take lie detector tests or discipline or terminate them for refusing to do so.

Perhaps the liveliest area of employment law in the United States at this writing is the increasing case by case restriction of the employment at will doctrine by the courts under the common law. Courts in some jurisdictions have held that employees can sue the employer for damages if they are terminated (1) in violation of public policy (as in "whistleblower" cases); (2) in violation of the employer's own policies that are found to be a part of the contract of employment (such as progressive steps in a discipline process set out in an employee handbook); (3) in violation of obligations of good faith and fair dealing that are implied in law to be part of any contract; (4) in a manner that is abusive. These exceptions to the employment at will doctrine are expanding rapidly on a case by case basis, although only the first two are recognized in most jurisdictions. The monetary damages assessed against employers in such cases have often been quite large. One state, Montana, has adopted legislation requiring cause for dismissal, and a proposed uniform state law has been developed by legal experts.

In the union sector employees have a broad contractual right to be disciplined or terminated only for "just cause." Virtually all collective bargaining agreements contain such a provision. Similarly universal are provisions requiring arbitration of unresolved claims that an employer breached such a just cause provision. It is in this sector that something like a systematic law of the obligations of employment has developed. Accordingly, the following discussions relate mainly to the rules and procedures that exist in the unionized sector. It should be kept in mind that labor arbitration is private and (at least in the private sector) voluntary. The rules we discuss thus arise outside the formal legal system. As a matter of contract law, however, courts routinely enforce agreements to arbitrate and the resulting arbitrators' decisions.

Contractual procedures in the unionized sector typically include a multistep grievance procedure. An employee's claim of unjust discipline or termination may pass through three, four, or even more levels of the union and management hierarchies before going to arbitration. Contracts provide for joint selection of an arbitrator and for sharing the arbitrator's fees and other expenses of arbitration. The chosen arbitrator conducts a hearing to take evidence and hear the parties' arguments. Hearings vary in formality and sometimes even involve a formal transcript of the testimony and briefs (written arguments). The arbitrator then renders a written opinion and award that may sustain, modify, or overturn the discipline. If the discharge was not for just cause, the arbitrator will usually order reinstatement with full or partial back pay. By agreement of the parties the award is final and binding. While there is no formal process of appeal to the courts, on rare occasions a party will attack an award in court as exceeding the arbitrator's authority, as contrary to public policy, or as biased or corrupt.

SUBSTANTIVE RULES OF EMPLOYMENT OBLIGATION

The substantive law of the employment obligation is somewhat elusive, even in the union sector. Its elusiveness stems mainly from the fact that there is neither statute nor case precedent in any formal sense. Arbitrators need not follow the decisions of other arbitrators in any previous case, although most consider themselves bound by decisions on the same issue under the same collective bargaining agreement. However, something like a common law has built up over the years, as published arbitration awards have established a set of customary and therefore expected results. Arbitrators do in fact tend to follow what other arbitrators have done in the past. Consequently, past decisions make it possible to predict what they will do when presented with a particular case. It is this body of arbitral actions to which we will refer in analyzing the specific issues addressed in this chapter.

We proceed in four steps. First, as background, we will describe the historic common law of the employment relationship as it relates to employee obligations and rights. Second, we will set out two contemporary efforts to summarize the rules used by modern arbitrators and will relate these to the historic common law. Third, we will consider in detail the rules that exist in the set of particular cases that we have chosen for analysis. Finally, we will tie these together into a set of statements about the law of industrial justice in the United States.

THE AMERICAN LAW OF MASTER AND SERVANT

To the extent that law reflects custom, we would expect current legal rules to derive from historic rules and practices in the society. In employment relations the law of master and servant, which is still extant, constitutes the oldest set of these. This law is applicable to employment contracts that are for a fixed period. It is only when the parties have not fixed the term of the employment relationship that the employer can terminate the employee at will. Where employment is for an agreed period, it can be terminated by either party only for those causes historically recognized under master and servant law.

It has long been true under the common law that the relationship of master and servant existed where one person was employed by another who had the "right of exercising control over the performance of the work, to the extent of prescribing the manner in which it shall be executed." That relationship contained an implied promise by the servant "to obey the lawful and reasonable orders of his master within the scope of his contract." Stated most baldly, "submission to the master's will is the law of the contract."[2] A necessary characteristic of the relationship is the power of the master to dismiss the servant.[3] As one writer put it, this is the right of the master to "expel the lazy drone from his family and leave him to his own beggarly condition."[4] One justification for the master's control is that the master is legally responsible for the consequences of the servant's actions. Another might be that this is part of the implied understanding of employment.

Recognized causes for termination of the master–servant relationship historically included the following: (1) "willful disobedience . . . of any lawful order"; (2) "gross moral misconduct, whether pecuniary or otherwise"; and (3) "habitual negligence in business, or conduct calculated seriously to injure his master's business."[5] Examples of specific causes include use of confidential information to the servant's advantage and the employer's detriment, absence without excuse, failure to perform work with due care and diligence if it is habitual or capable of causing serious damage, incompetency, and being disrespectful and insolent.[6] According to one author, immorality can be grounds for dismissal where the act is a crime or there is a public scandal, the question being whether the misconduct makes the servant "unfit to perform duties . . . or [is] prejudicial, or likely to prove prejudicial, to the business of the employer."[7]

It might be hypothesized that current law on employment termination and discipline in each country is rooted in the historic law of employment (termed "master and servant" law in the United States) in that country. If this is so, it will be possible to better understand differences among countries on the basis of differences in their historic legal frameworks. In the United States there exist at least some grounds for this hypothesis. First, there is some correlation between the bases for termination in the common law and those in the arbitral law. For instance, at the time of birth of the arbitral rules, the leading legal encyclopedia, *Corpus Juris,* contained language on causes for termination of the employment relationship that was quite similar to the arbitral law that developed.[8] Second, the master and servant rules preceded the arbitral rules in time. Third, it is reasonable to expect arbitrators to base their rules on the parties' expectations, and those expectations would have been shaped by the common law governing other employment relationships. Fourth, a large proportion of the early arbitrators were lawyers who presumably knew the law of master and servant, and were therefore knowledgeable of its rules. Fifty-seven percent of the arbitrators whose decisions are reported in the first volume of Labor Arbitration Reports (the standard reporting service for arbitrators' awards) were lawyers. These included some of the great names in the arbitration profession. One of these, Harry H. Platt, expressly cited a common law master and servant case for the proposition that good and sufficient cause had to be shown by a preponderance of the evidence in order for discharge to be upheld.[9] These facts furnish a sufficient basis for hypothesizing a link between the common and arbitral laws. However, the authors of this paper differ between us with respect to the degree to which this is true.

MODERN INTERPRETATIONS OF "JUST CAUSE"

The rules developed under collective bargaining agreements start out with two basic propositions. First, employers may discipline or terminate an employee only for "just cause." Second, the employer must generally use progressive discipline. Under progressive discipline penalties are applied that are of gradually increasing severity. Generally they involve oral warning, written warning, suspensions without pay, and termination, in that order. There is no authoritative general definition of what is a "major" offense (one for which progressive discipline may not be required), but it is generally agreed that insubordination, theft, and acts of violence are included in this category.

There are at least two approaches to an understanding of the meaning of "just cause" as the concept is used by modern American arbitrators. One can examine the historical context out of which the modern employment relationship arose, or inductively develop a general conception of just cause from arbitration awards. One of us, along with a coauthor, has argued that just cause is present only where an employee "has failed to meet his obligations under the fundamental understanding of the employment relationship." The employee's general obligation is the performance of satisfactory work, which includes: (1) regular attendance, (2) being obedient to reasonable work rules, (3) reasonable quality and quantity of work, and, (4) avoiding conduct, either on or off the job, that hinders the employer's ability to carry on the business effectively. In addition, for just cause to be present, the discipline must serve a legitimate interest of management. These interests are defined as including the rehabilitation of an employee, deterrence of undesirable conduct by the disciplined employee or others, and "protection of the employer's ability to operate the business successfully." Just cause also requires meeting the union's interest in guaranteeing fairness to employees. This includes "industrial due process," which consists of notice to employees of the conduct required and possible penalties, an employer decision based on facts after due investigation, and progressive discipline except in extreme cases. It also includes "industrial equal protection," where like cases are treated similarly, and individualized treatment, where the distinctive facts about the employee are given weight.[10] Another attempt to capture the essence of just cause has been made by Philip Selznick. According to Selznick, the heart of the matter is the avoidance of arbitrary treatment of employees by the employer. This means that the actions of the employer must be in pursuit of legitimate business ends and must be reasonably related to those ends. Employer action must also meet the test of moderation. That is, some consideration must be given to the economic interests and dignity of employees. Evenhandedness is required, as is the fitting of the penalty to the offense.[11] A similar definition comes from arbitrator Harry H. Platt, who says that the purpose is to "confirm the employer's right to discipline where its exercise is essential to the objective of efficiency, but also safeguard the interests of the discharged employee by making reasonably sure that the causes for discharge were just and equitable and such as would appeal to reasonable and fair-minded persons."[12]

The modern attempts to define just cause are useful efforts to make sense of what has always been a troublesome concept. They do get at the roots of the idea. Furthermore, when one seeks to identify the particular obligations that arise from being in the role of employee, the old master and servant law may also be valuable.

THE PARTICULAR OBLIGATIONS OF EMPLOYMENT

The substantive rules of the employment obligation are best understood and compared across national systems in relation to concrete cases. The balance of this chapter attempts to do this, and then to draw some general conclusions.

SUBORDINATION

Case Scenario

JD, a janitor at the A Manufacturing Company, is assigned the task of waxing office hallways. He completes one hallway.

His supervisor, FF, inspects the hallway and says to JD, "Do this floor again." JD replies "No," and walks away.

Analysis

This case involves a clear incident of insubordination. JD has been given an order. He has refused to obey it. This is a major offense in the United States system, which means that termination or other serious discipline may be appropriate for the first offense. The invariable rule in American industrial relations is "obey now, grieve later."[13] However, since this scenario poses a single incident of only moderate severity, few arbitrators would in fact sustain discipline more severe than a suspension without pay.[14]

Seriousness. Several factors related to the seriousness of the offense might affect the outcome. If the employee were abusive in his response, such as swearing at the supervisor, his fate would probably be sealed.[15] On the other hand, politeness on his part might decrease the penalty. Physical touching of the supervisor by the employee, such as pushing him away, would make it certain that termination would be upheld by an arbitrator. If this were shown to be the first incident of disobedience by the employee, his chances of escaping termination would be greater. The presence of other employees would exacerbate the offense because of the danger that the defiance of managerial authority would be contagious. The offense would also be more serious if the supervisor repeated the order, emphasized its importance, or expressly warned JD of the consequences of continued disobedience.

The employee's beliefs about the propriety of the order are not likely to affect the arbitrator's decision. It is true that a reasonable belief that the work would threaten the employee's health or safety (say, by causing lethal fumes) would support refusal of the order, of course.[16] However, a mere belief that the order contradicted company rules or was foolish or useless would not excuse his conduct or affect the penalty. Arbitrators take seriously the saying that "the shop floor is not a debating society," and, as noted above, the rule of "obey now, grieve later."[17]

Thus the employee might be held to obey even an order that offended his dignity—for example, a direction to scrub the floor with a toothbrush. (In such a situation, however, an arbitrator would be likely to treat the order as a provocation that would mitigate the penalty.) Similarly, that an order fell outside the employee's job description would provide no defense. Nor would the fact that the floor was already properly waxed. On the other hand, if the employee's offense impeded production the arbitrator would likely sustain more serious discipline than if it had had no effect.

Mitigation. Provocation would be the chief mitigating factor. If the supervisor called the employee an idiot when giving the order, for example, an arbitrator would view the subsequent disobedience as less serious.[18] Long seniority and good work and disciplinary records would also count in the employee's favor. If the employee were a union representative, his or her office might count as an aggravating factor on the ground that representatives have a special responsibility as role models to follow legitimate orders.

Enforceability. Several factors bear on enforceability. If the supervisor merely asks the employee to do the floor again, the employee may be able to effectively claim that he did not understand the request to be an order. Insubordination consists of *willful* disobedience, and if the employee is not aware that an order has been given, failure to comply with it cannot be willful.[19] If the arbitrator believes this to be the case, a termination would certainly not be upheld. However, if the employer proves that this is simply a matter of supervisory style, and that the employee understood full well that an order was given, the form of the supervisory direction will not mitigate the penalty. If the employer has previously tolerated disobedience by this or other employees, the arbitrator would not be likely to sustain any penalty greater than a warning.

SOBRIETY

Case Scenario

RR, a laborer on the loading dock of B Trucking Company, is observed by his supervisor, JB, reaching into the pocket of a coat that is hanging near his workplace. JB observes RR bring something to his mouth, appear to swallow, and then replace it in the coat. JB approaches RR and asks, "What are you drinking?" RR reaches into the pocket of the coat and hands JB a bottle that contains an alcoholic beverage. JB forms the opinion that RR's breath smells strongly of alcoholic spirits and that his eyes are unfocused.

Analysis

This is a clear case of the use of alcohol on the job, with some evidence of intoxication. On these facts an American arbitrator would uphold the imposition of some discipline, perhaps as severe as a suspension without pay. In the absence of exacerbating factors, most arbitrators would not find termination to be appropriate. There is, however, something of a split of authority on this, with some arbitrators willing to uphold termination for mere possession or consumption of alcohol on company premises.[20]

Seriousness. Several factors would affect the seriousness of the offense. A high degree of intoxication or the use of an illegal drug such as cocaine would of course aggravate the matter.[21] Actual or potential harm to other employees or to the employer's property would also aggravate it. So might the location of the offense—for example, if it took place in view of customers. Demonstrable harm to the employer such as the loss of a valued customer would also increase the seriousness. With any of these aggravating factors present, an arbitrator would very likely sustain a termination.

Mitigation. Mitigating factors might be important in this case. If the employee were to prove that he is an alcoholic who is undergoing treatment, termination might not be upheld, although a suspension might well be.[22] For some arbitrators alcoholism is a sickness that requires treatment, not punishment. For others, however, it is the conduct, not the cause, that determines whether discipline is appropriate.[23] In some industries, for example, brewing, drinking on the job is customary, and an arbitrator would not uphold discipline unless some exacerbating factors were present that made the offense more serious.

Enforceability. The employer's consistency or inconsistency in dealing with similar behavior would affect enforceability. If the employer had previously tolerated on-the-job drinking or drug use by employees or supervisors, no arbitrator would uphold serious discipline until the employer had warned employees of a change in policy. There need not be a formal rule against such conduct, since employees are expected to know that it is improper. However, some arbitrators might insist on such a rule before sustaining a termination unless the dangers to safety, property, or reputation were so obvious as to warn employees of the severest possible discipline.

344

SECURITY OF EMPLOYER'S PROPERTY

Case Scenario

PR, a clerk employed by C Gourmet Foods Company, is observed by two supervisors taking company products out of a packing box, concealing them on his person, and walking out the door with them. He is apprehended after he exits the store, and admits taking the products.

Analysis

This is a clear case of theft. Like insubordination, theft is a major offense which may justify termination even for a first occasion, unless there are mitigating factors. Even if there are mitigating factors, many arbitrators would still sustain a termination for a proven theft. Unlike many other types of offenses, however, discharge for theft produces a stigma that marks an employee for many years. As a result, most arbitrators insist that employers prove charges of theft by a higher degree of proof.[24]

Seriousness. There are several potentially important considerations. Some arbitrators would not sustain a termination if the value of the goods were extremely small, say under $1.00. The employer could counter this by demonstrating that the cumulative harm of many small thefts threatened its profitability. Thus telephone companies and retail stores have usually been able to enforce terminations for offenses that are individually minor. If the employee believed the goods to be scrap, an arbitrator might view the offense as less serious. Even so, some discipline would be in order because employees have no right to take any of the employer's property without permission.[25] On the other hand, arbitrators would be even more inclined to uphold termination if other employees knew of the theft, since a failure to punish it severely might tempt others to steal.

Mitigation. So serious is employee theft that mitigating factors would influence only a minority of arbitrators. Some might give decisive weight to extremely high seniority, say twenty years or more, particularly if the value of the stolen goods were small and if there were other mitigating factors. A few would reduce a termination to a lesser penalty in the case of a first offense if the employee stole because of some compelling need, such as medical treatment for a critically ill child.

Enforceability. Probably the only serious bar to enforceability

345

would be the previous failure of the employer to punish similar offenses with equal severity. If this were the case, an arbitrator would refuse to uphold a termination unless the employer had clearly warned the employee of the change in policy.

PEACEFUL WORKPLACE

Case Scenario

MM is a clerk in D Department Store. NN is another clerk in the same department store; he is physically larger than MM. While MM is moving some heavy equipment from one area to another NN says, "I'm surprised that you did not ask a real man like me to handle this job." MM, angered, strikes NN on the jaw, knocking him down. NN gets up and walks away.

Analysis

Fighting at work is a major offense, justifying termination. However, it is one where provocation and other circumstances are often viewed as important in determining the appropriate degree of punishment.[26] Given the bare facts of the case scenario, an arbitrator would probably uphold termination of MM.

Seriousness. There are a number of elements that affect the seriousness of this conduct. Of major importance is whether the disciplined employee was the aggressor. An employee who initiates violence is ordinarily terminated. Termination would not be appropriate for one who responds to an attack, but some lesser penalty might be if the victim fought when he could have escaped or used more force than required to defend himself. If the attacker used a dangerous weapon or caused a serious injury, an arbitrator would surely sustain a termination.[27] A number of other variations are possibly relevant. These include actual or potential damage to property, potential injury to other employees, interference with production, damage to the employer's business or reputation, and the merits of the dispute among the employees. These, however, are not as likely to determine the acceptable level of discipline.

Mitigation. Mitigating factors tend to be of limited importance in these cases. That the employee had no previous history of violence would probably not count for much. This would also be true for a history of peaceable relations among the employees

346

involved in the dispute, although a history of past disputes would enhance the chances that the arbitrator would sustain the discharge. Provocation does not justify fighting, but it may serve to reduce the degree of the discipline.[28] That the employee involved was an employee representative would not mitigate the offense, and might exacerbate it. High seniority, say of twenty years, would, however, cause many arbitrators to substitute a rather lengthy suspension, perhaps by reinstating the employee without back pay. In the typical case this would amount to a several month suspension without pay. In this case the provocation is not sufficient to excuse the attack, but a more serious provocation—say, a threat of physical harm or use of a racial slur—might cause an arbitrator to reduce the penalty.

Enforceability. About the only serious bar to enforceability would be inconsistent application of discipline in similar cases.

OFF-DUTY CONDUCT

Case Scenario

TT, head salesclerk for E Toy Store, participates in a white supremacist demonstration. He is arrested for disorderly behavior, and a photograph of him handcuffed to a post and snarling at police is printed in the local newspaper, along with his name and the name of his employer.

Analysis

Off-duty misconduct is an area of industrial discipline where the principles are clear but the applications are not. The rule adopted uniformly by American arbitrators is that the employee's conduct away from the job will be grounds for discipline only if it affects the employee's ability to perform the work, the willingness of other employees to work with the employee, or the business interests of the employer. As it is sometimes stated, there must be a "nexus," or connection, between the conduct and the job in order to justify discipline.[29]

In the scenario all of these conditions are potentially present, but have not been firmly proved. Given only these facts most arbitrators would not uphold discipline, although a minority of arbitrators would. However, it is often possible for the employer to prove damage to its business or unwillingness of others to work with the employee. In cases of extremely shocking misconduct nexus might be presumed, in which case the employer need not prove it explicitly.

Seriousness. A criminal conviction for off-duty misconduct will not by itself provide a basis for discipline. The seriousness of the matter turns on the harm it causes the employer's business interests; this is the so-called nexus requirement. The more serious and disreputable the crime, the more likely an arbitrator would presume the existence of a nexus between the conduct and the business. In most cases, however, the employer is expected to prove the nexus.[30] Thus termination is more likely to be sustained if the offense were physical assault rather than if it were merely disorderly conduct. Similarly, the employer's action is more likely to be upheld if news reports prominently mentioned the employer's name and if the incident occurred in a small town. Proof of nexus might require, for example, evidence that customers now avoid the business or that black employees refuse to work with TT. In any event, there must first be actual misconduct to trigger discipline; an employee may not be disciplined solely for expressing his opinions in a lawful demonstration.

Mitigation. As with other offenses, seniority is the principal mitigating factor. Very high seniority, of say twenty years, would cause some arbitrators to reduce a termination or at least to insist on very clear proof that the conduct hurt the employer's business.

Enforceability. Also as in other cases, consistency of discipline would be important. An employer which had overlooked similar conduct by other employees could not suddenly terminate TT without first alerting him that the rules had changed.

ATTENDANCE

Case Scenario

JJ is a nurse's aide at F Nursing Home. Because of an illness her attendance at work has been erratic for two years. During that period she has missed 30 percent of her scheduled working days. During the last month she has missed 20 percent of her scheduled working days. All of these absences were excused. She then misses three days of work, without notifying her employer, because she decides to extend her holiday.

348

Analysis

As in the case of off-duty conduct, the rule in absenteeism cases is clear in principle but difficult in application. The employer has a right to expect regular attendance at work. The failure of an employee to meet this expectation is grounds for termination. This is usually so whether or not the absences are the fault of the employee.[31] Termination because of excused absences such as documented sick leave is known as a "no fault" termination, and is not properly viewed as disciplinary in nature. Termination or punishment for unexcused absences, on the other hand, is disciplinary in nature, being based on intentional misconduct.

In the case of excused absences, whether termination is appropriate depends on whether there is a substantial probability that the employee will attend regularly in the future. This is determined on the basis of quantity, frequency, trend, and reasons for past absences, and on medical or other prognoses. In order to support termination it is also necessary that the employer give counseling or other warning to the employee that the absences may lead to termination, usually including progressive steps as if discipline were being imposed. Unexcused absences are simple minor disciplinary offenses. After progressive discipline termination can take place.[32]

The present case involves a common mixture of excused and unexcused absences. On these facts most arbitrators would sustain a lengthy suspension, say of five days or so, but would not sustain termination. Some arbitrators who have perhaps not fully considered the consequences might simply order reinstatement without any back pay. That, we believe, is wrong, since it imposes a suspension far longer than any rational employer would impose and makes the severity of the penalty turn on an irrelevant factor—the length of time required to resolve the dispute. Refusal to sustain termination in these cases often rests on a lack of evidence about the employee's future prospects, on the lack of counseling or progressive discipline, or the absence of a formal no-fault system on the use of excused absences. While being sufficient ground for some discipline, a single unexcused absence without notice to the employer would not be sufficiently serious to support termination.

Seriousness. As noted above, the factors relevant to seriousness of the conduct are number, length, and reasons for the absences, whether the absences were excused, the trend, and predictions for future attendance. For example, if the employer had persuasive medical testimony that the employee would not be able to attend work regularly, or the union had persuasive testimony to the opposite effect, this would probably determine the case. If the medical evidence conflicted, the outcome of the case might well depend upon which side the arbitrator found most convincing. The presence of some unexcused absences, as is true in our scenario, would increase the likelihood of termination being upheld.

Mitigation. Mitigating factors can be important. It is probably true that long seniority, good performance, and a good discipline record make a difference in whether a termination is upheld.[33] These factors may also indirectly influence the way that the arbitrator interprets other factors. Family needs of the employee are unlikely to be determinative of the outcome in these cases.

Enforceability. Enforceability mainly depends upon adequate warning and on consistency. If the employer fails to provide counseling or progressive discipline, an arbitrator will not likely uphold a termination. Consistent with the requirement of progressive discipline, a suspension would not be upheld without a previous warning. If the employer has failed to punish other employees with the same severity for the same conduct, the arbitrator will likely reduce the discipline to the level previously employed. In addition, rules on attendance requirements need to be reasonably specific and well communicated in order to support discipline.[34]

PERFORMANCE

Case Scenario

HH is a warehouseman for G Distributing Company. G has instituted a program that determines levels of productivity for warehousemen. This program meets accepted professional standards for such programs. Over a period of two months HH fails to produce at the prescribed levels, consistently falling 10 percent below the standard. He is warned that he will be terminated if he fails to improve his productivity within two weeks. He fails to do so. HH claims that the standards of the new system are impossible to meet. He proves that prior to the institution of the new system he was given above-average evaluations by his supervisor for producing at his current level, covering a period of ten years.

Analysis

Poor performance is a minor offense that can lead to termination after progressive discipline has been used. In order to give rise to discipline there must be a reasonable standard and the employee's performance must be significantly below that standard. Unless negligence or willful misconduct is involved, this is similar to excused but excessive absenteeism in that it is no fault. The employer has a right to insist that the employee produce at a reasonable level. An employee's failure to do so after being given a reasonable chance to perform at such a level can give rise to termination, even if the reasons for the failure are beyond the employee's control.[35]

Given only the facts in the scenario, an arbitrator would not uphold termination. This is because the employer has not proved that the deficiency was significantly below acceptable levels and did not use progressive discipline.

Seriousness. Several matters having to do with seriousness are relevant. As indicated above, performance 10 percent below a certain standard may or may not be seriously deficient. If the employer shows that the degree of performance deficiency is serious—let's say 40 percent below standard in our case—this would greatly increase the probability that a termination would be upheld. How much is enough to be sufficient? If overall production is substantially affected by this individual's performance, the conduct is more seriously deficient. If it is proved that there are demonstrated financial costs of, say, $200 per week, this would incline an arbitrator to conclude that the deficiency was significant. If the deficiency caused safety problems that resulted from production bottlenecks, this would lead one toward the conclusion that the deficiency was significant. If the employee's poor performance or the employer's failure to punish it previously have had an adverse effect upon other employees, this would also be relevant.

As in the case of no fault absenteeism, questions of prognosis of future conduct are relevant.[36] If the employee has been performing below standard for six months, the matter is more serious than if this has only been true for one week. If the trend of the employee's performance has been down rather than up, the conduct is more serious.

Mitigation. Seniority and good past performance are potential mitigating factors. Long seniority, say 20 years, would cause arbitrators to insist on adequate warning and remedial training, but if the employee is simply unable to perform, the employer is under no obligation to continue to employ him or her. Good past performance, particularly over a long period, would reinforce any tendency to avoid dismissal.

Enforceability. As to enforceability, the crucial question is generally the reasonableness of the standards of performance. In our scenario we have technical correctness. However, if an arbitrator concluded that the standards were not reasonable because they were proved not to be feasible, discipline for violating them would not be upheld.[37] This would probably depend upon the experience of other employees in meeting the standard. If it were proved that employees suffered physical detriment from performing at this level, this would argue powerfully for the unreasonableness of the standard.

In order to enforce the production standard, progressive discipline must be used, so that the employee has adequate warning of the need to improve.[38] As is true in other cases, it is also necessary that discipline be imposed uniformly.

LOYALTY

Case Scenario

JS, a teller for H Bank, during an appearance on a television consumer information program states that her employer regularly fails to advise customers when they make mistakes in favor of the bank, but promptly corrects mistakes made in favor of the customers.

Analysis

Disloyalty cases as exemplified by this scenario are rare in the United States. While there is agreement that employees owe a duty of loyalty to the employer, there have not been many cases in which this duty has been applied and articulated. One arbitrator, reviewing the cases, concluded that the following questions are relevant: (1) Was the act or conduct expressed orally or in writing? (2) Was the act or conduct directed toward persons within the private organization or outside the organization? (3) If the act or conduct was directed toward a customer or competitor, did it directly cause damage to the business or loss of business opportunity? (4) If the act was directed toward a governmental agency, did the employee exhaust available internal avenues of redress? (5) Were the statements reasonably believed to be true? (6) Was the tone malicious or slanderous? (7) Were "substantial personal rights of expression and citizenship" involved? (8) Did the employer condone this conduct in the past, and did the employer's policies put the employee on notice that such conduct might give rise to discipline?[39]

Assuming the employee reasonably believed the statements to be true and the employer had no specific rule prohibiting public comment about business matters, most arbitrators would not sustain a termination in this case. Many if not most would regard a warning as appropriate, however. This is somewhat akin to the recent "whistleblower" suits in which employees have won damages from their employers after being terminated for reporting the employer's illegal conduct to the authorities. It is therefore possible that in some jurisdictions a nonunionized employee in JS's situation might successfully sue the bank.

Seriousness. Since there is very little arbitral precedent, we can only speculate how variant facts might affect the seriousness of the offense. Evidence of significant harm to the employer's business would likely count against the employee. If the employer were in a field less dependent on a reputation for honesty, such as retailing, arbitrators might view the matter as less serious. If the employee were in a different job classification, the harm caused to the employer—and thus the seriousness of the offense—would be different; an auditor's charges, for example, would carry more weight and a janitor's less. Of course, if the employee made false charges either maliciously or without reasonable grounds for believing them true, termination would be a more reasonable response. Finally, if the employee's charges attacked the quality of the employer's product rather than allegedly illegal activity, discharge for disloyalty would be more likely to be upheld.[40]

Mitigation. High seniority, illegality of the employer's conduct, and failure of the employer to heed more private complaints would all count toward mitigation. That the employee made the charges because of some unrelated grievance would be no defense. Arbitrators would consider not only the specific incident causing the discharge but also "the employee's entire record of performance, attitude, and conduct."[41]

Enforceability. As to enforceability, the existence and reasonableness of employer rules in this area would be of considerable importance. If the employer had a formal rule prohibiting employees from making public information about the bank and its business, and it were clear that discipline would follow a violation of this rule, an arbitrator would likely uphold some discipline. Even so, arbitrators would be unwilling to sustain termination for a first offense. If the rule is so broad as to cover any communication, even if it has to do with illegal activity, it may be unreasonable and therefore unenforceable. On the other hand, if the rule provides that an employee must consult with management before revealing potentially damaging information to the public, thus giving the employer a chance to change wrong policies or at least to explain the practices to the employee, a violation would result in rather severe discipline, perhaps even including termination. To support discipline, the rule must be communicated to the employee and consistently enforced.

RESTRICT COLLECTIVE ACTION

Case Scenario

JJ, a machinist at I Manufacturing Company, becomes angry because he believes that his supervisor is treating him and other employees in a disrespectful manner. In protest, he persuades the other employees in his work group to leave work together in the middle of their scheduled work shift and not return until the next day.

Analysis

Leading what is known as a wildcat strike (one unauthorized by the union) is generally grounds for termination. This assumes the usual clause in the collective bargaining agreement in which the union agrees that it will not engage in strikes during the life of the collective bargaining agreement (which is normally one, two, or three years).[42] In the facts of the scenario an arbitrator would uphold termination of the leader of this collective refusal to work.

Seriousness. Several matters would influence the seriousness of the offense. Perhaps the most significant is the strike's impact.

One involving only a few employees for only a few minutes would obviously be less important than one involving the entire workforce over several days.[43] A high level of antagonism that produced violence or destruction of property would aggravate matters. If the employee were a leader rather than a follower, his or her offense would be more serious. Similarly, union leaders are held to a higher standard because of their positions of responsibility and their presumed greater knowledge of contractual obligations.[44] Arbitrators are unlikely to sustain the termination of mere followers, although they would merit a warning or a suspension.

Mitigation. In mitigation seniority, as usual, would be important. Long seniority of twenty years might save the employee from termination.[45] If the supervisor had in fact abused and insulted employees over a substantial period, say six months, this provocation would likely make termination insupportable, absent exacerbating factors. If, on the other hand, the supervisor's conduct consisted merely of ordering work to be done in ways that were contrary to custom or the collective bargaining agreement, this would probably not serve as a mitigating factor, as the rule of "obey now, grieve later" would apply. The proper remedy for such a problem is through the grievance process.

Enforceability. Enforceability could be affected by inconsistency of punishment for others involved in the same or similar incidents. On the other hand, it is appropriate for the employer to impose different penalties on employees with different degrees of involvement in the misconduct. As with most other forms of misconduct, the employer should demonstrate that the employee knew or should have known that his conduct violated the collective agreement and company rules.[46]

AVOID CONFLICT OF INTEREST

Case Scenario

IB, a systems analyst for J Company, has access to private computer systems of his employer. IB accepts a string of free-lance, relatively routine programming jobs for K Company, a competitor of his employer, performing work at his home.

Analysis

An employer may prohibit employees from moonlighting that presents a conflict of interest. Generally, any employment with a competitor is seen as conflicting with the obligations to the employer. It is necessary, however, to have a clear rule against such employment, and to give an employee an opportunity to quit that employment before imposing discipline. In the scenario, since there is no proof of a rule against this conduct and no prior warning, discipline more severe than an oral warning would not be appropriate.[47]

Seriousness. The seriousness of the conduct is potentially affected by a number of possible variations on our scenario. As noted above, the existence of a formal rule against working for competitors is a necessary condition for discipline. The seriousness of the conduct would be increased by such factors as a similarity between the types of work performed both places, the revelation of any trade secrets, use of skills in the second job that were learned in the first, the acquisition of an ownership interest in the competitor, negative effects on the primary employer's business such as loss of customers, and by the employee's access to highly secret and valuable information about the employer's business. Seriousness would also be increased if the second job were known to other employees or were a long-term one rather than a temporary or casual job. However, the existence of a reasonable rule and the failure of the employee to quit working for a competitor after warning would by themselves justify termination.[48] If the case did not involve a competitor, the other elements would become more important. In that situation the question would be one of effects upon the employer's business, primarily through loss of customers or the giving away of valuable secrets, because the employer must demonstrate some harm before regulating off-duty conduct.

Mitigation. In mitigation seniority would once again be of some importance. However, if the employee refused to quit work with a competitor after warning, termination would probably be upheld regardless of seniority. If the employee showed compelling financial need, such as money for expenses of an illness of a family member, this would reduce the likelihood of termination where the work was not for a competitor, because it would be difficult for the employer to demonstrate that its fears of harm outweighed the employee's need.

Enforceability. Enforceability considerations are of importance. A general rule, such as a prohibition against a conflict of interest, it is less likely to support discipline than one which clearly prohibited work for a competitor or one that required prior supervisory approval of a second job. As in the other cases, evenhanded application of the rule is essential.

CONCLUSIONS

All of the particular obligations of employment analyzed are of considerable importance in the United States. Perhaps the ones most tightly binding on employees are the obligations of subordination, sobriety, security of the employer's property, peacefulness, and restricting collective action. Violation of any of these can amount to a major offense. Also important but always requiring progressive discipline before termination for their violation are attendance and performance. Proper off-duty conduct, loyalty, and avoiding conflicts of interest are less well-defined obligations.

The obligation to be subordinate means that employees who refuse to obey orders can be terminated. Although many factors influence the application of this rule, it is generally applied rather strictly. The obligation to be sober is more situational, with the most severe penalties occurring where exacerbating factors are present. However, offenses involving illegal drugs are dealt with rather harshly, and the degree to which this is true is increasing. Security of the employer's property is, like subordination, an obligation that is often enforced even in situations where there are no exacerbating circumstances and where the outcome might seem quite harsh compared to the value of the property. Theft, even of goods of small value, is likely to lead to what American arbitrators call "industrial capital punishment"—termination. The obligation of peacefulness is applied with considerable rigor to employees who initiate physical violence, but is more situational for those who are attacked.

Off-duty misconduct has traditionally been one of the more difficult areas of industrial justice in the United States. This may be because there has been a tension between the modern rule and the historic rule under the law of master and servant, where the employee's obligations to the employer were somewhat broader. These cases often come down to troublesome issues of proof about effects upon the business of the employer. In drug cases the rule appears to be breaking down, with arbitrators willing to enforce employer rules against off-duty drug use even without proof of on-the-job effects.

Attendance cases are classic no-fault situations when all the employee's absences are excused. Here the key question is whether the employee is likely to attend work regularly in the future. If the answer to that question is no, the employee will probably be terminated if he or she has had proper notice and progressive "discipline." Where some or all of the absences are unexcused, there is a admixture of true discipline, as unexcused absences are intentional violations of the obligation to attend work. Often an unexcused absence will serve as a final straw which, added to excused absences, will lead to termination. Employer "no fault" or "point" systems which assign points to all absences, regardless of cause, and result in automatic termination upon the accumulation of a sufficient number of points have been upheld by some arbitrators but rejected by others as inherently unreasonable.

Performance cases are somewhat similar to excused absence cases, because they do not require proof of intentional misconduct in order to support discipline or termination. However, the employment relationship has as a central obligation the responsibility of the employee to be at work and to perform at a reasonable level. If the employee persistently fails in either of these, termination can occur.

Limitations upon collective action against the employer during the term of the collective bargaining agreement form a crucial aspect of the American system. Trade unions in the United States have made what more radical union movements would consider a pact with the devil, agreeing to accept a rule of law in place of the strike during the life of the collective bargaining agreement. The union's agreement not to strike is generally seen as the quid pro quo for the employer's agreement to be bound by an arbitrator's determination of disputes arising under the contract. Employees engaging in such strikes can be disciplined for their participation, although employers can, and usually do, impose the heaviest penalties upon strike leaders.

Loyalty and avoidance of conflicts of interest are handled as one might expect in a system that has a more economic and less social view of the employment relationship. That is, although these obligations exist, they are not as compelling as some of the others. Even in the nonunionized sector employees have some protection against being victimized for blowing the whistle on employer violations of the law.

When one looks to the historic law of master and servant, it appears that the modern law of just cause is somewhat similar to it and may be rooted in it. The general idea of employment as involving subordination is central to both. Care for the employer's property and the persons of fellow employees are included in both. Perhaps the greatest difference lies in such areas as off-duty conduct and loyalty. Whereas the traditional master and servant relationship involved a strong general duty that encompassed the employee's whole life, the modern arbitration rule limits this to a considerable degree. Although in drug cases this seems to be breaking down, the general arbitral rule is still that the employee's activities away from work are the employee's own business, unless it can be shown that the employer has suffered injury. This reflects a liberal, rather than a feudal, view of the employment relationship. In the nonunion sector we find a classical liberal relationship from both sides, although this operates largely to the advantage of the employer.

The substance of the employment obligation as it currently exists is summarized reasonably well in what Abrams and Nolan term the "fundamental understanding" under which the employee is to perform satisfactory work. Attendance, obedience to reasonable requirements, doing work of reasonable quality and quantity, and avoiding doing harm to the employer's business are now regarded in arbitration, as they have long been in the master and servant law, as obligations of employees. Selznick's observation that the heart of the matter is the avoidance of arbitrary treatment of employees is useful once one identifies the obligations and the legitimate goals of management in enforcing those obligations. These legitimate goals have long been the same—forwarding the business of the firm, with moderation.

The substantive rules of industrial justice in the United States reflect rather stark contrasts between the nonunionized and unionized sectors. In the nonunionized sector there is a growing body of limitations on the right of employers to terminate the employment relationship. However, these form a patchwork, not a systematic body of principles. In the unionized sector a systematic body of rules does exist. In that sector there is a fairly clear set of employment obligations. It should be noted, however, that the contrast in practice may not be as great as it is in the law, as nonunion grievance procedures and formal "open door policies" are growing in use. This consideration supports the need for intensive studies of the actual practices to supplement the kind of legal analysis represented by this chapter and others in this book.

NOTES

1. Hoyt Wheeler, "Management-Labour Relations in the USA," *International and Comparative Industrial Relations,* ed. Greg J. Bamber and Russell D. Lansbury (London: Allen & Unwin, 1987), 60–61.

2. C. B. Labatt, *Commentaries on the Law of Master and Servant,* vol. 1 (Rochester, NY: Lawyers Cooperative Publishing Co., 1913), 824–25.

3. Ibid., 69.

4. Charles Manley Smith, *A Treatise on the Law of Master and Servant* (Philadelphia: T. & J. W. Johnson, Law Booksellers, 1853), 69.

5. Ibid., 70.

6. Labatt, *Commentaries on the Law of Master and Servant,* 824–25, 866, 895, 902–07, 912–13, 926–27, 930.

7. Ibid., 920–22.

8. 39 *C.J.* Master and Servant, Secs. 79–90 (1925), 80-89.

9. *Campbell. Wyant & Cooper Foundry Co.,* 1 LA 263 (Harry H. Platt, 1945).

10. Roger I. Abrams and Dennis R. Nolan, "Toward a Theory of 'Just Cause' in Employee Discipline Cases," *Duke Law Journal* (1985): 611–12.

11. Philip Selznick, *Law, Society and Industrial Justice* (Berkeley: Russell Sage Foundation, 1969), 13, 164–66.

12. Walter E. Baer, *Discipline and Discharge under the Labor Agreement* (New York: American Management Association, 1972), 7–28.

13. Jerome H. Rattig, "Arbitrations on Discipline," *Arbitrating Labor Cases,* ed. Noel Levin, et al. (New York: Practicing Law Institute, 1974), 87–88.

14. James R. Redeker, *Discipline: Policies and Procedures* (Washington: Bureau of National Affairs, 1983), 179–80.

15. Jean T. McKelvey, "Discipline and Discharge," *Arbitration in Practice,* ed. Arnold M. Zack (Ithaca, NY: ILR Press, 1984), 43; Maurice S. Trotta, *Arbitration of Labor-Management Disputes* (New York: AMACOM, 1974), 288.

16. Redeker, *Discipline: Policies and Procedures,* 178–79.

17. Arnold M. Zack, *Grievance Arbitration* (Lexington, MA: Lexington Books, 1989), 112–13.

18. Redeker, *Discipline: Policies and Procedures,* 177–78.

19. Ibid., 175–76.

20. *Armstrong Rubber Co.,* 77 LA 775 (Adolph M. Koven, 1981); See generally, Adolph M. Koven and Susan L. Smith, *Alcohol-Related Misconduct* (San Diego: Coloracre Publications, 1984), and Tia Schneider and R. V. Denenberg, *Alcohol and Drugs: Issues in the Workplace* (Washington: Bureau of National Affairs, 1983).

21. Redeker, *Discipline: Policies and Procedures,* 147–57.

22. Ibid., 86–91; Schneider and Denenberg, *Alcohol and Drugs,* 4–6.

23. McKelvey, "Discipline and Discharge," 97.

24. Ibid., 94–95.

25. Zack, *Grievance Arbitration,* 98.

26. Trotta, *Arbitration of Labor-Management Disputes,* 275; Redeker, *Discipline: Policies and Procedures,* 207–11.

27. Redeker, *Discipline: Policies and Procedures,* 209–10.

28. Ibid., 208–09; McKelvey, "Discipline and Discharge," 96–97.

29. Abrams and Nolan, "Toward a Theory of 'Just Cause,'" 605–06; Noel Levin and Gerald Aksen, *Arbitrating Labor Cases* (New York: Practising Law Institute, 1974), 89–93.

30. Adolph Koven and Susan Smith, *Just Cause: The Seven Tests* (San Francisco: Coloracre Publications, 1985), 106–10.

31. Abrams and Nolan, "Toward a Theory of 'Just Cause,'" 613–14.

32. Redeker, *Discipline: Policies and Procedures,* 55–57.

33. *Menasha Corp.,* 71 LA 653 (George Roumell, 1978).

34. Redeker, *Discipline: Policies and Procedures,* 58–67.

35. Ibid., 220–29.

36. Zack, *Grievance Arbitration,* 101.

37. Redeker, *Discipline: Policies and Procedures,* 224–25.

38. Ibid., 222–23; McKelvey, "Discipline and Discharge," 91–92.

39. *Zellerbach Paper Co.*, 75 LA 869 (Joseph F. Gentile, 1980).

40. Redeker, *Discipline: Policies and Procedures*, 106.

41. Ibid., 99.

42. Ibid., 230–40; Trotta, *Arbitration of Labor-Management Disputes*, 269–75.

43. Redeker, *Discipline: Policies and Procedures*, 239.

44. Trotta, *Arbitration of Labor-Management Disputes*, 269.

45. Redeker, *Discipline: Policies and Procedures*, 239.

46. Trotta, *Arbitration of Labor-Management Disputes*, 270–71.

47. Redeker, *Discipline: Policies and Procedures*, 214–19.

48. Ibid., 218.

GENERAL COMMENTS

Integration and summarization of our work in this volume is highly challenging, largely because of the complexity of both the substantive subject matter and the interactions between it and the structures of our various industrial justice systems. Nevertheless, doing so offers as a reward a fuller understanding of this subject than is available when one only looks at national systems individually. If, as we believe, understanding is relating, then it is necessary to view each of these systems in the context of at least some other systems, and see how they relate to one another, in order to hope to understand any one of them. More importantly, if we are to understand industrial justice systems and the obligations of employment in a general way, it is necessary to compare their operation in a variety of settings.

The employment relationship, in which employee obligations and rights arise, has at its core the employee duty of subordination—the obligation to obey. This duty and others are generally enforced in the first instance through private justice systems internal to the employing organizations. However, in all national industrial justice systems the decisions made in the intrafirm system are reviewed by outside, extrafirm, authorities—either courts or independent neutrals appointed by employer and employee representatives. In all of our systems these extrafirm mechanisms have developed both procedures and substantive rules that serve the function of assuring that employee interests and rights are respected. Put another way, the boundaries of employer enforcement of the employment obligation are policed by these extrafirm mechanisms in order to ensure that employers stay within the bounds of legitimate employer interests and reasonableness and the requirements of public policy.

From our observation of the various national industrial justice systems in operation, we believe that it is possible to induce a single general guiding principle to inform judgments on whether particular behaviors are deserving of termination of employment or discipline. Yet there remains considerable diversity as to whether, and to what degree, employees are protected from termination without cause, the rules as to discipline, the sources and mechanisms for enforcement of employee protections, and the substantive content of particular obligations (subordination, loyalty, etc.).

We will initiate our consideration of these matters with an inquiry about the nature and origins of what appear to us to be the central concept (subordination) and accompanying process (private justice system) that underlie the employment relationship, from which the obligations of employment arise. We will then state what we believe to be a unifying principle that is capable of furnishing a rough guide to the operation of the obligations of employment. Comparisons will be made as to the general rules and procedures on termination of employment and employee discipline in our various countries. The extensiveness and intensiveness of particular obligations will be compared across countries. Finally, some broad conclusions will be drawn.

THE EMPLOYMENT RELATIONSHIP

In reviewing our national papers, we are struck by the ubiquity of subordination as the fundamental link in the relationship between employer and employee. Theoretically, one could imagine a multiplicity of other crucial principles for this relationship. For example, legal notions used in dealing with contracts for providing finished or semifinished goods or services could be utilized. Economics provides an alternative set of models from its perspective. The more recent ones include the fair wage hypothesis,[1] partial gift exchange,[2] implicit contracts,[3] and internal labor markets.[4] These views tend, however, to ignore subordination, which is the central reality of the legal relationship of employment that is reflected in our papers.

Starting from a basic sociological inducements/contribu-

364

tions model[5] may provide a framework that is more congenial to our analysis. We can view the employment relationship as the exchange of two bundles—material and immaterial inducements, and contributions. Most of the attention in industrial relations, as in economics, has traditionally focused on the material aspects of the relationship—the exchange of a wage for the application of competencies to effort. However, the immaterial components of the exchange are probably at least as important. For the employee these consist of inducements such as social status, both inside and outside the workplace, and some amount of self-realization through work. They include a certain number of rights provided by law or custom that may amount, to a degree that varies among countries, to ownership of the job.[6] Also included, in practice, is some assurance against unemployment and indulgence of occasional poor performance.

In exchange for the set of inducements that we have described, the employee contributes, above and beyond the narrow application of his or her competency to job tasks, a broad *subordination* and loyalty to the employer. Furthermore, the employee acquieses in the employer's right not only to manage, but also to impose punishment upon, the employee. It might be argued that where there is no right on the part of the employer to impose discipline short of dismissal, as in the Canadian non-union sector, there is no "punishment" involved, but rather the ending of a contractual relationship by its terms. However, it seems to us that even there the reality of termination of employment is, in substance, a kind of punishment of the employee.

It is an extraordinary situation in a free society for one individual to have the legal right to impose punishment on another in what amounts to a private system of justice. Interestingly, punishment may be imposed for matters that are unrelated to job performance, strictly defined. Broadly speaking, the only limit, albeit an important one, would appear to be that the behavior must have some impact on the employer's business.

It is interesting to speculate about where the employer's private justice power comes from. We believe that contractual explanations are insufficient, as are reasons limited to the requirements of productive efficiency, since the employer's disciplinary powers seem to often go beyond these. In reviewing the literature on this subject, one finds that the employer's authority in this is generally treated as existing sui generis, without its

365

source being systematically addressed. One does, however, find some suggestions as to possible sources. These include public policy or public order (government finds it convenient to implicitly transfer this power to employers in order that national output be maximized), custom and practice, property rights, community governance (requiring a leader with authority), exploitation (the employer buys labor power, not labor, and therefore has to extract surplus value by this means), and natural human inclinations.[7]

Whatever its source, it is clear that in all of these systems employers have the right to create and enforce a web of rules at the enterprise level that go beyond any regulation of employee behavior that the state makes. While often unilateral in their adoption and initial enforcement, they are nevertheless subject to constraints that derive from the extrafirm societal industrial justice system. It is those constraints with which this volume primarily deals.

A GUIDING PRINCIPLE OF INDUSTRIAL JUSTICE

Comparing across countries the general obligations and rights of employees, and the accompanying procedures and remedies, one finds the same fundamental rule enforced by different methods. The basic rule in all of these countries is that employees *must avoid behaviors that materially damage the functioning of the employment relationship.* The employment relationship has as its main social function the efficient production of goods or services. Its means of doing this is a hierarchical subordination relationship between human beings. It necessarily involves employees being entrusted with the property of, and often potentially damaging information about, their employers. In the modern organization work is a social activity, requiring cooperation with employees' peers as well as their superiors. Therefore, this peculiar relationship is damaged when it appears that employees are unlikely to perform the work of producing goods and services at a reasonable level, the authority relationship is impaired, or the personal relationship of trust and cooperation is destroyed. Also, since the end purpose of the employee's employment is the welfare of the employing enterprise, anything that does damage to the business frustrates the purposes of the relationship and thereby damages it.

INDUSTRIAL JUSTICE SYSTEMS
AND EMPLOYMENT OBLIGATIONS

All of our national systems of workplace justice regulate the substantive obligations of employment and the procedures for both their enforcement and challenges to their enforcement. These rules relate to both termination of employment and discipline short of dismissal. They derive from different sources and are enforced by different mechanisms.

TERMINATION OF EMPLOYMENT

The General Principle

It appears from our review of the various national systems in operation that when an employee acts in such a way as to destroy the foundation of trust and interpersonal cooperation on which the employment relationship is based, through either a single serious breach or an accumulation of nonserious ones, immediate termination is permitted under all of these systems. Discipline, and in some systems termination with notice, is the appropriate employer response to less fundamental damage to the relationship.

The general employee obligation not to destroy the foundation for the employment relationship and the employer's concomitant right to summarily terminate for breach of this obligation are explicit in the laws of some countries and only implicit in others. In Belgium the statute expressly provides for dismissal without notice where "further professional cooperation between the employer and the employee . . . became impossible." In France it is generally agreed that "serious" cause, which makes the employee susceptible to termination, means cause that prevents to some extent the continuation of the employment relationship without damage to the enterprise. In Spain, in addition to particular causes, the statute provides for termination for "bad faith or abuse of confidence." German law provides for extraordinary dismissal without notice only where it is "intolerable for either of the parties to respect the normal notice period." By statute in Italy a just cause for termination implies serious contractual violations or factors outside the employment relationship that eliminate trust between the parties, creating conditions that do not allow the employment relationship to continue but rather require its immediate termination. We are of the opinion that one can reasonably infer, either from the specific causes set out in statute or from common law or arbitral rules, that this is essentially the law in Australia, Canada, Israel, the United States (except for the non-unionized private sector) and the United Kingdom.

That it is destruction of interpersonal trust and cooperation that leads most directly to summary dismissal seems to reveal something basic about the employment relationship itself. There are many ways of viewing the employment relationship—as an economic exchange of commodities, as a political community, or as a social dominance hierarchy, among others. Here we see the crucial element being very personal individual relations. At the very least this should remind us of the necessity of remembering the humanity of the actors in the employment relationship and the importance in this human relationship of interpersonal feelings such as trust and the ability to act cooperatively one with another. That this is the law is perhaps of less interest than the likelihood that the law is based upon customs that have evolved over human history. It is interesting that in these different national cultures there is this common thread.

Necessity of Cause for Termination

National industrial justice systems vary as to whether termination of employment by the employer (for reasons other than those associated with the needs of the enterprise, i.e., layoff for economic reasons) can be done only for cause, can be made without cause if notice is given, or can be made without either cause or notice. They also vary as to the proportion of the labor force that is protected against termination without cause. Figure 1 depicts this.

In several of our countries termination of the employment relationship, even with notice, is lawful only if based upon justifiable reasons. Cause that gives rise to a lawful termination generally must be, in the words of the German law regarding termination with notice, justified by the "person or conduct of the worker" or redundancy. Countries having this requirement by statute are Belgium, Spain, Italy, Germany, France, and the United Kingdom (except for part-time and short-time workers, who can be terminated without cause with notice). The same requirement is made effective through collective bargaining in the unionized sectors of Canada, Israel, and the United States, and in Australia for the large majority of employees who are covered by industrial tribunal awards. In Israel there is the additional requirement that, for some employees, termination be a joint labor–management decision.

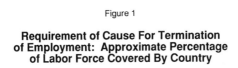

Figure 1

Requirement of Cause For Termination of Employment: Approximate Percentage of Labor Force Covered By Country

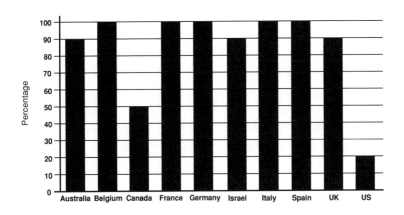

Termination with notice, even in the absence of cause, is lawful in the nonunion sector in most parts of Canada. In Australia and Israel this is also permitted (in Israel severance pay, rather than notice, is given), but only affects a relatively small number of employees because of the large proportion of employees protected under collective bargaining agreements (Israel) or industrial tribunal awards (Australia). In Israel there is also an obligation of employer good faith as to all employees. In Belgium no explicit notification of the cause for the termination need be given at the time of termination, if notice is given. The period of notice, which is determined by statute, can be quite substantial. Also, it is possible for employees to challenge a termination with notice as "abusive."

Among the countries in our study, termination of employment without notice, in the absence of cause, is permissible for employers only in the nonunionized private sector of the United

369

States. Aside from a set of very special exceptions, United States employers may fire employees at their discretion. The United States has the greatest contrast among groups of employees, with nonunionized workers having very little protection and unionized workers having strong protection.

It would appear from the above that there is a great deal of diversity among these countries in worker protection against unjustifiable termination. In some countries employees can be terminated only for cause. In others they can be terminated without cause, but notice is required if serious cause is not present. In one country some employees can be fired without either cause or notice. Yet one should be careful to recognize that this is not the whole story.

The diversity among countries as to protection against termination, while quite real, may be somewhat less important than it appears at first glance. This is because in all of them, with the exception of Italy (in firms with more than 50 employees or units of more than 15 employees within smaller firms), the unionized sector of the United States and the nonunionized sector and part of the unionized sector of Canada, employers can, with only special exceptions, successfully terminate employees without cause if they are willing to pay a price. Except for these countries the reinstatement remedy is available to employees only in the United Kingdom, and Germany, and mainly to shop stewards in France. In these last three countries, however, it is so rarely used as to not be of any real importance to the work force as a whole, although it may have symbolic impact. There is considerable variation among our countries as to the size of the price, and this may be quite significant. Nevertheless, the bottom line is that the employer can in fact terminate the employee's employment if it so wishes. The crucial question is the degree to which unjust dismissals are inhibited by the prospect of whatever sanctions exist in each country. This is a question of practice, not of law, and can only be answered by empirical research.

DISCIPLINE

The imposition of discipline short of discharge is an issue that is dealt with by the laws and collective bargaining agreements of several countries. This is regulated rather intensively by statute in Belgium, France, Italy, and Germany, and by collective bargaining agreements in Israel (in the Labour Code),

Canada, the United States and the United Kingdom. In Germany disciplinary penalty codes are made subject to co-determination, and are thus within the range of power of the works councils. In Italy collective bargaining agreements as well as statutes regulate employee discipline. In the American and Canadian unionized sectors, by virtue of collective bargaining agreement provisions, employees can only be disciplined for just cause. Although there is broad similarity among these regulations, there are some interesting differences.

In Italy the law on employee discipline has as one of its most visible aims ensuring the personal dignity of employees, generally forbidding such things as bodily searching employees and machine monitoring of performance. In at least some collective bargaining agreements, as shown by the example of the Italian metalworkers' contract, penalties are set out for particular kinds of misconduct (e.g., tardiness, minor insubordination). Italian law permits fines of no more than four hours pay and suspensions of not more than 10 days. Belgian law provides that employers are permitted to impose either moral sanctions (e.g., warnings) or pecuniary sanctions (e.g., fines), that an employee may be suspended from employment, and that employers are restricted to penalties that are set out in the firm's work rules. There are also procedural requirements that a Belgian employer must meet in imposing discipline.

French law provides that a penalty short of discharge can be imposed for "real" cause that is not sufficiently serious to warrant dismissal. An employer must meet a number of procedural requirements in imposing discipline. Disciplinary sanctions can be contested by employees in labor courts. The German penalty codes that are worked out between employers and works councils can, by law, lead only to the imposition of warnings and fines, not to dismissal. These procedures are subject to labor court review. In the United States and Canada collective bargaining agreements typically set out only the requirement that discipline be for just cause. The arbitral case law has worked out some rough principles as to what penalties are appropriate for what offenses. The general distinction in the United States, as in Canada (and the United Kingdom under employer disciplinary codes and collective agreements), is between major offenses, such as theft, that can lead to termination on first occurrence, and minor offenses, such as tardiness, that require progressive discipline.

371

SOURCES AND MECHANISMS FOR ASSERTION
OF EMPLOYEE RIGHTS

The other side of the same coin that holds employment obligations is the right of employees to be terminated or disciplined only under the conditions permitted by law. This right has different sources in different countries. It is based primarily in statute in Belgium, France, Germany, Italy, Spain, and the United Kingdom. In the other countries it is founded mainly upon collective agreements (the United States and Israel), collective agreements and the common law (Canada), or industrial tribunal awards (Australia). Enforcement of this right is through the courts (either ordinary courts or specialized labor tribunals) in most of our countries. However, in the United States and Canada arbitration is the most important enforcement mechanism, and in Israel bipartite committees serve this function.

THE PARTICULAR OBLIGATIONS OF EMPLOYMENT

At the outset of the project we collectively selected a set of obligations of employment that we believed were capable of being analyzed across all of our national industrial justice systems. It appears that these obligations did lend themselves to our analysis. With a single exception—abjuring collective action—all of the obligations that we selected apply, at least to some degree, in all of our national systems. This exception is itself of some interest.

In addition to selecting obligations, we specified theoretical factors and factual variations that we believed would affect the outcomes on the various obligations. Broadly speaking, this framework was usable.

There were some considerable differences among the factual variations as to their relevance in particular national systems. One of the more interesting differences in factual variations, falling under the factor of enforceability, is in Italy, where, alone among our countries, the view that generally prevails among judges (although there is some division among them on this point) is that there is no requirement of consistency of treatment on the part of the employer.

Another interesting systematic difference on a factual variation concerns the effect of the employee having the status of an employee representative. We classified this under the factor of possible mitigating conditions at the outset of the analysis. Indeed, in several countries it does appear that an employee representative is less likely to suffer termination. In Belgium there is a special procedure for dismissing a trade union representative for serious reason without notice. This procedure requires the employer to get the prior approval of a labor court. If the employer terminates a union representative and wrongfully fails to reinstate him or her, there are substantial financial penalties. In France an employee representative can be dismissed only after a special procedure involving authorization of the dismissal by the works council and labor inspector. Reinstatement is available as a remedy for wrongful termination. In Germany it is works council members who are given special protection, with the consent of the works council being a prerequisite to dismissal of one of its members, although a court can give approval if the works council refuses. In Spain there are special rules on the dismissal of employee representatives, and reinstatement is available as a remedy for wrongful dismissal. In Israel safety committee members are given special protection.

In all of our other countries except the United States the status of union representative is legally irrelevant, although it may be relevant as a practical matter, and in the United Kingdom there is even a nonbinding Code of Practice provision that states that a union representative should be dismissed only after consultation with a full-time union official. In the United States, and only there, union representatives not only have no special protection, but are likely to be held to a higher standard of conduct than other employees.

In our discussion of particular obligations here we will focus upon the general question of the relative strength of each obligation in each country. That is, the question is how intensive and extensive is the obligation of, say, subordination in each national system. In general, this is judged according to the likelihood of a violation of the obligation leading to immediate termination.

In this discussion of particular obligations, and in the balance of this chapter, when discussing national differences we will speak to the rules covering the majority of employees in the system unless we specifically indicate otherwise. The two exceptions to this rule are Canada and the United States, where the reference will be to the unionized sectors unless otherwise indicated.

SUBORDINATION

When one views the obligation of subordination in the light of a particular scenario involving possible insubordination, it becomes clear that it is easier to state that the obligation exists than it is to apply it. Our basic common scenario sets out a clear but relatively non-serious case of insubordination. An order has been given. The employee refuses to carry it out. This is insubordination, which strikes at the very heart of the employment relationship. One might expect, therefore, that the employee would be terminated. However, this is not clearly the case in most of the countries, and the result varies along several factors.

In all of our countries an occasion of relatively nonserious insubordination could, but probably would not, lead to termination, depending upon exacerbating and mitigating factors. Probably the most important variation in most of these countries would be the employee insisting on being insubordinate after being warned of the consequences or after repeated orders. In France the basic scenario would likely lead to termination, but with notice. In Spain and the United Kingdom the obligation may be at its weakest by this measure.

One interesting issue on which we find some national differences is whether it constitutes a disciplinary offense to refuse to obey an order that is outside the employee's job duties. In the United States it is an offense. In Canada the employee must obey now and grieve the erroneous work assignment later unless grieving later would be a useless act. In the case of Australia, Belgium, France, Italy, Spain, the United Kingdom, and Germany it appears that the employee might be excused from obeying such an order. In Canada, Israel and France the order being outside the employee's job duties might mitigate the offense. In France, Belgium, and Canada (nonunion sector) the employee would be entitled to declare the employment contract breached by the employer and demand notice or compensation.

Overall, the subordination obligation seems at its strongest in Canada and the United States. This contrasts with a relative laxity in the other English-speaking countries.

SOBRIETY

With respect to sobriety, there do appear to be some differences across countries, although these differences may end at the point where the employee's work is affected. Simply consuming alcoholic beverages or being intoxicated on the job is treated with greater or lesser severity in various countries.

In general, it appears to us that the obligation not to consume alcohol or be intoxicated is somewhat stronger in Australia, Belgium (where there is a statutory prohibition against having alcoholic beverages at the workplace), and France. It is an offense, but usually a minor one, in the United States, although some arbitrators treat it very severely. In Israel and Italy this offense appears very rarely. The obligation seems relatively weak in Canada, the United Kingdom and Germany, perhaps the United States, and especially weak in Spain (except as to the employee defense of chronic alcoholism, which Spain does not recognize). Drugs stronger than alcohol are dealt with especially severely in the United States, perhaps because of the serious and well-publicized drug problem in this country.

SECURITY OF EMPLOYER'S PROPERTY

The obligation to refrain from misappropriating the employer's property is probably the most severely and uniformly enforced of the duties. Theft is punished very harshly in all countries. This seems to be the case even where the value of the goods stolen is quite small. However, commentators from several countries indicate that mitigating circumstances might be considered in their systems. Israel appears to be especially severe, at least in the respect that unproven employer allegations of theft have served to support termination for theft.

It is interesting to speculate upon why the sanctity of the employer's property is such a strong and widely held principle. This may be inherent in the fact that the employment relationship by its very nature has to do with employees using the property of the employer, or the historic link between employer authority and property rights. It probably also relates to the fundamental breach of interpersonal trust involved in an act of theft. As noted above, those offenses that destroy this aspect of the employment relationship tend to be treated especially severely.

PEACEFUL WORKPLACE

The peace obligation is also one that is broadly considered to be tightly binding upon the employee. All of our countries seem to treat breaches of this duty very severely. It may, how-

375

ever, be the case that in Canada termination is less likely to be permitted under the particular facts of our scenario.

The basis for this obligation's being so intensive may be the necessarily social nature of work since the industrial revolution. If workers cannot work together in a cooperative fashion, the goal of the employment relationship—the production of goods and services—is plainly impossible. Here again, as with theft, essential interpersonal relationships are especially threatened.

OFF-DUTY CONDUCT

The obligation to conduct oneself properly off duty is perhaps the most difficult of the obligations with which to deal in practice. All countries appear to have the rule that employees are obliged not to conduct themselves in such a way that destroys their effectiveness as employees or injures their employers' businesses. Yet there is the rule, as the Australians say, that the employer and employee are "square at every payday." That is, employees should be free to act as they choose on their own time. The balancing of these two conflicting principles is necessarily problematic.

It may be that France is somewhat tougher in this respect than other countries, on the ground that there would be a loss of confidence in the employee in a case such as that given in the basic scenario. The Spanish catch-all offense of bad faith might also be broad enough to cover this, although it would be unlikely to lead to termination in a case such as the one given in our basic scenario.

This obligation speaks to the extensiveness of the obligations of employment. It defines the extent to which the employee has an obligation to the employer beyond the boundaries of working time. The postfeudal view of employment generally holds that free workers owe employers their labor and not their lives in general. Yet we see in all of these countries that something else is going on besides a narrow exchange of money for labor power. There seems to be a human relationship involved that is impossible to understand within the narrow boundaries of a contract for the supply of a commodity called labor.

ATTENDANCE

The consequences to an employee of a failure to attend work depend heavily upon whether the absence is justified or unjustified. With justified absences employee fault is not involved. It is clear that in none of our countries can justified absences give rise to termination unless they are substantial and continuing. In the case of unjustified absences intentional misconduct is present, and termination will result more readily.

There are substantial differences among our countries in the treatment of justified absences. Although nowhere are the rules very harsh, it would seem that several countries are especially lenient with respect to this obligation. In most of our countries—Australia, Canada, France, the United States, the United Kingdom, and Germany—the law is essentially that justified absences, including those caused by illness, can give rise to termination if they reach a point where the employment relationship is not, as a practical matter, operating on a full-time basis, and this appears unlikely to change in the future. However, in Belgium the contract of employment is suspended during illness. The employer can terminate the employee only when the incapacity lasts for more than six months. In such a case the statutorily mandated notice must be given. In Israel the rule under collective bargaining agreements seems very lenient as it is applied in practice, given the necessity for the worker representative to agree to the discipline in the first instance. In Italy dismissal is appropriate only after a very lengthy period or, in the case of sporadic illness, a large number of incidents. In Spain dismissal may occur, but compensation must be paid to the employee.

As to unjustified absences, there is also a good deal of variation. In Belgium, Canada, France, the United Kingdom, the United States, and Israel one instance of three days' unjustified absence would usually result in only discipline and not in discharge. In Australia and Spain three days' unjustified absence would lead to certain termination. In Germany and Italy one instance of a few days unjustified absence might or might not result in termination, depending upon its exact length. In Italy and Canada the length of the period varies according to the provisions of the particular collective bargaining agreement that is applicable. If the absence follows a holiday, this could lead to dismissal in Germany, and would be an exacerbating factor in the United States, Canada, and Belgium. It would lead to a loss of holiday pay in Israel.

PERFORMANCE

A pertinent distinction in the area of performance is between negligent or willful failure to perform (which is misconduct) and simple insufficient performance. The former is treated as intentional misconduct of some seriousness and treated accordingly. Even in the latter case, if the standards are reasonable and it reaches the point where it can fairly be said that "enough is enough," it can amount to nonfulfillment of either expected standards or contractual obligations. In such case termination with notice, after warnings, would be proper in many countries. This would clearly be true in Australia, the United Kingdom, the unionized United States, Belgium, Italy, and France. Overall this obligation may be somewhat weaker in Canada, Israel, and Germany. In Spain, although the employee might be lawfully dismissed, he or she might also be entitled to compensation.

A change in production methods and standards by the employer and punishment of an employee for failure to meet new higher standards raises a special issue. In some countries— for example, Belgium and France—employee representatives must be consulted before a change can be made. Failing this, in Belgium, Canada (nonunion sector), and France, the employee could consider himself or herself terminated and claim compensation, and in France could receive severance pay. In Australia and Germany such a change would have to be the result of collective negotiations. In the unionized sector of Canada an employee would have to be given a substantial period to adjust to the change before discipline for failing to meet the new standard would be appropriate. In the unionized United States and the United Kingdom the employer could change standards and dismiss for failure to meet them so long as the standards were reasonable and the employee had adequate notice and time to adjust. In Spain the prior agreement of a workers' representative or government officials to the change in standards would be necessary before an employee could be disciplined for failing to comply with it. Israeli law is the most lenient in this area, being highly unlikely to allow dismissal.

LOYALTY

The frequency of cases of disloyalty varies greatly from country to country. In Spain these cases are quite common. In the United States they are rare. Where they do occur, such cases often pose a troubling conflict between, on the one hand, the duty of loyalty and confidentiality of information obtained in employment which are necessary to retain the trust of the employer, and, on the other hand, the public interest. The balance between the two is tilted differently in different countries. In France, Germany, and Spain a pervasive duty of confidentiality and good faith is expected of employees, making dismissal in these cases likely to be upheld. Israel, usually more lenient toward employees, seems somewhat more harsh than many other countries in these cases. To the contrary, in Australia, under a set of facts showing disloyalty but involving unethical conduct by the employer, dismissal would be unlikely to be upheld. In many countries the result in a disloyalty case such as this would turn on exacerbating or mitigating factors. In Canada, France, the United Kingdom, the United States, and Belgium, and probably to some extent in the other countries, the rank of the employee, the lawfulness of the employer's practice, the damage to the employer's business, the existence of a rule, and statutory protections would all be important. In Italy the courts rather carefully and explicitly balance the interests involved.

In the nonunionized sector in the United States, protection of whistleblowers may be rather substantial as a matter of court-made common law. This may produce the anomalous result of nonunionized American employees, who are generally the least protected among our countries, being perhaps the best protected (along with American unionized employees) in the area of loyalty-related offenses.

RESTRICT COLLECTIVE ACTION

As to collective action, two dividing lines are important. One is between the theoretical existence or nonexistence of a legally protected right to strike. The other is the practical one between law and fact. In some countries, such as Spain, Italy, Belgium, Israel, and France, the law protects the right to strike, irrespective of union support. In these countries the individual contract of employment is generally considered to be suspended, not broken, by striking. But conditions on this right are imposed in Israel and in Spain, the breaking of which, at least by active militants, can give rise to sanctions. In France a walkout is permitted at any time, and sanctions against employees are unlaw-

379

ful so long as the action meets the definition of a strike, is not in the public sector, involves an actual work stoppage rather than an instance of working to rule, and is not for political reasons. Conversely, in Australia and the United Kingdom there is no protected right to strike. In Canada, the United States, and Germany this right is severely restricted by limiting conditions.

AVOID CONFLICT OF INTEREST

Simple moonlighting would probably be misconduct in some of our countries, but not in others. It appears to be generally punishable in Israel and Spain, and might be in the unionized United States and Canada if the employer has a clear and reasonable rule prohibiting it. In cases of working for a competitor, there may be applicable the pervasive duty of good faith and loyalty, a breach of which would justify dismissal in Australia and Germany. In Italy (depending upon the nature of the second job) and Belgium this may run afoul of the duty of noncompetition. If damage is caused to the employer's business, this might give rise to termination in France and the United Kingdom.

Like other types of off-duty conduct, this is an obligation that lies at the boundaries of the employment relationship, as it does not necessarily involve work performance. The existence of such obligations is perhaps the best proof of the employment relationship's going beyond a pure job nexus.

CONCLUSIONS

The crux of the employment obligation is the subordination of the employee to the will and interests of the employer, with limits. The limits are drawn somewhat differently in different countries, but generally are delineated by the boundaries of the legitimate business interests of the employer and the needs and dignity of the employees.

Insofar as the general law of the obligations of employment in our countries is concerned, there is a broad similarity. Employees are obligated to conduct themselves in such a way as to not destroy the fundamental rationale for the relationship. If they fail in this obligation, the employer may summarily dismiss them. Lesser offenses may give rise to discipline short of dismissal or dismissal with notice. Penalties are generally administered by a private system of industrial justice under the control of employers, subject to review by the courts or arbitrators.

One of the more interesting aspects of our analysis is the light that it sheds on the nature of the employment relationship itself. We find subordination at the heart of this relationship in the laws of all of our countries. This is hardly surprising, but significant nevertheless. What strikes us as most distinctive about what we induce from the laws of these several countries is the degree to which, within this subordinant affiliation, interpersonal human relations predominate over other aspects of this relationship, at least insofar as providing grounds for summarily terminating employment. We have a hierarchical subordination relationship, which has roots in the most primitive of human societies. We also have, in employment, such a relationship that in both custom and law can be traced back to the paternally dominated family. This relationship implies a great deal more than a market exchange of labor power for money. What this analysis of the law points up is the degree to which it is influenced by the close, intensely human, dynamics of trust and interpersonal cooperation. A problem may arise, however, from the one-sidedness of this dynamic in the modern employment relationship, which has these broader extraeconomic burdens resting entirely upon the employee. The ancient paternal relationship, and that under the old master and servant law, implied strong obligations on the part of the master that went beyond mere payment of a wage. Perhaps the modern human resources movement can be viewed as a new paternalism that seeks to restore the customary, and therefore expected, balance in this relationship.

With respect to the strength of particular obligations of employment among our various countries, a few interesting similarities and differences appear. As to the obligations of security of the employee's property, off-duty conduct, avoiding unjustified absences, and performance, there appears to be a great deal of similarity. As to maintaining a peaceful workplace, there is a broad similarity with the possible exception of Canada, where it may be weaker under some circumstances.

Differences among our countries are less clear. It does appear that, overall, the obligations of employment may be somewhat weaker in Belgium, Italy, and the United Kingdom, and somewhat stronger in Australia, Germany, and the United States. The subordination obligation seems to be at its strongest in Canada and the United States. The sobriety obligation seems weak in Canada, Germany, and Spain, and the offense is rare in

Israel and Italy. Attendance, insofar as justified absences are concerned, seems weaker in Belgium, Germany, Israel, and Spain. The loyalty obligation seems especially strong in France, Germany, and Spain. The obligation to abjure collective action seems especially weak or absent in Belgium, France, and Italy, and is also weak in Israel and Spain. It appears to be at its strongest in Australia, Canada, the United Kingdom, and perhaps the United States. The obligation to avoid a conflict of interest seems especially strong in Australia, Germany, Italy, and Spain. We should also not forget the uniquely unlimited obligations of employees in the nonunionized sector in the United States, where the rule is essentially one of employer prerogative.

Several subjects appear from our analysis to be worthy of further study. First, there is the question of practices and their consistency with the law. In addition to knowing what are in fact the practices, it would be interesting to know whether the differences that we have observed in the laws of our countries exist in practice as well. Second, there is the question of the differences made in practice by the existence of different remedies. Does the prospect of reinstatement inhibit employer action more than that of financial consequences? Third, an analysis of the law on an in-depth basis—obligation by obligation, rather than country by country, would be useful to help our understanding of these phenomena.

The picture of industrial justice that emerges from our analysis across ten countries is one that includes many interesting differences. However, the principal impression that we gain is one of broad commonality of the law of the obligations of employment, albeit enforced by a variety of mechanisms. It is, of course, impossible to say with any certainty why this is so. It may be, as stated by one of us in our oral discussions of these papers, that "the common economic order that we share is more important than common law or civil law" or other divergencies among our systems that separate us.

NOTES

1. George A. Ackerlof and Janet L. Yellen, "Fairness and Unemployment," *American Economic Review* 78, (1988): 44–49, and "The Fair-Wage Effort Hypothesis and Unemployment," *The Quarterly Journal of Economics* 105 (1990), 255–83.

2. George A. Ackerlof, "Labor Contracts as Partial Gift

Exchange," *The Quarterly Journal of Economics* 97 (1982): 543–69.

3. Costas Azariadis, "Implicit Contracts and Underemployment Equilibria," *Journal of Political Economy* 83 (1975): 1183–1202.

4. Peter C. Doeringer and Michael J. Piore, *Internal Labor Markets and Manpower Analysis* (Lexington, MA: Heath, 1971).

5. James C. March and Herbert A. Simon, *Organizations* (New York: Wiley, 1958).

6. Frederic Meyers, *Ownership of Jobs: A Comparative Study* (Los Angeles: Institute of Industrial Relations, UCLA, 1964).

7. Hoyt N. Wheeler, "Management from an Institutional/Biological Perspective," *Management under Differing Labour Market and Employment Systems*, ed. Gunter Dlugos, Wolfgang Dorow, and Klaus Weiermair (Berlin: Walter DeGruyter, 1988), pp. 95–105.

CONTRIBUTORS

Roy J. Adams	McMaster University, Canada
Bernard Adell	Queen's University, Canada
Werner K. Blenk	International Labour Office, Geneva, Switzerland
Brian Brooks	University of New South Wales, Australia
Chris Engels	Catholic University of Leuven, Belgium
Francesco Liso	University of Bari, Italy
Karl J. Mackie	University of Nottingham, England
Mordehai Mironi	Tel Aviv University, Israel
Dennis R. Nolan	University of South Carolina, United States
Antonio Ojeda-Aviles	University of Seville, Spain
Elena Pisani	American Embassy, Rome, Italy
Jacques Rojot	University of Paris I, Sorbonne, France
Hans Peter Viethen	Federal Ministry of Labour and Social Affairs, Germany
Hoyt N. Wheeler	University of South Carolina, United States

INDEX